Anatomy of Educational Innovation

Anatomy of Educational Innovation:

AN ORGANIZATIONAL ANALYSIS OF AN ELEMENTARY SCHOOL

LOUIS M. SMITH

Washington University
and
Cemrel, Inc.

PAT M. KEITH

Iowa State University

John Wiley & Sons, Inc., New York • London • Sydney • Toronto

Preface

As the manuscript of this book is being set in galleys and page proofs, the world of education—classrooms, schools, and ideas—continues in great ferment. Major reports such as *Crisis in the Classroom* and *Children and Their Primary Schools* are suggesting new waves of change to replace the now older modes advocated in the *Restoration of Learning* and *Education for All American Youth*.

Through all of this we are struck by the calm voice of Professor Maslow (1964) who has urged educational innovators to be "good reporters" and to tell the story of their attempts at change. A series of circumstances led us to be that limited part of a courageous and important attempt to remake public education, in the rather typical middle class suburban school district of Milford.* The setting was the Kensington School, a unique architectural structure with open-space laboratory suites, an instructional materials center, and a theatre, designed in what might be described as the square lines of classical Greek simplicity. The program exemplified the new elementary education of team teaching, individualized instruction, and multi-age groups. A broad strategy of innovation—the alternative of grandeur, the utilization of temporary systems, and minimal prior commitments—was devised and implemented. The intended outcome was pupil development toward maturity—a self-directed, internally motivated, and productive competence.

Elements of tragedy existed. Realities were often less than intentions. Organizational structures and processes contained complexities which were "latent, unanticipated, and unintended." Human nature seemed not so malleable as some people hoped and others feared. At the universities and the research and development centers, the scholarly world of professional education and social science, of which we are a part, has failed to do justice to the complicated problems involved in originating an innovative educa-

* The names of all persons and places have been coded to preserve anonymity.

tional organization. Investigators and theorists have not focused hard enough, long enough, nor carefully enough on the small and mundane as well as the large and important issues and problems necessary for idealistic practitioners to carry out their dreams. Our hope is that this monograph will fill some of those gaps. Presumably also, some readers will find public policy considerations, if not recommendations, in the discussion. For instance, the recent United States Office of Education's guidelines for the Experimental Schools Program states, "The program of each Experimental School must be implemented in the first year of operation rather than in stages over the 5 years." This opts for Kensington's point of view, what we have called "the alternative of grandeur," as an innovative strategy in contrast to a "gradualist" strategy. Our data suggest that this alternative posed a number of critical and difficult dilemmas for administrators and staff at Kensington. If the Office of Education holds to that requirement, five years from now considerably more should be known regarding a number of hypotheses generated in our case study.

As always, a number of individuals are important to the completion of a book, and to them we owe our thanks. Steven Spanman and Jerl Cohen, superintendent and curriculum director of the Milford Schools, invited us to be observers. Eugene Shelby, principal of Kensington School, and his faculty not only permitted us "to be around" but were supportive of our efforts to understand. Their concern for making the Kensington story known was reflected in our total freedom as investigators. Although our perceptions and interpretations were sometimes incongruent with theirs, we strove for accurate data and careful analysis. Responsibility for the final interpretations is ours. The United States Office of Education through its small contract program provided initial resources at a critical time. Our own organizational affiliations at Washington University, CEMREL, Inc., Webster College, and Iowa State University continue to reflect the best traditions of academic freedom and support. Our colleagues in these institutions exemplify the best in inquiry and concern for the improvement of public education. We owe special thanks to Paul F. Kleine, who participated with us in the initial stages of the project as an additional and valuable observer, and to Patricia Carpenter who, as typist, secretary, and general assistant, handled the innumerable problems that always threaten to keep a manuscript from becoming a book. Finally, Marilyn, Cathy, and Curtis graciously put up with the horrendous schedules and the seemingly never-ending quality of the field research, data analysis, and multiple drafts of the manuscript.

LOUIS M. SMITH
PAT M. KEITH

Contents

Anatomy of Educational Innovation

SECTION I

Introduction

CHAPTER 1

Overview

AN INTRODUCTORY EPILOGUE

By definition, epilogues are speeches, short poems, or the like that are addressed to the audience at the conclusion of a play and, hence, do not belong at the beginning, if at all, of a research monograph. In a sense, however, our research is a play that has ended. By giving a brief description of the ending, we hope to produce a set for the interpretation of the story. Some contemporary psychologists suggest that this can have significant results.

Kensington is a school. Now, two years after it began, it does not exist as it once did. The school board has changed; the superintendent, Steven Spanman, has resigned after a year's leave of absence; the curriculum director, Jerl Cohen, has been gone for a year; and the principal, Eugene Shelby, left in the middle of the semester of the second year. Only eight of the original teaching staff returned the second year; only two of the original group, it is rumored, will be back for the beginning of the third year.[1] The principal participants who played a part in the beginning of the school are recorded in Figure 1.1. In February of the second year, a going-away party was held for the principal. Several excerpts from the field notes[2] made after the announcement of the principal's departure illustrate further facets of the epilogue.

> Tonight the staff held a party for Eugene, the principal. He's due to leave the day after tomorrow for PS 2100 in Metropolis.
>
> Eugene commented briefly about the differences in the new position and the

[1] Later data indicate that there were only two; eventually one of the two also left. Almost all of the teachers who came the second year departed before the third year.

[2] The methodology of the study—participant observation—produced voluminous recorded accounts of the events of the school. The quotes are from these records and have received only minor editing for clarity.

Principal	Eugene Shelby	
Basic Skills Division	Wanda Ellison	Additions and Replacements
	Jean Emerson	Chris Hun
	Sue Norton	Sarah Jones
	Mary Radford	
	Elaine Ross	
	Carla Young	
Transition Division	Meg Adrian	
	Daniel Hun	
	Claire Nelson	
Independent Study Division	Kay Abbot	Substitutions and Replacements
	Jack Davis	Linda Dixon
	Liz Etzell	Ann Gage
	Irma Hall	Walt Larsen
	Bill Kirkham	Abbie Allen
	David Nichols	
	John Taylor	
	Alec Thurman	
Curriculum Materials Coordinator	Tom Mack	
Teaching Aides	Helen Beacon	
	Arthur Carroll	
	Joan Sidney	
	Marjorie Wald	
	Inez York	
Central Office Staff		
Superintendent	Steve Spanman	
Curriculum Director	Jerl Cohen	
Counselor	Joe Harlan	
Others	Howard Couden	
	Edwin Kaufman	
	Adolph Sullivan	
Consultants		
1. General	Dr. Leslie Roberts	
2. N.T.L.	Dr. Lois Erickson	
	Miss Lyn Karson	

Figure 1.1   Kensington faculty and significant others.

fact that the school will have state financing rather than local financing, and it also will not be so closely tied up with local control. As he talked, he was almost explicit about what I would call the reasons for the difficulty, and they center on the public opinion of the community and the lack of resources to carry out the task. He commented also that the director of the new project will be a friend of Steven Spanman, the superintendent. This produced in me a reaction—mainly of corroborating a feeling—that Steven will not return. He is taking care of his last major appointment and has made sure that he has a position. Jerl, the curriculum director, is now with the Olds Foundation.

John mentioned the fact that most of the teachers are thinking about leaving and many have already decided to do so. Of the old guard: he will leave for he hopes to have his dissertation completed; he has been working very hard on it. Apparently he has things straightened out with his advisor.[3] Meg and Jean are considering leaving; Meg would like to go to Florida. Jean's talking about going back to graduate school. In my brief conversation with Claire and Jean, they raised issues of the kinds of schools here in the Mid-west that accented things like team teaching. Wanda and Irma, the latter was not at the party tonight, seemed to be the only bets for people who will remain at the school. John thought that Wanda might go to another school in the district.

The party was quite an emotional undertaking. The faculty brought two presents for Eugene: a plaque and pen-set combination as well as a sweater. The plaque had a photoengraving of the floor plan of the school and a comment of appreciation to Eugene for his leadership in making Kensington a reality.

The feeling I had about the party was that the new staff members tended to be the ones in high prominence in the social interaction. . . . As I watched and listened, I had the feeling that there were no major or minor strands of conflict and hostility within the group. Obviously in this kind of a setting it would be hard to pick it up. I guess the major indicator I would look at here is the quality of the humor. The new coloring book didn't have the bite that I recalled the old one to have.[4] Similarly, as the people joked, the spirit was much more of we against them—the forces outside in the community which were trying to stifle the school and trying to attack the principal. I had the feeling as I talked alone with John that the villain in the eyes of the teachers this year was the district, which wouldn't support the basic idea that the school was trying to convey. He talked most earnestly about "It's been a good idea and there were some unfinished things to be done yet."

Some of the humor centered on the flagpole problem, which apparently is part of a series of community comments, and *Daily Sentinel,* one of the local newspapers, comments about the fact that the school doesn't fly a flag. Apparently the rope of the pulley is broken. Why it hasn't been fixed I don't know. The staff remarked about the newspaper article in the *Sentinel* in which a picture of the pond behind the school was featured, and a statement about a "slimy pond" at the "school of the year" was commented on. I couldn't pick up any overtones or any within-team struggles or conflicts. In fact, the reverse was true. John commented that the ISD group had a "strong and well-functioning team." Apparently the classes are pretty much self-contained

---

[3] Further information finds this not to be true. We analyze this in more detail in the section "All but the dissertation: the heavy burden."

[4] The "coloring books" were objects developed for staff parties; they indicated the creativity of the staff and the use of humor in focusing on significant episodes in the life of the school.

in the morning, as I'd heard before, and in the afternoon they have jointly scheduled the same classes and the staff swaps pupils; they have done some regrouping according to diagnostic tests. He commented that there had been some good instructing this year. Similarly, I heard no overtones of any problems that Meg and Claire were having, nor of any that Jean was having with the Basic Skills group. Wanda is in Kindergarten where she wanted to be, and apparently is quite happy there. . . . Also the feeling I get is that the total staff is a good bit more teaching and instruction oriented. For instance, one of the teachers in ISD came from a principalship and, according to John, is a highly organized and task-oriented guy. Also, there seems to be a good bit more experience on the part of a number of the staff members.

Some of the kinds of comments I've been making suggest that the first year in any organization is apt to be a tremendous trial in that it takes a good bit of sorting out to get ultimately a smooth-running unit (2/28, post-experimental year).

These observations were some of the ones recorded the year following the study. We had gone back to the district to be a part of a phase of the ending of the Kensington Story. We have commented about a number of issues, the full significance of which will be apparent only as one explores the full story of Kensington.

THE RESEARCH PROBLEM

The Initial Proposal

However, our study did not begin as an investigation of teacher turnover nor of administrative succession. It began as we suggested in our research proposal.

The problem[5] to be studied in this investigation contains several components. In its most general aspect, we are trying to capitalize on a rather unusual naturalistic event, the building of a new and uniquely designed elementary school building. Figure 1.2 contains the floor plan and design.

Although in a general sense, the question, What happens in such a novel situation?, is the focus of the research, the more specific problems to be analyzed are: (1) the development of the faculty social system; (2) the principal's role vis-à-vis the faculty social system; (3) the teachers' innovations in instruction; (4) the development of the school-wide pupil social system.

(1) In a prior investigation (Smith and Geoffrey, 1965, 1968), we were impressed with the importance of a faculty peer group as an element in the classroom teacher's decision making. The influence it exerted was not widely recognized in the building. The clique had been in operation for a number

---

[5] These materials are quoted verbatim from the research proposal funded by the United States Office of Education and Milford, the local school district.

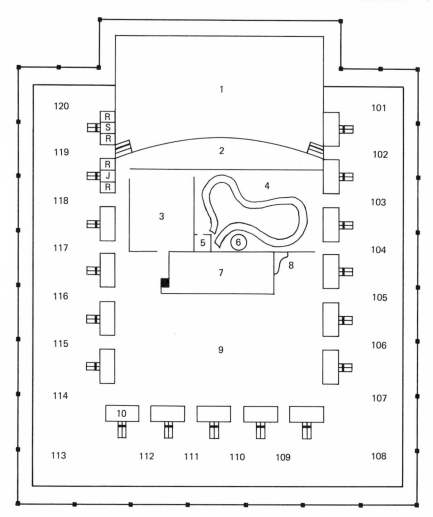

Figure 1.2 The floor plan of Kensington School. (1) Covered play shelter. (2) Stage. (3) Administrative suite. (4) Children's theatre. (5) Projection room. (6) Acting tower. (7) Curriculum center. (8) Aquarium. (9) Perception core. (10) Areas that contain rest rooms and janitorial or storage space. (101 to 120) Laboratory suites.

of years. In this study we shall have an opportunity to observe the formation of an entire faculty system (18 of the 23 teachers are new to the school district), to determine in what ways it is a totality, what and how cliques are formed, the influence processes, and the resulting impact, consonant or dissonant, on the teacher.

(2) In the proposed study, the principal's decision-making role will be a focal point in light of the novel building design, the demand for instructional innovation, and the majority of teachers new to the system. By capitalizing on these events, which should highlight the issues, we should be able to criticize and to extend the theory of decision making as it has been applied in education, for example, Halpin, *Administrative Theory in Education.*

(3) Typically, teachers entertain few dramatic changes of style, curriculum content, or classroom organization. The present setting in many ways is optimal for encouraging creativity in these areas. Such innovations with pupils lie at the heart of alterations in pupil outcomes. Observation should lead to the rethinking of models of teacher-pupil relationships. These models will be broader than many current ones, since they must encompass some of the "team" aspects and also the novel physical resources.

(4) The pupils' reactions in their new environment will be observed carefully. While one major focus will be on the developing sentiment toward the new school, activities such as independent study and social interactions will be considered also. Geographically, the large library-study room and the covered playground area will be the arenas for initial observation.

In short, although the study focuses on the impact of a unique school plant, and several specific areas of investigation have been suggested, the principal investigator's bias leans toward the broader goal of the development and integration of social science theory in education. In this regard, an attempt will be made to synthesize role theory, decision making theory, and social system theory as they explicate the functioning of this school.

Shelby's Initial View[6]

Although the above was our phrasing of the problem, Shelby, the principal, had his own views of the study. The field notes after our first extended interview related his perspective:

> One of the first questions I raised with him concerned what he thought might be of interest to the investigation, what kinds of questions might be answered. He was ready with an answer, and I infer that he had given some thought to the proposal and to what he wanted to see done. A number of issues were raised. One of them concerned his feeling that the physical plant was overemphasized in opposition to the educational innovations in the program that would be carried out. In this regard, he drew a brief diagram of the physical plant influencing curriculum, teacher behavior, and organizational factors. He thought the accent ought to be on the things that were influenced and that they were the most important. We talked about how the physical factors have been used as a hook on which to hang the proposal. He could understand that very readily. He presented an illustration, and he does this quite often

---

[6] Later in our discussion of the Institutional Plan we present Shelby's conception of the school, its goals, organization, and program.

as he talks, of a physical factor such as the item of movable desks. When one contrasts what happens in this kind of a classroom from classrooms where there are fixed desks, very often the results are negative in that the movable desks never get moved. In that sense they are not utilized at all. At this point our ideas met very closely, and I illustrated this with the concepts of opportunities and constraints, which seem to me to be important ideas in the discussion of classroom and school phenomena. These concepts do not appear in most learning experiments. Eugene suggested that they sounded somewhat like Kurt Lewin type concepts (8/9, prior to the first year).

As the study developed, the title of the research proposal, "Social Psychological Aspects of School Building Design," reflected only a part of our interest. Our subproblems of staff peer groups and administrator decision making remained significant. In addition, organizational development and formal doctrine became foci for analysis. Finally, we were to find social-systems ideas as the most fruitful and potent theoretical structures to handle the key substantive issue of educational innovation.

The Methodology

The investigation was a formulative or model-building study, and the principal method of data collection was participant observation. This was supplemented by informal interviews, intensive analysis of records, and verbatim accounts of meetings. Access to all documents had been given; this included faculty and parent school-council bulletins, committee reports, and district-wide curriculum materials. Observations were made of classroom interaction, the use of facilities, the total faculty meetings, the team meetings, the curriculum committee meetings, and the parent school-council meetings.

These varied observations enabled us to follow the development of the organization through three main periods of time. The first block was a four-week workshop prior to the beginning of school. In the months of September to December, the school's three academic divisions—the Independent Study Division (ISD), Transition Division, and Basic Skills Division—were temporarily housed in three widely separated facilities. From December to June, the divisions were located in the building designed for the program.

Maslow's statements about the need for observation and reporting of educational experiments seem relevant and most encouraging.

"In most such cases (experimental programs and schools) we wind up with a retrospective story of the program, the faith, the confident expectations, but with inadequate accounts of just what was done, how, and when and of just what happened and didn't happen as a result. . . . The real question is how we can make the best use of the 'natural experiments' that result when some courageous enthusiast with faith in his ideas wants to 'try something out' and is willing to gamble. . . . If only they were good reporters too . . . and regarded the 'write-up' as a part of the commitment!

"That is just about the way the ethnologist works: he doesn't design, control, manipulate, or change anything. Ultimately he is simply a non-interfering observer and a good reporter" (Maslow, 1965, p. 13).

Hopefully, we filled the roles of "a non-interfering observer and a good reporter."

Although we have written more intensively on participant observational procedures (Smith and Geoffrey, 1968; Smith, 1967; Smith and Pohland, 1969; Smith and Brock, 1970), several comments seem in order. In the original proposal the procedures were described in three short paragraphs:

> The general design follows the standard participant observational field study procedures as these have been described in W. F. Whyte's "Observational field work methods" in Jahoda, Deutsch, and Cook's *Research methods in social relations;* S. Kimball's "The method of natural history and educational research" in Spindler's *Education and anthropology;* and H. Becker's "Problems of inference and proof in participant observation" in the *American Sociological Review,* 1958.

> In terms of more specific design, these field note records of school and classroom events will be analyzed according to Becker's specific suggestions: (1) selection and definition of problems, concepts, and indices; (2) checking the frequency and distribution of phenomena; (3) construction of social system models; (4) final analysis and presentation of results (p. 653).

> Procedurally, the plan will be to have two persons, the principal investigator and research assistant, engaging in the observation. One of the two will be in the building at all times.[7]

[7] Although we were not there at "all" times, we did approximate this situation. In the summer workshop and through the first few weeks of September, Paul F. Kleine worked full time on the project. Smith and Keith (who was on a fellowship at the time) devoted almost full time to the project. During the study, school was in session 177 days from September to June. The workshop had involved four weeks in August. The observers have field notes from 153 *different* days at the school or in the district and 247 total entries. The latter indicates the overlap when both of us were in the field. Although it is possible to speak of 247 man-days of observation, this is faulty in the sense that some of the entries reflect part days and some reflect early morning to midnight days. One of our colleagues phrased it colloquially but cogently when he commented, "You were all over that school." The intensity of involvement is a key issue in the validity of the data.

The Outcomes: Description and Theory

The outcome of the research, by design and actual result, is twofold. We wanted to describe carefully and accurately the events that make up the beginning of an innovative school. Also we wanted to abstract from that description and to discuss the events in a more general theoretical language which would have applicability beyond the single particularistic case of Kensington. In this regard we have built "models," pictorial sketches of interrelated hypotheses, that explain our data and that, we argue, can be fruitful starting points for verificational research. To illustrate the description and theory, we present an initial view of the school and an initial interpretive model based on the epilogue at the beginning of the chapter.

The Initial View. The colored photographs of the school initially gave an image of a fairyland with its slightest hint of the unreal, since the external aspects of the building were those of an unusual rectangular columnar, white one-story structure that hinted at the simplicity of a Greek temple. This was our first view of the prospective Kensington School.

Inside, with no corridors, the areas at the center were juxtaposed to an outside covered walkway designed for casual strolling. Within, the description was completed with carpeting, colorful furnishings, and air conditioning. As if to insure their uniqueness, the areas were indicated by terminology as unusual as their shape—the nerve center, the perception core, the satellite kitchen, and the laboratory suites.

However, the uniqueness persisted even beyond the material manifestations, since they took on complete meaning only when regard was given to a program of "individualized learning" for which the facilities were especially designed. None of the techniques to be used as means was wholly new; it was the totality that boasted "newness." The program was to capture team teaching with all of its varying organizational possibilities—ungradedness, total democratic pupil-teacher decision making, absence of curriculum guides, and a learner-centered environment. The idea to prevail was primarily that of freedom from staid educational means which, in turn, would unleash both faculty and students from the difficulties of the traditional and move toward an "individualized learning program." On hearing of it, one was reminded of the similarities between the Kensington School and the Dewey School at the University of Chicago, Washburne's experimental revision of the Winnetka Schools, and Neill's Summerhill.

Yet, although the philosophies were similar, what was to be attempted in September was, for us, spatially nearer, administratively more accessible, currently in existence and, consequently, more feasible for study. In its totality the school was to be one of the first implementations in the United States of such a program with a corresponding building design. Also

Kensington was a public school with no emphasis on pupil selection. It was in a lower middle class suburban school district in a large metropolitan area in the Ohio River valley. What would happen in the way of its development as a social institution, its community response, and the carrying forth of the program in all its uniqueness were vital questions. The study approached the school from a social science perspective, using concepts from organization and systems theory. Drawing from the functional orientation, with its emphasis on social consequences of phenomena as well as their source and composition, the concepts of latent and manifest functions and dysfunctions were used to help organize and present the data as they relate to formal organizational doctrine, internal administrative structure, and facilities.

The Theoretical Intent. With some misgiving, we give an initial theoretical interpretation, the idealization of Eugene Shelby that appears in the epilogue. The reservations arise because these data are "soft," sketchy, and our analysis is highly speculative, in contrast to interpretations later in which the data are "hard" and the hypotheses are grounded well in the case, if not more generally in the real world. When Gouldner (1954a, 1954b) first analysed administrative succession in terms of the idealization of the earlier manager, he called it the "Rebecca Myth" after a similar phenomenon that was the central thesis of a novel by DuMaurier (1938). Our intent, throughout our analysis is to build on the descriptions captured in the field notes. This building involves (1) the "borrowing" of concepts, such as the idealization of an administrator, (2) the creating of new concepts, such as the "Bataan Phenomenon," (3) the linking of concepts into hypotheses, such as "increasing idealization of an administrator increases positive sentiments of Kensington's potential," and (4) the patterning of the hypotheses into pictorial models. Figure 1.3 presents such a pictorial model. This kind of intent is our understanding of the cumulative function of theory described by Merton (1957), practiced by Homans (1950), pictorialized by March and Simon (1958), rationalized by Zetterberg (1965), and extrapolated to educational theory by Smith and Geoffrey (1968).

Figure 1.3 should be read in this manner. At some point in time (T_3), the middle of the post-experimental year, several aspects of the social system could be isolated and described. The "Bataan Phenomenon"[8] refers to a kind of administrative turnover and includes the dual facets that Eugene was the last of the key administrative figures to leave, since Steven Spanman

---

[8] Our allusion here is to the charisma associated with General MacArthur's involuntary departure from the Philippines, his pursuit of the war in the Pacific, and his vow to return. Metaphorical labels such as "Bataan Phenomenon" have some obvious strengths and weaknesses.

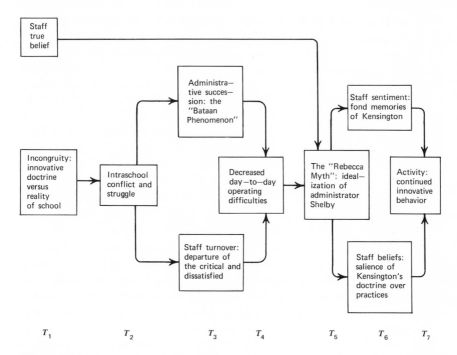

Figure 1.3 Complexities of staff turnover and administrative sucession at Kensington.

and Jerl Cohen, the superintendent and curriculum director of Milford, had both departed. Second, Eugene was not leaving spiritually, since his new position was with PS 2100 in Metropolis, a school designed for the future. In effect, he was going to continue the battle for the Kensington ideals, or as we described it metaphorically, the pursuit of the grail. We argue also that decreased day-to-day frustrations from the level of the prior year and the particular kind of staff turnover at the end of the prior year were important at T_3. We hypothesize that these elements lead to the idealization of Shelby, the formation of the "Rebecca Myth." This idealization contributes in turn to the staff's accenting of fond memories and to the selective recall and salience of the doctrine as opposed to the practices. For perspective we introduce an arbitrary T_1 in which an "innovative doctrine" or vision of the school was incongruent with the reality of the school (the practices) and led to a year of staff conflict and struggle (T_2). Similarly, there was a quality of true belief, what Hoffer describes as "fanatical faith," which characterized the staff in its selection and early socialization.

As we look back at Gouldner's analysis of "Old Doug," the Rebecca of the gypsum plant, we find essentially that in his case the myth arose out of worker resentment of management's rescinding of the indulgency pattern of supervision.

"In part, workers conjured up the past, comparing Peele with 'Old Doug,' as an effort to legitimate the crumbling indulgency pattern and to justify their resistance to Peele's changes. If the elements of the indulgency pattern were suspect and non-legitimate, the myth of 'Old Doug' became its guardian. The issue then need no longer be, 'This is what we want,' but could be stated, 'Old Doug did thus and so, and he was a good man.' The development of this myth illustrates the workers' response to a 'latent problem' and their use of informal rather than contractual solutions to meet Peele's violation of the indulgency pattern" (1954b, pp. 28–29).

As we have tried to analyze the Gouldner position more carefully we developed the model in Figure 1.4. The essence of this theory is a particular case of Homans' more general position: ". . . the higher the rank of a person within a group, the more nearly his activities conform to the norms of the group (1950, p. 141)." In Gouldner's instance the activities refer

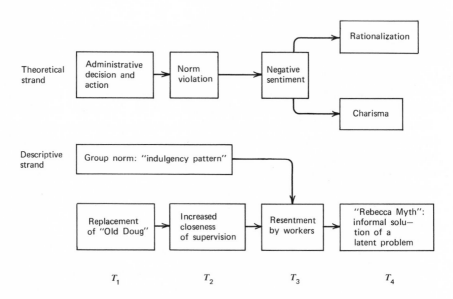

Figure 1.4 Gouldner's theory of the antecedents of the "Rebecca Myth" (after 1954b, pages 28 to 29).

to the incumbent of an administrative position in a particular formal organization, a gypsum factory. The sentiment is resentment. The "Rebecca Myth" is, in our terms, a group belief system that amounts to a rationalization developed when workers could not deal formally or contractually with the indulgency pattern, its violation, and their resentment.

The point we wish to make from our data is that the idealization of a departed leader can have additional roots and subtleties. We discuss in fuller detail later "the innovative doctrine" and "the reality of school." At this point, we can say that they indicate the background of hopes and aspirations that brought a certain kind of staff to Kensington and that they provide a context for the events of the year. The conflict and struggles also are important background factors raised later. At this point, we would highlight the "Bataan Phenomenon," our metaphor from World War II wherein the leader left the scene of the lost battle very late and went to continue the broader fight. Essentially we are arguing that charisma, of which the "Rebecca Myth" is a special instance, is truly a much more complex phenomenon than Gouldner's case indicates. In the context of an innovative organization it takes on considerable significance. Administrators who fight to the end and who leave, not for personal reasons but for a wider use of their talents in the cause of the group's broader purposes, tend to be idealized. In a sense, we are still arguing the broader Homanian hypothesis, positive sentiment (esteem) comes to him whose activities fulfill the norms of the group. Our data suggest also that this idealization has been facilitated by decreased frustrations in the second year (in contrast to the conflict and struggle the first year). This lessened frustration is interdependent with the kind of staff turnover: a departure of the more critical and the more disillusioned of the true believers. The remaining staff were the ones whose faith in the school was a firm commitment for reasons of the simple "rightness" of the ideology.[9]

In our analysis, in contrast to Gouldner's, we would accent a more complex set of dimensions surrounding the departure of the earlier administrator and the nature of the system at that time. Furthermore, the analysis suggests linkages between the "Rebecca Myth" and charisma the more general form of idealization of leaders.

CONCLUDING THE EPILOGUE

Once again we anticipate our data by sketching and analyzing aspects of the environment that contributed to Kensington's change. In a sense

[9] Later we shall say a good deal more about true belief and about a theory of personnel turnover.

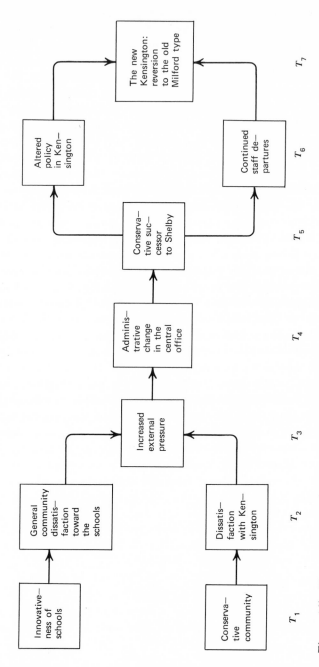

Figure 1.5 The social context of Kensington's administrative change.

we are seeking a conception that we can articulate, eventually, with the internal dynamics presented in Figure 1.3. In a very important sense, strands of events run parallel in time. Occasionally the strands run together, by chance or design, and have significant impact on each other. This multiplicity of events is important for the educational administrator, the social theorist, and the school patron as citizen. Descriptively our chain of events begins arbitrarily at T_1 in Figure 1.5, the social context of Kensington's administrative change. We might have chosen some prior time, a school board election, the appointment of the school superintendent, or an earlier community conflict over school policies. Suffice it to say, T_1 shows the incongruity of a conservative community and an innovative school system. This incongruity led to community dissatisfaction with the school system generally and with Kensington in particular. The dissatisfaction was expressed as pressure on and in the school board and resulted in administrative changes in the central office—Spanman's leave of absence and a more conservative successor. With Shelby's departure, a resignation accepted in midsemester, the central office chose a conservative successor. Policy shifts occurred in the school, since a principal has considerable power when he has the backing of the central office, and the staff turnover continued. New faculty were more traditional, and Kensington as both dream and reality was gone. The school was now in both philosophy and action a part of "the old Milford." Figure 1.5 sketches these events and ideas.

This then is what we are about. We observed for many hours over the course of the full school year. We lived with the staff from the first day of the summer workshop in August until the last formal meeting, a closing dinner party in June. We kept careful records on the day-to-day trials, accomplishments, tribulations, joys, and sorrows. We thought as hard and as well as we were able to understand Kensington as an individual case study and as an illustration of broad and significant issues in social science and education. This was our task and our privilege.

Origins of an Innovative Organization

CHAPTER 2

Formal Doctrine: Manifestations, Content, Dimensions, and Consequences

INTRODUCTION

Sometimes a picture of social reality becomes clearer by stepping back from the concrete images of day-to-day activities and events and by viewing the larger context into which the particulars fit. One part of this frame of reference is what we have called the "formal doctrine."[1] Our analysis proceeds this way. All groups and organizations, in the course of their development, build a point of view or perspective about themselves, their problems, and their environment. These points of view vary in the degree to which they are visionary, conscious, and codified. We have come to use the term "formal doctrine" to represent the complex combination of a point of view that is visionary, that is highly conscious, and that is highly codified. Ideology, a visionary theorizing, could serve about as well, although it tends not to emphasize the conscious and codified aspects. The doctrine includes an elaborated system of concepts, spelling out the entire structure of means and ends within an organization.

At Kensington, a number of events took place that demanded additional labels. These include mandate, institutional plan, and facade. A mandate is the formal charge or directive given by the legitimate authority. In the case of Kensington, it is the superintendent's directive.[2] The Institutional Plan is the particular conception of the doctrine as the principal, Mr. Shelby, had developed it prior to the August workshop. In its most

---

[1] This is an adaptation of Selznick's concept of "official doctrine," which appeared in *TVA and the Grass Roots* (1949).

[2] This might be pursued further in the sense that a superintendent has a mandate from the school board and, in turn, the board might have a mandate from the residents of the community. In the Milford District these two additional linkages contained complexities of prior political conflict.

articulate form, it appeared as a mimeographed document titled *Kensington Elementary School: Design for Individualized Instruction.*

In addition, Kensington's formal doctrine was codified in three other major documents: (1) the *Educational Specifications* developed for Kensington's architect, (2) a proposal to the Olds Foundation that was written by the curriculum director, and (3) a published document from the Architectural Design Institute (ADI) that described Kensington as an innovative school. In general, a high degree of consistency existed among these statements; however, each carried the slant of its particular purposes and authors.

An additional and important phrasing of the formal doctrine occurs in what we have called the facade, the formal doctrine as it was presented to the public. Even here further distinctions are required. The "public" is multiple; it includes the parents who are the immediate patrons of the school, the residents of the Milford School District, the broader audience of the subcommunities in the metropolitan area in which Milford exists and to which it compares itself and, also, the national community, which received images of Kensington through national magazines. In addition, one can discriminate between the lay audience and the professional audience, the latter being the numbers of educational personnel who visited Kensington, who heard about the school from the many spokesmen connected with it, or who read about it in the numerous professional articles that have been printed about the school.

Finally, one must speak of individual faculty member's conceptions or schemas. The school was many and sometimes different things to individual faculty members. As we shall learn, to some it was a reason for being, a total existence; for others it was mainly team teaching, or ungradedness, or individualized instruction. In effect, particular elements were abstracted and focused on by particular staff members.

As one asks oneself the question, "Why make such distinctions?" a number of answers occur. First, the doctrine varied in the world of Kensington. Second, the facade, that part which appeared in the national magazines, was often a series of special instances and fond hopes rather than the reality of the new school. Third, the principal's Institutional Plan was a culmination of considerable personal thought and was his image of what the school was to be made into through day-to-day interaction. It was not to be changed easily. Fourth, the doctrine served to buoy up spirits when the reality flagged. Fifth, the mandate from the superintendent to the faculty, "build a school," was in partial conflict with the principal's Institutional Plan, which had many aspects already indicated. Sixth, the individual staff conceptions, in accenting specific elements, often raised issues of conflict with the totality or other specific but different elements that another accented. Finally, and perhaps most important, the formal doctrine, especially in a new and developing school, suggests the means-means and means-ends relationships that become the structure of the school. In one sense, it is through varying interpretations, perceptions, and adaptations of doctrine that organizational structures are elaborated and changed.

SOURCES, MANIFESTATIONS, AND CONTENT OF THE DOCTRINE

The Mandate

In our theoretical analysis the initial mandate, or general set of directives issued to the principal and faculty, precedes the formal doctrine of the school and also specifies elements in the doctrine. The mandate was characterized, as observed in the superintendent's statements, by its long-range goals. Both in substance and goals, the mandate reflects what might be called the "new elementary education" of the 1960s. The doctrine developed and adopted by the Kensington School faculty was geared somewhat more to immediacy and to effecting a program at the beginning of the school year in September.

Much of the broader mandate of the Milford School District was presented by the superintendent at a total Kensington School faculty meeting on August 18. Some of the points noted below form a major part of the doctrine that was propagated and that performed various functions for the school. The ideas were a part of a five-year plan that contained several points. In outline form, from our notes, we find the superintendent saying:

> CURRICULUM. The curriculum is all pupil experiences while under the direction and supervision of the school. It depends on the goals and the kinds of adults we want. For example, we don't necessarily want adults who can name all 50 states, or 36 presidents, or who said the prayer in the Continental Congress. We want adults who have developed effective language techniques, life-long habits of continuous learning, and values which guide them as individuals and as members of society. We need communication and computation skills. Outside this there is no continuity. There is no instructional curriculum. We don't need to teach American history at fifth grade or individual states at fourth grade. The curriculum is determined by the needs of pupils. We don't need a crutch such as a text. We are looking for ways of organizing curriculum at Kensington School. The faculty will do this. There are no policies, no regulations, no gimmicks for you to use as an excuse. You are to determine it. The faculty is the curriculum.

> METHODS. (1) Individualize, (2) humanize, (3) dramatize, (4) socialize. Under the category of individualize, one must decide how to set objectives, plan, prepare, communicate, and evaluate and in doing these decide whether or not one is operating within the framework of the group or individual. Item two, humanize, refers to getting to know the students and respecting them.

Included in dramatizing, one emphasizes creativity, divergent thinking, and devices for handling wrong answers. Socializing deals with the learning of various roles for working in groups. The past week of group development (that is, the August T-groups) contributes to this.

TIME. (1) *The school day*. There should be varied lengths of time in the school day. In the elementary school some should come at 7:00, 8:00, and 9:00 and leave at 2:00, 3:00, and so forth. It is hoped that in the Kensington School there will be no bell and pupils can come when they want. We hope everyone will not leave at 3:30. (2) *The school year*. The twelve-month school year is advocated. The three months' vacation has outlived its usefulness. As an example, parents' vacations fit individual wants; they are able to resume their work when they return.

STUDENT AGES. Two-, three-, and four-year-olds should be able to come to and leave the school at varied times. All should not remain in school the same number of years.

PERSONNEL. (1) *Teachers*. The teachers are to break down walls and become learning consultants rather than the traditional dispensers of information. (2) *Pupils*. Instead of classroom units, there will be pupil units. There will not be 18 units of 30, but 550 units. It is to be a completely individualized program. There are to be multilevel materials.

PROTECTED SUBCULTURE. The idea of the Kensington School as a protected subculture. If we are to be change agents, we must develop subcultures. Group norms and pressures influence teachers. This subculture will protect good teachers from being influenced by group norms. By protecting subcultures, we may help the spread of ideas.

The presentation concluded with a quotation, "A man's reach should exceed his grasp or else what's a heaven for?" Thus, this was the mandate and framework within which the principal and faculty at Kensington proceeded to formulate their mode of operation. As consultant Roberts viewed it, and in his words, "This is a very peculiar charge: 'Go start a new school,' not 'Here are the books, go teach.'" In a most important sense the new elementary education was endorsed strongly by the superintendent. It should be pointed out also that the "start a new school" interpretation is even more open ended than were the illustrative items of content themselves as they were presented by Spanman. An implicit unasked and unanswered question remained: "Is the first priority on the configuration of the content of the mandate as presented by Spanman or on the resources of the staff members?"

Behind the superintendent's words of August 18 were earlier aspects of the intellectual content of Kensington. In January, the year before the opening of school, a district-wide proposal of the Milford schools was submitted to the Olds Foundation.[3] Broadly stated, it was a three-year "comprehensive project for developing a design for learning." To better understand the development of Kensington's doctrine, we review briefly the purposes of the proposed project. They included these statements:

1.   To reconstruct all areas of content into concepts, skills, and values.

2.   To develop experiences that will implement the learning of concepts, skills, and values.

3.   To investigate the changed roles of students and teachers in the school; that is, to change the relationship of teachers and pupils from one of dependence to one of self-realization.

4.   To decrease the time lag between the theoretical acceptance of proven new developments and the working acceptance of new developments in learning experiences.

5.   To develop a comprehensive rationale of criteria necessary to initiate change in an educational enterprise (pp. 10–12).

The project was to be in three stages. In Stage I, Kensington was to be one of two elementary schools with a prototype program. Stage II, as delineated in the proposal, would apply the program in the middle grades of all elementary schools. During Stage III, the program would be established system wide, kindergarten through high school. Although Kensington was a protected subculture and had a mandate of its own, the district also was assumed to be ready for change, and Kensington was to be a vital part of that plan.

As we have presented it, the mandate is a concrete and tangible part of Kensington's environment. As such, the mandate is important information for the organization and for its administrator. It ties an organization or system to the larger organization. Furthermore, and to anticipate a later discussion, the mandate aids in clarifying the "supportive-nonsupportive" dimension of the environment. As organizational alternatives are raised, explored, and evaluated, the mandate is the template indicating which alternatives will be supported, which will be rejected, or which will be responded to with lukewarm interest. We consider this an important specification of Simon's (1957) point that the next higher level of the larger organization specifies the decision premises of the immediately lower level of the organization. The implications for hierarchical control, for democratic school

---

[3] This proposal did not receive funding. At the time, we, the investigators, were not aware of the impact this would have on the resources available to carry out the tasks taken on by the Kensington School and the Milford District. Also, these events occurred before the heavy federal funding of innovation through Title III of the Elementary and Secondary Education Act.

administration, and for teacher-pupil relations are quite real and quite important.

The Building Specifications

Another aspect and source of the doctrine of the Kensington School developed from the "Specs," the *Building Specifications*. We make an analysis of this document into its social psychological components. From this we can view particularly the interplay of early conceptions of the program and the physical plant as they lead to the more general point of view of the school. In the building specifications the original rationale for the design is stated straightforwardly, although abstractly: "the ultimate goal is to enable all the children of all the people to develop to the limits of their potentiality. The educational program and the physical structure facilitate this. The program changes because society changes. The building remains; hence, it must be flexible and adaptable" (pp. 1–2). These statements reflect the special concern of the architect who is aware of the open-system qualities of an educational organization and the closed-system qualities of a structure made of concrete and steel. Even so, further ambiguity is introduced because of professional education's inability to speak precisely about the ends of educational endeavors.

Objectives. The general objectives are stated and restated a number of times in the *Specifications*. The words used vary considerably: (1) ". . . all the children of all the people to develop to the limits of their potentiality" (p. 2); (2) ". . . complete living in all phases of life" (p. 10); (3) ". . . become the architect of his own character" (p. 10); (4) ". . . self-realization" (p. 10); (5) ". . . development of the child intellectually, socially, emotionally, and physically" (p. 12).

The unique objectives of the school approach specificity in a statement from the *Specs:*

"The specific objectives of the educational program are: (1) to promote self-realization of the child by developing an inquiring mind; (2) to teach the basic fundamentals of reading, writing, speaking, and listening in the native tongue; (3) to learn the basic concepts of numbers and calculations; (4) to achieve habits of good health and citizenship; (5) to understand the use and influence of science at present and its implications for the future; (6) to develop an appreciation for beauty in art, literature, music, and nature; (7) to develop and guide children in the wise use of leisure time; (8) to inculcate an aesthetic appreciation and understanding of our cultural and spiritual values; (9) to develop self-respect and respect for human relationships towards friends, classmates, family, society and its institutions and laws; (10) to take pride in good workmanship and choice of occupation; (11) to be able to assume responsibility and cooperate effectively as a person within a group or society; (12) to develop maturity and insight in making decisions and in interpreting ideas" (pp. 9–10).

Objectives are ends of human endeavor. Such a simple statement belies the complexities lying within it. In our analysis we were struck by several aspects of objectives: (1) the ends have a time dimension varying from the present to the distant future, the oft-cited long-range and short-term quality; (2) activities can be classified as specific subgoals; (3) present activities can be classified as subgoals instrumental to distant goals; (4) goals vary on a generality-specificity continuum; (5) objectives differ in the degree to which they are written and formalized; (6) as goals become more specific, concrete, and immediate, agreement among individuals and groups of individuals becomes more difficult; (7) priorities among educational ends are not clear, and the criteria and mechanisms for establishing priorities and resolving conflict are not clear.

That these problems are not unique to Kensington is clear from Simon's statement:

"The fact that goals may be dependent for their force on other more distant ends leads to the arrangement of these goals in a hierarchy—each level to be considered as an end relative to the levels below it and as a means relative to the levels above it. Through the hierarchical structure of ends, behavior attains integration and consistency, for each member of a set of behavior alternatives is then weighed in terms of a comprehensive scale of values—the "ultimate" ends. In actual behavior, a high degree of conscious integration is seldom attained. Instead of a single branching hierarchy, the structure of conscious motives is usually a tangled web or, more precisely, a disconnected collection of elements only weakly and incompletely tied together; and the integration of these elements becomes progressively weaker as the higher levels of the hierarchy—the more final ends—are reached" (1957, p. 63).

If our analysis is correct, the difficulty in specification of goals in time and concreteness by the original planning group, by the superintendent, and by the principal has enabled us to move only tentatively to comparabilities in discussion of the building structure, the program of educational activities, and the structure of interaction among the significant participants. Educational and social theory have important problems that remain to be solved.

Physical Facilities. In our analytic framework the statement of general and specific objectives must be accompanied by a statement of means that have high probabilities of reaching the ends. The program of activities, the interactional structure of pupils, teachers and staff, and the building facilities provide a simple taxonomy for the analysis of means. The most general statement of the building dimension appears in the *Specifications:* "Consequently, a physical plan which is considerably different from and more comprehensive than the traditional elementary plant is required" (p. 12). The specific elaboration of this as a taxonomy of facilities in the *Specifications* does not suggest to us more comprehensiveness or greater difference from most school plant specifications. In outline form the statement is as follows.

1. Educational Spaces
   a. General purpose classrooms
   b. Special instructional areas
2. Auxiliary Spaces
3. Special Facilities
4. General Environment

In the analysis of educational space, the most pertinent comment for our purposes proceeds in this manner:

"In developing a design for the general purpose classroom a number of functions which are to be served by this space should be kept in mind. These functions are: 'home base' activities such as pupil accounting, guidance, individual schedule assignment, and storage of clothing; individual formal work; group formal work; individual informal work; and group informal activity" (p. 13).

At this point in the *Building Specifications* the analysis of interactional or organizational structure ("formal to informal work," individual to group work, and the interrelationships between the two) has arisen with mostly implicit relationships to the objectives. There has been no justification of these kinds of structures through linking the structures to the objectives. The closest the planners come to explicitness is the following introductory comment.

"Educational spaces should be designed for learning rather than for teaching. This is a way of pointing out that many of the things which have been taught in the elementary schools have not been learned. It is also true that much has been learned that no one intended to teach. Some of these latter things such as learning to dislike the school situation, and learning to live in an adult-dominated situation while being exposed to information about democracy, have been all too common" (pp. 12–13).

The special instructional areas include drama, art, music, physical education, large group activity, and the instructional materials center. The discussion of auxiliary facilities, special facilities, and general environment does not provide clear discriminations for the present investigators. In general, the items seem to involve attention to basic physical needs of the food, clothing, and shelter variety, and include food services, toilet facilities, temperature and lighting control, and the like. They do provide, however, an occasion for the educational specifications committee to introduce another general interactional variable, "the teaching-learning process."[4]

Flexibility is stated as a key dimension in the Kensington School specifications. This conceptual label possesses several different definitions, and it is used in several different arguments. The essential ingredient in the definition seems to be ease of change. A flexible building, then, is a building that can be changed easily. Presumably, the changes are instituted in terms of varying purposes. The prospectus speaks of four kinds of flexibility: (1) daily flexibility, (2) frequent flexibility, (3) infrequent flexibility, (4) long-range flexibility. The first refers to day-to-day changes residing in items such as movable furniture and equipment and movable walls or partitions. The middle two categories are the ones that imply change for periods of days or weeks, and the latter category implies major and more permanent additions, deletions, and alterations.

Daily flexibility becomes critical in the momentary planning by teachers and pupils. As teachers have multiple purposes and as they try to attain them in the same physical locale, then the facility needs to be flexible. Similarly, as teachers change their goals, flexible facilities are advantageous. The ability to make additions onto the building to handle increased enrollments would be an example of long-range flexibility. One might question whether Kensington's shape and internal design would permit this kind of addition. Presumably, a building may have a high degree of one kind of flexibility and a low degree of other kinds.

Social Structure. Social structure, in its initial formulation, is primarily an activity structure and an interactional structure. Certain kinds of tasks are carried out and certain relationships exist among the persons involved. The building specifications suggest at several points the nature of the dimensions involved and their presumed interrelationships. We have diagrammed in Figure 2.1 the relationship among general environmental conditions, the social psychological variables of groups, and individual outcomes.

Also from the *Specs,* we have abstracted references to other social psychological variables that presumably interrelate with building structure and facilitate the earlier stated goals. They include organizational formats "not restricted to the traditional grade lines of K to 6" (p. 10). This is an

---

[4] Didactic instruction seems to be their intent although it is not defined.

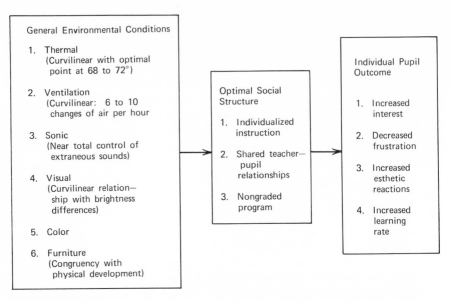

Figure 2.1 Assumed relationships between physical facilities (general environmental conditions), social psychological variables, and individual pupil outcomes (Specifications, pages 20 to 27).

early acknowledgment of the nongraded structures that were to be made concrete in the three divisions: Basic Skills, Transition, and ISD. In the *Specs* clear demarcations are not made into our broad categories of activity structure and interaction structure. Rather, a half dozen more specific interpretations are made that define the social structure of the school:

1. ". . . a program flexible enough to provide for individual differences of pupils."
2. ". . . schedules arranged according to needs and interests of each pupil."
3. ". . . guidance of pupils into experiences of successful living."
4. "Purposes and methods will be shared by pupils and teachers."
5. "Pupils will carry out projects individually as well as in small groups and large groups."
6. "Learning assignments will be individualized . . . ." (pp. 10–11)

Notice that organizational structures such as team teaching receive no mention in the *Specs*. Verbs such as inform, explain, instruct, and tell also are noticeably less prominent in the *Specs* than nouns such as projects and activities. Thus, guides for teacher activity and interaction structures

that presumably would facilitate planning and development of flexible programs, schedules, grouping of pupils, and individualized learning were not
explicit in the specifications.

The Institutional Plan[5]

Introduction. The "Institutional Plan" was the design of the school in
the mind of the principal. The observers first heard of it in the preworkshop
discussions they had in getting the research underway. The staff became
aware during the middle of the T-group week. The summary notes reflected
the observer's interpretation at the time.

> Eugene's comments about the school really came like a blast at lunch yester-
> day.[6] His feelings about the "Institutional Plan" and the continual reiteration
> of this raised skepticism, at least, in a few of the people. This I would judge
> partly by the expressions on their faces and partly by the later comments,
> for instance, one of the staff's asking about how flexible the Institutional Plan
> is. I keep getting a very strong image of Eugene as someone who wants to
> be a democratically oriented school administrator and, yet, who has an ego-in-
> volved idea that he sees as more vital and more real and more ideal than
> anything else that might be arrived at. In this sense he seems to be a man
> with more faith in his own idea (which is a very interesting and very exciting
> one, I think) than in the possibility of this group of people arriving at a
> better Institutional Plan. Most of this we won't really know about until next
> week when the individuals start working in their areas and elements of the
> plan become open for interpretation in the light of very specific things that
> must be implemented with the pupils. For instance, one staff member has
> already made some digs, on occasion in the group, about the notion of effective
> or "fully functioning" children. She equates this conception with a bland ad-
> justment concept and a denial of individual idiosyncrasies. I would guess that
> other staff also have some special interpretations here (8/12).

The ten-page statement traced briefly the history of some of the purposes
and methods of education in the United States. In this account, historical

---

[5] Seldom have we seen as sophisticated a statement made by public school personnel.
Using broader professional standards as a criterion for analysis and evaluation is
to some degree as unfair as it is also a measure of our esteem for Kensington's
attempt to think through The New Elementary Education.

[6] The field notes, and especially those we have called the Summary Observations
and Interpretations, contain a good bit of the observers' interpretations, emotional
reactions, and inferences, often in quite colloquial language. In general, we have
left them this way for the readability and the evocative images they generate.
The notes also enable the reader to judge aspects of our methodology, especially
the way evidence is sorted and conceptual issues are generated. Also, although
there are comments that might strike some readers as excessively eulogistic or critical,
they were our aids in moving to the long-term goal of phrasing the Kensington
experience from the vantage point or perspective of each of its individual members.

interpretations were made. For instance, in the early 19th century personal instruction was used to prepare limited numbers of children for secondary education. It was in the latter part of the 19th century, with the coming of the mass education philosophy, that group instruction developed. Operating this way, the needs of the individual pupil were subordinated to efficient school administration and organization. In the 20th century more individualized, flexible programs, that were achieved by grouping based on rate of learning, were tried. These programs were in response to the limitations of the group approach to teaching. We notice that Shelby, writing in the Institutional Plan, felt that these programs had hampered a more broadly conceived individualized instruction at the elementary school level.

"Attempts which have been made to individualize instruction have concentrated on rate of learning and have failed to take into account the entire teaching-learning situation which includes talents, needs, interests, readiness, backgrounds, and motivation of students, as well as effective instructional materials and methods.

"Subjects have been presented in isolation with little or no emphasis upon interrelatedness of areas of instruction" (p. 2).

We now give a resumé of the content of the Institutional Plan of the Kensington School. This is what was presented to visiting educators, parents, reporters, and other interested persons. Also, as we have indicated, this particular document served as the staff's first formal contact with the new school's program.

Objectives and Assumptions. The general objectives for the elementary school formulated in the plan were these:

"1.   To assist pupils to become fully functioning mature human beings.

2.   To meet the needs of individual differences by providing a differentiated program (rather than merely a differentiated rate for progressing through a uniform program).

3.   To provide the skills, the structures, and the understandings which will enable pupils to identify worthwhile goals for themselves, and to work independently toward their attainment" (p. 4).

The school's function, according to the plan, was to establish and to implement a program that would assist in reaching the goals or objectives. Accordingly, the instructional program was based on two assumptions. The first idea was that learning results only from experience. Experience was defined as "what happened within an individual as a consequence of his living in or transacting with his environment." A second assumption was that it is impossible to structure a particular experience; only the environment can be structured in such a way that the desired experience is likely to occur. These assumptions implied that the Kensington School had a twofold task: decisions must be made as to experiences considered desirable for the pupil, and ways must be located for structuring the learning environment so that these experiences are likely to evolve. The pupils at the Kensington School were to take active parts in both of the processes.

There was to be no one central focus such as textbook-centeredness, pupil-centeredness, or teacher-centeredness; instead, numerous facets of the school were to shape the learning environment. Learning was viewed as an interactive process that varied from individual to individual. These ideas were a part of the rationale utilized in decision making as it related to curriculum, teacher-pupil roles, the organization of the school, the building and facilities, and the instructional materials.

Curriculum. The Kensington School placed primary emphasis on process development as opposed to content development. What was designated as the "spiral curriculum" in which concepts, skills, and values were the central elements aided in this shift in emphasis. The document stated that:

"Concepts, skills, and values form the unifying threads around which learning experiences are provided. Referred to as the 'spiral curriculum,' this approach places major emphasis on process development rather than content development. Although ample provision is made for individualization of the curriculum, continuity, sequence, and integration of knowledge are facilitated through the use of curriculum guides which have been developed. Since organization of knowledge really takes place in the mind of the learner, the structure of the curriculum does not determine directly what is learned by pupils, but influences learning indirectly through helping to shape the learning 'milieu' for pupils" (p. 7).

Later, and in considerable detail, we shall present the staff's attempts to translate these ideas into day-to-day events in the lives of the children.

Redefinition of Teacher-Pupil Roles. The document emphasized that more was involved in accomplishing the objectives of the school than just slicing subject matter in a variety of ways. The contributions of the behavioral sciences to a recognition of vital human forces in the teaching-learning process that are of concern when planning educational programs were cited. Human factors such as motivation, perception, discipline, communication, and thinking were designated as important in the acquisition of knowledge as well as in the development of the pupils into fully-functioning human beings, which it will be remembered was one of the general objectives. The application of these processes brought about the recognition of a need for a change in the traditional teacher-pupil roles and in the organizational climate in which this interaction occurs. Figure 2.2 shows the change in emphasis in teacher-pupil roles.

From	*To*
Passive, reactive pupils	Active, initiating pupils
Pupil followership	Pupil leadership
Restriction of pupils	Freedom for pupils
External discipline	Self-discipline
External motivation	Self-motivation
Group activities	Individual activities
Restricting pupil interaction	Encouraging pupil interaction
Teacher responsibility for teaching	Pupil responsibility for learning
Teacher planning	Teacher-pupil planning
Teacher evaluation	Teacher-pupil evaluation
Teacher as a dispenser of knowledge	Teacher as catalyst for inquiry
Teacher as controller of pupils	Teacher as organizer for learning
Identical roles for teachers	Differentiated roles for teachers
Closed, rigid social climate	Open, flexible social climate

Figure 2.2   The Institutional Plan's redefinition of teacher-pupil roles (p. 8).

Although our field notes contain no staff references to the work of H. H. Anderson and his colleagues, and the Institutional Plan does not footnote their contributions (1945, 1946a, 1946b), it seems fair to say that the redefinition of teacher-pupil roles is congruent with Anderson's continuum of dominative to integrative social contacts between teachers and children. Similarly, the pupil behaviors of spontaneity, self-initiation, and activity are within his conceptual framework. In the second-to-last item in Figure 2.2 the shift from identical to differentiated teachers' roles is a new element introduced, but even here Anderson's conception of "inviting differences" seems relevant.

Organization of the Kensington School. "Organization of teachers and pupils assumes a different perspective when viewed in terms of implementing a new approach to the attainment of refocused objectives. As with all other elements of the school, organization is merely (designed-intended) for the purpose of facilitating the educational program. The appropriateness of the form of organization employed is dependent upon the function of the school" (p. 8).[7]

The doctrine surrounding the organization stresses flexibility. Teacher-pupil organization has as its base "planned flexibility." "Both horizontal and vertical organization of the school are, therefore, designed to provide the framework within which is possible the frequent reorganization of pupils

---

[7] The frequent reorganization that became a reality outside the document is examined elsewhere as to its latent and manifest functions when the program became a part of teacher-pupil interaction and confronted the community full-blown for the first time.

and teachers for meaningful instructional activities" (p. 9). Vertical organization is considered as referring to the sequence of progression through the school and is closely related to the concept of gradedness. In the past, in most schools sequence has not been viewed as problematic; however, the failure elsewhere to recognize that there are numerous sequences is pointed out in the document. The Kensington School avoids organizing on the basis of "rigidly defined 'levels' " or six lock-step grades. The vertical organization has three basic divisions, and there is opportunity for flexibility within and between divisions. The three divisions—Basic Skills, Transition, and Independent Study (ISD)—are planned to perform differentiated functions. The organization within, horizontal organization, is also differentiated for maximum effectiveness. Much of this is summarized in Figure 2.3, a summary table from the Institutional Plan.

As has been shown, much of the doctrine emphasized the flexibility of both the building and the instructional program. The provision for individual differences of students to the extent of schedules arranged according to the needs and interests of each pupil, which represented the "highly individualized" program, was descriptive of the school's intentions.

Schemas of Individual Faculty Members

In effect, we have presented a number of instances of the formal doctrine as individual conceptions, since the mandate reflected the superintendent's position, the foundation request was written primarily by the curriculum director, and the Institutional Plan was the principal's formal statement of his view of the doctrine. However, the data suggest strongly, as will a reading of later descriptive aspects of this monograph, that each faculty member held his own view or schema of Kensington. Typically, each schema seemed to be generated out of personal needs and goals, early conversations about the school (especially with Spanman and Shelby), and early documents. As the faculty convened in August, the individual and common experiences of each seemed to shape the conceptions a step or two further. As the divisions and teams went their individual ways, both geographically and instructionally, individual members were privy to only partial experiences of the totality. The channels of informal communication were interlocked through living arrangements, for example, one of the Basic Skills-4 team members lived with an ISD teacher and another lived with a Transition teacher. Although these circumstances, and devices such as monthly Saturday morning staff meetings and frequent staff bulletins, served communication functions, people saw and heard only limited parts of the totality. The researchers were frequently the object of "What's going on over at . . . ?" type of questions. Most of these questions were parried with a variety of responses. For example: "Why? What have you heard?"

Function of the Elementary School	Designed to develop the learner as an individual and as a member of society.		
Means of Fulfilling Function	Focus on learning generalizations basic to the disciplines and on ways of knowing and thinking. Emphasis on the individual.		
Organizational Structure	Vertical organization consisting of three sequential divisions: Basic Skills, Transition, and Independent Study.		
	Basic Skills Division	Transition Division	Independent Study Division
Distinctive Function of Division	To provide the basic communication, computation, and social skills essential for acquiring knowledge and for developing as mature human beings.	To teach pupils to work within the structure of the school to pursue knowledge independently.	To assist pupils pursue meaningful knowledge about the world in which they live.
Means of Fulfilling	Through the use of sequential learning activities and materials.	Through the development of the classroom group as an effective social system for attaining institutional goals.	Through the provision of a systematic framework that allows pupils to utilize extensive human and material resources for learning.
Basic Unit of Organization	Classes within the division (self-contained classrooms).	Small groups within classes within the division.	Individuals within the division.
Organizational Structure of the Division	Vertical (sequential levels), with intraclass flexibility for instruction.	Horizontal, with flexible vertical organization for instruction in skill subjects.	Complete horizontal and vertical flexibility for instruction.
Pupil Progress	Differentiated rates of progress according to individual needs and abilities. Reassignment of pupils within division and to next division whenever appropriate.	Provisions for variations in program according to individual needs and abilities. Reassignment of pupils within division and to next division whenever appropriate.	Provision for variations in program according to individual needs and abilities. Reassignment of pupils to secondary school at end of fifth, sixth, or seventh grade.

Figure 2.3 Summary of Kensington's Formal Doctrine (p. 10 of Institutional Plan).

36

Perhaps, the most critical doctrinal outcome for the organization was the inability of a number of the individual conceptions to become merged into a common enough framework, an agreed on interpretation of the doctrine. Individual and subgroup interpretations of this doctrine were involved as we report shortly in the early schism between the two teams in Basic Skills, in the coalition aspects of Transition, and in the continuing conflict in ISD. Differences as to teaching methods, materials, pupil control, and staff organization were prevalent. The staff was verbal and articulate in isolating and elaborating "reasonable but incompatible" individual interpretations of what Kensington should stand for. As these intertwined with other personality variables and with episodes in the school's evolving social processes (such as the T-groups), they contributed to the complex puzzle that was Kensington. These processes are diagrammed in Figure 2.4.

Summary

In a sense, we are caught between these different but highly overlapping statements. On the one hand, they were sources of the formal doctrine; on the other hand, they were statements of it. In effect, there was no

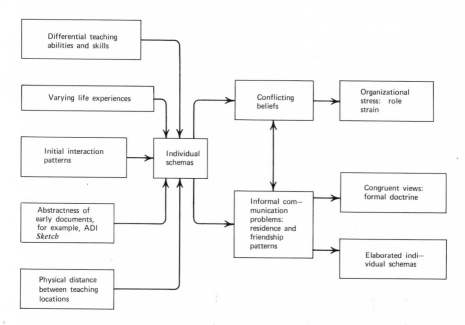

Figure 2.4 The antecedents and consequences of individual faculty schemas of Kensington doctrine.

one clear and totally accepted statement of the doctrine. As we cite in other parts of our analysis, even more variety occurred in the conceptions of the doctrine as they were held by individual staff members. As in the parable, the elephant was less than an elephant as the five men clutched it in the dark, and thus it was as the faculty members viewed the Kensington School.

STRUCTURAL DIMENSIONS OF THE DOCTRINE

As we analyze the doctrine apart from its substantive content, several structural dimensions seem significant. They include the degree of formalization, the degree of abstractness, the degree of consistency, and the degree of affectivity.

Formalization. We have described in detail the nature and content of the Kensington "point of view," its formal doctrine. As we tried to formulate the conception in terms of a continuum, we found that the rephrasing as formalized doctrine, the degree to which the "point of view" is systematized and codified, seemed significant. Kensington had a high degree of this formalization. Presumably, some schools have a considerably less articulated doctrine.

The antecedents of this high degree of formalization seem to focus on a number of conditions. First, that the school was new and had an innovative thrust seemed crucial as we looked at our data. Because it was different, it had to explain itself. In trying to explain itself, a formal statement of its point of view developed. The Milford School District also sought outside funds continuously, for example, the Architectural Design Institute (ADI) for building resources and the Olds Foundation request for general support. Requests from such sources demanded written statements, and this enhanced the formalization of "what one is trying to do."

Within the Milford leadership, for example, the superintendent, the curriculum director, and the Kensington principal, a strong desire existed to have an impact on American education. These men, individually and collectively, perceived weaknesses in present-day educational practices. They had vivid images of a better mode of operation. Not only did they seek to put these into practice, but also they talked and wrote about their ideas. Such behavior helped to shape a more formalized doctrine. Also, and particularly within the Kensington faculty, Shelby had strong codifying and analytical motivation. He tried to make conscious a wide realm of school activity.

Finally, we saw the community conflict as an important aspect of the move toward a formalized doctrine. The Milford District had had a reputation for many years as a community that has fought over its school pro-

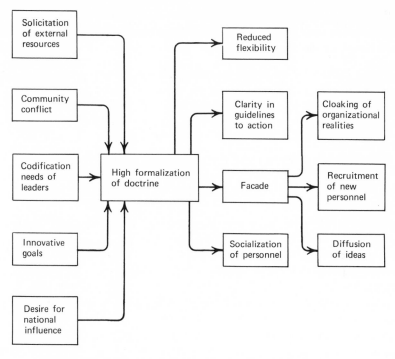

Figure 2.5   The implications of the formalization of the doctrine.

gram.[8] Tentatively, we would argue that the superintendent's early attempts to build a social base at the district level pushed him to verbalize and codify his position. Later, Shelby was forced in this same way by the patrons of the school who wanted to know "what was going on."

These relations have been sketched in Figure 2.5.

Although he was commenting on TVA, Selznick seemed to capture the interrelationships among the several sources of the doctrine as they were part of Kensington.

"This quest for an ideology, for doctrinal nourishment, while general, is uneven. Organizations established in a stable context, with assured futures, do not feel the same urgencies as those born of turmoil and set down to fend for themselves in undefined ways among institutions fearful and resistant. As in individuals, insecurity summons ideological reinforcements.

---

[8] Although we have not pursued this in detail, the district had a notorious record of bond and tax problems and squabbles in firing, rehiring, and then retiring the superintendent who was Spanman's predecessor.

The TVA was particularly susceptible to this kind of insecurity because it was not the spontaneous product of the institutions in its area of operation" (1949, p. 48).

Also in Figure 2.5 we hypothesize some of the consequences of a formalized doctrine. It provided a guide to action. It aided in socializing new members. It told them what the school was all about. Shelby made wide use of the Institutional Plan during the summer workshop. As the formal doctrine departed from the reality of the organization and was presented to the public, it became what we have called the facade. This facade became a cloak or screen covering the realities of organizational practices. This, too, had some exceedingly important implications. Finally, the doctrine and its counterpart, the facade, had implications in recruiting new staff.

Affective Tone. Doctrines can be analyzed, irrespective of their content, in terms of the degree to which they have affective or emotional qualities. Here we would distinguish between the doctrine's goals that necessarily commit the organization to implicit value systems which, in our judgment, are ultimately acts of faith in affectively endorsing certain ends in life and the degree to which the doctrine is phrased in terms of emotional appeals that seek to persuade on irrelevant or highly tenuous grounds. Operationally, we presume one might measure doctrinal documents on this affective-tone dimension by engaging in content analysis, using as a format the usually described propagandistic emotional appeals.

In the Institutional Plan, the principal's document, the affective tone is present but moderate, at least, in comparison to the Architectural Design Institute's (ADI) account. For instance, the former states as a conclusion:

"Rather than organizing on the basis of six lock-step grades, or even greater number of rigidly defined 'levels,' as many 'non-graded' schools do, the vertical organization of Kensington Elementary School consists of three basic divisions with ample opportunity for flexibility between and within these divisions. Referred to as the Basic Skills Division, Transition Division, and Independent Study Division, these organizational units are designed to serve differentiated functions. The horizontal organization, or organization within each division, is consequently differentiated for maximum effectiveness" (p. 9).

Similarly Figure 2.2, the "From-To" diagram, contains a number of affectively oriented educational statements. The document from ADI contains even more significant attempts to excite the reader.

"The initial impact is embodied in the simplicity of the building design, calling forth an image of an earlier era of civilization. A Parthenon whose qualities contribute to an effect of organically articulated form rather than mere massiveness, of subtle refinement rather than gross power. A building whose shape is in fact a prototype of evolutionary progress in educational growth. It is a facility offering facility and speed, mobility and flexibility to a nongraded, organic, fluid approach to inquiry" (p. 2).

Such a glowing account, that is, a high degree of doctrinal affectivity, seems to have a number of consequences. They include, for instance, a visibility, a stimulus for enthusiasm, and a less than critical quality of thinking. We sketch a broader model of relevant hypotheses as Figure 2.6.

In short, the affective tone, especially as we have seen it in the ADI publication, and later with the appearance of the facade, suggested two important cautions to us. We have renewed our suspicions of written accounts that seem to strive to excite the reader. Also, we have renewed our concern regarding potential incongruencies between the doctrine in its many forms and the organizational reality lying beneath it.

Integration. The degree to which the content of the formal doctrine is

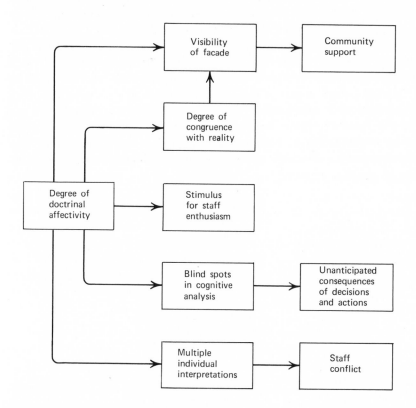

Figure 2.6 The implications of the affective tone dimensions of the formal doctrine.

consistent or integrated seems another dimension worthy of further investigation. Several illustrations proved almost classical in our observations. One of the major goals was individual pupil decision making. A major subgoal was an organizational structure that involved team teaching. The experienced teachers reacted frequently and spontaneously that they were able to provide more individual pupil decision making in their self-contained classrooms of prior years than they could in a team where their behavior was contingent on their teaching peers instead of upon their pupils. Relevant excerpts from the field notes appear in several parts of the report: the descriptive accounts of Kensington (Chapters 3 and 5) and the more systematic analysis of team teaching (Chapter 7).

Another illustration of inconsistency within the doctrine appears in the deification of the group and of the individual. The doctrine argues for group consensus as an ultimate goal and individual development as an ultimate goal. The point we make here is similar to Spindler's (1955) analysis of the transformation within American culture from traditional to emergent values. Kensington had internalized within its doctrine intense commitments to values of individuality and social processes. On what occasions and in what situations one value or the other took precedence was not clear. The rules about rules or norms about norms remained a critical problem throughout the year. The social and personal conflict predicted by Spindler became a part of Kensington. In effect, the doctrine was giving simultaneous and incompatible signals or directions to the teachers and provoking conflict within and between them. Neither the staff nor the broader establishment of American Education has entertained strong analytic attention to this kind of issue. In terms of testable hypotheses, we offer the model in Figure 2.7.

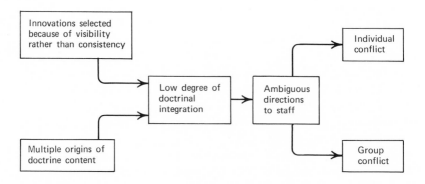

Figure 2.7 Hypotheses surrounding doctrinal integration.

Abstractness. Doctrine may vary also in the degree to which it is abstract or concrete. Kensington's doctrine accented the abstract. Issues were treated at a lofty and general level. For instance, explicit concrete definitions of "individualized instruction" and "fully-functioning pupils" did not receive final or agreed on concrete operational definitions. Individualized instruction could be a carefully guided tutorial experience in which the teacher communicated specific concepts to a single pupil, or it could be a self-selected learning experience engaged in by one or more pupils. As a language system is abstract, it permits legitimate but varying concrete interpretations. A doctrine with considerable abstractness hypothetically can provoke a wide range of these interpretations. This problem arose even when it seemed that considerable specificity had been obtained with respect to teaming, resource specialists, and academic counselors.

As we indicate shortly, Kensington had a further complication in terms of the individual faculty-member styles of problem solving. Early in the summer workshop, some members wanted to deal with "nuts and bolts" while others preferred the broader philosophical questions and an accompanying deductive strategy and tactics for problem solving. The abstractness of the doctrine seemed to be both cause and effect in enlarging that issue. Similarly, the doctrinal content contained abstract statements of teacher power to make educational decisions but little specificity regarding means for doing this. In addition, the peculiar quality of educational methods having little concrete evidence of effectiveness played into the abstract quality of the doctrine also (see Figure 2.8).

Complexity. Doctrines vary in the degree to which they are simple as opposed to being complex or complicated. We hypothesize that increasing intellectual ability and increasing compulsivity of influential group members produce an organizational point of view that has many parts, elements, and nuances. Kensington's doctrine had a number of elements and each element, for instance, the nature of pupil-teacher interaction, had a series of components listed in great detail, as we show in Figure 2.2.

Scope. Related to the complexity of the doctrine is the doctrine's pervasiveness or scope, that is, how much of organizational life is covered by the doctrine. In Kensington's case it was large. Specification in goals covered the total child and specification in procedures covered the whole day and a multitude of ways of behaving—teaming, ungradedness, no textbooks, and the like. This quality of doctrinal scope has implications for personal commitment to the organization by its members. The important consequences of this characteristic are amplified in a later chapter.

Flexibility. Flexibility has at least two kinds of subissues connected with it. One of them is the flexibility or rigidity with which individuals hold to the specific content of the doctrine. For instance, during the summer

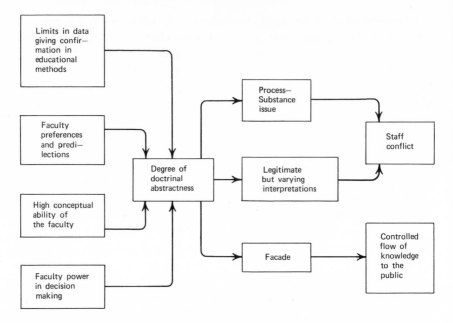

Figure 2.8 The relationships of the abstractness dimensions of the formal doctrine.

workshop early in Kensington's history, Shelby was most reluctant to depart from the Institutional Plan and to create with the faculty new and different structures. The other subissue, and a central one for the point concerning flexibility, is the degree of changeableness of the doctrine. For instance, to cloak the point in good and bad words, a doctrine that is unyielding or unchangeable is "rigid" and a doctrine which changes constantly is "overly pliant" or "vacillatory." The "right" amount of changeableness is "flexible." We would hypothesize that doctrines vary in the degree to which they are changeable, and this has important consequences for the organization whose social structure and activities are changing rapidly as was that of Kensington.

The issues in the relationship between administrative behavior and the doctrinal flexibility are highlighted in Selznick's comment from *TVA and the Grass Roots.*

"Among the many and pressing responsibilities of leadership, there arises the need to develop a Weltanschauung, a general view of the organization's position and role among its contemporaries. For organizations are not unlike personalities: the search for stability and meaning, for security, is unremitting. It is a search which seems to find a natural conclusion in the achievement of a set of morally sustaining ideas, ideas which lend support to decisions which must rest on compromise and restraint. Organizations, like men, are at crucial times involved in an attempt to close the gap between what they wish to do and what they can do. It is natural that, in due course, the struggle should be resolved in favor of a reconciliation between the desire and the ability. This new equilibrium may find its formulation and its sustenance in ideas which reflect a softened view of the world. The ethic of revolt, of thoroughgoing change, assumes that human and institutional materials are readily malleable and that disaffection from current modes of thought and patterns of behavior can be long sustained in action. But leadership must heed the danger of strain and disaster as recalcitrance and inertia exert their unceasing pressures; in doing so, it may see wisdom in the avowal of loyalty to prevailing codes and established structures. The choice, indeed, may often lie between adjustment and organizational suicide" (1949, pp. 48–49).

In the early spring of the year, the successes of parts of the program (especially in Basic Skills), the nourishment of enthusiasm through outside attention, and the Milford district-wide attempts for a large-scale curriculum project contributed to the heightening of the Curriculum Committee's activity and a return to doctrinal considerations instead of to an expenditure of energy and resources on the day-to-day programmatic aspects of instructional materials and procedures. Kensington's choice, as it were, was to *not* change the doctrine.

Uniqueness. Doctrines vary along a dimension of "run-of-the-mill" to uniqueness. As one looks at a number of schools, one can observe an important variation on this dimension. Kensington's ideology was not commonplace; its point of view was unusual in the variety of ways about which we have talked at length already and that we shall discuss especially in the next chapters. A unique doctrine along with other aspects of uniqueness, for example, the physical structure of the building, makes the school visible, attracts a particular kind of staff, mobilizes energies, and may well evoke a higher ratio of unanticipated to anticipated consequences of purposive organizational activity.

CONSEQUENCES OF THE DOCTRINE

As with all of our analyses, the models specifying antecedents and consequences indicate multiple hypotheses. These relationships seem viable in our data, and we offer them as testable propositions for the realities of other educational organizations. As we developed further the analysis of the formal doctrine, it seemed to fall comfortably into the context provided by our general conception of manifest and latent functions and dysfunctions.

Manifest Functions

Guide to Action. A formal doctrine contains statements of goals and objectives toward which one strives. Also it contains subgoals to be approached "on the way" toward the more general and ultimate objectives. Similarly, it contains specification of means, that is, alternatives of action, of social structure, and of procedures that contain high probabilities of attaining the goals. In effect, it is a plan—a guide to individual action and group activity. Kensington's formal doctrine possessed this manifest function. The building was built according to the building specifications. The August workshop was run according to the Institutional Plan. Although school was opened in temporary quarters, the dimensions of the beginning, as we shall describe shortly, occurred in terms of divisional and team understandings and interpretations of the doctrine. The doctrine had a potency that could not be denied. The structures fostered by the doctrine often contained a number of dysfuntions, as we discuss in detail at other points in the book.

Group Norms. Formal doctrine in its ultimate sense becomes the codified policies and rules of the bureaucracy as stated in the manuals of standard operating procedures. Group norms reflect the same kinds of issues, except that they usually are the informal statements of "the way we do things around here." The congruence of these two systems has been the subject of a fair amount of research and discussion. Relatively less has been said of the interdependency in the development of each. One of the more graphic illustrations was reported by Arensberg and McGregor (1942) and reanalyzed by Homans in *The Human Group* (1950). As the "electrical equipment company" was analyzed in the latter volume, the formal organizational charts reflected an earlier period in the organization's history, but the company norms reflected the issues of a number of years of survival during difficult and complex environmental shifts (for example, the economic depression of the 1930s). The authors as consultants argued for a reshaping of the doctrine to fit the current norms and procedural activities.

At Kensington, we have the exciting case of multiple statements of the doctrine prior to the interaction of the staff and students who were to be the incumbents of the organization. These statements, especially the Institutional Plan, and the forcefulness of the principal as author of the Plan and as the central and most powerful member of the staff, provided the basic framework in which norms were to develop. The issues in the doctrine were the issues with which the faculty struggled throughout the year.

In Jackson's (1960) terms, norms did not crystallize within the staff. Staff turnover was at a high rate even before the end of the first year, for example, Kirkham was replaced and Larsen, his replacement, was temporary. Linda joined the ISD staff at midyear. Jack became ill in the spring and was replaced for several months by Lee, a long-term substitute. Elaine was married at midyear and left in the spring; Sarah took her place. The conflict and interpersonal difficulties contributed heavily to this lack of norm crystallization. Some subgroups did work well together and friendship groups developed also. They tended to give a picture of norm ambiguity, a special case of low crystallization.

Latent Dysfunctions

Cloaking of Organizational Realities. A well-codified and an abstract doctrine has a number of dysfunctions. One of them is the cloaking of organizational realities.[9] In this usage we argue that every organization to some degree masks its internal functioning to its public. We hypothesize that the more formalized the doctrine becomes and the more internal problems that exist, the greater the degree of masking that will occur. By internal problems we mean, at Kensington, the severe staff conflict, especially in the Independent Study Division, and the difficulties the divisions had in implementing the program as defined initially. Additional impetus to the cloaking of activities was the continuous "battle" with, at least, a minority of vocal parents and district residents whose biases toward traditional education were in conflict with one or more of the innovative elements of the program.

As consequences, inaccuracies in perception of the realities of the school and parental frustrations developed. This, in turn, prevented the building of long-term support for the school as well as for the district leadership. These implications are diagrammed in Figure 2.9.

Self-Deception. At least since the Freudian revolution, language systems have been viewed as possible vehicles for self-deception, rationalizations. An ideology or group belief with its concomitant social support possesses the increased strength to carry out consequences such as self-deception. In his trenchant style, Hoffer (1951) draws the picture of the extreme condition in the relation of doctrine to self-deception.

"All active mass movements strive, therefore, to interpose a fact proof screen between the faithful and the realities of the world. They do this by claiming that the ultimate and absolute truth is already embodied in their doctrine and that there is no truth or certitude outside it. The facts

---

[9] This point is essentially Selznick's (1949). Corroboration in the Kensington case extends the generality of the argument.

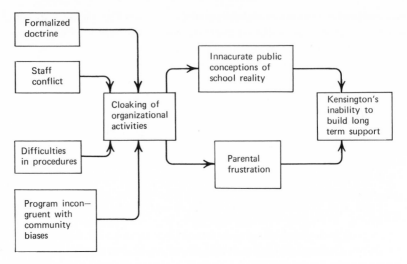

Figure 2.9 The antecedents and consequences of cloaking organizational activities.

on which the true believer bases his conclusions must not be derived from his experience or observation but from holy writ" (p. 75).

The modal member of Kensington was not this extreme, although some individual staff members were. As we analyze in detail later in the discussion entitled "On true belief in an innovative organization," Kensington did have such a quality about it. The formal doctrine seems to contribute to the masking of reality with regard to the members of the system.

In retrospect, as we reflect on the party described in the introductory epilogue, a number of the elements described in Festinger et al., *When Prophecy Fails* (1956), seem to have occurred at Kensington. Strong belief, commitment in action, specific implementation or ties to the real world, disconfirmations, and social support were critical elements. For at least a minority of the staff (witness the comments by John and Jean in Chapter One) [10] the phenomenon described by Festinger occurred.

The Facade: Functions and Dysfunctions

The events that determine major aspects of an organization's social structure vary in the degree to which they begin as fortuitous and mundane conditions. Also they vary in the degree to which they are outside the immediate control of the participants in the system. The dislodged pebble

---

[10] At this point in time, the numbers are not easy to ascertain informally. Post-experimental Year II contacts suggest that this could be a majority phenomenon.

that cumulates into an avalanche is not a bad analogy. One piece of the facade, a public face of Kensington, relates to the *Daily Star's* cover story. Another piece lies in the hundreds of visitors who spent part of a day in the building. Just before Christmas the data were these:

> The day, generally, has been an interesting one. A *Daily Star* news reporter was nosing around to get information for a Sunday supplement feature story for sometime in January. The photographer will be here the first week in January. It will be interesting to see what comes of this in terms of the public image of the school as opposed to the more personal, private day-to-day image that we have been developing. Eugene also was showing around some friends of his who are school people in Canada. Today's Bulletin carried with it also a statement about observers in this school and the need to plan for these people and schedule them. I'm struck by the facade that they must see on these one-day shots. I quizzed the reporter as to the genesis of the story and apparently the Sunday supplement news editor lives in this part of town and has seen and been familiar with the development of the building and thought it might be a good idea. It apparently was as informal as that. He commented also that they have a difficult time getting newsworthy and particularly photography-worthy articles on schools and this one is especially appropriate for that (12/23).

As we use the concept, facade refers to the image that the school presents to the several publics. Kensington was a highly visible school. Prior to our study, the board hired a superintendent who was articulate and bright, a "comer," to use a colloquial phrase. He held strong interests in developing in the Milford School District a unique, novel, and ultra-contemporary educational program. Kensington was a major part of this. Through the consultants at ADI, and their publications, the school attained an initial visibility.[11] Thus, the first image of the school was projected. As this attracted increased attention, further aspects of the formal doctrine were needed, were available, and were utilized to present the image of the school. As awards were won for architectural design, popular news media began to describe the program, which was equally unique. The process accelerated.

Theoretically, the uniqueness of the physical structure of the building and the superintendent's intentions for national leadership by Milford created an initial visibility. With this visibility came increased attention and the need for a codified point of view—the formal doctrine. However, as our descriptive materials will indicate, the day-to-day functioning reality

---

[11] A potent part of the doctrine, especially as it shades into the facade, is the sketch of the school produced by the Architectural Design Institute. Since its major focus is on the building *qua* building, we analyze it in detail in a later chapter. However, we do need to mention that it was available and part of the ideological milieu in which the Kensington reality developed.

was not totally congruent with the doctrine. This led to the special "public face" which centered on intentions, "what we are trying to do," and on special atypical concrete instances that illustrated these intentions.

The facade produced many important outcomes. On the one hand, the local and national acclaim was a hearty stimulant to flagging faculty spirits. The newspaper and magazine accounts brought commentary about "our school" from parents, relatives, and friends. The complex process of social approval and identity development for the individual staff member in relationship to his occupation of teaching seemed highly significant. The energizing aspect was noted early in January:

> Today was the day that the *Daily Star* photographer was out in the Milford School District and at Kensington. How much he was a "causal agent" I don't know and how much resides in the fact that I observed the Basic Skills team of four, but today the school looked and operated much more like a thriving, ongoing enterprise. As I walked in I noted that the bicycles were being put over on the side where the kids had been instructed to put them. The play area had been hosed down and was relatively clean and the heaters, except for two or three, were all working. The perception core was full of busy kids who were reading, working on reports, and active in this regard rather than fussing with the models and playing with games. The language arts program in the Basic Skills team moved readily, easily, and with a real flair, as well as seemingly with important learning outcomes for the children. As I walked out of the building, John had his mats on the stage of the play area and the kids were tumbling and were doing exercises. The photographer was taking pictures of the children with the colorful backdrop of the wall behind the staging area. Perhaps the school was just putting its best foot forward for the visitors and the photographer. Be that as it may, when the best foot forward is so put, it is a very good one (1/6).

By the cloaking of organizational realities, we have reference to a biased or partial picture of the organization. The field notes contained references to *National Weekly's* article on the school. The journalist spent a week in the school in January, and the feature article appeared in early summer after the first year of the school's operation.

> As I read the article I am struck by a feeling I had in earlier public presentations: although most of the material in the article is true, there is an erroneous conception developed through the lack of what is said. For instance, the title of the article reads "A school where children teach themselves." Without question, in some parts of ISD a number of children are engaged in such activities and are teaching themselves. This seems particularly true in David's and Linda's rooms. This is most certainly *not* true in the Basic Skills, in Transition, and in at least half of ISD. Similarly, the subheading of the article: "Strange things happen within this strange looking building. With teachers only leading the way, kids from 6 to 12 decide whether to do advanced math, study the

philosophy of communism, or measure the diameter of the sun. Best of all, says the school, they are learning to learn." Without question, there has been some election of math, although one would need to define carefully "advanced," if this were to be applicable. Also without question, some of the children studied the philosophy of communism. And I imagine some of them discussed measuring the diameter of the sun, although I have no direct recollection of this. The majority of the children did not do any one of these three things. Among the major options, which the author did not suggest and which many of the pupils elected, were spending considerable time working with the tape recorders, playing with the art supplies, and passing the time of day (6/24, post-experimental year).

Other critical comments we would make on the public image are: inadequate discriminations between intention and reality in the program, the isolation of atypical teachers who were not representative of the majority, and inadequate normative data to make comparisons of such items as frequency of discipline problems. Hypotheses concerning the sources and consequences of the facade are presented in Figure 2.10. Elements in the diagram, for

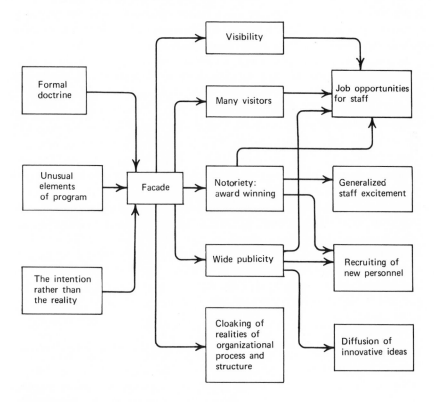

Figure 2.10 The implications of the facade.

example, the formal doctrine, must be integrated with prior discussion for additional antecedents and implications.

CONCLUSIONS

Our conclusions follow simply from the description and analysis. One needs a concept such as formal doctrine to talk fully and incisively about Kensington. Presumably, schools will vary in the degree to which they possess a visionary, conscious, and codified ideology. Second, in some instances, antecedents to the doctrine will exist in the form of mandates, as with Kensington. Other schools, especially new ones, will have building specifications that play dual roles—as antecedents of doctrine and later as another manifestation and sometimes contending operational definition of the doctrine. Third, organizational positions soon possess incumbents who interpret mandates, building specifications, and foundation proposals in terms of their own cognitive maps and professional schemas. In some situations this may be formalized to the point of a written "Institutional Plan." In the instance of Kensington this was a forceful and potent position paper. As we shall see later, it was a major determinant of the principal's decision making, a guide to the faculty, a source of conflict, and a major issue in the dilemmas of democratic administration.

To complement our observations and analysis we give a brief summary of Selznick's position on "official doctrine" as he presented it in his study of the Tennessee Valley Authority. This discussion we have codified in Figure 2.11. Such a model indicates similarities across organizations and is suggestive for a more extended comparative organizational theory. The genesis of his "official doctrine" lay in a hostile environment, an ideological vacuum, and a need for communication within the organization. The antecedents of Kensington's formal doctrine overlapped only partially. The consequences, too, seem only partially common.

Perhaps schools differ from regional governmental organizations, or perhaps it is innovative schools that differ from innovative regional governmental organizations. Or maybe it is just Kensington and TVA that we are contrasting. Nonetheless, the doctrinal functions of internal communication and orderly flow of directives did not occur at Kensington. The abstractness of the formal doctrine—even when these abstractions were specified as carefully as the principal tried in the Institutional Plan—still could not communicate. The laments of the proponents of behavioral objectives (Bloom et al., 1956) and operational definitions (Boring, 1945) were not heard. Even the voice of the tired traditional teacher saying, "This year we are going to go through the text from page 1 to page 250," has its own kind of concrete appeal. In spite of prodigious effort, common

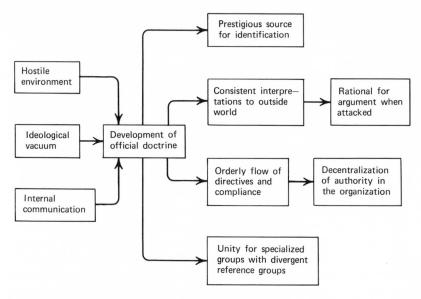

Figure 2.11 A model clarifying Selznick's reasoning concerning TVA's official doctrine (pages 47 to 52).

guidelines that guided did not exist; the language of school organization, teaching, and goals for pupils remains metaphorical and literary but neither practical nor scientific.

Our attempt to sketch dimensions of the doctrine has been exploratory, yet influential in our own thinking. As we have stated at a number of points our models seem to reflect well many of the specifics of our case. The degree to which they are more generally true awaits systematic verificational research. However, to the educational administrator to whom this book is, in part, directed, we urge that he think his way through his problems with an eye alerted for dimensions similar to ours and with his ear tuned for latent consequences similar to the ones we found.

Finally, we think the facade concept is most important. The organizational face presented to the public—especially in popular newspapers and magazines—did not reflect the reality of the school. These discrepancies have led us toward skepticism and caution with respect to any "feature" story about educational matters. Administrators who seriously try to keep up with the Jones District—or its facade—seem to be creating a new kind of problem while they are attempting to solve the original one.

CHAPTER 3

Innovative Organizational Socialization: the Summer Workshop

Although Kensington had been developing for several years, it began, in a real sense, for the staff in August. The teachers' first formal contact as a group occurred then. The four weeks between August 10 and September 8, the official opening of the schools, constituted a workshop and served as a period of initial socialization. As will be described in some detail, the activities were varied and the implications of those days in August were crucial for the development of the school as a social system. A month-long workshop was a major educational innovation in itself and an important part of the overall Milford innovation strategy.[1]

The first five days were spent in Training Groups led by representatives from the National Training Laboratory (NTL). Two sessions per day involved the total staff and the remainder of the time consisted of group meetings. The training groups were viewed by the leader as a form of planning for the coming year. The staff was to "begin to be a group"; they were to get to know one another, to learn each other's resources, and to learn to work together.

Monday, the first day of the second week, began what the principal called the "big day," the end of the preliminaries of general planning (by all kinds of other persons and committees), and the beginning of intimate work by the staff. The week contained also a more intensive welcome, which we characterized earlier as the mandate, by the Milford superintendent, Dr. Steven Spanman; total staff discussion led by the principal; the arrival of a consultant, Dr. Roberts, from City University; and the beginnings of a working committee structure. The latter included horizontal committees, divided according to age levels of the children—Basic Skills Division (first and second grades), Transition Division (third grade), and

[1] The workshop was supported by local funds; Title III resources were still a year or two away.

Independent Study Division (fourth through sixth grades)—and vertical curriculum committees, in science, language arts, social studies, and mathematics. A more general committee, the Curriculum Coordinating Committee (CCC) was established. Finally, considerable time was allocated to individual work by the teacher. Each teacher kept an activity log that was turned in to the principal and that provided information for him.

Much the same pattern was followed during the third week.

Although the same activities were continued during the fourth week, the focus shifted toward preparation for the temporary physical quarters and planning by the teams who would be working together. The new school building had not been finished on schedule; consequently, Basic Skills would be housed in six rooms at Milford High School, Transition would be in Hillside, a neighboring elementary school, and ISD would be in the gym of the Milford Junior High School. Also the broader environment impinged on Kensington. The total district staff came alive as they prepared for their teaching responsibilities in the September beginning of another school year. The Kensington staff spent two evenings meeting with parents in a discussion of the school and its program.

On Tuesday, after Labor Day, school began.

The Faculty

Although we do not have data on faculty composition of new schools and, consequently, cannot make rigorous comparisons, our belief is that the Kensington staff was unusual and unique. First, the majority of the teachers were new to the school district. They were recruited from the breadth of the Midwest—the Gulf of Mexico to Lake Michigan. This meant that they were not only new to each other but also to the procedures and practices of Milford. In the eyes of the administration this meant they could be trained directly in the new procedures instead of having to break old habits and patterns prior to retraining.

Following through on the same concern with breaking old ways, the staff was relatively inexperienced. Seven of the original twenty-one[2] had had no teaching experience beyond student teaching, an apprenticeship, or internship. Although two of the teachers had had more than 20 years of experience, most of the remainder of the staff had taught less than five years; even some of the ones who were older had come to teaching late, after raising their families. Interestingly also, three of the group had had almost no training or experience with elementary children; they had

[2] The numbers varied; we have not counted the four teacher aides who played vital roles, nor the kindergarten teacher who took no part in the summer and fall program. We did count the guidance counselor who was quite active in August and throughout the school year.

trained for secondary education in one of the content areas. The group in ISD, especially the resource people, had been selected because of intensive training in a speciality: science, mathematics, social studies, language arts, and physical education.

The staff seemed very able intellectually. Three of the group had all their doctoral course work finished and needed only a dissertation. All of these three had taught at the college level; one additional staff member held a part-time, Saturday morning college position, a Principles and Methods of Teaching course. Most of the staff had M.A.'s (some through an M.A.T. internship program). The quality of the intellectual life and discussions among the staff in committee and faculty meetings we found impressive relative to our contacts with other elementary schools.

Attitudinally, the faculty was characterized by one of the central office staff as "not a Republican in the group." Although our conversations and informal interaction suggested this was not true for several, the majority reflected a liberal Democratic political orientation. More specifically, however, the group did have high scores on the *Minnesota Teacher Attitude Inventory* (MTAI) (Cook et al., 1951); the median fell at the 85 percentile on the national norms for elementary teachers. On the *Teacher Conceptions of the Educative Process* (Wehling, 1964; Wehling and Charters, 1969), the faculty scored high on pupil autonomy, teacher consideration, adjustment as a goal, content integration, and closeness of teacher-pupil relationships. Although the validity of these measures of teacher schemas, beliefs, and attitudes might be questioned, they have achieved widespread usage. According to the intentions of the test authors, such scores indicate that the Kensington staff was chosen in harmony with the formal doctrine. The high MTAI scores reflect teachers who are:

". . . able to maintain a state of harmonious relations with his pupils characterized by mutual affection and sympathetic understanding. The pupils should like the teacher and enjoy school work. The teacher should like the children and enjoy teaching. Situations requiring disciplinary action should rarely occur. The teacher and pupils should work together in a social atmosphere of cooperative endeavor, of intense interest in the work of the day, and with a feeling of security growing from a permissive atmosphere of freedom to think, act and speak one's mind with mutual respect for the feelings, rights and abilities of others" (Cook et al., 1951, p. 3).

The Wehling-Charters scales indicate that the Kensington teachers valued pupil autonomy as both an end and as means. They saw pupil personal-social adjustment as an important goal. The academic content should be relevant and integrated. Teachers should be psychologically close to the pupils and considerate of their wishes, needs, and interests.

The summary field notes from the first few days of the workshop capture further emotional and attitudinal characteristics of the faculty.

There is a very real aura of "We can do it and what we're doing is very important. It's very much in the creative front line of educational practice and innovation." This is all very striking for the teachers were trained in a variety of places. Several of them came from City Teachers College and spoke glowingly of their program there which was in contrast to many of the others who came from "better universities" and the comments they had about their education programs. There are some real questions as to why these people haven't been stifled the way some of the preservice education students were in other situations. Most certainly there is an ability factor here, for these people seem more than a little bit bright, and some of them seem very, very able. It is also critical to get a notion of Eugene's background, since yesterday he commented that he had spent last summer as a supervisor in the Harvard-Lexington program. Apparently he had kicked around in and about this kind of a program for some time.

Another thing that I'm struck with, and it may be just because I don't know our own students as well, is the degree to which these people, and particularly the young ones, are excited by the kind of thing that they are doing in education. Our students at City University just do not carry this flavor of excitement. I am struck, too, by how much of this, and the references to which they appeal, especially people of the order of John Goodlad, are unknown and are not widely discussed, at least among the staff at City University. For instance, my colleagues, if they mention Goodlad, usually mention him in a condemning fashion. We have, in effect, abandoned this kind of approach or set of variables and, at least in my case, without having considered the evidence, which my colleagues would probably say did not exist, and without careful argument about the programs.[3] I guess the point I want to make is that there is an excitement about teaching and about the things that they are going to be trying, even though they are not very specific and clear about this yet, that pervades the place and that I just have not seen in any degree at City University. Such an influence or consequence alone would seem to me to be so meritorious as to argue for its inclusion almost regardless of the validity of the position. That one will need to be straightened out in some detail (8/11).

Of the original group, nine were men. All but one of them were married. Of the twelve women, seven were not married. In only one instance were both husband and wife members of the Kensington faculty. Such a high percentage of men on an elementary staff also seems unusual.

The staff contained five noncertificated personnel, four married women,

---

[3] This conflict between an innovative-creative orientation to teacher education and a reflective-analytic orientation strikes us as a major latent issue in professional education.

and a young man just graduated from high school. He served as audiovisual technician; the women served in the capacities of secretary, library clerk, teacher aide, and instructional clerk. They were all new to their positions. At the time, this extensive use of aides and paraprofessionals was also quite novel. Later, during the fall semester, four student teachers from local colleges were a part of the staff. They were finishing the final year of their teacher training programs. Again, although we do not have comparative statistics, this seems to be a large number relative to the total staff size.

Although other personnel, from the central office, custodial staff, and cafeteria personnel, were part of the story, they tended not to be central actors. As the staff changed during the year and new persons played a vital part, we have introduced them in the following chapters.

In short, the administrators of Milford had assembled an unusual group to staff the Kensington School. They were young and inexperienced, but bright, enthusiastic, and attitudinally focused on the central tenets of the new elementary education. An initial congruence with the formal doctrine had been achieved.

The T-Group Workshop

Training Groups, described by the NTL trainer as "the exciting venture of learning to become a group," began the first day of the workshop. The focus on Training Groups arose primarily through the efforts of the principal, Mr. Shelby. The T-group activity involves a unique kind of learning experience in which a number of persons meet together and the activity of the group develops out of the growing relationships among the members of the group. The training is intended to make individuals more perceptive of group processes and their own personal relationships within the group.[4] General sessions alternating with the T-groups were to combine lectures, discussions, and training exercises using human relations problems.

Considerable discussion among Shelby, the principal; Cohen, the district curriculum director; and the two NTL trainers arose in the decision regarding the constitution of the two T-groups. The alternatives considered were a split by division (ISD versus TD and BSD) or a vertical split; the

[4] This approach has been the subject of considerable controversy in education and the behavioral sciences. Contrary positions are found in reports such as Whyte (1953), Bradford et al. (1964), and Miles (1959). Shelby had had only indirect contact with T-group training. He had been involved in a human relations oriented school administration training program. The investigators themselves have been skeptical as shown in earlier writings (Smith, 1959; Smith and Hudgins, 1964; Smith and Geoffrey, 1968). More recently, sensitivity training and confrontation groups have been in vogue in professional and lay circles (Birnbaum, 1969).

latter form was selected. The principal was to be in one group and one of the older, more experienced staff members, Tom Mack, the curriculum materials coordinator, would be in the other. The men and women were divided about equally.

An additional degree of novelty of this experience became apparent in the discussion Sunday evening before the workshop began.

> Another point that came out at this time was that neither Lyn nor Lois, the trainers, had had an experience with just this kind of situation before, that is, in the sense that they were working with groups of people who are now an aggregate and have not worked together and who ultimately will become a long-standing and continuing group. Each of them has worked more with *ad hoc* groups and secondarily with groups that had a history and would remain together. But the no-history phenomenon seems a very unique one[5] (8/10, 7:00 A.M).

In effect, a group of people who had not known each other before and who were to work together all year in a formal organization, a public school, would be spending their first week together in a T-group setting.

The schedule of the Training Groups was much the same for each day of the first five days of the workshop. In the morning hours, the two groups met independently; after lunch, there was a total group lecture and discussion. The lecture content on Monday centered on people's varying perceptions and expectations; the genesis of these differences, for example, past experience; and the consequences of the differences, for example, conflicting values and loyalties. The discussion was lively and controversial. After a brief coffee break, the T-groups met for the remainder of Monday afternoon, until approximately 5:00 P.M.

The content of the day's T-group discussions involved getting acquainted, raising questions about specific aspects of Kensington, and the giving of interpretive comments by the NTL trainers on aspects of group process. In one group, the initial focus lay on the problems of status and authority in both teacher-teacher relationships and teacher-principal relationships. For example, a possible dichotomy of younger versus older teachers was raised. Being free to challenge the principal and to call him by his first name were examples of the latter. In the other group, in the middle of a discussion of leadership, one teacher interrupted with, "I don't care who is leader. I'm interested in 'nuts and bolts,' what will go on in Kensington." The situation was entangled in two additional ways. Earlier, another teacher had commented that the training groups lacked reality in that they did not have a task. Later, one teacher argued that they should develop their

---

[5] Later searches of the literature, Bradford et al. (1964) and Glidewell (1966), indicate this was an unexplored dimension of T-group theory and practice.

own expectations. He was supported by comments such as "We, the staff, are the architects." In contrast, another felt that they should await direction from the superintendent and principal.

The T-group was not a situation responded to with indifference and docility. A brief summary comment recorded late Wednesday after the third day is typical:

> The morning T-group session and the afternoon T-group session each had its dramatic high point. In the morning it involved a fracas between David, Joe, and Lyn. David was opening himself up catharsis fashion. Joe made an interpretive comment that cut right through to the nature of David's personality. This material was on tape and Lyn cut in about this point, indicating that it was much more clinical and therapeutic than processual, and it had gone beyond the limits of what she felt qualified to handle. Feedback this afternoon from Paul indicates that Tom thought that she should not have turned off the tape recorder. His feeling was that it was personal but not disabling and that she could not handle the material intellectually instead of emotionally. Paul also reports the other group perceives our group as having all of the aggressive leadership and the fireworks. They feel that there isn't any leadership in their group. Paul sees this as centering on the inhibiting role of Eugene. Paul reports also a noon conversation in which Jack was very angry in talking with Dan about the salary revelations that have occurred and the fact that he was under misinformation. Most of the locals were under misinterpretation also about the $300 that they would make this summer (8/12).

The more extended theoretical analysis of these events will be developed in a later chapter.

During the remainder of the week of Training Groups, attention centered on analytic observations of group behavior, discussions of group-related variables (individual effectiveness in groups and its determinants), problem solving, communication, decision making, and leadership. Authority and the contrast between the authority structure of Kensington and that in other elementary schools was considered.

Not unrelated to authority and decision making, the concept of the "Institutional Plan" was introduced by the principal, Shelby, during the week of the Training Groups. The Institutional Plan was presented as a given, and it was indicated that a serious problem would arise if personal goals were radically different from the plan. He indicated that effort had been made to select staff that would in effect erase the line of differences. The givens were commitments by the school district to persons or institutions both outside the school and outside the district, such as the United States Office of Education. Also, in response to those interested in "nuts and bolts" and task concerns, the principal led an extended question-answer session on the new building (which would not be ready for opening day), materials, supplies, procedures, and the like. Questions of audiovisual use, music schedules, and modern math in the curriculum were answered as undetermined as yet; their solution was a goal of the summer workshop.

At the end of the week, when the T-groups reconvened for the last time, the intensity of the emotionality was indicated further as the groups talked through the pro's and con's of continuing to meet during the course of the year. For several of the group, the experience had been a dramatic revelation of self and an intense development of empathy. Others viewed it as a social situation leading to further important social situations at Kensington. At 2:20 P.M. the total group met for the discussion of issues in forming a new group, establishing working relationships, and ambiguous and unknown aspects of the teaching role. To facilitate the transition into the following weeks, the three divisions—Basic Skills, Transition, and ISD—met independently. The groups engaged in tentative exploration of themselves, the T-group experience, Kensington's program, and the temporary facilities. Prior to adjournment, the groups met together for summary discussions.

George Homans (1950) argues that the interaction demanded of people by the formal organization spills over, becomes elaborated, as sentiments of mutual liking are perceived. This elaboration takes the form of new activities, increased interaction, and more broadly based sentiments. This was the case at Kensington. The field notes on Wednesday contain an entry that indicates some of the early sentiments:

> Part of this morning's T-group conversation centered about the salary problem and its effects on teacher relationships. Jack was rather surprised to learn that others knew his contractual agreement with the Milford School District. In the course of the discussion with Eugene, some of the women made known that they were not aware of the fact that they were being paid to attend this workshop. Jack expressed some concern in the morning workshop that the rest of the staff was fully aware of his exact salary picture. During coffee this discussion was carried on at greater length. He stated in very clear terms that it made him very aggravated to know this. Dan was also present and both he and Jack agreed that it was their opinion that this is an entirely personal matter and no concern of anyone's as to their salary (8/12).

Later in the same day's notes, the cross currents of subgroup interaction and evaluation were reported.

> During lunch I participated in a conversation with Liz, Elaine, and Dan. By consensus of opinion these three felt that it would have been advisable to begin the group action by working on an actual problem instead of by studying group processes. Elaine stated that she would have preferred working on an

actual problem such as the curriculum and then coming back to studying group processes at a later time to analyze what they had done (8/12).

Still later in the notes of the same day a "minor" event was reported.

At the conclusion of today's T-group, Jack left the room, thereby somewhat disrupting the conversation of the group. It was undecided whether to continue. However, the conversation did continue and was centered on this main point: Should they analyze the day's discussion or should they wait until the entire group reconvenes tomorrow morning? The group gradually began discussing activities of the afternoon session and Lois, the trainer, interrupted to remind them that they had suggested to wait until tomorrow morning's session. By group consensus they decided that this was the wiser plan; consequently, they adjourned (8/12).

The salary issue concerned not only the Kensington staff but other teachers in the district who thought it "unfair" that Kensington teachers were paid above the stated training and experience guidelines. The concern over the T-groups and alternative ways of beginning the workshop was to crystallize later into a conflict between the "substantive" versus the "process" staff orientations. The final point, when do we stop talking about school "business," who must be included in these discussions, and who determines when faculty come and go, were issues about which no precedent existed, and which were to be a part of the issues of influence and decision making in the school.

Although our major analysis of the implications of the T-group experience appears in the next chapter, we can report that one immediate reaction of the teachers was that of considerable discomfort. The first item of the first Staff Bulletin on Tuesday, August 11, stated the response this way:

"We are very pleased with the progress of the staff orientation workshop. *Although a group development laboratory is never a comfortable thing to participate in* [our italics], it should prove helpful to us as we work together during the year to provide a forward-looking educational program. As important as the many tasks for preparing for opening of school are, we believe that the development of good working relationships among the staff is of primary importance" (Bulletin no. 1, 8/11).

The last item of the second Bulletin, issued on Friday of the first week, summarized the reaction.

"We would like to extend a special word of appreciation to the directors of our group development laboratory, Dr. Lois Erickson and Miss Lyn Karson. *We will not deny the frustration of the experience, but undoubtedly it will prove to have been most profitable as we work toward our goals this year* [our italics] . . . . Thanks again for your contributions in providing experiences which will certainly be long remembered" (Bulletin no. 2, 8/14).

The Middle Two Weeks

The Big Day. The second Monday, August 17, was described as the "big day," the beginning of intensive substantive discussion and planning for the year. The principal chaired the total staff meeting. Initial discussion centered on several major items, one of which was the interdependence of the program parts. The principal developed a lengthy analogy that contrasted the functions, methods, and parts of a T-Bird and a Model-T Ford as he spoke of Kensington and traditional education. Commitment by the staff was stressed. This was analyzed as issues of staff selection and the congruency between individual philosophy and instructional objectives. Also, a contrast was made between traditional authority and a "rational approach," which was to be used at Kensington. These were construed as conditions developing commitment. The principal accented the latter. The introductory remarks of the principal stressed skill in implementing the program, the necessity for making mistakes, and the possibility of staff growth. "The Institutional Plan," the principal's document, was raised as "a skeleton of the program, and the staff is to put hair on it." Finally, he suggested that differences and disagreements should be open and explicit. They should be "out on the table," as had been accented in the previous week.

The remainder of the pre-coffee discussion centered on two mimeographed sheets containing job descriptions of the academic counselor and the subject specialist and a third sheet that illustrated the administrative organization of Kensington. They are reproduced as Figures 3.1, 3.2, and 3.3. These documents provoked a brief discussion that focused on (1) an administrative organization different from the single, self-contained class as a means to handle individual differences of pupils; (2) who makes what decisions regarding the academic program; (3) criteria of progress from division to division; (4) Goodlad's (1963) models of instruction, A, B, and C; (5) Kensington as an attempt to be a "C" school; (6) the nature and kinds of educational objectives for Kensington with the emphasis in the affective (self-motivation) and complex intellectual skills areas; and (7) decisions yet to be made regarding particular books, materials, and supplies.

Further aspects of the schedule were clarified. For the remainder of the workshop the faculty was to meet as they deemed necessary—by divisions and in curriculum committees. They were free to schedule themselves and their meetings, and they were to note the times on a bulletin board. Subsequent to this, faculty members were asked to indicate which of the following

August 14

Job Description for Subject Specialist

Primary Responsibilities:
>   Curriculum organization
>   Developing independent learning activities and materials
>   Developing instructional activities and materials
>   Providing individual and group instruction in subject areas
>   Using diagnostic instruments in subject areas
>   Using evaluative instruments in subject areas

Secondary Responsibilities:
>   Assisting with curriculum organization
>   Developing independent learning activities and materials
>   Developing instructional activities
>   Developing instructional activities and materials
>   Providing instruction in subject areas

Although pupils will be under the direction of both an Academic Counselor and Subject Specialist, final responsibility for making decisions pertaining to pupils rests with the Academic Counselor.

Figure 3.1   Kensington job description for resource specialists.

KENSINGTON ELEMENTARY SCHOOL

August 14

Job Description for Academic Counselors

Primary Responsibilities:
>   Grouping of pupils
>   Scheduling of pupil activities
>   Evaluation of pupil activities
>   Diagnosis of learning difficulties
>   Dealing with pupil problems (behavior, attendance, illness)
>   Evaluation and reporting of pupil progress
>   Administering standardized tests
>   Maintaining pupil records
>   Assisting pupils with independent learning activities

Secondary Responsibilities:
>   Assisting with curriculum organization
>   Developing independent learning activities and materials
>   Developing instructional activities and materials
>   Providing instruction in subject areas

Although pupils will be under the direction of both an Academic Counselor and Subject Specialist, final responsibility for making decisions pertaining to pupils rests with the Academic Counselor.

Figure 3.2   Kensington job description for academic counselor.

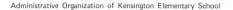

Administrative Organization of Kensington Elementary School

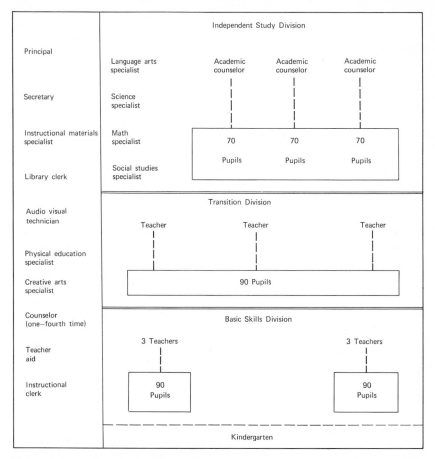

Figure 3.3   The initial statement of Kensington's administrative organization (8/17).

committees they would like to be on: (1) materials and facilities, (2) curriculum coordination, or (3) curriculum subcommittees in (a) language arts, (b) mathematics, (c) social studies, (d) science, (e) creative arts, and (f) physical education.

A final item concerned "practicing what we preach." The staff was to be on individual schedules with the principal as their "academic counselor." They were asked to fill out daily logs (see Figure 3.4) on their activities. Discussion ensued as to who would read the logs, and at the suggestion of a staff member they decided, in order to facilitate communication, to have them open to everyone.

KENSINGTON ELEMENTARY SCHOOL

Date: _____

Log of Daily Activities

Name _____ Division _____ Acad. Coun. _____

(Please record all activities in which you have engaged today. Include what you did, the approximate length of time, whom you worked with, and your own evaluation of or reaction to the activity.)

_____
_____
_____
_____
_____
_____
_____
_____
_____
_____
_____
_____
_____
_____
_____
_____

Figure 3.4   The daily log to be filled in by the staff during the workshop (8/17).

As is pointed out elsewhere, the logs completed by the faculty were identical in form to those required of students a few weeks later. Thus, in the second week of the workshop, primary attention was given to substantive concerns. At midweek Dr. Leslie Roberts from City University met with the faculty and began an extended consulting arrangement.

The Institutional Plan: A Phrasing of the Formal Doctrine. Earlier we had a good bit to say about the formal doctrine, the codified ideology of Kensington. The antecedents of the doctrine, the dimensions of the doctrine, and the consequences were part of that analysis. During the weeks of the workshop, the Institutional Plan, Shelby's statement of the doctrine, became the focus of considerable discussion as well as the major operational plan for the development of the school. Briefly, the central thrust of the school was to assist pupils in becoming "fully functioning mature human beings." This goal was to be reached through "individualized instruction." The latter was not to be merely differentiation in rate of presentation of material, but differentiation in content as well, that is, according to the needs of the individual child. The curriculum was described as "spiral," and it was to accent processes instead of content. The materials were to be individualized rather than packaged as textbooks. Teacher-pupil relations were to be reformulated from categories such as "restriction of pupils" to "freedom for pupils," from "teacher responsibility for teaching" to "pupil responsibility for learning," and from a "closed, rigid social climate" to an "open, flexible social climate." The organization was to move from six rigidly defined levels or grades to three divisions. Within the divisions, teachers were to play differentiated roles. In turn, the pupils were to change from being "passive" and "reactive" to being "active" and "initiating."

The Divisions. The divisions, or as they came to be called by the staff: Basic Skills, Transition, and ISD, were an important and early defined division of labor. These groups began working together in the second week of the August workshop. Instead of describing in detail the development of the divisions, we present an introductory overview from the observer's notes of his perception of the way things stood as of mid-workshop, 4:00 P.M., Tuesday, August 25.

> I had a chance to spend a fair amount of time with the Transition Division. By all odds, they are the most smoothly functioning team in the school at this point. Each in his own quiet, unpretentious way makes suggestions to which the others listen as they go about shaping up a program. Apparently they are interested and pleased in what they have been doing for they do not want to bring another person into their group now. They explicitly told this to Eugene, the principal. Shifting them to their temporary quarters in Hillside School came about with no great difficulty in terms of Eugene's suggestion, or in terms of their acceding to it. My guess is that they will be a very task-oriented set of teachers who will have all kinds of interesting things for the kids and who will blend their own suggestions and initiation with the suggestions and initiations of activities from the pupils. They seem to make judgments on a reasonable common-sense professional background basis. The only major inhibiting factor that I see at this point is that Claire and Dan have not taught extensively. Meg may be a bulwark here if she is as good as I would guess she is.

> The Basic Skills group seem to be laboring with the consultant, Leslie Roberts, who is pushing them hard, and who seems not to understand that they are now a team of four and a team of two rather than a six-man team. Carla seems very set in her ways and is going to do what she wants to do, and apparently Mary will integrate without too much difficulty. The other team looks like it might go also. My guess is that Elaine is an old warhorse who is a very experienced, a very agile, and a very interesting teacher. Jean has

had enough experience to know her way around, and Wanda seems also to be a very stable person. It seems that they will be able to carry Sue well enough until she learns the ropes. If she turns out to have some talent for working with young children, the group then should be able to move along without too much difficulty.

As I summarize the teams, it becomes very interesting that the major reservation seems to lie within the Independent Study Division. Paul reports that David was in a quiet and unhappy looking mood all day today. He also reports, as I think I indicated earlier, that Liz has made all kinds of comments of her unhappiness with David and with the way in which the group is going. Perhaps this is the item that upset David. I have no data on that. As I recall now, one of the gals called David on a couple of things yesterday. They had to do with his railroading the group. This may be also a reason for his quietness. In this group also, Irma is very unhappy, and she is apparently thinking of dropping out of the team. She feels she is less adequate for it now than she was when she discussed it last spring with Eugene. She has been unable to get any kind of a structured role so that she will know what she's going to be doing. Although nothing arose today that I saw or heard about, Kay has a continuing problem of wanting to support David and at the same time seeming to side intellectually with some of the people in the disciplines. This makes her seem to vacillate back and forth between varying points of view. Jack seems to be frustrated in terms of wanting to act like a principal and run the meeting. He and Alec look like people who have interests in teaching rather than in some of the other kinds of activity that teachers might be called on to do. Alec has had minimal experience.

The staff left a bit earlier than usual this afternoon. Maybe it is my own feeling, but it seemed to me that everyone looked pretty tired. Unfortunately, the group has had so little experience generally and almost none in extended team teaching that they are now at the point of waiting and seeing how things begin to develop. They don't realize the kinds of preparation, à la Joe Grannis' chapter in the Shaplin and Olds (1964) book, in which they might be engaged that would be helpful for the long term haul this semester and year.

Also, they still have many procedural problems on how to work together. This seems, in part, to be a function of Eugene's inability to realize that the school is part of a bureaucracy and must have some of these overtones and, second, that the week of "sensitivity training" is having all kinds of negative transfer effects (8/25).

The Committees. Although the first week was characterized by the staff as the T-group week, the later weeks of the workshop were dominated by the committees and the divisions. Cumulatively these events had their immediate consequences and also their longer effects. The number of committees and committee assignments was quite large and contained overlapping memberships:

1. Curriculum Coordinating Committee (7 members)
2. Curriculum Subcommittees
    a. Language Arts   (4)
    b. Mathematics   (4)
    c. Science   (4)
    d. Social Studies   (5)
    e. Creative Arts   (5)
3. Facilities Committee   (4)
4. Research Committee   (5)

Some of the complications of the committee structure appeared in the summary notes early in the third week.

> One of Paul's first comments was of the order, "What goes on in the central committee?"[6] His observations, independent of anything I told him, were that the role of the central committee seemed to have changed dramatically, and that it has taken on a number of different functions that it did not have before. He was curious as to how these changes had come about. Specifically, the kinds of things that he mentioned centered on what he called the committee serving as a sort of an assistant principal to Eugene. In effect, they have considerable power and they are being used as an instrument for a variety of policies. I asked him directly about Eugene's behavior, and he commented that Eugene, in effect, was leading the meeting and was running it. I asked him "like an administrator?" and he commented, "yes." This, in effect, corroborates the behavior I saw earlier in the morning in the same committee. Paul indicated several specifics: listing the agenda items, instrumenting them, and terminating discussion on items when he thought there had been sufficient discussion. To my direct question, Did he sit around and wait for an agenda to develop as has occurred in other meetings, Paul responded "no" (8/25).

The summary notes record not only shifts in leadership styles and role within the faculty, but also the complications of dissatisfaction, disagreement, and ineffectiveness. We began a paragraph with a prediction.

> Both of us keep expecting the lid to blow off the whole place when the anxiety of the first day finally mounts with the realization that they aren't organized. This is our prediction, however. Related to it now is a conversation with one of the teachers who is extremely irritated at several things: (1) what she perceived to be railroading of items, (2) the inability of anybody to get anything done in the committees, and (3) the tremendous amount of committees that she is on—at least, three. A close to verbatim quote went something like,

---

[6] A later name for the curriculum coordinating committee.

"If things don't straighten out very soon, I'll pack up my bag and go home."
This was followed by "you can quote me too" (8/25).

Without presenting our detailed documentation, suffice it to say that
the committees did not produce authoritative position papers. The dilemma
of a totally individualized child-selected curriculum as opposed to a structured and sequenced set of experiences formulated by adults was not resolved by the curriculum subcommittees. The curriculum coordinating committee had a turbulent history, changed its name to the central committee,
and became, during the workshop, the arena for most of the open struggle
for power and leadership in the school.

The Kirkham Affair. On Friday, August 25, at the end of the third
week, Kensington underwent its most significant trauma: Bill Kirkham
was removed as a member of the staff.

The action occurred, formally, during the ISD team meeting. The stated
reasons were that his point of view was too different and that he blocked
the smooth functioning of the team. Varying opinions existed about the
genesis of the action. Some of the staff were more cognizant and involved
than the others. Some thought the action had been handled well; others
did not think so. There was some feeling that the unsettled team leader
role was critical. Some thought that Leslie Roberts behaved inappropriately
in his consultant role. Others believed the dismissal arose as a scapegoating
mechanism because of the failure of the team to progress. Some thought
that Bill and his curriculum ideas were a personal threat to Eugene. There
was talk that Bill did not know it was coming, that he thought it was
arranged before the Friday meeting, and that there was more to it than
appeared on the surface.

These events we have conceptualized as a series of antecedent variables:
intrateam conflict and ineffectiveness, norm violation by the consultant,
leadership inconsistency, potential threat to authority, and differential
knowledge and involvement by team members. We would hypothesize that
increasing amounts of these variables precipitated the dramatic personnel
change. Major consequences to Kensington were both immediate and long
term. Although, in a sense, incalculable, the ramifications will appear
throughout this book. We speak of only two at this point. First, there
was a decrease in the quantity and quality of organizational resources.
Kirkham was an experienced teacher. At such a time, late in the summer,
Kensington was never able to obtain a competent, experienced replacement
for the year. For a while, Walt Larsen filled in, but he never was socialized
into the ISD group, and he performed only marginally until he was released.
John Taylor, the physical education specialist, was dragooned into becoming
a temporary academic counselor. This provoked some ill feeling in the
other divisions (to which he had a responsibility) and reduced resources

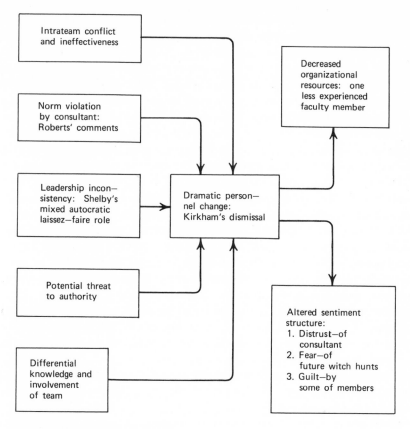

Figure 3.5 The Kirkham affair.

in that phase of the program's concern for the totality of the child's personal development. Second, within the ISD team, major shifts occurred in the group-sentiment structure. Specifically, an increase in distrust, especially toward the consultant, developed. An atmosphere of fear occurred as rumors of future witch-hunts seeped or exploded through parts of the team. Finally, guilt was now a part of the group, as some members of the team had second thoughts about the event. Figure 3.5 diagrams these hypotheses.

The Final Week of the Workshop

Time falls naturally into weekly units that have ascertainable beginnings and endings. Events often correspond to this naturalness, although August's lingering one more day into the new week seemed to carry overtones of the prior three weeks. Although the Milford District was mobilizing itself through a district-wide teachers' meeting, which the Kensington staff attended, and Kensington was to have its first evening parent meeting, the spirit of William Kirkham remained.

After the district-wide morning exercises of speeches, introductions of new staff, and announcements relevant to the whole district, the Kensington teachers as well as the other teachers returned to their individual schools. On Monday afternoon, Shelby met with the ISD teachers and they spent a half-hour discussing aspects and implications of Kirkham's removal. They then moved to the task of delineating a new organizational pattern. The academic counselor and subject matter resource specialist roles reached "clarity" around points such as: (a) the academic counselor will concern himself with the totality of the child's development; the subject matter specialist primarily will concern himself with development in that resource area; and (b) the academic counselor will decide whether the child, for instance, goes to science, but will not decide what will be done in science. Shelby commented that the biggest responsibility of the academic counselor in the first month would be helping the pupils learn to work independently and interdependently. Decisions were reached to have the children form groups of six as the basic unit. Irma and David were to be the academic counselors. John yielded to pressure to become a "temporary" academic counselor, and this was changed later to an assistant academic counselor. Liz and Kay became assistant academic counselors and resource persons in language arts and social studies, respectively. Jack and Alec remained resource persons. In the eyes of one of the staff, ISD was working better with Shelby's active leadership.

On Monday evening, two parent meetings were held in Milford. One, a large protest meeting, reflected continuing community and district conflict with the public schools. The specific issue involved a book and fee assessment that had been levied against each pupil. The roots of the community conflict had a long history: a prior superintendent who had been fired and rehired, a split in the school board, and a reputation in the regional area as "a district with problems."

The second meeting, which was repeated on Tuesday and Wednesday evenings, was a Kensington parents' night in which the principal and staff sought to explain the program. In a pleasant style the principal spoke of the need for understanding between the parents and staff, the organizational structure of the building whose goal was to facilitate individualized learning, and the materials, books, and equipment that they would have available in the school. The parents expressed concern and confusion regarding bus schedules and knowing where and how the very young children would be transported to the temporary facilities. Other questions included promotion, grading, and report cards. There were distinct variations in overall hostility of parents; Monday night was quite strong, although the other meeting went more smoothly. We discuss this in more detail in a later section on the organization and its environment.

As teams and as individuals, the staff continued preparations during the middle days of the week. The Basic Skills Division was meeting explicitly as a team of two and a team of four.[7] The BSD-4 team had drawn and cut out a "magic bus" which was to be a focus of initial activities. They were having a difficult time handling it because of a lack of bulletin board surface in their temporary quarters. Perhaps underestimating their accomplishments, they spoke of the day as "not very stimulating or productive." The Transition team worked on their plans for the coming week while the tile men resurfaced the floor in their large room (which had been a storage area for Hillside and the Milford School District) and the glaziers replaced glass broken from vandalism and informal play in the adjacent area behind the school. The ISD team alternated between working separately on specific tasks and meeting as a group. It was on Wednesday morning in the team meeting that the pupil Training Groups idea, initiated by Shelby and responded to warmly by David, was instituted after a brief discussion of discipline and the need for pupils to move from external discipline to internal controls and to the self-initiation of activities.

The Wednesday discussion, as recorded in the field notes, went this way:

DAVID. We must internalize the goals of Kensington in the child and I think this can best be done by group process.

KAY. I agree very much, but will just discussion in small groups do this? This would be abstract.

DAVID. I think discipline is not abstract. It is a very real issue. Children will come to a variety of conclusions and I would question how they came to this decision.

EUGENE. I feel a teacher will be needed with the group like Lyn and Lois [the August trainers] were with us. Perhaps you could take a small group.

DAVID. I don't care. I do think it is most important though.

[David questions the group as to their response.]

ALEC. I can see it at first, but I feel it requires close supervision—I think it's part of the goals of the school, but I don't think they can do without us at first.

EUGENE. How about letting David do this in small groups for the first few weeks and you all take the rest of this.

Shelby suggested that the faculty have one of the trainers, who was

[7] Several alternative team structures, 2, 2, 2, and 3, 3, as well as the 4, 2 arrangements were considered. The 4, 2 resolution solved the most serious aspects of interpersonal staff conflict within the Basic Skills Division.

in their August training-group session, come in and assist them with the pupil training groups. Kay and Alec expressed positive sentiments toward the idea of bringing in a trained person; however, David, who hoped to be most instrumental in setting up and continuing the groups, voiced less approval than did the others.

It is important to note the support that Shelby gave to the plan and his backing of David. The principal suggested two sessions per day of one-and-one-half hours each, and he also volunteered his help. Illustrative of his enthusiasm at the time was his mentioning of several persons at City University who might come in and work with them during the first week's training.

At the same time, the presumed flexibility of the program was indicated. The field notes continued:

> DAVID. Do we start the groups the first day?
>
> EUGENE. You could. That's the beauty of this. You all don't have to do all things.
>
> DAVID. I have trouble. I want everyone to agree on everything in our group and I guess it won't always be that way.

David asked for feedback as to why the team was rather "cool" to his suggestions on "group process."

> IRMA. I feel children are too immature at this by themselves.
>
> LIZ. I think you gave us too much information.
>
> ALEC. I felt it was important but I didn't want to do it.
>
> LIZ. I feel we're segmenting the children too much. If my group doesn't work right should I send them to David or call David in?
>
> DAVID. No, if you can handle it, fine; if you want help, I'll be glad to help.
>
> LIZ. We started calling it group therapy. We must tell them it's not a counseling group.
>
> KAY. There's been a lot of this in psychology the last few years. It's spooky business for kids; it's scary.
>
> LIZ. [to David] You must realize it's on group process. Lois [the NTL trainer] told us it's not group therapy. Don't try to help on individual problems.
>
> DAVID. I don't see this as a function of a T-group. Do you think I might tend to do this?
>
> LIZ. Yes.
>
> DAVID. Then they go from training groups in the morning to academic counseling in the afternoon.

It was decided by the ISD faculty that the students would participate in training-group sessions conducted by David Nichols. As was indicated in his earlier statements, David was a strong advocate of this method.

On subsequent days there was discussion as to how to present the idea of training groups to the students. Liz said, "I supposed it would be entirely vocal—David would arise to call 'Follow me.'" Irma commented: "Yes, like a trumpet." The discussion in the team meeting continued:

> KAY. We could say, since we're doing work in groups at Kensington, we think we should know how groups operate.
>
> DAVID. Good, sure you don't want to run a T-group? I hope they let us make tapes; it's never been done before.
>
> ALEC. Are you going to pull them out of groups that have done tasks? How will you choose the groups?
>
> DAVID. I've not definitely decided. I definitely don't want natural groups.
>
> ALEC. I'd like for David to pick out groups at the beginning and put them in task groups. Does this have top priority? If you want him, he goes? [He refers to the composition of training groups.]
>
> DAVID. I'd like to say yes, but that's not my decision. It's our decision. They can't miss more than one a day [refers to T-group meeting].
>
> ALEC. I've lost all you have said . . . thought it was imperative that they be there.

Thus, late in the final week of the workshop, the Independent Study Division reorganized itself to meet an important objective, socialization of pupils toward the ideals of internal initiation of activities and of self-discipline. In so doing, they produced a new team role and a new structure in which to work.

On Thursday, September 3, the day began with what was described as a "nuts and bolts" meeting for the entire staff. The discussions included a number of specific items: (1) Kirkham's replacement (Walt Larsen) was introduced as an assistant teacher. (2) The several teacher aides who were to have vertical responsibilities, that is, with the entire staff, were reassigned to have primary responsibilities by divisions in the separate geographical locations. Each team was instructed to work out its own routines with the aides. (3) Parents who refused to pay district-wide fees were to be given a list of supplies to buy. (4) A letter to the parents on bus schedules would go out the first day. The buses would be on a double run, and the Kensington children would be picked up at 8:55 A.M. in the morning and at 4:15 P.M. in the evening. (Joan Sidney, the aide who had been working on this and on attendance, and who had the precise information, was not present because of her husband's illness.) (5) The furniture was to be delivered today. (6) The textbooks, which have been donated mostly from American Book Company (ABC), were the only ones available and could be checked out today. Similarly, encyclopedias, globes, individualized materials such as the SRA Reading and Writing Laboratories, the Cycloteachers, and the like were available. (7) Expendable materials would be handled on a temporary borrowing procedure. Each team should meet with aides and work out procedures. (8) Individual storybooks would be checked out six per teacher. Tom commented that the library books would be in tomorrow, and he would be working all weekend. Discussion ensued on the allocation of funds for library books rather than for textbooks.

At 9:20 A.M. the meeting adjourned for coffee and a small birthday cake for Meg, who was surprised and a bit embarrassed. Later, most of the staff gathered in the junior high school gym, which was the central materials headquarters. The ISD team, working from David's sketch, was organizing the space and was beginning to move furniture about. Trapezoidal tables would be used for study tables, and individual desks would be used as pupil stations.

> 10:45 A.M. As I watch I'm impressed with the confusion. There is one maintenance man assigned to Kensington, according to Tom. Jean commented that what they needed was a half-dozen strong high school boys. . . . From the Junior High School custodian's eyes, things are chaotic and will remain so until the first of the year. He cited the delay in getting into the new junior high building three years ago (9/3).

During the last two days of the week, the ISD team met to solve the particularized and specific aspects of duties, schedules, the geography of the gym, and other specific matters.

The split of the Basic Skills Division into a team of two and a team of four was complete by the last week of the workshop. Both groups were temporarily housed in the Milford high school building. A comment in the notes summarizes, in part, the last day of preparations.

> Mary and Carla (the team of two) are probably the most highly organized and the most far along in their planning and in their preparation for Tuesday. They will have two rooms over in the high school. The one room is large enough to hold all 60 of their children, and they have it divided up very nicely and very neatly. They both plan on being in the room together. The other room will be mostly their literature and reading and independent work area. The kids will be brought over here by one or the other of them as the day and the week progress. Some will be allowed to come in by themselves and work independently. They have decided that they will alternate with the groups.

Into the notes, the observer put an interpretation and hypothesis that caught more of the later team dynamics than he realized at the time.

> Also, as I observed them sorting out books, I was struck again by the fact that Carla is very directive and very dominating of Mary. She tells her what

to do, which things to carry, which things to write down, and which things to put where. Mary tended to do these without question. Later when Mary was showing me around the larger room, she commented about the way they were working. A large tree they have on the north wall, on which they will place cutouts of words children learn, was originally suggested by her, so she reported to me, and Carla then suggested that they make a huge one for the wall, and then another suggestion built on another suggestion, and so on. The point that she was making is that each of them contributed ideas that seemed to complement the other and make it work together. It seems to me that she has told me this kind of story a number of times, each time almost protesting that she, too, has something to say about what's going on. Again, it seems as if it's usually in the context of Carla ordering her about. I still view this as a latent and a very important conflict that could erupt if Mary ever were to find an alternative to turn to that she could be secure in, and that would be with someone who is probably as effective in the classroom as Carla is.[8]

They have their walls decorated with pictures that, Mary explained, were cut out from a workbook and with the letters of the alphabet around the room. In the main room they also have science displays and exhibits and also an aquarium and other objects. All in all, it looks very attractive. They also have picked off some of the ABC books and the workbooks in reading, social studies books, and the like. My guess is that they will be able to operate very easily, and very quickly and without much to-do once the day starts. It will be a very good standard program, probably the best of any of the teams, but probably with little innovation.

The other part of the Basic Skills team is moving along, although much less rapidly. They are apparently getting considerable help from Dan's wife, Chris, who has been hired for a part-time position. Organizationally, they are ready for the first day but not for much more. As it stands now, the team will be divided into four rooms with the children and the teachers set for the first day. Each room will be given a color. Each room also will become an activity-type room in the sense that reading will be going on in one, creative arts in another, a messy room in another, and so on. The rooms themselves are currently taking on the decoration and structure of an exciting primary department. Elaine has brought along a puppet booth and literally dozens of puppets that she works with very effectively. She gave us a demonstration of the alligator and a pet dog. Pictures are going up, lines are being put on the floor, and so forth. Jean was putting some of the strips down, and Sue was coloring them, while Elaine was working on some other materials, and Wanda was putting stuff on bulletin boards. They have not commandeered

---

[8] Later discussion and research in team composition must attend to the complex issues of the prediction of team cohesiveness and effectiveness. Mary and Carla had known each other for several years and had taught in the same elementary school, but they had not teamed before.

any extra help as Mary and Carla had done. The latter have a teen-age boy, a former pupil of Carla's, helping out, and also a high school teacher from upstairs who is a special friend of Mary's. It is interesting to observe that the hired help for moving has been on a catch-as-catch-can basis, not only here but also over at the Hillside center where a group of junior high kids have been helping through Dan's efforts (3:30 P.M., 9/3).

In short, each team was moving toward the following Tuesday when the pupils would arrive. A variety of planning and preparatory action had taken place.

The month's workshop, which began with total school activity in the analysis of group functioning, was now concluding with individual team efforts to handle specific and concrete problems of the first days of school. The faculty, which began as a group atypical of most elementary school staffs, had spent a month in preparation for their major responsibility, providing an education for 500 elementary children during the coming year. As we have indicated, this month raised many issues, created some important changes, and established aspects of the structure that was to prevail during the year.

CHAPTER 4

Conceptualizing Organizational Origins and Development

INTRODUCTION

Tucked away in a volume on leadership as statesmanship, Selznick (1957) presents a brief discussion of three developmental problems in the origins of an organization: the selection of a social base, the building of an institutional core, and the formalization of procedure. These tasks confront the organization with initial and critical policy decisions. For our analysis, they provide us with an introduction to the origins of organizational development. Selznick comments in regard to the first conception:

"The early phase of an institution's life is marked by a scrutiny of its own capabilities, and of its environment, to discover where its resources are and on whom it is dependent. The achievement of stability is influenced by this appraisal; and the future evolution of the institution is largely conditioned by the commitments generated in this basic decision" (1957, p. 104).

With respect to Kensington, we shall have more to say as we analyze the school's relationship to "the everpresent environment." For the moment, we would indicate that the lot of Kensington was cast with Spanman, the new superintendent; and his assistant, Cohen, the curriculum director. Shelby, the principal, was part of the new guard of Milford, and his school was a major element in the new program. The dependency here was so great that the superintendent's departure, a temporary one-year leave that later became permanent, and the curriculum director's departure at the end of the first year were mortal blows. Although no one knew it at the time, one might argue that that was the moment that Kensington died.

"Building the institutional core" is the second task suggested by Selznick. Creating an initially homogeneous staff has a variety of consequences:

"(1) . . . indoctrinate newcomers along desired lines. (2) . . . provide assurance that decision making will conform, in spirit as well as letter, to policies that may have to be formulated abstractly or vaguely. (3) The development of derivative policies and detailed application of general rules will thus be guided by a shared general perspective" (1957, p. 104).

Selznick argues that selective recruiting and shared experiences provide twin procedures for handling the problem. In regard to these issues, he makes generalizations that our data suggest must be sharply limited or qualified.

"The creation of an institutional core is partly a matter of selective recruiting . . . . By choosing key personnel from a particular social group, the earlier conditioning of the individuals becomes a valuable resource for the new organization" (p. 105).

In a new organization that is an innovative one, the criteria for selection are considerably more ambiguous, since the nature of the desired earlier learning is not clear. The option of accenting highly recommended but inexperienced teachers and the aspiration to train them in the new directions seems, in hindsight, to have resulted in a host of consequences, many of which were dysfunctional for Kensington. Also, as we talk of true belief in an innovative organization, important self-selective personality factors seem to operate in terms of availability for recruitment to an innovative setting.

Selznick's further generalizations regarding the building of an institutional core are interesting in the light of the data from Kensington.

"But core building involves more than selective recruiting. Indoctrination and the sharing of key experiences—especially internal conflicts and other crises—will help to create a unified group and give the organization a special identity" (pp. 105–106).

Indoctrination, or socialization, occurred in the summer workshop. The T-groups, the division, team, and committee meetings, and the Institutional Plan all contributed toward the imbuing of principles and doctrines. Interwoven and extending into and throughout the year, internal conflicts and crises occurred. They did give Kensington a special identity, but they did not create a unity. Our guess would be that for unity to be achieved an organization must be successful in the eyes of the participants and in the eyes of significant others. That is the sine qua non. If one has that, then internal conflicts and crises provide stimuli for high emotion that has a positive, exciting quality to it, and such sentiments then can lead to unity and identity. Our observations of the "Bataan phenomenon" in the introductory epilogue suggest additional intricacies and qualifications to Selznick's more general statement.

When he speaks of "formalization," the third developmental problem, Selznick comments:

"The organization reduces its dependence on the personal attributes of the participants by making supervision more routine and by externalizing discipline and incentive" (1957, pp. 106–107).

Implicit in his statement is a concern for When? and Where? and How soon? formalization is attained within the organization. The gains from early formalization are clarity in communication and command. The losses are limitations in flexibility, open-endedness, and freedom for leadership decisions. Kensington presented several unique twists regarding formalization. First, a high degree of formalization existed early in the manifestation of the formal doctrine known as the Institutional Plan. As we argued elsewhere, formalization of this kind may have come too early. Second, the doctrine itself accented flexibility as an important subgoal. Third, a variety of experiences, for example, the T-groups, accented a lack of formalization in interpersonal relationships. Fourth, Shelby exhibited contrasting leadership modes of total nondirectiveness to unswerving commitment to elements in the Institutional Plan. Fifth, styles of the staff varied from almost total personal autonomy to high willingness to accept organizational or subgroup perspectives. In short, formalization was not of a single piece at Kensington, and the consequences were multiple as well. The economy of formalization of social structure, that is, having an organizational history, is not to be underestimated.

FORMALIZATION AND INTERNAL RESOURCES

Some Necessary Distinctions

School personnel, probably like people in general, usually do not appreciate what it means for an organization to have a history. To possess a past is to have a social structure or "sets of alternative actions, or tendencies to act in certain ways . . . and the constraints that specify or limit these alternative actions," as one recent social scientist phrases it (Buckley, 1967). A major part of the origin of an organization centers on generating or building these sets of alternatives and the constraints that define them. We believe that this is the essence of Selznick's conception of formalization and we propose to explore it in additional detail, in the context of the origins of an innovative school organization.[1]

Because our organization is an elementary school, we have a special case.[2] As compared with other organizations, a school has a rather interesting social structure. A major dichotomy exists in the age of its members, since the adults are concentrated into a subgroup of teachers and administrators. In addition to age, one also finds power, freedom, knowledge, and maturity concentrated among the adults. This adult faculty is also a minority. Also the school is a part of a larger organization, the school district. The school's purposes are a particular kind of socialization. Its technical base is open to high debate. Its environmental relations are political with local control. In such manners a school is a special kind of organization. Hypothetically, the processes of formalization will vary because of these differences. A well-developed comparative theory of organizations would have solved some of our problems here.

As often occurs in trying to formulate a difficult problem, the resolution, in retrospect, is absurdly simple. Organizational change is a broad rubric requiring its own set of concepts. It might be analyzed into purposive and nonpurposive antecedents. The beginning of a new organization is a special case of organizational change. Consequently, principles appropriate to organizational origins ought to be special instances of the more general principles of organizational change. Similarly, developing an old organization is a special case of purposive organizational change. Maintaining an innovative organization, by definition, involves dealing with planned change. Starting an innovative organization is a compounding of the two special cases of genesis and innovation.

Although no organizations are autonomous in the sense of being independent of their environments, organizations do vary in the degree to which they are subunits of larger organizations. Once again, Kensington was unique. As a public school, it is a unit of the larger Milford School District. But it had a special relationship to the district; it was a "protected subculture." Relatively, it moved freely of many organizational constraints of the larger organization. It set many of its own goals and almost all of its procedures. It was probably as autonomous as any public school ever is. These unique aspects had special implications for the origins issues.

---

[1] Although we did not call it formalization, we explored at some length the similar problems faced by a teacher who begins work with a new class in the fall of the year (Smith and Geoffrey, 1968, pp. 47–86).

[2] Although we did not utilize Hemphill's (1956) scheme of group dimensions, it would be applicable in supporting this analysis.

For instance, if a natural history of an autonomous organization were described, we presume it would have small beginnings—few participants, limited resources, and trial-and-error procedures for reaching its goals. The required decisions would be relatively simple and, as they occurred, they would be cumulated, examined, and formalized into social structure. Over time, specialized roles would develop, routine activities would be instigated almost automatically to recurring stimuli, and the members of the organization would be able to tell an outsider or newcomer about "the way things are done here." In time, the latter might carry a righteous or normative quality as well. The organization would attain a coordination of an artistic sort, much like the smoothness one sees in a highly skilled psychomotor performance such as diving, gymnastics, or golf. Considerable time and energy resources are involved in making the innumerable decisions that accumulate into a social structure which then serves to guide and to direct the participants and leads to economy in goal attainment.

Thus, at another level, this complex adaptive process may be viewed as involving "a source of variety against which to draw, a number of selective mechanisms that sift and test this environmental variety against some criteria of viability, and processes that tend to bind and perpetuate the selected variety for some length of time" (Buckley, 1967, p. 128). Although the genesis of formalization may be gradual or rapid, we hypothesize that a new but autonomous organization moves through such a process of decisions, trial and error, activities, gradual growth, and formalization.

In the general case, a school that has been created whole, in respect to full size of members, staff and pupils, and without a history does not initially have a social structure; but it does have ties with a parent organization. It is not totally an autonomous organization. Without this social structure, the new organization generally appeals more frequently to procedures and available documents, such as the formal doctrine, from the larger parent organization. Because Kensington was a "protected subculture," the ties to the larger organization, the Milford School District, were deliberately less than usual. In this sense, Kensington was more like an autonomous organization. Because the school was deliberately mandated to be innovative, the impact of the district's structure was also reduced.

The history-less, near-autonomous, innovative organization faces immediately a continuous series of decisions to the "problems of the moment." Inevitably, because of the complexity of the human condition, these decisions are conflicting to some degree. At its worst, on the one hand, this can precipitate staff confusion, frustration and, in many instances, emotionality. A lack of experience in key activities can be critical. The task of making the decisions especially in a "democratic" style can be a tremendously time-consuming and fatiguing process and can drain resources from other aspects of the organization. Each of these in turn can generate meetings and conferences and more drain in time and energy, a vicious circle that can be severely debilitating.

In an educational organization, major consequences can occur in the resulting confusion and disturbances in teacher-pupil relations. No one knows for sure just what to do; directions are not clear; and control of pupils is jeopardized. This is coupled with limited time and energy for preparation as a result of other meetings. In sum, the most severe consequence, a kind of anxiety, is created. Meeting a group of youngsters when procedures in teacher-pupil relations are confused, and when one has inadequately prepared for the lessons, qualifies as such a consequence. In part, we are anticipating later portions of our descriptive narrative, the early weeks of school in September.

Resource Limits: A Major Unanticipated Consequence of Formalization Processes

Early in August, a major problem began to arise at Kensington. It involved the expense in time, energy, personnel, and materials related to beginning this new, relatively autonomous, and innovative organization. Essentially, we are saying that all organizational change carries heavy demands for resources. Our special case of change, the origins of an innovative organization, makes the heaviest demands. If these resources have not been budgeted or if they are unavailable for other reasons, the organization lies in peril. An early observation and interpretation stated it this way:

> Another item that came up in my discussion with Eugene concerned the lack of administrative assistance that he has. For an elementary school in which the principal just "keeps the wheels turning" and things going as they are, he doesn't really need a lot of assistance. That's an hypothesis. But for an elementary school in which the principal is trying to change a number of things, then it seems to me that he needs someone to help coordinate, communicate, follow through, and carry out the numerous and almost endless little details and chores. Eugene doesn't have anybody to do this, and he is being pushed back into a terrible corner with his other work and with keeping the program moving. This is related to Larry's[3] point about having in the background of any innovative attempt sufficient budgeted resources to pick up all the slack and all of the difficulties that are bound to arise from unanticipated consequences. Administratively, it seems to me that Kensington School is headed for that kind of problem also. An assistant principal could handle some of this, or it might also be handled with the team leaders playing a

---

[3] The observer is recalling one item from many highly significant and meaningful conversations with a former colleague, Professor Laurence Iannaccone.

much more influential role in this set of tasks. Part of the problem locally may fall around the inability of Eugene to delegate responsibility (8/18).

In short, we hypothesize that the phenomenon of beginning an organization, and especially an innovative organization, requires more resources than usual, and second, that the unanticipated consequences of each purposive social action will require an added increment of resources. Finally, we argue, the Kensington planners did not anticipate to the required degree either of these demands. In this discussion we believe that we are saying much the same thing as Etzioni (1966) in his use of the concept "take-off."

"The concept of take-off, borrowed from aerodynamics, is applied to the first stage of epigenesis to distinguish the initiation point from where the continuation of the process becomes self-sustained" (p. 38).

As he extends the analogy, he speaks of the resources needed for self-maintenance.

"The image is one of a plane that first starts its engines and begins rolling, still supported by the runway, until it accumulates enough momemtum to 'take-off,' to continue in motion 'on its own,' generating the forces that carry it to higher altitudes and greater speeds. The analogue is that through accumulation, while relying on external support, the necessary condition for autonomous action is produced" (p. 38).

At Kensington, the resources available for creating organizational structures and processes were limited. This aspect of Kensington's newness remained all year.

In addition, Kensington had several unique dimensions that intensified the consequences. These aspects can be drawn from our earlier descriptions also. They include: (1) the nature of the immediate goals themselves, for example, individualized instruction; (2) the lack of teaching experience; (3) the newness in many organizational patterns such as team teaching about which the profession has limited intimate and generalizable knowledge; (4) the "upside-down" authority structure; (5) the intrastaff conflict and negative sentiment; and (6) the more extended activities, for example, the Curriculum Committee and the staff research program.

Furthermore, we would hypothesize that the successful operation of an organization that lacks a set of formal procedures is greatly dependent on the use of verbal skills. The style of the team meetings grew from that of the early T-group training sessions. Interpersonal communication was of utmost importance. The analysis of past events, the diagnosis of student and faculty problems, the reactions to community sentiments, the clarification of intermediate and long-range goals, the means of attaining objectives, the ways to preserve the uniqueness of the school, and a minimum concentration on the "nuts and bolts" of the organization characterized a typical meeting. The records of the decision-making process indicate some of the communication problems. Discussions seemed to vary among, at least, four levels. The first was the theoretical; the second, the "nuts and bolts"; the third, interpersonal relations; and the fourth, personal anxiety.

Some of the great time demands of a system of this nature have been pointed out. Other than the time spent in instruction and contact with the children during the day, there were numerous meetings, many of which were both long and frequent. There were team, subteam, and total staff meetings. All of them were in addition to the regular teacher-pupil responsibilities, and they were not during school hours. It was not unusual for a team meeting to last three-and-one-half hours to four hours. Parent meetings, the parent-school organization, and the Curriculum Committee sessions also were attended in some cases by all staff members and in the latter two instances by a part of the faculty.

There were innumerable antecedents for what appeared to be the extraordinary amount of time devoted to the school. Kensington was new with no traditions and norms of its own to look to, to find security in, or to modify. Even more dramatic was the fact that the staff was to develop plans and patterns to follow with little or no help from other less innovative systems. Seldom were Kensington's reference groups functioning elementary school organizations. More usually, university-based scholars or selected "schools of thought" that represented what was to be attempted at Kensington filled the role. In a sense, ideas were their referents rather than schools already in operation. This is doubtless true of anything that is really innovative. However, many aspects of Kensington had been developed and utilized before the attempt to integrate them into an innovative whole in the Milford District.

Thus, with its absence of previously developed norms, procedures, and the attempt to modify what had been viewed earlier by other practitioners as solutions to procedural and instructional problems, perhaps it is not surprising that "building" the many intangible and agreed-on ways of doing things required so much time.

The notes provide various pieces of information as to the reaction of the families of the staff and, in turn, the faculty member's statements about their families. A half-dozen of them would include: (1) one member allegedly bought a color TV because of his many nights away; (2) another's wife commented about seldom seeing him and he jokingly responded that he was going to have to get a divorce if he weren't home more; and

(3) other married staff's objections to a lot of evening and weekend meetings because of ill spouses and outside responsibilities in the district and in the larger community. A number of the faculty were unmarried; they tended to be strong advocates of the school's philosophy, and they were able to spend evenings and extra time on academic matters. Initially, they were also very interested in the Curriculum Committee, which met frequently and for several hours at a time. However, as the year progressed even they were less willing to devote large blocks of time to long team and committee meetings. The Saturday staff meetings also contributed to the time pressures. There also seemed to be an unspoken faith in contact and duration of contact with the building, with the ideas it represented, and with fellow faculty members. Yet, the believers in this same faith came to realize the millstonelike quality of the exhaustion and frustration that may come without respite from a responsibility and mandate so great as, "Go build a school," and the organizational corollary, "develop a formal structure" in which this will occur. We summarize these conceptions in Figure 4.1. As the figure shows, a number of events drained Kensington's

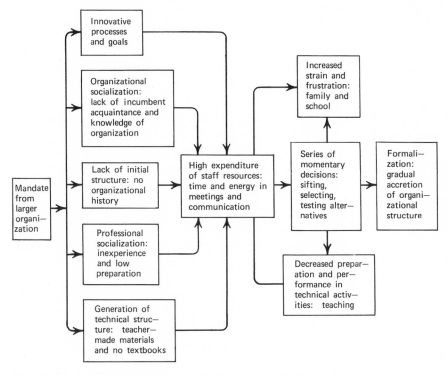

Figure 4.1 A miniature theory of resources and formalization at Kensington.

resources. The processes leading to the selecting and testing of alternatives from the environment and emphasizing congruency with the mandate from the district level were critical. These expenditures were increased by the requisites accompanying implementation of innovative processes and goals. Also, as noted elsewhere, the low level of experience and formal teacher training combined with the lack of acquaintance among the staff and the lack of information about mutual capabilities, interests, and productivity to make further drains on scarce resources.

Often the alternatives that were selected were subject to conflicting interpretations, an outcome of high ambiguity about teacher-pupil role behaviors and increased strain and frustration for the staff. Less time was available for preparation of materials for teaching which, in turn, was reflected in the performance in the classroom.

Although formalization at most provides a range within which certain activities may be performed, the continuous sifting and testing of elements from the environment made accretion of procedures most gradual. Continuous remapping and reorganization of variety and alternatives, as pointed out in previous chapters, became the norm. The lack of consistent policy and procedures placed an increased emphasis on verbal communication and interaction of the staff. The frequency and length of school and team meetings is cited elsewhere. They, in turn, with their great demands on time and energy produced interpersonal difficulties at home and school.

And as we shall describe later, at Kensington "the processes which tend to bind and perpetuate the selected variety for some length of time (Buckley, 1967, p. 128)" were not forthcoming for all of the school, the divisions, and the teams until less innovative forms of organization (for example, self-contained classrooms) were among the sets of alternatives selected. In the interim, increased strain, frustration, and emotionality were expressed by the staff, and the time spent in preparing for performance in the classroom was reduced.

BUILDING AN INSTITUTIONAL CORE

A major determinant of formalization is building an institutional core, a staff unified, homogeneous, and with an identity, thus Selznick argues. By tentatively accepting this, we can ask for hypotheses clarifying the relationship of building an institutional core to the phenomenon of formalization from the data of our special case, the origination of an innovative organization. Our efforts will focus on two broad domains: (I) an analysis of the T-grouping experience, a very important innovative procedure for organizational socialization; and (II) "true belief," a way of focusing on faculty sentiment in an innovative organization.

I T-Grouping: Innovative Organizational Socialization

Of all the analyses and interpretations, one of the ones we hesitated about most involved the T-group.[4] As we have indicated elsewhere, our intent has been to create hypotheses that fit our case—our accumulated field notes. The hypotheses are offered then for wider testing and verification. The following analysis is an attempt to conceptualize T-group experience with an aggregate of staff new to each other, yet on their way to becoming a working unit.

Our problem of putting additional meaning in the interpretation of the training experience begins in the phrasing of the issue. Instead of asking the simple question, T-groups—pro or con?, we would ask, "What happens to an organization when the participants come together for the first time, engage in T-group activities for a week, and then must work intimately together for the next ten months?" To the best of our knowledge (Miles, 1959; Bradford et al., 1964; Glidewell, 1966) research has not been directed to this kind of problem. However, training groups are being formed with members of the same organization (Katz and Kahn, 1966). Miles (1964), in his discussion of temporary systems, presents a taxonomy that includes temporary staff and client, and permanent staff and temporary client, but does not present intensively the quasi-temporary system in which the client is permanent but the staff is temporary, actually the more usual consultant case. Nor does he handle the special case of the time at which the meeting occurs in the history of the organization. The intent of our discussion is to describe and to interpret this special case of T-group experience.

Initial Aspects

During the first week of the month's workshop a number of events took place that were intertwined with the T-group experience. Some occurred in the meetings per se, and some occurred formally and informally along the way. We have tried to analyze and categorize them around several broad rubrics consistent with our general conception of organizations.

Negation of Formal Status. The T-group experience was new to the members of the Kensington faculty. In the judgment of the observers, the experience was dramatic and influential. For instance, although informality was built into Kensington in a variety of ways, the T-group experience contributed to this. As we have indicated, at the first meeting the faculty was grouped vertically, that is across divisions, into two groups,

---

[4] This refers to a skepticism we have had through the years and is illustrated in our analysis of teacher-leader behavior in Smith (1959), Smith and Hudgins (1964), and Smith and Geoffrey (1968).

and the principal was a member of one group. It was at this point that he shifted his role to that of a peer, a member of his group. During a meeting containing a discussion of status barriers and problems accompanying them, he gave them the option of calling him whatever they felt most comfortable using—by title or by first name. One of the members quickly suggested that they call him by his first name; this was accepted by members of both groups, and throughout the year the principal was addressed by his first name.

This move toward informality had its limits, however. The principal's formal position was a factor that was impossible to overcome totally.[5] This is true, we believe, because of the complexity of the special authority encompassed in the role, which we analyze in detail later, and partly because of the perceptions teachers have of principals. The summary notes that report on the conversations between the observers reflect this:

> I have had little chance to talk with Eugene about the progress of the workshop or, for that matter, about anything else in the program. Paul tells me that the principal's presence in the other group raised considerable difficulty with the group's progress. When they split into small subgroups and he was not in one group, that group made tremendous progress in discussion and in moving toward a series of analyses (8/12).

Delineation of the Faithful and the Skeptical: Public Testimonials. Early Tuesday morning, the observer recorded several items of interest:

> Follow-up comments on yesterday seem necessary. One of these centers on the selection of people for the school. While I haven't had a chance to check it out carefully in the field notes,[6] it seems to me that almost everyone has made a testimonial of some kind of extreme faith in the new school and what it is trying to do. The contrast here with the group of teachers at the Washington School[7] is also very, very marked. The cruciality of this variable should not be neglected and should be highlighted in the general write-up of the report. It, coupled with the principal's enthusiasm and with his own very unique conception of the nature of elementary school organization and instruction, is an important variable (8/11).

Our interpretation suggested that the T-group experience provided an opportunity for making public deeply-held feelings and beliefs. As we indicate

---

[5] Independently of our analysis, our colleague, Professor Edwin Bridges, neatly tested experimentally a similar conception and found the same inhibiting effect of the elementary principal with his staff (Bridges, 1966).

[6] The reference here is to a split between field notes, a stenographic *in situ* account, and summary observations and interpretations, lengthy dictated notes made at various times of the day but out of the setting.

[7] This is a reference to an earlier intensive analysis of a classroom in a slum school (Smith and Geoffrey, 1968).

elsewhere, the staff selection in an innovative school, the sentiment of enthusiasm, and the principal's Institutional Plan were salient early. Opportunities for expressions of faith, in one sense, helped to make somewhat
less nebulous the organizational structure that was to become Kensington;
however, the public testimonial statements also fostered an over-aggrandizement of Kensington. In reality many of the intangible doctrinal aspects—the
verbal assessments and descriptions, both written and unwritten—of the
facade were reinforced in this manner. The further importance of such
public statements and acts of group members has been clarified by Festinger
et al. (1956) in their account entitled *When Prophecy Fails.*

Personal Revelation. As we have indicated, the T-group experience was
dramatic and influential. One aspect included what we have called personal
revelation, the offering of intimate details of one's personal life. In Chapter
2 we described episodes of catharsis-type comments, psychiatric-type interpretations, and emotional rebuttals and defensiveness. There were discussions of the personal details of one's self system. Also there were discussions
of several kinds of personal salary negotiations. For instance, the extra
pay for the workshop and the breaking of the fixed salary scale, years
of experience, and amount of training, in order to attract some of the
staff, were items of comment.

Toward the close of the workshop, several weeks after the T-group experience, the observer recorded this interpretation.

> In one sense, the first week has opened up all of these other issues about
> who I am, where I am going, etc., which then can be used prejudicially toward
> one another. For instance, Bill Kirkham's obvious ambition might have been
> held under better check and better control if he had not revealed his "true
> goals" because of this softening up process. The question I have really is:
> Could he have worked with this group as a functioning member even though
> he held these other ambitions more latently? On the surface my guess would
> be that he could. It seems to me that this would be possible for Jack Davis
> also. And, in one sense, it seems to be that he's defined his role that way.
> He will not be involved as an assistant academic counselor although the ma-
> jority of the others will be. Another idea that this has cued off concerns the
> report that several of the people had been developing strategies for resisting
> Bill and dealing with him in many of the things that he was proposing (8/31).

The aftereffects of self-revelation, for example, vulnerability, frustration,
and anxiety (especially among the ISD team members), were to be felt
all year long. In that respect, the T-groups legitimated individual catharsis.
The input of this information had consequences for the individual making
the statements, the individuals attending to the statements, and the organization that now contained the information as part of its accumulating
history.

Emotionality: Sentiments as Group Tasks. Many items could be used to illustrate the principle that the T-group provokes high emotionality among its members. One part of this occurred as the T-group trainer interpreted a group member's behavior and pushed him toward insight and resolution. In the summary notes, the observer recorded the episode in this fashion:

> Perhaps the most dramatic incident occurred late in the afternoon when the leader began interpreting some of the behavior of the members of the group. She accused one member of not learning from his experience of yesterday and taking over the group again at noon, as he had, and of making decisions for the group. This led to a good bit of defensiveness on his part and soon opened up another who commented how angry he had been at this. He related how he hadn't said anything and he wasn't going to say anything all afternoon and how he had responded only on the direct request of the first. He was mad at himself for doing this also. The leader "egged them on," with more interpretation and also urging, to have the second ask the first how he felt rather than just assume that the first would be unhappy if the second had made a comment. This took three or four urgings. A number of people chimed in during this.

> Later, one member ultimately called them all "chicken" for not wanting to fill out the questionnaires regarding the T-group functioning. The leader made a very dramatic interpretation of a third's behavior, which was rejected almost completely. At the close of the meeting, the first commented to the second that he hoped they could sit down and talk for a while today because they were going to have to work together all year this year. Most everyone seemed to be provoked at each other or at the whole training program by the time the day was over. Paul commented about much of the general hostility that existed in the other group and how most of it seemed to be directed toward the leader rather than toward each other. As far as I can tell, very little hostility is directed toward the other leader at this time (8/12).

In one respect, being socialized in this fashion made the task of divesting suggestions and ideas from the idiosyncratic characteristics of their originators even more difficult. Making affect manifest, in a group working together through time, does not necessarily insure in later task sessions that it will "make way" for the presentation of substantive concerns. High emotionality, generally acknowledged to be minimized by formalization of organizational procedures, was highlighted and, in part, legitimized by the early training groups at Kensington.

The Degree of Acquaintance. As one might suspect from our discussions of testimonials, high sentiment, and personal revelation, the T-groups produced also an intimacy, a high degree of acquaintance among the staff. The observer reflected on the contrast in this and a group workshop of which he had been a part.

Another phenomenon that really hit me was the discussion that several of the staff had during one of the small group sessions. The depth and the ease with which they could talk with one another at this point is truly very remarkable. The function of the T-group in having people share a variety of more personal and intimate aspects of their lives as they bear on the school creates, or at least seems to create in this particular instance, a kind of Bill Mauldin *Up Front* degree of rapport, for they have been at war and have fought together. They were pretty sick of having so much small group-connected things, and Sue particularly commented that she wants to go off for a month without any connection with the group. Bill Kirkham is talking about the possible kinds of sedition that he can engage in, which strikes me as very unusual for him, although it might not be. This might be contrasted with another group I participated in, which, in some respects, never did get far enough along after six weeks to discuss issues very well together (8/13).

Thus, in an instance where a staff is unacquainted, a training group experience seems to be a method whereby participants may learn certain aspects of one another in a relatively short time. However, overinvolvement in the intimate, personal facets of group members' lives can be a hazard. Later, as is pointed out elsewhere, these intense personal dimensions often seemed to reappear as obstacles in working together.

The T-Group's Longer Reach

The T-group experience, as we have described it, was a potent experience during its week of operation. In our judgment, its potency reached far beyond the first few days. In this section we trace out the further implications of the experience. As we have described in our methodological section, the ultimate test of our interpretation must lie in the accumulation of similar cases and ultimately in experimental analysis. Nonetheless, we can relate data from our notebooks, our interpretations at the time, and, now, later reflections.

Content-less-ness of the T-Group? We argue that the T-group has a special kind of content instead of being content-less. At Kensington what it seemed to do was to cause some people to "play out their hands" in an unfamiliar game or in an unfamiliar way. In general, this then set up a social structure that was not transferable to the central tasks of the elementary school, even an innovative one such as Kensington. Our initial speculations are mixed with earlier problems and several lines of inquiry:

This is another aspect of the T-group experience that intrigued me very much. Insofar as there is not an agenda, the major resource, to use their term, upon which one can draw is an individual's own identity, stability, and general empathy. There may be some other factors such as one's more self-oriented needs. The kind of thing I think I'm saying is that you may get a selection of some kind of an index of maturity coming out of this kind of group which typically you don't get as quickly or as dramatically, if at all, from other groups. Once again, Tom seems to be the guy who is coming out on top in this. My guess is that Kirkham is not able to do this and that he is much more visible as somebody trying to feather his own nest and push his own status. That may be more my own personal bias than the group's bias, although I doubt it. His "take charge" kind of attitude, which may have been very effective in rural Ohio, somehow just is falling flat here. His deflation is apt to provoke some very serious problems.

My interest in seeing the development of a faculty social system is coming to pass in very fine fashion. It makes me wonder how much of this kind of thing occurred at some distant point in the past at the Washington School downtown. My guess is that once the group had achieved some kind of initial stability, the sort of thing that I witnessed regarding Mr. Alton is about as close as this would ever come.[8] Then the individual must struggle with the group rather than struggle with the aggregate as the aggregate tries to become a group.

I would have some real questions as to whether this is the best kind of experience to start off with, or whether it would be better to work a week and then have this and then work a couple of more weeks. Paul and I raised a point somewhat similar to this when we talked about having some subject matter much less sensitive than the individuals' own egos and the developing group structure as the immediate task at hand. This just loads the dice for a high affective involvement and possibly the setting up of hostilities and sensitivities that will be forever in getting dissipated. It's an interesting question as to whether there are any data whatsoever on the T-group experience as it applies to a new group that is not an *ad hoc* group but that will have long-term continuing relationships with one another. Also this was a new experience for the training staff. Lois, the first Sunday night, said that she had never worked with a group exactly like this in just this kind of situation. Lynn had not either (8/12).

We have spoken about the high emotionality of the T-group experience. The serious problems associated with Kirkham's removal were described earlier. The consternation over task focus versus process focus remained throughout the year. The social structure that developed during the group sessions was in most respects not applicable to the tasks specified in the mandate of "building a school." This social structure often contrasted with the highly formalized doctrine.

The Process-Substance Dichotomy. When approaching a new task like that of starting a school, people vary in their preferences. Some want to

---

[8] Once again, the observer plays the new data against the earlier project (Smith and Geoffrey, 1968). Alton is a teacher who tended to be rejected by his peers in the faculty of the Washington School.

explore verbally the totality and some want to begin on a particular concrete problem and let this take them to the more general issues as well as to other concrete problems. In retrospect, this variation in style of approach to large significant novel problems seems to be a most important dimension of human personality. One facet, although not the central aspect, was caught partially in the observer's notes in the Sunday night planning session:

> Another item that occurred which left me a little bit uncomfortable was the lack of concern about the immediate desires of the people for a lot of information about the new school and about what they would be doing and how they would be doing it. Eugene has put this off until the second or third week rather than having it in the first week. This is a very interesting commentary on the staff as the staff perceives him for the moment. It will be interesting to see how much of this keeps cropping up in the discussions as we go along. Lois' notion here was that informational questions could be treated and answered as they arose. She had not bought the cult so directly that she felt it was impossible to do this. Lynn was even more open about it and talked about the value of having an informed member who could act as a resource on certain questions of fact (8/10).

Ultimately what was created was a schism between those faculty members who wanted to talk about the school in general—its objectives, its ideology, and its broader contribution—and those who wanted to talk about specific roles, specific duties, and day-to-day items of "What am I going to do?" A variety of dimensions seem to run through this: the realist versus the idealist, the practical versus the dreamer, substance versus process, and deductive versus inductive.

A major hypothesis we would offer states that neither the global nor the concrete leads to "better" solutions. In effect, we would argue that each ultimately digresses into the other, in the give and take of group interaction. Essentially there are assumptions of compromise, taking turns in expressing opinions and points of view, and freedom to participate. Our data suggested that the T-groups accented one line of approach. In effect it provided a normative pattern by reinforcing the processual and abstractly oriented individuals, and delaying and frustrating the concrete and substantively oriented individuals. This tended to develop subgroups in the faculty, to make the easy give and take between individuals more difficult, and to set the occasion for serious conflict which was to erupt later. The notes suggest this:

> At noon I had a brief conversation with Bill about his experience in the T-group. He has never done this before, and the way he talked left it clear that he wasn't very happy with it. Paul told me that his conversations with Jack, Bill, and Dan indicated that they also were getting concerned about having a whole week of this when in their eyes there was so much work to

be done. I did talk briefly with Dan at lunch, and he commented about the concern for group process without regard for content. He argued that the kind of content, or what I would call the task, would probably make a good bit of difference in the way in which the activity was carried out. He wondered about how generalizable the experience would be in that regard. As far as I know, he hasn't taught except for practice teaching.

One of the more interesting things that happened in the discussion this morning concerns David's holding to the notion of getting the objectives laid out before you can talk about the specifics. On the one hand, it seems to me that this is one sensible way to make decisions and lies behind some of the comments that we are making in our analysis of decision making. It also strikes me that he has a strong intolerance for the fact that some people have to operate in a different style. Specifically, it conflicts with Jack Davis' interest in going from a set of concrete examples to a more general framework. If you like, one could make a case that this inductive approach is actually more in accord with the Kensington set of goals than actually starting out rationally with a broad set of goals. Later Jack raised the possibility of people retaining convictions and yielding to action which makes the compromise move along. This issue was one that got considerable discussion earlier and one on which they couldn't reach any fundamental agreement. This fits in with the earlier comment, since David seems unable to accept other people's methods of approach and to make compromises and to work with them. My guess is that he would interpret this as a lack of authenticity and also as a lack of being his real self. This kind of inability could lead to real havoc with the Independent Study Division (8/12).

The T-group experience in conjunction with the problem-solving styles formalized the dichotomization of the staff and introduced serious frustration to the "inductives." This in turn led to intense staff conflict and helped precipitate what was to be a permanent schism in the ISD and the ousting of Bill Kirkham, which we have called the Kirkham incident.

Avoidance of the Mechanics. One of the consequences of the T-group experience, the doctrine, the enthusiasm, and the biases of several of the influential persons on the staff was an avoidance of the procedural means, the "nuts and bolts" issues, as the staff came to call them.

A number of items came up late this morning and over lunch. For instance, at the lunch hour I raised the direct question, at seemingly an appropriate time, as to whether there would be report cards at the Kensington School. None of the group—Tom, Bill, David, Liz, Alec, or Jack—knew whether there would be report cards. They are all, or nearly all, operating on the assumption that the cumulative records with anecdotal comments and work samples would be used to show the parents the kinds of things that the children are doing. No one has any notion as to who would carry out the parental conferring.

As they responded, no one in the group seemingly has thought much about it or tested it out very extensively. There also is a lack of clarity on articulating with other schools regarding transfers in and transfers out (8/19).

Later that same day the observer commented:

Another point that keeps coming up and reflects my own bias about organization and administration is the need for mechanisms to attain certain kinds of goals or ends. This was perhaps best illustrated in a discussion this morning with Sue and Liz and Alec about the phenomenon of their overlapping interest in the integration of knowledge being presented to the students. The several people involved in the conversation were all agreed that content integration[9] was important. There was some agreement that part of the content integration would be a consequence of a basic attitude that would prevail throughout the school. However, there was little discussion and seemingly little awareness of what I would call the mechanisms to help make this happen. Specifically, I mean the kind of planning that would go on, the kind of distribution of the time of the teachers and the students, the pinpointing of responsibility for initiating and following through on agreements, and so forth. This may be part of the negative transfer from last week. But, as far as I can tell, there is practically no concern on the part of the younger people about this phenomenon. There seems to be some pleasant assumption that once we all get to know each other, then it will automatically happen. This is precisely what I don't agree with. Perhaps this viewpoint reflects my more general concern for the mundane. There are some exceptions to this in the Independent Study Division. I think the major people who would take exception are Jack and Irma and perhaps Alec. The Basic Skills Division might also be exempt from this. The Transition people have not really spoken enough for me to know. Perhaps the more significant notion is that there is a time and place for both. The staff who are resisting feel that we haven't gotten to that time or that place as yet (8/19).

As our early descriptive accounts indicate, the workshop time did not progress rapidly and easily with these concerns. Critical procedural decisions were being made late in the August workshop. Therefore, it may be hypothesized that in an innovative attempt in which procedural details are initially unspecified, further avoidance of mechanics (that is, lack of attention to planning, scheduling, grouping, subject matter concerns, distribution of materials, and spatial arrangements) becomes a key variable for the consideration of organizational consequences. As was indicated previously, the training groups fostered processual concerns and, in part, legitimized the avoidance of planning for specific and concrete organizational activities and tasks.

[9] That this value was held schoolwide was supported by the test data from the Wehling-Charters *Conceptions of the Educational Process*. The staff scored high on the dimension "Integration of Content."

Individual Captivation. Although the T-groups captivated several of the staff, David found it most congenial. It permitted him to engage in broad philosophical discussions, in explorations in the quest of self-understanding, and in entry into close personal relationships with fellow staff members. The approach to learning, which the unstructured position provided, fit his point of view in working with children. Generally, this consisted of informal relationships between teacher and student, a minimum of didactic or usual instructional behavior with large groups of children, and a high regard for the internal motivation for learning. It blended neatly with his perception of the Kensington doctrine of individualized instruction and gave a substance to the vaguely defined role of academic counselor. As our descriptive account indicated, it led, also, during the first week to a new element in the ISD (Independent Study Division) program, T-grouping or group processes with the children. The intent here was to aid the children in exploring their interpersonal relationships which, in turn, would enable them to function more fully as individuals and as members of ISD teams. The pupil T-groups produced a number of unintended organizational consequences.

Summary. In our judgment the T-group experience was a very powerful technique. The timing within the year, the close relationship to parts of the formal doctrine, and the salience for individual staff members were part of the context. The implications were both immediate and long term. A number of our most significant hypotheses regarding this innovation at Kensington are summarized in Figure 4.2.

It is possible to view the events of Kensington at a considerably more abstract and general theoretical level. For example, if innovative attempts, such as our case of Kensington School, are characterized by what March and Simon (1958) call unprogrammed activity, then uncertainty as a variable is more potent and the presence of uncontrolled outcomes is greater than in traditional programs. Less is known about the variation in inputs; that is, when a large number of innovative elements are introduced, priorities in terms of degrees of influence are more difficult to assess. As is noted elsewhere, high uncertainty also may be accompanied by a degree of vulnerability, an openness to outside threats, not present in settings in which participants may be better able to specify both inputs and outcomes. In one sense, the training groups, as Figure 4.2 shows, were implemented to reduce uncertainty about both group functioning and individual performance with the group. Search behavior such as this has been treated by some analysts as a quest for identity, a search for knowledge or information that identifies at the levels of the individual, the group, and the organization (Klapp, 1969). Also, the training groups were selected as a part of the formal socialization of members to enable them to become

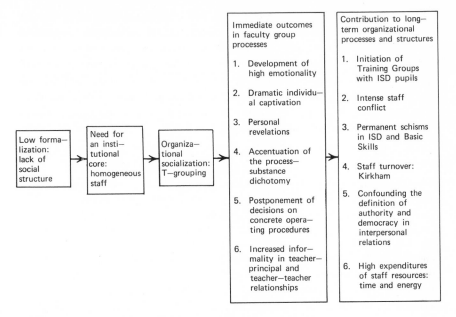

Figure 4.2   The context of T-grouping at Kensington.

a part of the quest for a "new" elementary education. Although the quest may be treated at this point as an organizational goal, our later discussion dealing with true belief also explores its ramifications for the individual participant.

In short, these events of early August and the accompanying analysis suggest some of the nuances in the building of an institutional core in an educational organization which has an innovative thrust. With such a focus, one perceives clearly a number of problems that organizational theorists and administrative practitioners would do well to anticipate.

II   True Belief: Staff Sentiment in an Innovative Organization

Introductory Perspective

The use of the T-group as a means of building an institutional core, a homogeneity of outlook and sentiments, was an important part of Kensington's strategy and program. But people come to organizations with existing sentiments. If our data from Kensington can be generalized,[10] we would

[10] Once again we point out that our view of case studies, for instance, this description and analysis of Kensington, is to suggest hypotheses, not to present supported propositions. We have treated this in greater detail in Smith and Geoffrey (1968) and Smith and Pohland (1969). Glaser and Strauss (1967) make a similar analysis.

suggest that the sentiments brought to a highly innovative organization are a special, different, and idiosyncratic kind and, as such, are an important aspect of the anatomy of such an organization. As we were a part of the Kensington experience and as we tried to analyze it, the emotional quality loomed large. From the first day of the summer workshop the observers noted the quality of excitement, enthusiasm, and high aspiration. This section of the analysis becomes a consideration of sentiment, a broad rubric that has been defined by Homans (1950):

"Now let us go back to our passage again and consider another set of words and phrases: sentiments of affection, affective content of sympathy, respect, pride, antagonism, affective history, scorn, sentimental nostalgia. . . . Here we shall call them all *sentiments,* largely because that word has been used in a less specialized sense than some of the others, and we shall speak of *sentiment* as an element of social behavior" (pp. 37–38).

Our particular concern is with sentiment within the dynamics of a beginning, innovative organization that is also a part of a larger organization, the Milford School District, and a larger system of ideas that we have called the "new elementary education."

In a seminal book, *The True Believer,* Eric Hoffer states the proposition: "Some kind of widespread enthusiasm or excitement is apparently needed for the realization of vast and rapid change . . ."(p. 13). Elsewhere he describes the extreme of enthusiasm and excitement as embodied in an individual: ". . . the true believer—the man of fanatical faith who is ready to sacrifice his life for a holy cause . . ."(p. 10). The parallels between our observations of sentiments in an innovative school and Hoffer's more general argument suggested an important opportunity for mutual stimulation. Our developing analysis could test the conception offered by Hoffer, and his ideas could serve as guides for additional insights. As always, the field notes arbitrate the differences.

Finally, in attempting to understand how the sentiment of true belief functioned in a beginning organization, Klapp's (1969) consideration of the sources and attributes of crusades and crusaders helps. Some of his interpretations correspond to what we observed, but others suggest additional hypotheses that need verification. A crusade may refer to "any remedial enterprise undertaken with zeal and enthusiasm." Both in terms of its program being a remedial one and the great enthusiasm that accompanied implementation of the ideas, the events surrounding Kensington resembled those of a crusade.

The role of a crusader or participant in a movement, such as the new elementary education of which Kensington was a part, encompasses a combination of behaviors and sentiments that contrast with the ones considered characteristic of the "typical" employee or incumbent in an organizational position. The task "rises above ordinary life because it requires one to leave business-as-usual and commit himself earnestly to something he believes in deeply" (Klapp, p. 257). The uniqueness, the separateness, the differentness, the intensity of the sentiments and behaviors of the individual engaged in an enterprise of this kind must be emphasized. Thus, it is both the remedial effort with its extraordinary intents and the accompanying zeal and enthusiasm that help define the role of the crusader. As such, this corresponds to Hoffer's concept of true belief.

Kensington exemplified well how a crusade may differ from a movement aimed at only practical results. At one level the school was a program organized to institutionalize the "new elementary education." At another, it was a movement to develop and to extend a set of beliefs surrounding change processes in general and elementary education in particular. It is at the latter level that the elements of a crusade are most clearly illustrated.

Aspects of true belief were formalized in various elements of the doctrine and facade, as we have indicated previously. In this way, true belief and its concomitants extend beyond any practical attempt and are maintained in the face of failure. Although a part of the crusader's role, if he is engaged in a demonstration of his ideas, may be to bring the reality in line with his stated attempts, the facade incorporates the hopes and dreams that the humdrum of the mundane may deteriorate. Thus the paramount effort is addressed to the maintenance, advocation, and high visibility of the facade. As well as bolstering one's own efforts, it is the embodiment of aspects of a grail that others may be persuaded to seek. It is the doctrine, the facade, and their subtleties, for example, shared beliefs in their validity, the rituals that preserved and cultivated them for their presentation to those who do "not yet know," that provided reassurance in the face of no demonstrable evidence for their potential successes and even in the presence of failure. It is this "true belief" in the ultimate vitality of the elements of the doctrine and facade that enables participants to speak of "next year," "when I go to ————, I'll do . . . " and seek further for opportunities to continue their mission. From the doctrine and facade, comes the motivation to carry on beyond what real, day-to-day results seem to justify. In the instance of Kensington, after a major restructuring of ISD's organization, comments such as, "Well, we've lost a battle, but not the war," illustrate the vitality of the ideas connected with the doctrine and facade even in the face of retraction and regrouping in the realities of the school. The language of "sentiments," especially as developed by Hoffer and Klapp, has its own kind of sensational quality. Our earlier descriptive accounts should help persuade the reader that Kensington might be viewed legitimately from that perspective. An early quote from the field notes, long before Hoffer and Klapp were part of our intellectual armamentarium, adds to that creditability.

> We talked at some length also about two more of his consultants, a man named Roberts and a man named Schwartz from City University. The former will be involved in curriculum and program and will be here for several days. The latter, who has interest in music education and the total curriculum, will not be coming apparently because of the financial impossibilities. Eugene spoke somewhat derogatorily of this. Apparently he thought the man should come out of the goodness of his heart or out of his own interest in the development of his own ideas in such a context as this (8/9).

What we called "goodness of his heart" and "own interest" we would phrase now as part of the morality of true belief. In our judgment, inducement-contribution theories of organization (March and Simon, 1958) have hardly touched the complexities of the attraction of personnel in innovative organizations. The principal's comments about a potential consultant clarify one aspect. Perhaps another appropriate intellectual lever is Etzioni's (1961) conception of the normative organization. Recruitment of true believers would fit this point of view.

Dimensions of True Belief

In short, sentiments, true belief, and crusading provide an initial perspective for clarifying a very important aspect of Kensington. Elaboration of this aspect of the origins of an innovative organization seems most critical. Essentially we shall pursue our data and relevant theory as we seek hypotheses linking the dimensions of true belief to other aspects of the organization.

The Need for Remedial Effort. An "image of evil" is an aspect of crusades, as noted by Klapp and others, and provides a basis for the direction of the participant's efforts. Furthermore the notion of "wrongs-to-be-righted" provides a background for faith in the new solutions that, in turn, justifies the subsequent troubles and risk. Kensington rejected things as they were and proposed in varying degrees of detail the characteristics of a new order. In our data a great deal of the formal doctrine illustrated the wrongs and "evils" of traditional education that Kensington was to alter and replace. The superintendent's initial remarks to the staff workshop was a clarion. The content of the parent meetings incorporated the ills that Kensington was to eradicate. The building Specs chastised the discrepancy between what is taught and what is learned. The Institutional Plan's "from-to" page that redefined teacher-pupil roles, as shown in Chapter 2, indicated clearly many of the aspects of traditional elementary education that the majority of those at Kensington wished to change. Closely associated with these proposals were alterations in educational process, content, materials, and building design. Thus, a part of the crusader's role is to call attention to existing "wrongs-to-be-righted" and to propose solutions for them. The data from Kensington are clear.

Total Commitment. When one commits oneself to an organization, one pledges or binds a portion of his time, energy, skills, and loyalty. Typically, the organization reciprocates in the form of financial compensation, recognition, and other items valuable to an individual. By total commitment we mean an increase in time and energy beyond the formally contracted "eight hours per day" and beyond the professional knowledges and skills possessed by the staff. Satisfactions and rewards that typically come from investing time and energy in family, friends, church, clubs, community services, hobbies, and recreational pursuits are relinquished and diverted into the organization.

As we have indicated, one hypothesis we offer is that this develops, in part, as a consequence of high enthusiasm. In Kensington, the ideology surrounding the development of the fully-functioning pupil contributed to it as well. The socially integrative stance is personally expensive to actualize. At the end of the second week, the observer noted:

> During our coffee break discussion, I raised the question of the norms about how much time they should be spending on school problems and how long the day would be, and how and when they would carry out the time for planning, and the like. There isn't much clarity on this, but the girls who responded indicated that they were literally working on school problems all the time. One of the schisms here is that the group with no family and no social life independent of the school, as yet, literally are involved through most of their waking existence. Most of them saw this as, over the long run, not desirable. Specifically, in terms of planning, Kay thought they might be having team meetings before school around 8:00 and curriculum and other such meetings at some time off and on during the day.

Ten days later, the observer speculated in a similar vein.

> Theoretically, perhaps one of the most crucial issues that I see now lies in the degree of personal involvement that one needs to carry out the task of teaching. How much of one's life needs to be committed to the task, how much of it needs to be open, and what kinds of agreements do you need rather than some superficial methods of working together? For instance, if the roles can be spelled out bureaucratically, and if one agrees to those roles, is that the sum and substance of it and does there need to be other than minimal personal involvement beyond that? In one sense, the first week has opened all of these concerns and a number of other issues about who I am, where I am going, and the like.

However, the staff at Kensington rejected any aspects of bureaucracy, which might have delimited the range and amount of commitment or that might have formalized and specified behavioral expectations. The acceptance of egalitarianism and the eschewing of bureaucractic dimensions is not surprising in that a feeling of righteousness and of being called on to work for a higher purpose, that is, a performance beyond the requirements of ordinary duty, is a part of the sentiment structure of the crusader. As Klapp (1969) states:

"We find a great range between bureaucracy, which is lacking in the ability to intensify feelings, and violent forms of 'fun' or conflict or crusades which give a person a chance to prove himself by commitment, encounters, and ordeals"(p. 45).

"In general, bureaucracy has no crusading spirit." (p. 269).

In this sense, at Kensington there was initially little of the "alienation" or meaninglessness frequently attributed to many kinds and settings of work. Work "beyond the call of duty" was the norm.

Theoretically, the consequences of total commitment become significant at Kensington when one considers the independently developing strand of social conflict and interpersonal hostility. Among the costs and constraints of total commitment are vulnerability and risk. For although "zeal or caring beyond matter-of-fact job requirements is the beginning of a crusading spirit, fanaticism is its end point." Fanaticism implies "unreasoning zeal" and may hamper the task of evangelism, a part of the role behavior of any crusader. However, also, total commitment is a requisite for performing as a crusader, since crusading is "called for only when the job is so difficult and extraordinary that *heroic* energies must be mobilized . . . " (Klapp, 1969, p. 267). The overall innovation strategy, the alternative of grandeur,[11] opted for at Kensington was such a position and required this kind of mobilization. The tasks involved extraordinary expenditures of time, effort, creativity, and loyalty.

Moreover, when one's total reward and satisfaction structure is tied to one source, failure of that source through events within or beyond one's own control and potency can have severe consequences. As hostility increased, as portions of the program failed, as administrative support changed, several faculty members were subjected to intense frustration, anxiety, severe personal debilitation, and withdrawal. At this point, again, the function of faith was illustrated, for a movement such as this needs something good enough to justify the problems, the trouble, and the risk. A majority of the staff at Kensington possessed this faith in the "new

---

[11] A description and analysis of this broad innovative strategy appears in Chapter Eleven.

elementary education." We present a summary schema of these relationships in Figure 4.3.

High Aspirations. In his discussion of cooperative teaching, Shaplin (1965) attributes to teaming what seems to belong more to innovativeness and true belief.

"One of the major confusions in the team-teaching movement has been the tendency to claim all-embracing objectives and goals, on a grandiose scale, phrased in the most general terms. The goals of the team must be consistent with its size and capability" (p. 17).

At Kensington, the teams were caught, to some degree, on the high aspiration and limited resources dilemma, but more basically it was the entire school that was entangled. With overtones from the various statements of the formal doctrine and with concrete efforts in the committees of the workshop era and, later, in the regular total staff meetings and, especially, in the curriculum meetings, Kensington attempted important and large alterations in American education. The extensiveness of the change, the sweeping away of the old, the implementation of the new, and a rejection of a gradualist strategy illustrate our point.

The exceedingly high aspirations that may characterize participants of

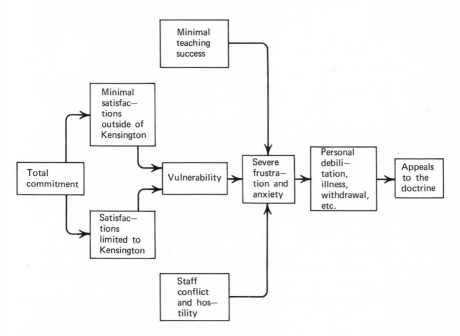

Figure 4.3 The consequences of total commitment.

a movement correspond to the specifications incorporated in the grail and, in this case, the doctrine and the facade. These high aspirations, which possibly would be deemed unrealistic by those with minimal crusading spirit, may lead to over-aggrandizement of the attempt on the part of the participants in a movement that has a practical level—teaching school. This, in turn, may support fallacious assumptions about the capabilities of participants in lieu of time, ability, and work demands. As we have analyzed in our discussion of resources, the requirements for the kind of task that they attempted involved time and a specialized personnel far beyond that which is available to a school district, much less a single school, even one as well endowed as Kensington.

A Framework for Faith. Interestingly, Kensington, not only by being a part of a larger school system but also by design, tried to be a rational organization. But even in rational organizations there are problems that defy rationality. The selection of ultimate goals is considered by most organizational analysts to be a valuational instead of a rational process (Simon, 1957). The tremendous complexity of some educational decisions requires one to settle some issues arbitrarily. At such times, it seems convenient to have agreement on "gods and bibles," that is, on who are the experts and ultimate authorities. We found this developing at several points.

On Monday morning, August 17, the principal discussed the curriculum and the overall framework. In doing this, he made explicit reference to *Planning and Organizing for Teaching,* a book by Goodlad (1963) in the NEA (National Education Association) "Project Instruction." The field notes report it this way:

> There are several models. Bill gives a mimeo summary. Eugene thanks Bill and develops the ideas: "Model A—The function is to cover and inculcate a body of material. The organization of the school is by grades. In Model B there is a prescribed body of knowledge by levels. There are no grades but 12 to 20 levels. It attempts to deal with individual differences by rate of progress. Model C has a different function—learner centered, ways of knowing and thinking, a conceptual approach to learning, function of effective functioning individual. Needs a different organization; Kensington follows this model. What are the implications for curriculum? What do pupils need for junior high—these books? concepts? skills? 'Here again I suspect we have wide differences. If junior high teacher complains the student doesn't know the solar system, I'm tempted to say I don't care. I don't think we have a prescribed body of subject matter' " (8/17).

The next day the observer recorded similar data:

> Another item that came up this morning in a before-school discussion concerned the kind of intellectual authority to which the teachers and the pupils in the building appeal and some notion of how this develops. So far the ASCD

Yearbooks on *Knowing, Perceiving, and Becoming,* and the one on *Individualizing Instruction* are two critical volumes. Another set of volumes are the NEA reports of people like Goodlad. Today one of the books that I noticed was Berelson and Steiner's *Human Behavior,* which David was carrying with him (8/18).

As we have tried to analyze this, the heart of the issue seems to be twofold: first, by definition, the nature of goals is an affirmation of faith, at least, at the ultimate level. Particular goals can be rationalized as means to the ultimate goals. Second, problems rapidly become very complex. This complexity is often cut through most easily by accepting the analysis made by an authority.[12] The processes of resolution and acceptance seem facilitated by the combined influence of the principal, the district curriculum director, the Institutional Plan, and the formal doctrine.

When ideas are the primary referents, rather than existing organizations, or when there is a blending of the two, additional emphasis is focused on the selection, reading, and interpretation of written materials. In addition, the doctrine, and the published sources are sought as arbitrators of issues. Thus, in an innovative setting, emphasizing uniqueness, a great deal of faith may come to be placed in the theoretical statements of "experts" and "authorities." At Kensington both informally and in meetings, much time and effort were given to discussion and to the consideration of various ideas and positions perceived as both authoritative and applicable to the school. At this point, the extent of ideological consistency or inconsistency is highly visible.

The problems of ideological inconsistency developed early, which seems likely to happen in any new movement. Time and criticism move most positions toward consistency or toward separation into groups with more congruent belief systems. High enthusiasm in August led to the holding of beliefs that were only partially consistent. Other aspects of the doctrine contributed to the inconsistencies, as we commented in the second chapter. In addition, there was conflict between ideas held by an individual and the ones shared by the other members of the group. The extent to which one or the other would be adhered to in the day-to-day operation of the school was also an issue. The emphasis of the training groups on individual search behavior and the team teaching's focus on cooperative behavior and the issues of coordination and control produced ideological constraints that were never resolved. These quests and searches, whether printed or interpersonal, involve highly

[12] In a very recent analysis, an SSRC committee (1969) argues that this is a very general and basic social process that occurs as individuals and groups face difficult decisions. Our data would suggest that the high enthusiasm of true belief accentuates the process.

idiosyncratic interactions with the environment. In one sense, this, too, is juxtaposed to the coordination and synchronization required by cooperative behavior. For the professional crusader, these constraints may be an onus to be avoided. In the case of one division at Kensington, the teams were dissolved and the individuals pursued their own courses. The issue seems particularly critical in education when individual development, in the context of a group setting, occurs. When reference groups are predominantly ideational and subject to differing interpretations and applications, as are most creeds, further concern develops.

Jargon. At Kensington, little was called by a usual name. Teachers were not teachers; they were academic counselors and resource specialists. Classrooms were laboratory suites, and the library was the perception core. Grade levels were gone and divisions—Basic Skills, Transition, and Independent Study—replaced them. A jargon, the technical vocabulary of a science, art, trade, sect, profession, or other special group, arose. Although, in part, necessary for the novel and unique aspects of the organization, it had a variety of additional functions.

One of the negative aspects was caught in the August field notes, as a member of the staff reflected on the new terminology:

> She feels that the entire group has been brainwashed. She likened it to the communist attempt at brainwashing people. She gave a specific instance, the failure of staff members to use certain terminology. She did not feel that one could use words such as textbook, teach, curriculum, subject matter, and other special words. She further stated that if one could say the same things only in different words it would be quite acceptable. She said, "If this isn't brainwashing, I don't know what is." She further mentioned that when she got finished with this year, there would be three words that she would never use again. These words are conceptualize, fully-functioning, and process (8/26).

Cultish aspects of jargon arose early in the program. Comments critical of traditional education appeared in labels such as "two by four" education. This is education that is restricted to the four walls of a self-contained classroom and the two covers of a textbook. As shorthand, it carried the emotional meaning of the true belief. One might argue that it foreclosed analytical thought and careful judgment.

The field notes reflect the observer's concerns in trying to view this clearly.

> The program of the school is so clouded with cliches and razzle-dazzle that it is very difficult to see clearly what will happen to the children. There will be a variety of team-teaching kinds of things going on. I can never get very much in the way of specific answers as to how this will be handled, who will be doing what, and who will coordinate them, and so on. A number

of people have been hired who will be team leaders, as well as the "house coordinator," who is an experienced principal. Whether or not this will wash is a very interesting question. It is very difficult to cut through the published and dittoed materials on the program. There seems to be a very strong assumption that the individual children after the third grade will be behaving in a way that looks to me to be very much like that of independently working college students. They will be on a variety of projects of their own choosing and of mutual choosing with the teachers. There is a strong stress on individual and independent work. I am not sure how this is going to function and what the requisite skills will be for this (12/20, pre-experimental year).

Given a combination of Kensington's novel building and organization, which reflected the creativity of a number of planners, and the sentiments of enthusiasm and true belief on the part of the staff, the role of jargon was multifaceted and had a number of implications for the participants. The jargon served as a rallying point for some of the staff, created an issue of contention for others, and provided copy for news media and contributed to the facade. For visitors and parents, it dramatized the innovative qualities and the uniqueness of the organization. On occasion, it hindered concrete thinking and the evaluation of the school and its program.

However, beyond a practical program, there are those things that the members of the movement have that outsiders do not readily see and appreciate, for example, beliefs, assumptions, sacred values, meanings, grail symbols, and the like. In the case of Kensington these attributes were the nuances of belief concerning the assumptions made in the Institutional Plan and doctrine, the interpretation and the adaptations of the writings of "authorities" and "experts," and the experiences revealed in the training groups; these elements and others were knitted together and shared via the jargon. Not only did the verbal symbols synthesize beliefs and experiences but they added to the mystique as well.

Resistance to Criticism: the Unassailable Belief. An unassailable belief is an idea that is held so strongly and closely that it is unyielding to intellectual attack or analysis. In August, after his first interview with Shelby, the interviewer recorded a paragraph in the field notes:

It is now 3:15 P.M. I have just spent almost four-and-one-half hours with Eugene, the Principal of the Kensington School. Summarily I might comment that our discussions moved from a general coolness and skepticism to the development of what I think is going to be quite real warmth, rapport, and ease of working together. The initial coolness centered around, I think, my skepticism and close questioning as to how the program would work and how it would function. Eugene is very committed to the whole idea and is very excited about it. It seems as if he were jolted by the fact that someone who is to be intimately involved might really question the whole purpose and approach of the discussion. Along about the first one-third, we got this clarified in that I made a comment that I had just come out of a very traditional situation and, also, that part of my gambit was to be critical and skeptical so as to push him to speak more definitively about what he was going to do and how the building was going to function. As the discussion moved on, I began to catch some of his excitement. Also we began to find a commonality in non-school issues on which we have some basic agreement (8/8).

Such conviction seems to create a charisma among the staff that furthers the commitment and the enthusiasm. We argue also that blind spots are created and that some issues are not thought through.

Although most of the data we have drawn on in this section were obtained in August, we insert information from a May conversation with one of the staff.

His comments range back to the early part of the year and the fact that they were "hurt" by the first month over in the gymnasium in the high school. He also commented about the naïveté, particularly of the ISD teachers. He was not prone to exclude himself from this naïveté also. A very important point it seems to me needs to be drawn out of this in that the whole group possessed a kind of an illusion about what they were and about what they were going to do, and how it was going to happen. The older and wiser heads, such as Irma and Tom, either did not express themselves forcefully or they, too, were deluded (5/18).

The constellation of inexperience, differential influence, and unassailable beliefs seems most noteworthy. The notion of the unassailable belief helps explain an unwillingness to compromise, a part of the role of the crusader. Such unwillingness to compromise was reflected early in the year in the events surrounding the Kirkham incident. Discussions concerning his replacement became entangled in whether the new individual would be "oriented toward our goals," which was a primary reason for Kirkham's dismissal. The inclusive-exclusive dimensions of the groups' perception of themselves proved most limiting in bringing in other personnel. The under-utilization of Walt Larson, the first of the long-term substitutes, as we described earlier, seemed very significant in the development of the Independent Study Division. Later David Nichols' strict adherence to the doctrine was described by erstwhile team members as "uncompromising." Interestingly, as indicated in a previous section, any vestiges of "bureaucracy," with its emphasis on structure and standardization were shunned as being inflexible. The building facilities and the program were phrased formally in terms of flexibility and adaptibility. In contrast, the belief systems of some of the staff proved to be highly resistant to compromise and change.

Futuristic Orientation. As Crest, the innovative psychiatric hospital (Stotland and Kobler, 1965), was spurred on by hope, enthusiasm, and the possibility of future success, thus was Kensington. The futuristic orientation that was adopted in the first few months of school continued throughout the year, although the focus changed considerably.

In retrospect, a latent function of the three-month temporary housing becomes clear. The new building became the point on which faculty sights were set and the frame of reference by which current behavior was weighed and by which it was evaluated. In some aspects the building and the anticipated influence that it was to exert grew to enlarged proportions. In part, it was not unrealistic, since the physical design was to serve as one means for adherence to the doctrine. The anticipation of the new building was a cause for hope and a renewal of enthusiasm in the face of increasing intrafaculty pressures. However, for some of the staff it was viewed as a panacea for interpersonal difficulties. Given this condition, for a time the hope expressed in the beauty and uniqueness of the building seemed to serve as a balm to lessen faculty tensions.

The noise, drudgery, and very close physical proximity of the first few months in the temporary quarters contributed to a partial esprit de corps among the staff. This enabled them to present a united facade to the parents, even when the interpersonal difficulties were greatly shaping and modifying the organizational structure, as we will present shortly in the data on the reorganization in ISD. The field notes contain some of the informal staff comments early in the fall. Shelby seemed to express faith and hope in the building as being likely to influence change in the behavior of both teachers and students. He commented that, "Some parents are expecting problems to be solved in the new building; some will be better and some worse." Yet, Jack Davis, while in the temporary quarters, stated that, "It's hard for me to get real excited here because of the new building." Tom asked, "Do you feel things will be less acute in the new building?" and Jack replied, "Yes, a larger area, more things to do, more places to go, etc. Things should be helped with the new situation. Kids and parents are looking forward to it. There might be more room for movement. I don't know." Then Davis added, "I think they (the parents) will give us until then. They're being fair; but if nothing changes, they'll be disappointed."

In effect, hope in the future seemed to flow from inexperience in August, and from frustration in the early fall. The dimension of hope and its concomitants, as in the case of true belief, extended beyond the forays and accomplishments at Kensington. As we pointed out in the introductory epilogue, hope was finally displaced, out of the Milford District and into PS 2100, where Eugene went in February of the second year, and into the more limited individual careers and opportunities of the staff. In this way a futuristic orientation interacted with the one of faith and true belief in the ideas embodied in the "new elementary education."

Humor. Although much of our data have supported the observations of Klapp (1969), they do not confirm his concerns with humor and detachment. In delineating some of the characteristics of crusaders, he describes the crusader as taking himself seriously, lacking humor and ironic detachment toward his role, and being so utterly committed that he lacks role distance. At Kensington, beginning early in the year, humor was an integral part of the staff esprit de corps. Early humor was exemplified by "fully-functioning-Freddy," the ideal pupil product of the school. At the close of the year, a coloring-book that lampooned the attempts of the staff to make parts of the program work was developed. It was a compendium of humor throughout the year. In this way humor, much as jargon, as we indicated previously, is a part of those characteristics the crusaders have which outsiders do not readily see nor appreciate.

Thus, humor was not absent and in most instances it grew from being able to stand back and reflect on events occurring at Kensington. In contrast to an absence of detachment and self-analysis, as suggested by Klapp, much time was devoted to verbalizing and rationalizing reasons for behavior. The cycle of questioning and explanation had its sources in both the training groups and in team teaching as a whole, which requires greater rationalization of one's intents and provides visibility of behavior. Although many of the staff were committed to the trappings of the new elementary education, they were able to employ a kind of self-consciousness to their work at Kensington and to state many of the difficulties surrounding the attempt to innovate on a grand scale. In all of this, humor remained as a major facet of Kensington.

Inexperience, Naïveté, and True Belief. The man on the street, the practical man, and the man of affairs, all seem to utilize a concept such as "experience" as they think about their organizations. Social scientists (for example, March and Simon, 1958; Blau and Scott, 1962), tend to make less use of it and have not engaged in intensive theoretical reduction of the concept. In the Kensington story, it loomed large. Recall our brief introduction to the staff. Of the 21 original members, seven had not taught. One of the 14 who had taught was removed before school began and replaced by an inexperienced substitute. Nine additional staff members, five aides, and four student teachers had had minimal or no work experience in the public schools.

The interrelationships among enthusiasm, training, and knowledge arose dramatically as substantive issues in pedagogy appeared during the workshop.

Another phenomenon that has struck me is that everyone in this workshop is devoting time and attention to professional matters in a way that I, personally, have never seen in our undergraduate elementary education students or by a school faculty. In this sense, the motivation is really intense and strong, and the people are willing to devote considerable energy with the task at hand. There are some interesting aspects about this because this is done within the limitations of their ability and their training. I cringe with the notion of how much more these people ought to know about reading, how much more they ought to know about social studies methods, and how inadequate most of their training has been as they talk about it, and how crucial it might be for what they are doing. Without question, the teacher education profession, at least as I know it, is really confused. Yet, the drama of this kind of involvement is quite exciting (8/21).

Analytically, several aspects seem crucial. In part, the administrative authorities had deliberately planned the organization in this manner. They did not want old solutions to educational problems. In their own words, they believed that it would be easier to train inexperienced personnel in new approaches than to retrain experienced persons. Experience, in this usage, seems to be a broad personality variable including schema dimensions such as awareness of problems and classical solutions to problems. Additionally, we argue, it contains trait and skill dimensions in executing these solutions and a high probability of success in this execution. For instance, if a child or class is having difficulty in understanding a concept in science or social studies, classical solutions would suggest that the teacher present a relevant illustration, exercise, or book passage to be read. Besides knowing the specific illustration, content, or title, the experienced teacher would know that it was "sure fire," that it had a high probability of reaching the goal, because she had sorted these through with previous trial and error. She would have a residual set of solutions. The inexperienced teacher probably would have a less wide repertory, although this seems linked closely with a more general creativity dimension, considerably less high-probability solutions, and probably less confidence in her tactics. Insofar as confidence produces cues of a self-fulfilling prophecy sort—both pupil compliance and pupil confidence of success—it becomes exceedingly important.[13]

As we have indicated, a further aspect of teacher motivation and commitment, beyond specific confidence, is the high enthusiasm for the cause, the ideology, which we found in a greater degree in the inexperienced as opposed to the experienced teachers.

The inexperience dimension had implications for organizational structure, status, and influence early in the summer workshop. Organizational

[13] Elaborations of these ideas appear in statements we have made regarding teacher training (Connor and Smith, 1967; Smith, 1968).

planning, skill in group discussion, and the ability for mobilization of agree-ment which were important in August may be considerably different from teaching. Early we hypothesized:

> One other hypothesis I would offer concerns the problem that is going to face the people when they have the children there with them. It seems to me that the individuals who are going to make out best are those who know a tremendous amount and who can make this readily available without much prior preparation. This suggests that men like Jack may be a very fundamen-tally important person at that time, where at this point he is not. Whether David can stand this kind of instructional pressure or whether Kay or Liz can, I don't know. Part of the question I would raise is that they have not taught and do not have the wealth of illustrations, materials, and procedures, at their fingertips that would make this very much simpler. In this sense, it's not a question of brightness, it's more a question of specific tactics and procedures.

In summary, at Kensington there was the pervasive desire for novel solutions to old educational problems. It was believed that inexperienced persons would be better able and more willing to seek and to implement new ways of going about the process of teaching. The initial sentiments of the inexperienced members of the staff were those of confidence, enthusiasm, and genuine support of the doctrine. Their commitment and willingness to invest great amounts of effort in the program exemplified their true belief in the tenets of the movement. However, in the practical aspects of the enterprise, the inexperienced persons had limited skills in teaching, little knowledge of "sure fire" techniques applicable to the classroom, and minimal awareness of the wide range of problems that may accompany the day-to-day activities of teaching. All of these point to the low level of information characteristic of many of the participants. Although the ideational qualities of the mandate "Go build a school" were mastered, the information input about the practical aspects was limited.

At the level of application, these factors interacted to produce problems in the classroom and eroded some of the original confidence and enthusiasm; frustration, anxiety, and discouragement increased. However, through the most dismaying times at the practical level, the field notes taken at the team meetings, the curriculum meetings, and of informal contacts indicate continued faith in the ultimate principles of the doctrine. This illustrates the resilience of inexperience and buoyancy of the true believer. Likely the most stringent trial of a novice crusader is survival of the often impairing blows of experience. The professional true believer has triumphed!

Although Klapp does not speak specifically of inexperience he points to "an inherent naïveté in crusading, so that at a certain point in sophistication people might find it impossible to believe that they could restore their identities or their society by such means" (1969, p. 310). Partial understanding and highly-bounded rationality may be requisites for participation in a crusade. Hoffer suggests "ignorance of the difficulties" entailed in change as a characteristic of participants. At another point in time, with more experience, information, and sophistication, the naïveté of inexperience might diminish and might preclude the attempt to provide individualized programs for 200 children in a gymnasium, write curricula and prepare materials for all curricular areas for K through 6, reject textbooks, and master team teaching, all in the space of nine months.

Conclusion. Hoffer (1951) ties together several aspects of sentiment in an organization as he describes facets of the *True Believer,* the man of fanatical faith who is ready to sacrifice his life for a holy cause:

> "For men to plunge headlong into an undertaking of vast change, they must be intensely discontented yet not destitute, and they must have the feeling that by the possession of some potent doctrine, infallible leader or some new technique, they have access to a source of irresistible power. They must also have an extravagant conception of the prospects and potentialities of the future. Finally, they must be wholly ignorant of the difficulties involved in their vast undertaking. Experience is a handicap" (p. 20).[14]

In the judgment of our case, his account underemphasizes the positive attraction of healthy people trying to make a better world. True believers come for many reasons. Some seem to have a relatively simple faith in working toward educational ideals that they hold sincerely and uncomplicatedly. Others perceive, quite clearly and consciously, the possibilities of combining their faith and their careers. Others seem to be searching for identity and a positive self-concept, as Klapp suggests. Although Kensington had those who were "intensely discontented" and "those who crave to be rid of an unwanted self," the majority were finding a freedom and an opportunity to create that is usually not available in the public schools—either from administrative fiat or from informal faculty "understandings." In addition, innovative organizations will have serious continuity problems because the staff will go on new quests. This departure is due, in part, to their high visibility and to being "bought" or competed for, combined with the commitment to advance the tenets of the movement. The grail is elusive; the quest is eternal. As shown earlier, Hoffer's analysis of potent doctrine, infallible leader, new techniques, extravagant conceptions of the future, ignorance of the difficulties, and the role of inexperience have a

---

[14] We are indebted to Professor Edwin Bridges for suggesting initially the parallels in this particular passage from Hoffer.

telling validity. He who would engage in large-scale innovative programs must be cognizant of the role of true belief that is endemic to the process.

The Broader Implications of True Belief

Broadening and Continuing the Crusade. The sentiment of intense commitment to the "rightness" of the cause enables participants to go forth with a sense of mission. Klapp observes that there is a "determination to go ahead in spite of lack of public support, even with public opposition." This was amply illustrated by the data from Kensington. We discuss in other sections of the book the various publics of an organization. Although Kensington was considered by some of the district officials initially as a protected subculture, it was less and less protected as time passed. A mission to say something about the "new elementary education" both locally and nationally was undertaken. Public opposition was evident, both among professionals and parents. However, for the crusader with true belief in the cause, this enhances the responsibility to fight an evil that others do not perceive. That one has discovered and is assailing that which is not perceived as injurious by others is further testament to the need for the movement. In this way, responses of opposition and apathy from one's public may be viewed as reinforcement for the mission. Thus, for those who truly believe, failure conceived as opposition or lack of support from one's publics and constituents is unknown, it only serves to legitimate the tasks of evangelism.

Socialization, Visability, and Mobility. Our data illustrate well how a movement such as Kensington was a part of what may be viewed as providing a form of socialization for the neophyte crusader. Reference to some early notes indicates how involvement at Kensington was viewed as a preparatory training for innovative tasks yet to come:

> This has been a very full day and it is difficult to get all the details in that one must. One of the kinds of things that seems to me to be most relevant is trying to state initially why people have come to the Kensington School. The general motives and goals became more and more explicit as the day wore on. For instance, Tom is working in the curriculum and instruction area and has about completed a doctorate. He has several years experience as a teacher, as a visiting teacher, and as a school principal. Actually five years in the latter. This kind of experience in the Kensington School as the key man in the Perception Core area will give him a very unique experience that will enable him to move to almost any teacher's college curriculum and instruction department in the country. And probably with a very good salary and with a very unique position. Almost the exact same thing can be said for the "other administrator" in our small group, Bill. He's on the make, and he wants to move ultimately into a college curriculum position. He is working on his doctorate at State University. Running through the entire group, includ-

ing these two people, is some desire to get finally into a position where they could carry out teaching operations in line with the kinds of theory and preaching they have been doing. This, when the kids come into the building, should make a very interesting day of reckoning for some of them. One or two look more like individuals who are trying to solve their own personal problems. Wanda and Jean look like individuals who have taught a while, although in Jean's case just a few years, and are interested in being able to implement some of the things that they were not able to do in the other building. Another seems more like a hostile subject matter specialist who is going to show all of the stupid education professors just how it should have been done. Kay apparently had a very enjoyable, exciting experience in her internship and seemingly wants to elaborate and to build on this (8/10).

Later the same day, I chatted a few minutes about a number of things with Bill. He raised the problem that I might be interested in the personal goals of the people on the staff. Alec and John were around at the time. In effect, he was saying that many of the people were using the school as a jumping-off place for later things. He argues that this determines some of the things, for example, makes a difference, in what he does, because he will ultimately move on from here. It is interesting that I had been raising the same notion in my notes this morning. He came from a position of principal, which is hard for a number of people to understand. Alec reported some Welcome Wagon person making such comments to his wife. John raised the same kind of notion that many of his friends from Ohio were skeptical as to why he would be coming here in that he has finished all of his course work for his doctorate and also has had a couple of years college teaching experience (8/10).

"From the . . . view of the recruit, the crusade is a role opportunity: to form oneself according to a pattern not ordinarily available, to rise to a higher level of input (commitment) and output (heroism), to test oneself by mortal encounter and engagement; above all, then, to find a new conception of oneself" (Klapp, 1969, p. 269).

The unique role opportunities were available, and exceedingly high inputs and engagement were requisites. As shown in the notes, commitment was to the movement for the new elementary education, and Kensington was an important but temporary training ground, a step for many of the staff as they searched to create careers as professional innovators. Commitment was to issues and ideas as well as to anything as place-bound as the generation of social structure of a beginning, fledgling organization. The ideas were portable, applicable elsewhere, and the educational world was waiting, as exemplified by the many visiting educators, the written inquiries, and the coverage by the media both in educational and popular publications.

In a more general sense, this fits the notion that not the "destination but the journey is important; though you do not get there, you may have experienced something along the way that is significant" (Klapp, p. 293).

The emphasis on the processual instead of on the substantive which was prevalent at Kensington merged well with the career intentions of the staff, their belief systems, and the means taken by some to find new identities. Thus, a participant may experience and may refine his expertise as a proponent of a movement. Indeed, part of one's role is to become a better crusader for something that extends beyond the framework of any one institution. Our account, in Chapter 1, of the "Bataan phenomenon" and the esteem accorded to Shelby, who was moving to a new position to carry out further aspects of the ideology, well illustrates the point.

Beyond Milford. During the August teachers meeting, the Milford School District followed the standard ritual of having a program with an out-of-town speaker who trades glowing epithets with the superintendent. Spanman introduced the speaker as an educational statesman of "ideas and integrity." The speaker, in turn, lauded the superintendent and the bright spots of Milford. He talked of the significance of teaching, "a job to build a dream on." The observer, who had attended opening night and had seen the play before, suggested an hypothesis which, although a bit cynical, still extends the conceptualization of issues in true belief and innovation.

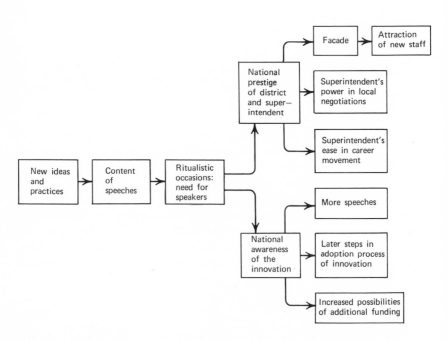

Figure 4.4   The dynamics of educational innovation in the context of true belief.

As I listen to him I get some feeling for the reasons that fads develop in education. These characters need something new and different to talk about as they journey around. They reach so many people that a "new" idea can be spread rapidly. Superintendents and others looking for fame can grab hold and offer their school as a case in point (8/31).

As lecturers and speakers have strong needs of this sort, the visible and newsworthy item is a potent reinforcer. The fame accruing to the innovator is not to be denied either. A symbiotic relationship such as this seems a potent underpinning of our discussion of the "facade." Unfortunately, in the perspective of the investigators, such a relationship may germinate, develop, and flower, independent of any assessment of the explicit goals of the innovation itself and the degree to which these objectives are actually reached. Although explicable and understandable from the vantage point of a social psychological interpretation of behavioral theory, it leaves a good bit to be desired from a value-oriented theory of education. Some of the implications appear in Figure 4.4. We are suggesting here that a dynamic exists external to the main arena, the school itself, and that part of the nature of "the broader content of true belief" lies in these outside persons who are caught up in their own system of psychological forces and, as a consequence, help create, extend, and perpetuate innovations such as Kensington.

Conclusion

A general theory of the building of an institutional core in an innovative organization remains a major unfinished task from our analysis of Kensington. Interdependencies exist among (1) schools as a particular kind of organization, (2) innovative schools as a special organizational subcase, (3) self-selection to innovative schools of persons characterized by a quality of true belief, (4) the emotional qualities inherent in a socialization procedure such as T-groups, and (5) the broader context of innovation in the national educational Zeitgeist. Our data and analysis would suggest that educational administrators, parents, and interested citizens cannot ignore these issues as they try to improve public education in the abstract case and individual public schools in the particular case.

SELECTION OF A SOCIAL BASE

The organization's relationship to its environment precedes, or at least provides, a context for the building of an institutional core that in turn precedes, or provides, a context for formalization. We have spoken of Kensington's problems in formalization and of its strategies, tactics, and problems in building an institutional core. Briefly we now consider Kensington's relationship to its environment.

"On Being Out Front": An Initial Description and Conceptualization of the Social Base

There is an old story which suggests that the leader of a parade should be out in front of the marching bands and the other members of his entourage. However, if he gets too far in front, he no longer leads the parade; the group may well be following someone else. This seems particularly applicable to the problems of an innovative school and its general leadership. We caught a taste of this in the early field notes.

> I also heard about the in-group or ruling clique or "club," as it is called, which exists in the school system. Essentially this is Spanman, Eugene, and Jerl. It also will include most of the Kensington staff ultimately. There may be one or two others. In a system with, at least, one high school and two junior highs and nine elementary schools this is an awfully small core, it seems to me at this point. It raises some question about the stability of the whole enterprise. It also raises some question in my own mind about an elitist conception of leadership. They are way out ahead of their school district, of their staff, and of the community. The balance between how much ahead of the parade and how much their strength derives from the group that one leads is open to real question here. Some of this came up at another point in the evening as both Jerl and Eugene made comments about the degree to which the community is informed about what is going on. Apparently there are a number of half-truths circulating about the nature of the school. Essentially these are omission errors rather than commission errors. For instance, they talked some about the ungraded aspect of the school but talked very little about the almost total permissiveness of the curriculum in social studies and

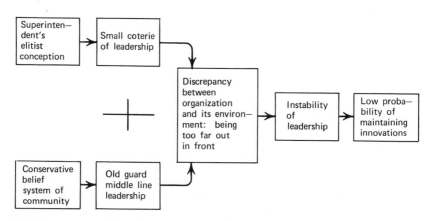

Figure 4.5 The issues in an innovative organization's social base.

in science. They feel the parents would not understand what they are trying to do. Apparently they have talked among themselves a good bit about how much should be communicated to the parents before the actual operation and opening of the school (8/9).

In short, we were raising hypotheses concerning aspects of what Selznick would call the "social base." The educational leadership seemed apart from the district patrons. The core of the leadership seemed small relative to the size of the school organization. The district seemed only partially aware of the changes underway in general in Milford and at Kensington in particular. All this seems to have significance for the probabilities that innovation will be maintained. Figure 4.5 summarizes these hypotheses.

The Multiple Facets of the Environment

At a very concrete level, one of the most striking generalizations is that the social environment has a number of discriminable parts. Each of these parts is a miniature social system in itself. These systems have interdependencies among themselves as well as with Kensington. In our case, the central office of the Milford Schools, the group of elementary principals, the school board, the district patrons, and the Kensington patrons had significant influence on the school. As we discuss the facade, the relevant publics, as parts of the social environment, expand to include the local, state, and national educational establishments as well as the national audience that reads the mass media.

The Divided Central Office. Although evidence of district-wide problems occurred all year and in many forms, we viewed them dramatically in December.

> Eugene told of conflict between himself and Howard from the central office. The latter wants to have more to do with the building than Eugene wants him to have. There have been a whole series of incidents. Last summer Eugene happened to be around when the order went out for the chairs in the school. He ordered three sizes and Howard had wanted to order six sizes. It was not clear to me whose decision it really was and apparently it's not clear generally. Eugene made a comment that Steven had changed some over the course of the last six months since August. When I asked him to pin down the change, he mentioned that he was turning many things over to Howard, Adolph, and Calvin. As I see it, the essence of this is that the superintendent is working through the formal, established channels and, also, may be trying to tighten the total ship in terms of the community problems that he has. For Eugene, this means that the superintendent rides the fence on issues instead of giving him total support for whatever he wants to do. This may mean that there is some equivocation and the two may not be seeing things so congruently any more. Other points of conflict between Howard and Eugene lie in the size of the chairs that will be out in the perception core. Eugene wants

them all the same size because the tables are all the same height and Howard wants them of different heights. When I asked Eugene who officially had responsibility for the building and, in effect, when the keys were turned over, he didn't have a clear answer. He made a guess that it was supposed to be his last July when he became principal of the building. The feeling I have is that this is another area in which Steven has not only not been clear in operating through channels but has been vacillating back and forth, and that nobody really knows who is responsible for what. Another area of conflict has occurred, since the plans were officially set, and Howard's committee was dissolved, and the more recent evolution of changes in the building. In effect, we have two people for whom the school is "their baby." The system seems rife with conflict.

These points suggest once again that one of the necessary subsequent studies is to look carefully at the total district and the impact that this has on the particular school building. This general confusion that appears to exist at the district level seems to be transmitted right on down into the Kensington School. Another case in point of the district influence on the school, and what may be some very negative consequences in terms of the program, is the fact that Howard pushed for the move to the new building to come early. According to one comment, and I heard it on at least one other occasion, Howard had promised the building would be ready by Thanksgiving, and he was caught wanting to maintain this and to maintain his position with the school board. The pressure was more personal in this sense rather than the need for the junior high facilities. If this is the case, and if it could have been made open and honest, then they could have moved one of the other divisions first and could have gotten it settled in that fashion. But when he had to take the rationalization, if it be a rationalization, of the junior high space problem, then it sewed up a whole series of other events that now have come about in a very dramatic and unhappy order.[15]

Another illustration of the lack of clarity in the system generally and in the impact of the district on the building concerns the fact that Jack perceives his role as science consultant in the district as being more significant than Eugene views it. Eugene says that the district work should be supplementary to total responsibility to the building. Which days Jack is released depends really on Eugene's beneficence. What it does, though, is to put the people in ambiguous spots in that Jack has to keep asking for favors, which is always a dangerous phenomenon, instead of having the right or his due in terms of having days off to work on the district material. As we talked about the flavor of this, it is quite different from what occurred early in the year. As it stands now, this is a recurring problem (12/10).

In effect, these and other decisions concerning materials, supplies, and money had a pronounced impact on the growth and development of Ken-

---

[15] The descriptive narrative of these events occurs in Chapter 5.

sington. Particularly, they seem to relate to the early conception of the school as a protected subculture and to the present reality; perceptions of what Kensington was and should be varied greatly among the district officials. These divergences, coupled with the ones internal to the staff, proved to be difficult taskmasters for the beginning organization.

The Elementary Principals. In most school districts that we have come to know well, we have been struck by the potency of the group of elementary school principals. In general, they seem to form an important reference group for the individual principal. The principal's decisions regarding his building seem to be conditioned by the impact of this group, as well as his own building staff. His evaluation of the success of his building program seems to be set by the norms of this group of principal colleagues. To the best of our knowledge, little systematic theoretical analysis or empirical data are available on these colleaguial cliques of principals. In the Milford District such a group of peers existed; however, Shelby was not a part of it. They were of the "old guard," and they viewed him as a deviant newcomer.

A lack of relationship with a group of this kind means one is not part of the informal informational grapevine. Also one does not have a group of equals involved in essentially the same set of problems, for instance, administering a building, with whom to turn for the informal give and take of advice and relevant perspectives. Also, in most districts the principals have a strong policy-making function, since they have the intimate contacts with the community through the parents and they are prime channels for the flow of information up the hierarchy to the central decision makers. Similarly, they are the key line officers for implementing the flow of policy decisions and commands from the superintendent and his central staff. Although we have little data on these issues, our impressions were that a minimization of these forces occurred early in the year and that there was an increasing strength of these forces later in the year. A careful description and analysis of the dynamics of this would have been an important supplement to our present discussion. Also, in subsequent years the intended diffusion process of Kensington's innovations to the other schools would have been fascinating if our tentative analysis of Shelby's relationship to the others is substantially correct.

The interdependence of Shelby and the other elementary principals, and the involvement of a high-ranking central office administrator, Jerl Cohen, appears in the field notes.

> Another interesting phenomenon to this point is the fact that, although we are concerned with the one building, Kensington, by focusing at this level one gets involved immediately in the interrelationship with other buildings

and with the broader part of the system. The sequence that is important here concerns moving from an understanding of the classroom and the need to go outside of it to the total building to gain a perspective.[16] Now when we are at the building level the interlocking between other buildings becomes very critical. In this regard, part of the discussion centered on the impact that Jerl Cohen's presence might have on the rest of the system. If he spends this much time with the Kensington School, then what would the other eight principals think about their relative status and their relative needs. Both Eugene and Jerl are sensitive to this. The problem is a very fascinating one of looking at the same sets of issues from the vantage points of people who are placed in different positions within the system. Small wonder that there often is confusion and misunderstanding among people in different spatial and hierarchical positions.

The Kensington Patrons. At a number of points we have indicated aspects of the relationship between Kensington and its patrons, another part of Kensington's environment. Although the nuances were intriguing and fascinating, the story is too long to be presented here. The major subgroups we would accent are: (1) a small loyal group who worked with the school throughout the year to help translate the ideals into day-to-day practices; (2) another small group who were opposed to the ideals in the doctrine and its correlated practices and who tried to get the school to look like their image of a more traditional elementary school; and (3) a large group of patrons who knew very little about the school and what was happening in its program. Much of the parental involvement occurred in the patrons organization and in open staff-patron meetings at the school.

The Kensington program intended close working relationships between home and school. On Wednesday, September 16, during the second week of school, an open house was held for the ISD parents. The notes, dictated late that evening, clarify additional aspects of Kensington.

> I have come from a long parent-teachers meeting at the Kensington School. As I listened to the program develop, it seemed to me, logically, that one way of organizing the notes would be to list and comment on the questions that were asked. As the evening wore on, I also had a number of more general-ized affective as well as cognitive responses. For instance, I had the very strong impression that the parents were asking quite specific, quite pertinent, and quite thorny questions. It seemed to me that almost universally they were right on the point. Second, I had the feeling that the parents, although they varied in the degree of hostility and support they had toward the program, were very sincere and very concerned about their children. Third, I kept won-dering what educational psychology as a science of behavior had to say to these teachers and to these parents. The phrasing of the questions, the problems

---

[16] This is a reference to our earlier work, *The Complexities of an Urban Classroom,* and our need to understand the dynamics of the faculty peer culture.

that were being attended to, and the complexity defy most of the current theory and research.

More specifically then to the notes on the questions that were being asked. First, one man asked: How do the teachers know what the individual children are doing? He raised it in the context of Alec's math program in which Alec had 200 students. He just did not see how it could be possible in those conditions. Alec's answer here, it seems, was caught on the program of a week ago, the program this week, and the ideal program. Nowhere did he or anyone else make clear the fact that these were three different kinds of programs and some of them could not be defended easily. The questions could not be answered and the issues defended on one aspect where they could on another. Second, one woman asked why they had physical education (PE) everyday even though they have the short program.[17] As far as I know, the staff had not thought about the educational soundness of PE in the shortened program. The PE program seemed like a very reasonable and plausible alternative and, as it is set up now, basically it gives every teacher a free period in which to do other work and to have a cup of coffee. Although it would involve some messy scheduling problems, it also suggests the very viable way to alter the program to get more instructional time or T-group-type time into the program. Third, there was a question raised about how the children make up the time that's lost in the T-groups. No one, however, asked whether the T-group was a wise idea or not. Fourth, a parent asked about the spelling program and when the children would get specific instruction in this. This typically was handled by both Irma and Eugene in terms of the words the kids actually used and of learning how to spell them. Fifth, the question was raised of communicating with parents about the child's difficulties and the procedure for this. Here the parent-conference answer was not wholly viable because the teachers each have 200 kids and they cannot have 200 conferences. In this also, it seems that the alteration of the program to its current status left many aspects undefendable in the same way that last week's part of the program left many aspects undefendable. For instance, conferences would be the academic counselor's job, yet now they do not have academic counselors. The staff was hooked on all kinds of ifs, and buts, and ands. Sixth, the question was raised about what happens to the kids if these two years, or however long, turn out to be a failure. Here, again, the risk aspect was just not faced up to. Seventh, the question was raised about what would happen to the kids if they went into junior high school this next year. This got everybody involved in a discussion about the rumors that the whole system was moving toward the Kensington-type program. When Eugene indicated this, he immediately was faced with the question of how fast and when and what would happen at Hillside Elementary School next year. He was called on to make more specific answers than he had any information about and had any ability to

[17] This was a reference to the shortened school day that was instituted for a while in the temporary quarters, which later drew unfavorable judgment from the State Department, and which finally was rescinded.

answer. Eighth, there was considerable discussion about one of the math assignments that Alec had made that ran about 16 or 20 pages. He apparently had left it open-ended as to when they would have it done, and one man's daughter was very conscientious and did not know whether she should have it all done by tomorrow or whether it should take a longer period of time. The father was very upset about this lack of clarity. There was a question raised also about the kids who were put off into the special section, and the possible repercussions of this. This is an interesting one in that little consideration was given to what the children thought or what the other children thought. (My personal guess would be, and it's rather a superficial one, that there has been so much hubbub and shifting and changing around that there is little or no discrimination by the children toward each other on the basis of anything of this kind. In that sense, when everything is confused and from the children's point of view, I suppose, quite disorganized, it's impossible to feel that you are being discriminated against. You never know for sure just exactly what's happening to anybody else.)

There was also in the group considerable support for the school. Some of this was of a backhanded sort in that one couple commented about how unhappy they have been with St. Mary's School which has had a new math program every year for the last three years, and about which their daughter was terribly confused. Others, obviously, were caught by the excitement of the possibilities of the program and were urging "patience," "let's see," and "give them more than a week and a half." Blended into this were comments indicating the very strong aspirations many of these parents have for the children. For instance, many of the parents want their children to have advantages that they did not have. They want them to compensate for mistakes they feel were made in their own educational program. They want them to be able to accomplish things that they themselves have not accomplished. Related to this also, it seemed to me, were problems that the parents were having with their children or problems that the kids had had in the school or in other schools. This was perhaps best typified by the man who carried the brunt of the dissatisfaction. He has a son in junior high school who apparently is a real goof off and will not do a damn thing. He also has a daughter who is overly conscientious and is concerned that everything be right. He's mad at the Milford Junior High School and their program; he's mad at Kensington and their program and, my guess would be, he will be unhappy all along the line no matter what happened to his children insofar as it did not shift them from these two extreme sorts of responses (9/16).

The school was involved intimately with the parents. At the evening meetings difficult questions were raised. Although a few parents seemed to be displacing their hostility on a convenient target, most seemed to have a picture of the public school as a vehicle for the better life that they wanted for their children. They wanted to be sure that the new program would facilitate this major goal.

The Milford Patrons. The story of the Milford patrons is an amplification of the school board story. In the local metropolitan area, the Milford District has had a history and a reputation of conflict. The prior superintendent came and went out of the picture several times before Spanman was selected. The district had grown several times over in size in the last decade. The new arrivals, lower-middle-class whites, wanted better homes and better schools than they thought they could obtain in the nearby central city, which was becoming rapidly a black ghetto. They projected aspirations for their children that seemed, at times, to be higher than the district-wide ability tests and the family socioeconomic status indicated were feasible. However, our data here were too limited to suggest very intensive analyses and generalizations.

The Nonunanimous Board. Although we attended only a few meetings of the school board, the observations were supplemented with conversations and with observations of board members on other occasions. Uniformly, the majority decisions supported the Spanman administration. Uniformly, there was minority opposition in verbal exchanges, if not in voting. Late in the year as rumors as well as an actuality of Spanman's leave of absence for the coming year occurred, the board began to have significant impact on Kensington. For instance, the Milford principals' freedom to allocate funds for teacher aides instead of for certified teachers was disallowed. Late in the year, Kensington suffered heavily from this controversy. In short, the board was split over the grand design for Milford and split over the specific program at Kensington. As such, it illustrates well another face of the multiple facets of Kensington's environment.

Alternative Conceptualization of the Environment

Our data, as we have reported them from the field notes, suggest that further conceptualization of the organization's environment must be made if we are to clarify the nature of Selznick's social base problem in the origins of innovative organizations. Dill (1962) raises two broader metatheoretical stances for carrying out such an analysis:

"Most of the work of developing an adequate theory of environmental influences on organizational behavior lies ahead. Considerable work is now being done, and two directions of study seem particularly promising. One is an attempt to dimensionalize variables of human personality and intelligence. This requires considerable faith in the adequacy of such techniques as factor analysis and the linearly independent dimensions that such techniques generate to represent significant influences on other variables that we want to study. Such faith abounds, though; and some imaginative steps have been taken. . . .

"The second direction of investigation is more consistent with the approach that I have suggested here. This is the effort to conceptualize individuals or organizations as information processing systems and then to simulate, usually with the aid of electronic computers and related 'hardware,' the environment to which they are exposed. . . . The trick in building a model of the environment under such circumstances is not in isolating characteristic factors or dimensions, but in writing programs and setting up systems to generate and to present information to an individual or an organization in the same manner that the 'real world' would" (pp. 107, 109).

In part, the kind of theoretical stance one takes depends on the kinds of questions one hopes to answer or the kind of problems one hopes to solve.

Dimensional Analysis. Dimensional analysis helps one see the structure of the environment. For instance, as we described the multiple facets of Kensington's environment we might argue that the latent dimension is one of complexity, that is heterogeneous (high complexity) to homogeneous (low complexity). A highly complex environment probably entails the development of multiple goals, multiple activities, and multiple faces and facades. This suggests, too, the possibility that consistency and formalization in an organization will be difficult to achieve and that leadership and resources will have to be allocated here. In short, we are arguing that relationships will exist between such an environmental condition and each of the variables contained within one's conception of the organization.

In Figure 4.6, we suggest several further dimensions that seemed latent in the field notes. The supportive-nonsupportive variable interacts with the complexity dimension. Some parts of the environment, the superintendent, were strongly supportive while other parts, for instance the divided central office, were less supportive. The environment was not stable. As the year wore on Kensington's environment changed. The departure of the superintendent had a major impact on the school. This changing administrative structure illustrates also the issue of potency and involvement of the environment or, at least, part of it. Members of the divided central

1. Complexity: homogeneous—heterogeneous
2. Supportive: supportive—neutral—hostile
3. Stability: stable—transitional—dynamic
4. Potency: potent—impotent
5. Involvement: involved—detached

Figure 4.6 Environmental dimensions at Kensington.

office were differentially involved and, particularly with the superintendent's departure, they became much more potent elements in the environment.

The Environment as Information. Most of our analysis of the "environment-as-information" model occurs in a later chapter in which we deal with the administration of Kensington. At this moment, we would stress several essential but often latent aspects of this point of view.

In the environment-as-information position there is an irrevocable tie with a time dimension. At time one (T_1) the environment presents itself to the organization. The organization processes the information and then acts at time two (T_2). Meanwhile, the environment changes through its dynamics, insofar as it is composed of organizations and individuals, and changes also because of its scanning of organizational action at time two. Consequently, the environment may be different at time three when the organization scans again. The handling of processes, changes over time, is an important and difficult methodological, theoretical, and practical problem.[18]

Implicit also in this conception is the phenomenon of social exchange. The organization requires resources in which to carry out its work to reach its goals. A business organization exchanges products or outputs for money which it exchanges in turn for further inputs. A school district through its board and superintendent provides an education to the pupils of the geographical area and, in turn, receives financial resources for hiring teachers, buying books, maintaining buildings, and so forth. An individual school, such as Kensington, competes with the other schools of the district for supplies, equipment, teachers, aides, and other resources. Each school provides intermediary services in terms of organization and program and terminal services in instructing pupils. These outputs are exchanged for some portion of the general resources. In effect, the goals of the organization are set in terms of the needs of the environment, that is, for what the environment is willing to exchange its outputs. These environmental outputs become resources for the organization. As we discuss later, Kensington was a "protected subculture," which meant that special rules governed the exchange between the school and its environment.

Thompson (1967) develops several concepts to enhance the environment-as-information analysis.[19] Task environment splits the total environment into that part which is especially relevant to the organization in

---

[18] Our attempts to grapple with this same theoretical issue as applied to teaching appear initially in Smith and Geoffrey (1968), and more elaborately, in Chapter 3, "As Events Move Through Time: Classroom Processes," of Smith and Brock (1970).

[19] In addition, Thompson (1967) develops a highly differentiated theory of "organizations in action" from this general vantage point.

the sense of influencing inputs or being influenced by outputs and into that part which is left over. Domain refers to what the organization will or will not do in relationship with the interacting parts of its environment. As a general rubric, it locates the organization within its environment and in terms of inputs and outputs. Domain consensus is the common view of the organization as held by the relevant others who compose the environment.

At Kensington, the most important element of the environment was the superintendent, Steven Spanman, and his immediate deputy, Jerl Cohen. Shelby was their intimate colleague and associate. The mandate, which we described previously, was the most significant item of information in Kensington's environment. It stated the initial terms of Kensington's existence both as a support and as an outline for goals and organizational structure. The Institutional Plan was Shelby's response to the mandate. In turn, this response became a stimulus and a guide to the later action, processes, and structure of Kensington. It led to recruitment and socialization procedures, that is, forming the institutional core. Indirectly, the mandate and Institutional Plan contributed, along with the developing institutional core, to both formalization and to the problems in formalization of Kensington's organizational structure.

SUMMARY

The origins of a developing and changing organization are most interesting phenomena to observe. The problems of selecting a social base, building an institutional core, and formalizing procedures were issues that faced Kensington as a beginning organization. In a very brief statement, which we discovered long after we had made our observations and developed our analyses, we found Stinchcombe (1965) discussing the "liability of newness."[20] He says:

". . . there are poorly understood conditions that affect the comparative death rates of new and old organizations. As a general rule, a higher proportion of new organizations fail than old. This is particularly true of new organizational *forms,* so that *if an alternative requires new organization,* it has to be much more beneficial than the old before the flow of benefits compensates for the relative weakness of the newer social structure" (p. 148).

---

[20] Our colleague, Paul A. Pohland (1970), not only suggested the reference but is exploring in detail the conception as it relates to "An Interorganizational Analysis of an Innovative Educational Program."

His analysis suggests four major factors that are appropriate as summary generalizations for our data:

"(a) New organizations, especially new types of organizations, generally involve new roles, which have to be learned" (p. 148).

Our notes and analysis, not only in this chapter but throughout the book, reiterate in a multitude of concrete ways the truth of this principle.

"(b) The process of inventing new roles, the determination of their mutual relations and of structuring the field of rewards and sanctions so as to get maximum performance, have high costs in time, worry, conflict, and temporary inefficiency" (p. 148).

Time and energy appear and reappear as underestimated expenditures of limited resources. Similarly, anxiety, conflict, and difficulties in goal attainment were rampant.

"(c) New organizations must rely heavily on social relations among strangers. This means that relations of trust are much more precarious in new than old organizations . . ." (p. 150).

Kensington developed and used a number of procedures in recruiting and socializing to help cope with this problem, but it remained an issue. Further aspects are raised both explicitly and implicitly in a later chapter as we discuss "Dilemmas in Democratic Administration."

"(d) One of the main resources of old organizations is a set of stable ties to those who use organizational services" (p. 150).

The linkages with the environment of parents, central office personnel, and other schools in the district, we have observed to be multiple and often conflicting. Some of them were deliberate and part of the innovative strategy, and some were unintended consequences of new organizational structures.

In short, we are arguing that Conceptualizing Organizational Origins and Development is a case study in the "liability of newness." As a single case, Kensington had a number of idiosyncratic aspects that gave a subtlety and vividness to the phenomena. The resources, the multifaceted environment, and the absence of a social structure are ways of talking about the same issues. At this point we encourage the reader to return to the descriptive chapters in which we narrated briefly the origin, development, and change at Kensington.

SECTION **III**

Substantive Issues in Educational Innovation

CHAPTER 5

The Realities of Kensington's Innovative Teacher-Pupil Relationships

As the mandate, Institutional Plan, and the discussions in the summer workshop have indicated, the relationships between teacher and pupil were to be innovative. Although "nontraditional" describes these relationships to some extent, a number of quite abstract terms were used. Nongraded, individualized, democratic, pupil centered, flexible, shared, open, purposive, free, and supportive indicate their tenor. Instead of attempting to clarify these terms, we remain at the "data level" in presenting a descriptive narrative of two critical points in this strand of the Kensington experience. The opening days of school in the temporary quarters and the move to the new building in December were important times.

THE INITIAL CONFRONTATION WITH THE PUPILS

The opening of school, the initial confrontation with the pupils on Tuesday, September the 8, began the second major phase of Kensington. The month's workshop, a major innovation in itself, had come and gone and with it the T-grouping, the many committees, and the varied planning. The physical plant of the new school had not been finished. Predictions for the completion ranged from several weeks to a semester. The divisions were to go their geographically separate ways, since they were housed in three temporary settings: Milford High School, Milford Junior High School, and Hillside Elementary School. The distinctions between "normal" school beginnings,[1] about which there is almost no careful literature with which to make comparisons, the processes unique to the Kensington formal doctrine and program, and the consequences of the temporary setting remain difficult to tease apart.

[1] See Chapter Two of Smith and Geoffrey (1968).

ISD: THE INDEPENDENT STUDY DIVISION

Day One

School began in the refurbished gymnasium at 9:10 A.M. as the first busload of children arrived. The final organization of the room, dittoing of instruction sheets, and so forth had occurred during the weekend. The efforts, energy, and direction of David Nichols were paramount in this preparation.

The temporary physical plan in which the Independent Study Division began operation left a good bit to be desired. The main area was a large open gymnasium, located in Milford's Junior High School. Highboy and lowboy cabinets were available for partial dividers, and other moveable facilities were accessible. In the room without permanent walls were 200 students, roughly from age nine to eleven. With them, according to the formal statement, were two academic counselors, four academic resource persons, one physical education resource person, a materials specialist, and an audiovisual technician. In addition to the gymnasium, the Independent Study Division also had use of a wide corridor with windows along each side. Faculty desks were placed in the hallway along with some tables for individual study and projects, and one area for instruction. A stairwell leading to the basement also was used for pupil Training Groups and small instructional groups. The playing floor of the gymnasium was covered with pieces of plywood that were taped together and that, with wear, would begin to pull apart. The student rest rooms were shared with junior high school pupils and were located in the main part of the building away from the gymnasium.

All of the teachers arrived early with the exception of Walt Larsen, Kirkham's replacement, who came at 9:15 A.M. The staff spread themselves out to usher the children from the buses, through the hallways, and into groups of six located somewhere in the large room at the children's own discretion. Most of these groups seemed to fall along sex lines, and along age and grade levels, as well as friendship. The following field notes capture in general the interaction of the first day in the Independent Study Division.

> 9:20 A.M. A quick check of station area indicates that most of the groups of 6's are along sex lines. Only one group in about ten is mixed at this point Kids move down the line reasonably easily. Jack and Kay help. John and Walt get the athletic equipment sorted out.

> The noise level continues to rise slowly as the number of children increases. The temperature and humidity also seem to be increasing gradually. Liz, for instance, is very warm and predicts some of the kids will be ill.

9:27 A.M. At least one parent is angry over buses: "I've been trying to find out for two weeks," she comments.

Tom and Arthur are in the hall. Alec is at the door. Kay and Jack are at the tables. Irma is in her room. Mrs. Beacon is at her desk, registering, etc.

9:30 A.M. About one-half dozen tables are empty. Probably one more busload is due in. The teachers are milling about. Walt is still filling out a schedule. A mother is here with her son and with a baby in arms. She talks to Irma. Leaves her son. Tom drinks a cup of coffee. Kay asks me if I've got "chaos" written down yet.

9:40 A.M. I'm in back of David's area. Kay, Liz, David, Jack, and Alec circulate from table to table helping the groups get started. Kay does this with consummate skill. Tom is in to help also. The teachers are all very warm. The children gradually get the idea of what to do and start making name tags.

9:43 A.M. John and Irma break their group into two parts. John has his in south hall. Irma stays in the gym. She has them pull out the blue sheet on miscellaneous information and begins to explain its contents.[2]

Later in the morning, after a cup of coffee, the observer tried to grapple with the totality of the sense impressions coming in upon him.

10:45 A.M. I'm back from coffee. The sign-up for classes is going full blast, 8 to 10 groups. David is holding his first T-group. They're reading the *Weekly Reader* or a similar paper. A brief survey indicates the kids are milling all about the gym; the sign-up area is jammed. Half-a-dozen kids are in line at the water fountain; some exploratory behavior in and out among the high- and lowboy cabinets begins. Also there is some horseplay—poking, tripping, and hide and seek. Some children sit at tables and gaze about. The 11:00 A.M. T-groups start to assemble. David directs Arthur to tell them to wait in Area 3. Some of the kids, one group of girls, are playing volleyball on the playground. Jack, Kay, Alec, Arthur, etc., help kids sign up.

11:02 A.M. As I wander about and talk with individual groups, most seem to have some of the scheduling accomplished. A few sit and wait because the sign-up area is too crowded. Some of the younger kids seem especially lost. One group of older boys is frustrated because they have four things in but can't work in the fifth—which is P.E.

To this point, the only formal instructional activity I've seen is David's group reading the *Weekly Reader*. All the others are trying to solve scheduling problems. So far no tempers are frayed nor do I see any serious discipline problems. Teachers help by going from group to group and trying to keep kids moving along on the schedules. Major instructional acitivty will be this afternoon.

[2] The explanations involved sheets of paper that indicated classes and class times for instruction. They were attached to the bulletin boards on the movable highboys. Pupils were to sign for classes, scheduling both hours and days.

The noise—mostly the chatter of the kids—continues unabated. I personally am about to get a headache.

11:10 A.M. The gaining of attention of a total group, that is, the ones cared for by an academic counselor, is extremely difficult. Irma taps pencil on desk but this is pretty much in vain. Her group picks up chairs and moves to the resource area. She obtains cooperation easily, talks quietly to individuals, dyads, and triads.

A final excerpt from the field notes continues our attempt to picture concretely the way the first morning went.

11:35 A.M. I'm spending just a moment or two in David's T-group. No one says anything. He sits. The kids (4 boys and 3 girls) writhe around literally and look like chained, muted animals. They don't seem to know what's happening. They look like they want to leave the situation. Some keep looking down toward sign-up boards. Mostly they look restless, uncomfortable, bored, and hot.

11:50 A.M. I continue to circulate. Several groups in the north area of the gym have obtained reading books and are making desultory overtures at reading. One girl comments—"This doesn't seem like school." Another child reads a copy of *Children's Digest* that she brought from home. Some of the boys draw airplanes and tank war scenes. There is a tremendous amount of listless behavior. Kids are sitting and not quite knowing what to do. At this moment only 2 of the 15 groups I see are reading.

12:05 P.M. On the south side three groups are reading. Four groups (3 of boys, and 1 of girls and boys) have come up with modeling clay. They're excited as they pound, roll, and form the clay. Snakes, lady in a bathtub, and a pistol are some of the products. The kids push the forms into a glob and make something else. In general, there seems to be less of the listless type behavior here. John and Irma keep at it steadily. On the other side, David is with his T-group; Jack sits in the hall to prevent kids from going to the rest room during the junior high lunch hour. Alec and Liz have been at sign-up boards. Kay is tiring.[3]

The TV is on over by the south wall.

Late in the afternoon, the observer returned from brief stops with Transition and Basic Skills. The notes indicated the close of the day in ISD.

3:30 P.M. Back at the junior high and ISD.

Confusion still reigns. Kay has just left her group because they would not do anything. Alec is teaching a math lesson. Essentially, he is asking "How many ways can you write the number 10?" He's got a long list of eights on the board: $4 + 4 = 8$, $5 + 3 = 8$, $3 + 5 = 8$, etc. The assignment for tomorrow is the ten's. They can make posters or other art-type projects. He wants

---

[3] She was hampered all fall from a summer bout of infectious mononucleosis; her physical stamina was not at her pre-illness level.

them to bring these in next time, and he tells them of games and other activities that they can do in resource center. He asks them to schedule him once or twice more this week. A minority of the kids seem right with him. Many, however, seem vague and far away. Background noise is loud. Some kids are running, etc. He asks them to plan when they want to come in and what they want to talk about. He'll have a schedule ready tomorrow for the remainder of the week. He tosses out a variety of suggestions.

3:45 P.M. The group breaks up to go back to pupil stations, the desks where they store their materials.

3:55 P.M. In Irma's section, most of the children are filling out their work sheets.[4] She and John move among the children and help them by answering questions and giving directions. As I wandered about, a group of boys were at each TV set. Size varied from about two to twelve. A few of the older and brighter kids seem able to handle freedom and work along on their log sheets. Others talk and wander.

4:05 P.M. The staff seems exhausted. David indicates there will be an 8:00 A.M. staff meeting tomorrow morning. The children are practically unsupervised. Irma is at a CTA (Community Teachers Association) meeting. Tom has a half-dozen pupils he's talking to. Liz is wandering still. Jack has been out in the hall. Arthur and Mrs. Beacon distribute bus tickets and an envelope regarding health (I think). Alec also has kept away from stations. The noise continues full blast. A few kids sign up for things.

The teachers have reported that the kids forget times they have signed up for. A few comment that they do not want any more language arts, etc.

There has been some scattered painting with watercolors, and a few of the pictures have been posted about. Some of the kids have watched a lot of TV, some have stood in the cool south stairway. There has been very little P.E. this afternoon. No one has been on the field since I've been back. I checked, and Walt has scratched off the last hour and one half.

4:13 P.M. Kids start toward the doors. The buses are not here as yet. Almost all of the kids have *a* book and their packet of papers.

4:20 P.M. The kids are lined up in the north hall for the buses. No one knows when or where the buses will come. Alec handles the major disciplining of quieting them and calling out bus sections. David, Tom, and aides help line up the kids.

4:45 P.M. Buses arrive.

The observer noted early in the morning of the first day that the children were all "well dressed and well scrubbed." Later he commented on their social behavior:

It's now 5:00 P.M. The buses were one-half hour late and did not arrive until 4:45. The kids stood around in the hall and some in the gym for the half

---

[4] They are the daily logs indicating the pupils' activities.

hour as they waited for the buses. Essentially they were a very orderly bunch who did not raise much difficulty at all. I'm continuously struck at how different the children are from those last year at the Washington School (see Smith and Geoffrey, 1968). The nonsense and the horseplay of a year ago just doesn't appear at this school. The defiance, the surliness, and the hostility are not present. Here, the teachers can leave the children unsupervised and they don't break out in fighting, name calling, and antagonisms. The "instinct of aggression" has been either bred out or trained out of these children. This contrast is one of the most instructive things thus far about the experience here at Kensington (9/8).

Continuous Reorganization

The Independent Study Division did not reach a simple equilibrium. Continuous reorganization of both staff and pupils was the mode of approach as long as they remained in the temporary quarters. Each change, as we shall argue later, brought a series of unanticipated consequences with which the division then had to cope. We enumerate the sequence of changes and include brief excerpts of notes to define this aspect of ISD.

The Original Organizational Structure. In the discussion of the preschool workshop, the framework of ISD was spelled out. Basically, the Institutional Plan and supplementary documents (Figures 3.1, 3.2, and 3.3) specified that there would be three academic counselors and four resource persons. Each counselor was to engage in diagnosing, grouping, scheduling, and evaluating approximately 70 pupils. The resource or subject matter specialists were to provide individual and group instruction, develop instructional activities and materials, and engage in curriculum organization. With the removal of Kirkham at the end of the third week of the summer workshop, and with the brief but significant delay in replacing him, ISD reorganized into its opening framework.

The Second Structure. The crucial elements of the second structure, the first reorganization, we have described partially in the events of the first day. The pupils were organized into groups of six. The groups scheduled their activities on sign-up sheets posted in the central area of the gym. Some of the pupils spent a part of the day in Training Groups. At the close of the second day of school, September 9, plans were made to change this structure.

The possibility that students might not yet be able to work in a program that emphasized considerable pupil responsibility had not been fully taken into account. When the staff spoke of changing pupil roles, they seldom considered equipping the students with techniques that would insure facility in performing the new roles. In effect, the immediate student performance was overestimated. This was most clearly illustrated to the staff by the difficulties in writing the student logs and the difficulties with group scheduling. The logs were a daily record kept by each student. They included what classes he attended, something about what he had done, and his feelings about the work. Each student was to have one-half hour at the end of the day to complete his log. With regard to the first day and the logs, one teacher observed that she "had a good many who couldn't write and they talked about how they couldn't fill them in." Another mentioned that some of the younger students were unable to fill in logs by themselves and "hardly with supervision." Still another noted that there was "no trouble when they're with one of us. The other time is hardest."

A further part of initial pupil difficulties involved the scheduling of classes. Subsequent problems were viewed by some of the faculty as having their origins in procedures the students were to follow. How the pupils were to "sign up" for instruction was not uniformly perceived by the faculty. Originally the students were to be grouped by friendship instead of by interest; however, some were not in groups and, thus, were unable to schedule with a group. They were described as "running around a lot and not having schedule forms." Group membership was seen as a problem: "Some are not functioning with the group at all." The scheduling was, phrased in the doctrine, a "strategy for making sure pupils assume responsibility." However, as pupil confusion related to scheduling within groups came to be viewed as problematic, there were differences among the faculty as to whether programming should be focused on the group or the individual. Even within the groups, as was noted, there were difficulties involving the laxness of pupil acceptance of responsibility. John expressed a general sentiment based on the observation of the students the first two days of school: "Most haven't experienced this (scheduling). Some had a ball watching TV. I know a girl who spent two hours viewing it." Jack and Alec agreed about the children who had been watching television. The transcription below shows the way most of the ISD Team were handling similar situations in the early days of school:

DAVID (in response to John). What did you do?

JOHN. I asked about their groups. I tried to question them about the best use of time.

DAVID. That's my feeling and approach. I ask to meet that group for 15 minutes and try to work it out in the structure of the group.

JOHN. Up to a point this works . . . Lots needs to be done if it will function at all. The group is the basic unit if it's significant.

DAVID. I tried to make it clear. It is important that they learn. Group pressure is strong.

ALEC. One boy was in a T-group half the morning; three others were in the other half. The group can't function at all.

EUGENE. The small group is not the best basic unit.

ALEC. I told them not to come as a group, but to schedule as individuals according to interests.

Even when students were permitted to "sign up" individually regardless of the action of their group, some were still unable to perform the procedure. Prior to the decision to have a self-contained classroom for those who had not mastered scheduling and the preparation of logs, Eugene stated that, "You get freedom when you assume responsibility. Should we have controls and put some in a situation until they do?" Jack asked: "Could we develop a list of pupils for a self-contained setting? Would that solve the problem for those who can't assume responsibility?" The discussion continued:

DAVID. I have no objection, but do not place them indiscriminately. Some are struggling like hell.

EUGENE. Where's the burden of proof? Will we put them in before they've had a chance to prove themselves?

TOM. This is the way we work with children at home.

IRMA. When do we start? First we had no brakes and then we put them on. We started with no controls. It's lots harder now. It's easier to loosen up rather than tighten up.

EUGENE (much later). Can we identify pupils for a structured setting? (Tom cites a case in which two students are holding up fourteen).

EUGENE. How many are like this?

TOM. About 20 percent . . . They haven't had the training. Maybe we should back up and give it to them.

ALEC. Some need one teacher. They're not ready.

EUGENE. We've said pupils are responsible. We might have to reverse it.

TOM. It doesn't have to be all year, David.

ALEC. One teacher and some of us coming in would be a big step for some.

EUGENE. I asked Irma privately if she'd be willing to take it. She said, 'yes.'

Thus, in response to the number of students who were unable to schedule instruction, engage in independent study, and move in the program, at the close of Day 2 the ISD team decided on a self-contained room.

It was decided that the identification of pupils for the self-contained group would begin the following day. Irma's group was to have access to the math resource person 40 minutes daily and the science resource person three days a week.

These skill difficulties were not the only problems experienced by some of the students. The planning and coordination of instructional periods, Training Groups, and other student activities were dealt with in a number of lengthy staff team meetings. There were no precedents with which to compare and to contrast the current attempt. Staff coordination problems were pronounced. Although the following segment indicates early considerations on the implementation of student scheduling, it also points to the lack of clarity concerning procedural matters.

> LIZ. If you have a 45-minute period . . .
>
> ALEC. How can you have a 45-minute period?
>
> LIZ. Well, if you let them schedule their own.
>
> IRMA. What about the group plan? Are we going to let them stay in groups?
>
> ALEC. Yes, but they may work independently.
>
> (Observer: David points out that they may not be able to keep permanent groups, since they are not "flexible"—more security at first—permanent groups—can form subgroups.)
>
> DAVID. It is going to require skills in scheduling . . . I hadn't realized it is essential to the whole thing . . . should we schedule the first week and go from there?
>
> (Observer: Liz doesn't know exactly how much time she needs. Kay wants 30-minute time periods at first. David wants a schedule so that periods can vary from 15 minutes to an hour; a time schedule sheet to schedule groups for 15 minutes to an hour.)

As a consequence of the difficulties, individual scheduling replaced group "signing up" in an attempt to keep closer check on pupil activity. In the course of this, David defended group scheduling on the basis of its social aspects and on its enabling students to learn to work in groups. Others believed that the groups would form naturally and favored letting social groups come as they would. David, on the other hand, continued to maintain that children should leave groups only by mutual consent with pupil groupings and that they should learn how to cope. His view was opposed by Shelby, Tom, Alec, and Irma.

The decision to change the scheduling was announced to the students to be effected the following week. In reply to a student's question about the problem of pupils erasing others' names from schedule sheets, Alec replied: "This freedom we don't have. We can't erase names. I hope it doesn't happen again. We don't want to have to tell you everything you do. . . . For that reason don't erase them. If the group is filled up, tell the instructor."

The early difficulties of the students, in part, highlight the absence of clearly defined decision-making areas for the faculty. At least two of the faculty and the principal were unsure as to what their roles were. At the second day's meeting, Mr. Shelby spoke of the lack of clarity in his role. He cited it as a "personal problem" and that he did not know "whether to lead, be a resource person, or just a member of the group." The materials specialist also pointed out several times that he recognized things that needed attention, but he did not know whether or not they were in his area of jurisdiction. A part of this lack of clarity seems to have grown from the initial assumption that the faculty structure would entail no hierarchy but, instead, all would have equivalent opportunities for decision making and action. The role of Walt Larsen, Kirkham's replacement, also was undefined. The impact of the ambiguity of the situation became more pronounced as the reorganization in ISD was attempted.

By the time of the second reorganization, there had been two major deviations from the initial plan with respect to allocation and organization of the faculty. The first involved David, who originally was to have been a full-time academic counselor, and who became the director of the student Training Groups. As is indicated elsewhere, faculty sentiments toward the continuation and value of the Training Group sessions varied. When Irma, who with David was to have been the other academic counselor, was assigned a self-contained group, the organizational structure was further changed. The consequences of these two deviations from the original plan were not clearly foreseen.

The Third Structure. During a lengthy team meeting (until 7:30 P.M.) decisions were made that further altered the organization of both the faculty and the students. Each of the resource people was to have a designated teaching station at which he worked consistently; during the course of a day he was to meet 40 to 45 students in each of four sessions in his subject matter area. In addition to this, he was to spend time with Irma's pupils in the self-contained group. Another change centered on John, the physical education resource person; at this time he was freed to assume his duties as a full-time resource person in physical education. The children were to be in a six-block schedule: language arts, science, mathematics, social studies, physical education, and Training Groups. David's total schedule was student Training Groups; these left him free in the afternoon. As a contrast, both the math and the physical education resource persons were having difficulties finding the free time to eat lunch and to spend time with the self-contained group, which was taking their free period.

The above changes were essentially a shift to large group instruction, which the program initially had sought to avoid. The modification was made at Principal Shelby's suggestion, which, in turn, was made in part in response to parental reaction. The faculty members, however, viewed the changes as being effected primarily under Shelby's impetus. As the statements below indicate, teacher sentiments with respect to the instructional changes were varied as of September 14.

> TOM. We've lost a battle but not the war. I fear the school would have blown up. I see it as necessary if the school is going to continue.
>
> (Observer: At this point in the development of the team, Tom seemed to fill an unofficial role of coordinator and acting principal.)
>
> KAY. I'm quite opposed. I don't like the large group instruction, and it doesn't fit what I want to do.
>
> JACK. I'm in agreement. This is more what I wanted anyway. I can't see how you can run a program any other way.
>
> LIZ. I'm unhappy that I don't have materials with which to work.
>
> ALEC. I see it as a necessary setback. I will have some of my groups on independent projects immediately.
>
> JOHN. I'm pleased to be back in physical education. Someone else suggested it, but I am in agreement.

David was in agreement with those who viewed large group instruction as a necessity at that point. At the time, he was still engaged as T-group trainer, was happy with the position, and regarded it as essential. Some days later other staff members expressed the feeling that David's Training Groups gave him a lighter load than they, and they subsequently voted to discontinue the groups.

Walt Larsen was not present at the meetings. Shelby had told Walt that he did not have to attend team meetings in that he might be at Kensington four days or four weeks. The consequences of the failure to make an attempt to integrate Walt into the ISD team were pronounced. His ill-defined role has already been mentioned, yet he was criticized by many of the faculty for not assuming a definite stance in the organization. Presumably he might have been a valuable asset in the weeks following the reorganization when, in effect, both academic counselors directed their energies elsewhere to Training Groups and to the self-contained room. However, he had no directive or job definition within which to operate.

Statements cannot be made as to what his effectiveness might have been had his position been clarified; however, the fact remains that few attempts were made to "build him into the faculty" and, if anything, were discouraged. He, in turn, showed little or no initiative. This seems a significant issue in staff utilization at a time when extra personnel were needed. These events also had the effect of perpetuating misgivings about the dismissal of Kirkham.

Summary: The Continuous Coping with Unanticipated Consequences

At one point in our data analysis we thought of subtitling the book, "organizational change, the continuous coping with latent and unanticipated consequences." The thesis we perceived was that each resolution of a tremendously difficult and complex problem created a host of consequences, new problems which, at best, had only been partially foreseen. ISD's third structure was soon to give way with the dissolution of the self-contained class and the elimination of the Training Groups. Rumors were rife concerning the removal of some of the ISD staff and also the replacement of ISD staff with one or more of the Basic Skills staff. Neither of these events came to pass. However, the dissatisfaction with the instructional program and the continued serious interpersonal staff conflict and hostility led, on November 3, to another major reorganization of ISD into two teams. The gym was split into the North and the South. This separation was accompanied by the physical closing of a high gymnasium room divider and seemed of great importance. Later, further changes occurred as the North team split once again into a self-contained classroom and a team of two. The program in both sides of ISD included some "teaming" in the sense of joint planning and some departmentalization, although most of the instruction occurred in the context of the self-contained classroom.

The consequences varied from mundane to major. All seemed to pose special problems. Selections from the field notes illustrate them.

> One of the more striking aspects of the team meeting of ISD centered on the impact of the split into two teams on minor events, such as the availability of tempra paints, and whether they should be stored in a central unit, and whether there would be any left if they were stored in a central unit. This kept raising the "fair share" type of issue. The unit about which people organize their thoughts is now a team of three rather than an individual of one or a team of six. Books, supplies, passageways, time for lunch, entrances and exits, and the like, all need to be reconsidered and settled (11/7).

Several of the more significant consequences were noted a short time later.

> At the close of the day I had a chance to chat briefly with Liz, Kay, and Alec, individually and together. The North Side seems to have resolved its division into three relatively self-contained classrooms. This distresses Liz to a very great extent and Kay almost not at all. Kay foresees a shift coming shortly as they begin to move about for instructional purposes. As a language arts specialist, Liz, literally, is not prepared to teach elementary in all the subject matter areas and just does not know what to do. She has little conception of how to organize and to set up a science program or to organize and to set up a math program, and so forth. She is a very interesting example of someone trained for a speciality, and then the speciality collapses. Now she must be an all-purpose kind of person and she does not have the skills or the knowledge to carry it out. Earlier, when the teams had been compared on experience, it wasn't experience so much that was critical but, instead,

the lack of training on the part of some, especially Liz. Added to this is the fact that David has very strong preferences not to instruct at all; these two in combination give the team its unhappy flavor. They do have an important foothold on the discipline problem, which they may or may not realize. The classes were much more orderly on the North Side than I've ever seen them. This is especially true of Liz's group. Now would seem to be an optimal time for her to strike and develop "challenging" lessons. She apparently does not have the resources to do it; the school, the team, and Eugene are not there to provide it. Some very simple instructional help in a repetitive style of traditional teaching could get the instructional program off the ground (11/11).

The observers hypothesized further regarding the conceptual issues involved in the organizational change. Initially, the researchers phrased the problem as the impact of the internal system back on the external system. Or, in other terms, the impact of the informal organization on the formal structure or formal organization.

With almost no consideration to the explicit problems of the learning objectives for pupils, and of the means of reaching them, the reorganization was brought about because various team members had considerable difficulty working with each other. We should point out also that there was some concern about the departmentalization and the fact that this was a far cry from the team setup that most of them had desired initially. It redid the formal structure in the sense of eliminating academic counselors and making everyone an instructor. It shifted the movement of the students through the school day to a very different pattern. Specialization is retained with physical education but with practically no one else. Until things settle down to some extent, they will approach their teaching in this self-contained fashion. There are consequences in terms of the way kids go to lunch and with whom they eat. There are also consequences with regard to which students are working together. A variety of aspects of friendship structure patterns have been broken up. Several kids have commented within earshot of the observers that they wish they were with their friends or could they switch and be with their friends. Some of this is within North and South, and some of it is between North and South. Some of the same old language arts difficulties on the South Side recur with Jack and Alec, especially when Jack has to teach some of these things. Although the South Side three may have an easy and friendly social and ideological compatability, they may get hung up also on the specialization skills that do not fit the current situation.

The interplay in other schools and situations between the domination of the textbook for (1) a vehicle that puts you through areas that you do not know well, and (2) as an easy set of program decisions that then saves you time for other things, or just saves you time in terms of the heavy wear and tear of teaching, seems more and more cogent. Part of the parameters of this seem to be how many things can one be creative about and excited about at one time. Is it better to do a major exciting, innovative job in language arts and social studies and give a kind of ride in science and math, or in another two areas, or one or three, rather than in six or seven? This seems particularly true for a new teacher who has, I guess, a number of things to learn (11/11).

Thus, the third reorganization involved major changes in the organization of the faculty, resulting in essentially two teams of three. This division left the teams unbalanced in terms of faculty specialization and preparation. For example, the North team had no one highly skilled in math and science; the difficulties arising from this lack of specialization were coupled with the absence of standard textbooks. Problems of the allocation and storage of materials and supplies also increased. The erection of a wall between the two teams enhanced the difficulties relating to pupil movement. Access to lunch, rest rooms, and library facilities for students on the South was gained only by going through the full length of the North team area. Also the supervision of pupils became more difficult, since instead of all sharing responsibility in some way for the entire group, after the division, students could be designated as "ours" and "theirs." Thus, the third reorganization had far-reaching implications for spatial, interpersonal, and organizational variables. The systemic quality of the issues ranging from the alteration of the formal doctrine to role specialization of faculty is readily apparent.

Subsequent to the North-South division (split), the North team of three divided leaving a team of two and one self-contained room. The latter division had its source primarily in differences of belief about the degree of structure the instructional program should have. Two of the team members wanted a designated time for instruction in specific subject matter areas, but one wanted students to be permitted to schedule activities independently at any time After being unable to reach a compromise on procedure, they decided on the two-one split. The ramifications of this decision are indicated in a later chapter.

TRANSITION DIVISION

The Transition Division had a team of three teachers and approximately 90 students. In the temporary quarters they were provided with one large room and two additional classrooms. The summary notes indicate some of the primary concerns of the team in the first few days of the early part of the year.

The Transition teachers indicated at the end of the first day that nothing had gone right. The buses did not come until almost 5:00 P.M., which made it a very long workday because some of the students started arriving before 9:00 A.M. that morning.

The principal came by from ISD and said: "Don't ask how things went. Things can go no way except getting better; the situation is certainly not hopeless."

Both Meg and Claire agreed that possibly the next day they would use more traditional methods. The next day one of the team remarked, "Today we rule the students; whereas, yesterday they ruled."

Meg feels that not enough transfer exists between the work that goes on in the smaller groups and that which takes place in the group of 90. Yesterday, for one hour and a half, 60 of the students remained in one room while the others went out for reading courses. Meg and Claire feel that this (the activity of the 60) was busy work and a waste of time; however, Dan feels that it was not wasted, that it was a good experience for the students.

Claire mentioned that they may go toward the more traditional, at least, for a while. It seems that both she and Meg will move in that direction. It is difficult to locate quite where Dan is standing or really just what he wants to do. He seems to disagree with some of the things that they have been saying, especially concerning what they saw as busy work and the more traditional methods; however, thus far he has offered few alternatives from which to choose.

Claire feels that the students are never busy. Meg describes the noise as "chaos," and she feels that most of it is their fault, i.e. the fault of the teachers, because they are not quite sure what they are trying to do and they have not been able to facilitate the activities that they have initiated. Another remarks that she feels stupid when she stands before a group and talks and yet knows that no one hears because they are talking so loud themselves. She says that the activities have not been fitted to the children, and part of this is because they haven't really got to know the children. Their failure to know the children is attributed to groups that are too large and of inconsistent membership. She observed that the children do not know how to use time and that they are tired of not doing anything. They also feel that there is not enough carry over and new activity.

Meg and Claire want to break into smaller groups; however, Dan holds out for the larger group for a while. He thinks that there are certain tasks that can combat what has been causing the trouble in the larger groups. When asked about specific tasks, he suggests some kind of ditto materials possibly taken from second grade workbooks because they are not quite sure yet where the children are reading or at what level they are doing their other work. Claire pointed out that thus far there are not any library books. However, Dan went to find out that they will be able to use the library on Monday.

They discussed the reading activity that was held in the afternoon, and they finally concluded that things were so noisy that it really was not a fair test of the students' reading levels. Meg thinks that the teachers must know at what level students are reading before they try to prepare any seat work activities that are of any value other than providing busy work. Claire noted that students' shifting back and forth between teachers makes for difficulty in co-ordinating assignments.

Some discussion centered on the arrangement of desks and chairs and the allocation of space in the large room. Meg pointed out that one reason why they are not functioning any better than they are at the present time is because they have kids, as she says, "wall to wall" and that there are no interest centers as such; everyone is just thrown together.

This led to a further consideration of pupil groups and organization. At the close of a lengthy meeting, they decided to assign thirty students to each team member. At the same time, each noted that this division of students is contrary to the Kensington philosophy, which none of them is sure will work (9/10).

Thus the primary concerns of the Transition Division centered about the size and structure of pupil groups, the assessment of student skills, the types of activity, the allocation of space, and the coordination of teacher effort. However, the shortage of materials, few library books, and few text-books were also reflected in the instructional program that developed. But overshadowing the early days of the Transition Program were numerous comments made by the faculty who measured their present classroom prac-tices with what they had interpreted as the doctrine of an individualized educational program.

BASIC SKILLS DIVISION

Early in the second week of the summer workshop, Basic Skills had split into a team of two and a team of four. The reasons lay generally in staff disagreement and conflict concerning the significance of teaching experience, the importance and legitimacy of basal readers in an in-dividualized program, and several personal issues. As we have indicated, the work of the two teams was carried out independently.

Basic Skills: Team 4

The field notes at noon on the first day indicated that the team of four had an array of major and minor problems.

> I just spoke briefly to one of the teachers about her conception of the next few days or weeks. She said that she hopes they will be split into reading groups very shortly because she is all set and ready to go. She felt that the others in the subgroup of four were not yet ready to divide, but she feels there is no other way to proceed. She stated that she had suggested several times that they divide into reading groups either vertically or horizontally and that they begin the work of teaching an individualized reading program. She felt that the group had not picked up her cues and said that she could

only wait and hope that they would do so soon. It appears that the team will be forced into a division of this kind quite shortly. They were very much confused today and had a difficult time in holding the children's interest for a long period of time. Compounding their problems are the physical surroundings which are at best inconvenient. The lunch procedure promises to be one of the major difficulties. The time was switched about six times as Jean put it, and right now she did not know when it would be. When I left at 1:10 P.M. the first child had not yet entered. They had planned to get in as early as 12:30 or 12:40 (9/8).

Midweek. Notes from the middle of the week indicate that the Basic Skills Division was rapidly becoming aware of the nuances of team teaching.

The subgroup 4 seemingly gained more insight to facilitate the teaching of reading. They were to end their period at 10:45. At 10:45 the entire Team-4 had planned to go outside for P.E. activities. Sue came to Wanda, Jean, and Elaine and told them that their activities with the second grade were so helpful and beneficial that they did not wish to break at this time. They wanted to keep their group a while longer. Neither of the three teachers wished to oppose this, so they said, "All right, go ahead." This left the problem of what to do with the schedule that had been previously agreed on by the team at last night's meeting. Wanda said, "I'll take all 70 of the first graders outside for P.E." This left Elaine and Jean free to take a break. I spoke to them for 10 or 15 minutes about the problems attendant to this kind of spur-of-the-moment decision making. In this discussion both Jean and Elaine saw very clearly the problems that this brings about. Jean mentioned that this *lack* of structure bound her a great deal. I asked for further clarity. She said, in something close to this fashion, "In my own self-contained classroom, I had all the freedom in the world. I could extend a learning experience, or shorten it, or cut it out completely if I wished. Here, I'm forced into a rigid schedule." She said that it seems very odd and yet the freedom that they wanted was the thing that inhibited them and made them more rigid. Elaine agreed that 25 children and a self-contained classroom would be far superior for the very objectives that they wish to achieve. They both felt that decisions as the one Sue and Chris had made were sometimes beneficial to the group making the decision, but it certainly disrupted matters for the rest of the children. Elaine gave the example that perhaps a group of 15 children were involved in a very meaningful learning experience and, therefore, the teacher of these 15 would simply arbitrarily state that the period would be extended for an extra 30 minutes. Although this may be fine for the group of 15, the group of 55 would have to find some makeshift busy work to kill time.

Last night, the Basic Skills group met after the day's sessions. All seemed very tired and very confused. The bus schedule was in a state of turmoil. They were ready for the children to leave at about 3:50 P.M. but had to wait until at least 4:30 or 4:40 before they actually cleared the building. After the children were gone the group met in subgroups of two and four. Chris met with the subgroup of four. After some informal discussion of how confused the day's activities were, Chris suggested that they were all rather "wilted" and that perhaps they had better meet in the morning. Wanda would have none of this. She said, "Absolutely not. I will not go home until I know what I'm going to do tomorrow. I will not go through another day like today." The main discussion centered on grouping or not grouping the children and what type of group to use. Wanda held out very firmly for the need for reading groups on ability levels. She suggested that they separate first graders from second graders and then group within each grade. Jean and Sue were not quite ready to break down into first and second grades. They seemed to want to hold on to a more novel approach to education but do not quite know how. Chris felt they could continue the present division for a few days at least until they had given the children a chance to settle down. Wanda was pushing very hard for a division in ability groupings for the next day. Elaine seemed sure that today had not worked well but did not quite know how best to proceed. Some of the disscussion centered on whether the children should have assigned desks—Sue and Jean holding out for a freer home base. Wanda was not overly impressed with tradition at this point; she just wanted to get some teaching done. The group finally decided to spend one hour in this morning session divided into first and second grades for a language arts period.

Chris and Sue will take the second grade group and have a large reading group. They will be doing free reading with some discussion of the material. Elaine, Jean, and Wanda will take the first graders in random selection and attempt to evaluate their readiness or reading level. I feel pretty sure that Wanda will continue to push for ability groupings even within the grade level; however, it will take a little more time to evaluate the children and to divide them in this manner. They are still holding on to their random groupings across grades (9/9).

Later notes indicate that there were some continuing problems with grouping. Also great effort was made to avoid the fate of a self-contained classroom.

Some summary thoughts concerning last night's Basic Skills team meeting. Jean appeared to give the most leadership in last night's meeting. She threw out many of the big questions that needed to be discussed. It seemed that once issues were brought out, they were not followed to conclusion. This seems to stem, again in part, from everyone's inability to follow a point to conclusion for fear of not getting group consensus or some other such group process problem. The Basic Skills subgroup 4 seemed to stack up somewhat in this fashion. Wanda, Elaine, and Jean, all three, seemed very dissatisfied with their own classroom work thus far. Elaine and Wanda seem to make statements in unison on several occasions that reflected their views of their own deficiencies up to this point. Wanda is quite convinced that it is because of the unworkability of the four-man team. She has tried to insert this on several occasions but received little support. Elaine also feels it is not working but does not seem quite as sure as Wanda that it cannot work. Several statements were made to the effect that they had subscribed to this type of philosophy for several years and, in fact, were much more successful in the traditional self-contained classroom than they have been in attempting to implement this at Kensington. Sue seems to steer clear of any removal of the subgroup of four. She does not want to get tied to a two-man team. She seemed to dread even more the thought of a self-contained classroom. Jean's position is a striving for some workable plan for their group that would not mean self-contained classrooms and also would not mean departmentalization. She wants a little flexibility in that she could utilize the strength of another teacher; however, she deplores the rigidity of attempting to conform to a fixed time schedule. Jean seems to have the right questions, but seemingly no one has the right answers. Chris is quite content with the way things are going and, in fact, said that they had made a lot of progress and that she would like to work out a few of the bugs in the program but, in general, she thought that things had gone quite well.

Wanda appeared quite concerned with the general behavior of the children. She stated last night that they were wilder than any children she had ever seen. In part, she wants to have more control of the children in their walking from classroom to classroom, in going to the lunchroom, to the bathroom, and the like. Sue expressed her interest in having no part of this arrangement. She said that the children will simply learn, and very soon, that they will want to walk from one class to another. Wanda is still most concerned about the image of teacher as controller and, as such, wishes a great deal more structure. Chris mentioned that the Basic Skills subgroup 2 had a much smoother operation. She noted that the teachers led the children from class to class and had the children sitting down quietly before they left them. She didn't seem to place any value judgment on this (9/15).

Thus, in addition to the limited temporary physical facilities and the coordination of their schedules with the ones of the high school in which they were temporarily located, Basic Skills-4 were not without their differences with respect to ideas about student grouping, teaching method, and choice of subject matter. As is indicated in the notes, the form that teacher-pupil organization would take was not delineated in detail at the outset of the Basic Skills-4 program. Varying sentiments were expressed about possible alternatives; they ranged from defending the self-contained classroom to advocating the elimination of fixed time schedules, which were viewed as rigid and inflexible. Also the self-evaluations of their performance as a team were just as disparate; some indicated approval of the program, but others felt that much improvement, if not revamping, was needed.

Basic Skills: Team 2

On September 7, the day before the pupils arrived, the research staff summarized and interpreted their views of Basic Skills Team-2.

> Subteam 2 seems to be working quite smoothly on the surface. Carla is a strong teacher, having taught 27 years in the elementary and, especially, in the primary field. She has never had a year off from teaching since she began as a two-year graduate 27 years ago. This lengthy experience has given her the feeling, and perhaps rightfully so, that she has experienced about every aspect of teacher-pupil behavior that is possible. She is quite firm and set in her ways and makes most of the decisions for this subgroup.
>
> Mary at times seems quite firm and able to make up her own mind and yet, at other times, seems quite willing to go along with Carla. Both have little patience for the so-called "discussion or process" method of the workshop. Both feel that the larger team meetings are a waste of time and both feel that much more can be done by working in small groups. I feel that this subgroup of two will have little contact with the other subteam of four in the Basic Skills Division. It will be interesting if the group that supposedly is departing the farthest from the Institutional Plan will perhaps work the smoothest and most efficiently. It will depend a great deal on how busy Eugene is with the other phases of the school program, especially the Independent Study Division, whether or not he will have time to supervise the Basic Skills. I am sure that he would not be pleased with the fact that they will be conducting what very well could be a double self-contained classroom atmosphere. I also feel that this subgroup of two will have a very definite plan in mind by the time the entire school gets into the new Kensington building. It will be very difficult at this time to revamp and to reorganize the Basic Skills into any other division than it now has, namely, a subgroup of four and a subgroup of two.
>
> This group will house all the pupils in their section in one of the classrooms having 60 desks in one room. They will then use the second room that is assigned to them for small group activity, such as reading groups, creative art, music, and the like. It would appear that these two teachers will work rather effectively together, introducing a good "traditional" atmosphere for the children (9/7).

In effect, the predictions were borne out. Number work began in the first days and beginning work in set theory of the new math was not far behind. The basal reading materials, *On Your Way,* were distributed and in use very quickly also. The program was academic oriented but traditional. Later conversations solidified the coherence of predictions, teaching style, and points of view.

> Yesterday after sessions on Thursday I spent some time talking to Carla and Mary. Both of them feel that the rest of the Basic Skills plus Transition and

Independent Study seem to be going in a direction of which they do not approve. It seems that neither of these two teachers would strongly support the Kensington philosophy if confronted by one of the patrons. Mary had compared the vagueness of Kensington with the solidity of her own child in the Jefferson School. She stated that he had come home with a sheet which very clearly outlined the goals and the expectations that they hope to achieve. By contrast she felt Kensington had not done this in any way. I attempted to remain neutral by stating that I did not know which of the two I would prefer. Evidently they read my statement to be a criticism of Kensington's vagueness and both laughed out loud at this comment. Carla considers herself a middle-of-the-roader and stated that she has been the same type of person in her self-contained classroom for the last 10 years or so.

I feel that both Carla and Mary's having taught fourth grade last year poses certain real problems for their adjustment to the first grade. Mary stated that she was very tired and tense working with the little folks. She said that she did not realize that so much lead up was necessary. She stated, "They cannot even write their own name and I even had to teach them how to use a jump-rope outside." She commented that she wishes she had stayed in the Transition Division as she had previously wanted to (9/11).

Thus, subteam 2 developed independently of the rest of the Basic Skills Division and, in effect, apart from the total school both in terms of actual classroom behavior and ideology. Communication between the subteams was quite limited, and Eugene focused little attention on the subteam. Later the split into two subteams came to be rationalized as a facet of the doctrine, with team 2 described as an expanded self-contained classroom. For whatever reasons, it was a characteristic of Kensington and its doctrine that such wide variation in structure and method were permitted.

SOME EARLY INTERPRETATIONS

Although the field notes contain a wealth of further detail on the fall day-to-day events of Kensington, it seems more feasible at this point to say a few general things that later will be considered in the more detailed analysis.

From the beginning, as is pointed out in an earlier description of the three temporary physical plants, study and instruction were somewhat altered and structured by the makeshift facilities. A significant amount of materials and equipment had not arrived by the opening of school. This deficit was especially critical at Kensington where textbooks and "traditional" teacher helps were discouraged which, in turn, placed even greater emphasis on para-instructional supplies, increased the pressure on the materials specialist, and heightened faculty tension in the face of a shortage of materials. The latter was especially important, since the faculty was to serve as the means to create the majority of the learning tasks to be used with pupils.

Attempts at coordination of bus times with the existing district schools resulted in uncertainties, long waits, and growing parental disapproval. With no formally agreed-on procedure whereby students were to be dismissed, the variability of the schedule emphasized internal problems in the ISD. With 200 children in one room, this lack of uniformity increased faculty tensions. Coupled with this was the fact that once decisions were made, members failed to adhere to them, and in other instances all were not informed as to the action to take. As becomes clearer elsewhere in this book, often when there was ample access to and knowledge about facilities and materials, deficiencies in the structure precluded their satisfactory use.

Another factor that required adjustment on the part of both faculty and students was the noise level. It was high in all of the divisions, and the staff was unable to speak loudly enough to be heard by all of the children. Initially, in the Basic Skills Division, teachers had to do the reading instead of the students. This minimized opportunities for pupil oral reading. In the Transition Division three whistles were in evidence, and in the ISD Liz, among others, was losing her voice and she "couldn't hear herself." Even though he expected it to be a problem, Tom noted that, "the noise level was a good bit higher than he had anticipated." In a later section we consider more fully issues such as "openness to extraneous stimuli."

Combined with the difficulties in quelling the noise was the sheer number of children that each staff member under the initial organizational plan was required to contact and to come to know. Learning the names of 200 children and something about each, as would be expected from the "usual" elementary teacher, seemed an insurmountable task at Kensington.

An early and continuing problem was that the majority of children were unable to devise and to carry out individual plans of work. Their being capable of doing this was crucial to the success of "individualized" study— an integral part of the Kensington program. This deficit, along with a lack of materials and limited teacher time and preparation, took an early toll and, in turn, was an incentive for the poor use of pupil time that both parents and some faculty came to view as a "waste." In addition, the children lacked adequate skills to work together in groups, which was another necessary capability to function well at Kensington. The wandering and milling about in the gym continued and were accompanied by clay throwing, paper air planes, further misuse of materials (most usually confined to individual tables), and a general restlessness.

Time demands of the program also were increasingly great. Since this is discussed in other parts of the book, a brief mention is sufficient here. Team, subteam, and planning meetings began to take several hours a week before or after school and in the evenings. The Transition Division, in part, was unable to find the time to plan enough activities for a large group and resolved the problem by dividing the students into three groups.

Another area that contributed to creating disillusionment was the repeated and continuing dilemma of reorganization. The sources of the reorganizations lay generally in some of the problems mentioned previously and in parental reaction. Conditions that preceded the various organizational modifications and their apparent "failure," in part, made for dissatisfaction and a lowering of morale. The frequent reorganizations emphasized movement from specialists to generalists among the staff. This was in conflict. with the original positions they were given when hired.

We observed previously that many were selected for their specialities, skills, and training for secondary education. Yet a few weeks after school began, faculty members with at best two areas of competency were teaching a variety of subjects as would have been the case in a self-contained classroom. Other than its being an unfortunate use of manpower, this condition deviated from the original plan for the school and added to the growing faculty disappointment and consequent morale problems.

By October, much of the August and September enthusiasm was partially translated into disillusionment, either of a personal or a team nature. A number of internal and external facets of the organization were instrumental in altering the initial hope. Several in the ISD were very discouraged; two members of the Basic Skills team were thinking of quitting at midterm. In addition to this, the notes indicate that "almost everybody is giving serious thought to not coming back next year" (10/23). As the introductory epilogue points out, this is in fact what did happen.

There were many reasons for the early despair. Some of the faculty were more vocal and the basis of their grievances more easily observable. Kay is recorded as "very tired and discouraged." She's sick of the dust, dirt, the confusion, and the lack of order. She's also tired of the noise. One teacher was asked whether or not she had talked with the principal. She replied, "No, not directly; it's his baby, and you can't tell a person that his baby is no good." She was also displeased with the departmentalized organization that the ISD had developed and "would just as soon have her own self-contained classroom."

David was also experiencing progressive disillusionment and disenchantment. He noted three primary areas of dissatisfaction: (1) the shift from process, (2) the loss of the student T-groups, and (3) the inability of the team to function as a group. His vehemence against formal instruction and his refusal to "teach" in the usual sense of the word was known by the faculty; however, our discussion clearly shows the strength of his feelings was put to the test by the third reorganization.

Eugene was also troubled. His discontent centered primarily on four areas, none of which were mutually exclusive: (1) the "sterile program" being offered in some of the classes, (2) his personal anxiety, (3) the deficiencies of the faculty, and (4) his relationship with one of the consultants. He saw the problems as crossing division lines but as stopping short of encompassing any one entire division. At this time he described his feelings as those of "general apprehension and anxiousness" (10/14). A week later he again noted that he was not "functioning very well" and "was not getting as much done as he had hoped to do." One specific item expresses some of his general feelings. In commenting about the interpretation and feedback of materials from the recordings on the consultant's research projects, Eugene indicated that they would probably have to be done by him. Although he was trained and competent to do this, when he was feeling tense and nervous this got communicated also, and the situation did not go so well.

His feelings about the inadequacies of the staff were also still much in evidence. He specifically mentioned one teacher and her inability as an instructor or leader. Later he was considering her release. What seems to be of importance is that little attempt was made to help the faltering team members. In fact, the several reorganizations placed some staff members at an even greater disadvantage.

Eugene's discontent with Roberts, the consultant, began early in their relationship and continued until the relationship was terminated during the second semester. Eugene notes that their rapport was "not good" and that the conversations "flitted around from topic to topic, rather than seriously moving in and attacking basic issues." He reported that he confronted Roberts with questions of bad rapport, and that they "could never get anywhere because of that," and that he wanted to "talk about his feelings" in regard to this. He perceived Roberts as listening only briefly and then shifting the conversation to something else.

These then are some of the sources of early discouragement experienced by the staff. Following the thread of these early difficulties through the remaining months of school, to the demise of some and the irresolution of others, indicates that one of the overshadowing issues was the departure of the school from the expectations stated in the doctrine. The notes confirm that most of the faculty expressed concern and, in some respects, disappointment over their failure to adhere more closely to the doctrine. The subsequent organizational development in light of these sentiments is described in later chapters.

THE MOVE TO THE NEW BUILDING

Introduction. On Wednesday, November 25, the staff bulletin contained this item:

"Moving date. Rapid progress is being made on the building, but there are still many things to be done before it will be ready for pupils. Although we may start moving some things in next week, it does not appear that the building will be ready for pupils until the following week. No definite date has been set, but we shall see."

The next bulletin, No. 24, the following Tuesday, carried the specifications:

"Moving arrangements. As of this moment (1:52 P.M.) plans have been made to move the office and the ISD into the new building on Thursday and Friday of this week. Cabinetry and equipment will be moved Thursday and Friday morning, and pupil desks and chairs will be moved Friday afternoon. ISD pupils will be dismissed at 1:00 P.M. Friday. They should be instructed to take all personal belongings and books, etc., home with them.

"The same arrangements will be followed for the BSD and TD the following week, December 10 and 11."

The bare announcements of the move convey little of the flesh and blood of the move itself. The children were engaged in busy work; the literal aches and pains of the staff were evident. The interplay of long-term and short-term commitments was visible also. The notes indicate the tenor of these events.

As I looked around the room the kids seemed to be engaged in a whole variety of busy-work type activities and holding actions. Some of them were working with SRA materials, some were watching ETV or films and some of them were listlessly sitting. Others were playing magic-square type games. Liz had on the overhead projector a picture of the Kensington School and was, in effect, telling them about where they would be going and what they would do. John was still looking kind of depressed about the move. He's not going to teach his Transition PE class this afternoon so that he can come over and get his materials and equipment arranged. He also commented that Tom has sprained his back and has some difficulties.[5]

Kay told me also that there was some discussion about whether the Saturday team meeting would be at the new building or whether it would be in the central offices as originally designated. She's eager to get over and begin work on the setup for Monday. John also talked in that same vein. Kay did not

[5] This was a recurrence of "back problems" which had plagued him some years before and which were to be troublesome during the next few months.

have any idea what was going to be on the agenda of the staff meeting and it was her hope that it was not going to take all morning.

In Transition, Claire raised several times questions as to why the kids were not excused from school and time given to the move. Mrs. Beacon commented that the most desirable time would be on Monday. She just does not see how they are going to be ready for the kids then.

It's now 3:00 P.M. and I'm leaving the new building for the day. David just came over a few minutes ago, and Liz and Kay came by for a few minutes more recently. I caught part of a brief discussion among Liz, Kay, Tom, and Irma. The topic centered on the problem of the instructional areas and, initially, whether there would be chairs and tables there. Tom said "eventually" but he didn't know whether they'd be ready by Monday. Liz, with a very strained and nervous laugh, commented that she was interested in eventually but was concerned about Monday. This led into a discussion of the utilization of the areas. Irma suggested that she and Alec and Jack had talked about the possibility of having one area belong to one team and the other area belong to the other team and share the third space—on a sign-up basis. There are some potential problems in this because the Transition Division apparently is to have access to those extra spaces also. One obvious solution would be for each of the teams to have one additional space. This will have some disadvantages in that the North team has two subteams—David versus Kay and Liz—and Transition has in reality two subteams—Dan versus Meg and Claire.

Eugene had a telephone conversation with the principal of an adjacent school. He was discussing the custodian, which they shared, and whether it would be possible to have him come over to Kensington tomorrow morning to help arrange furniture.

The teachers are scrubbing out cabinets. Irma has a bucket of soapy water and is working on them. David has been working with a screwdriver and a pair of pliers trying to get the shelving back in shape in the cabinets. During the loading and unloading of materials and furniture everything had been piled over in the center of the ISD area in the new building and the teachers were not free to have one person on the sending end and one on the receiving end to allocate what goes where and to whom things belong. Consequently the men, when they brought it, could not put it where it belonged; instead, they just let it plop into one big pile. Similarly, people are doing things such as cleaning cabinets and repairing shelves when the basic job seemingly ought to be to get the furniture moved into some kind of rough, approximate area, and the details can be cleaned up later or on another day. They will not be at all ready for the children's furniture when it arrives in the next 30 minutes or so. John is having difficulty finding space. When I saw him later, he had kind of a slaphappy mood about him and was looking over the basement room, which was full of paint buckets, a saw, and some other equipment and was a long cry from being cleaned up. It would be my guess that two men could not clean the thing out in the next two hours this afternoon.

Another item concerns David's asking the kids to volunteer, if they wished, to help tomorrow afternoon. He said about twelve were going to be coming in. He was concerned about what their parents would think of their coming in to help fix up the school. My reaction to him was that the parents would not mind at all if the kids wanted to. The point I didn't raise, and the one that seems most significant, will be the attitudes of the other teachers. My guess is that some will be unhappy just having the kids around and that others will be envious in that they did not get any kids to come in and help them.

Apropos of the whole organizational structure, and the affect toward it, it's appropriate to observe that neither of the student teachers, I guess, nor the permanent substitute showed up to help. On the one hand, you would think that they would want to and, on the other hand, one would think that they ought to. Perhaps the basic truth of it is the reflection on the satisfactions and the cohesion of the team, or the lack thereof (12/4).

Staff Reservations. Although the staff reactions to the move had a general cast of frustration and apprehension, there were individual nuances. For instance, one teacher commented to the observer:

She expressed a personal and private opinion which she had not talked about to the rest of the staff concerning what she calls respect for property. This arose when I made a comment about how pretty the building was and she returned that she felt unhappy about letting the kids in the building for fear of what they will do to it. She considers respect for property as one of the fundamental aspects of our society and she views these kids as not having it. Interpretively, to me, what she's saying suggests that important impact of the nature of the freedom that they have given the children and how this has led to a misuse and wasting of materials and resources and to the lack of concern about the "nice things" that they have in the school. This point should be made in conjunction with one that is in the notes earlier somewhere about how different I saw these kids as compared to the downtown kids at the beginning of the year, especially in regard to their hostility and to their destructive behavior, which I saw here as much less (12/4).

The overall reaction of the ISD staff was stated this way in the notes late on Friday afternoon.

The contrast in the sentiments of the professional staff to the sentiments of the nonprofessional staff, Mrs. Beacon, Arthur, and Inez, is one of a kind of grouchy gloominess versus childish excitedness in the latter. It ought to be a very happy occasion and, instead, it is a very painful one, and this seems a very real tragedy (12/4).

The Children's Reactions. The notes during the afternoon of the first day, Monday, December 7, indicate the children's response to the new quarters.

In summary, all in all it seemed as if the move went very smoothly. The basic reaction I have about the children and their reactions to the building is one of high excitement and high positive affect toward the building. The building looks new, it feels new, it smells new. It is difficult for me to take out my own excitement and parcel it out from the reactions of the children. As I watched them, they were eager to have a tour of the building, they were eager to see the different parts, they explored around, they wanted to know all about it. The carpets were well received in that the children kicked off their shoes and walked around in their stocking feet a good bit of the time (12/7).

Continuities in program and teacher style occurred as well in conjunction with the new physical quarters.

Only a minimal amount of academic work occurred in the South Side group. Jack had on the board, as I left, an assignment for a theme on their first day at shcool. At lunch he had commented that they had done a little oral reading. The lunch hour went amazingly well from my point of view.[6] I had expected considerable confusion over this. The children were allowed to go to lunch a little before noon, shortly after the lines were set up, and they tended to go by class and by small numbers within classes. There seemed to be no difficulty with this at all. Mostly, they ate back in their classrooms under the supervision of their teachers, although there was some flexibility in this, since Linda, one of the student teachers, ate with Irma's group while Irma ate up in the curriculum lab. There were no long lines nor jam ups at the tables. They are eating 45 minutes to an hour before they did at the other building, which will make a very, very long afternoon. David's group already is behaving as they have in the other building, and they have been relatively unruffled by the change. His mode of operation looks a good bit like what Gouldner was calling the indulgency pattern in the gypsum plant. As I watched them this morning, there were one or two, especially a boy named George, who spent a good bit of time watching educational television, which David had running almost continuously. Another couple or several children were painting and doing art activities. Another one or two were working on SRA materials and a few more were wandering here and there and a few were working with cycloteachers. It's going to take a very careful and quantitative check and count to find out the number of kids who were engaging in academic-type activities and were busy this way as opposed to those who are just spending time. Liz's bunch remains the noisiest and the most "out of control" of the children (12/7).

In short, the two groups just mentioned were examples of the variation in pupil behavior that existed at Kensington. Overtly this aspect of the social structure changed little with the move to the new building.

[6] As we describe later, the lunch program was individualized also; no cafeteria or lunchroom existed in the new school. The problems in the flow of pupils increased dramatically as we describe later.

The Arrival of Basic Skills and Transition. On Monday, December 14, the total staff and all the children were in the new building. In general, it was an exciting time for these pupils and the staff as well.

> The day began surprisingly well. The children in Basic Skills and Transition were very excited and were pleased to be in the new school. This seemed to be reflected in the things that they did, the excitement with which they walked around, the questions they asked about the building, and the efficacy of the implied threats that "if you are not quiet, you won't be able to walk with us," which several of the staff used. There was a consistent lack of traffic in the perception core except right up to the end. Just before I left, the Basic Skills kids were out there with Chris and were looking for library books. I took a trip through ISD before I left, really before I had my last cup of coffee, and the view suggested that most of the people were pushing hard toward instructional programming (12/14).

On the following day, the flavor is maintained:

> Lunch was kind of fun in that people kept adding to and leaving the group as they had free time. It started out with Liz alone, then Meg and I arrived; shortly thereafter Liz left and she was replaced by Claire and later Jean and Wanda and Kay, and then alternately David, Linda, and Pat joined. Jean thought today was going better than yesterday because yesterday she was still suffering from a long and fatiguing weekend. Her patience ran out on her yesterday afternoon, she said. Wanda sees today as not better than yesterday because the kids have lost their focus and nobody seems to know where they are going or what they are doing. Much joking back and forth; for instance, when Wanda and Sue and Jean were planning and arranging schedules for this afternoon, Claire made a comment very close to "last minute planning, huh?" Wanda talked about all the problems with the red tape and the rules in terms of trying to get things done. If she can't find a wastepaper basket and some other things, she's going to "steal" one. Meg was furious with one of the aides who would hardly budge in terms of doing some work for her. As she put it to Jean, she cannot understand how the Basic Skills staff could have lived with her for 3 or 4 months as they have at Basic Skills. She said she never would have gotten anything if Tom had not come by. There was additional good humor as Dan came by wondering if Meg had seen his lunch. She told him where it was. Later she told the rest of us that she spent 5 to 10 minutes this morning going around from child to child trying to find out whose lunch this bag was. Later Dan indicated that the kids were teasing that Terrifico had eaten it. Sue was by, scrounging lunch off of several of the people, since she is on a diet and does not want to eat, yet she's hungry.
>
> Wanda showed us how to cut out and make an elephant out of candycane and paper. It was quite novel and quite tricky. She learned this at a local nursery school. During this same interlude Meg commented that she had a number of different kinds of patterns and that the others in Basic Skills were

quite welcome to borrow them. This kind of trading seems to be an important part of the school. It extends the notion of the increased repertory as part of the experienced teacher personality. If they could once get things organized, this sharing of ideas could increase at a great rate and be most helpful to the newer teachers and to those with less skills in several areas (12/15).

The issues surrounding both formal and informal helping relationships are a part of the later analysis. Time limitations for materials construction by the staff, even with frequent exchanges in some of the teams were, as the later discussion indicates, quite severe.

The Detached Perspective: A Summary. Methodologically, we instituted, by chance as we recall, an interesting procedure. From time to time, a research assistant who had been involved intimately in the first weeks of the summer workshop returned to see old friends and to observe the developments of the school. Although we did not realize it at the time, this provided a different kind of data. Although our major efforts were on the minutiae of social psychological analysis, we obtained a view of the proverbial forest instead of the trees. Illustratively, the notes contained these comments during the first week of the move into the new building.

> My quick conversation with Paul centered on his feeling, (1) that they had no program yet, and (2) that their spirit was broken. Both of these points seem to me to be well taken. He commented also on sitting in on a discussion of religion with some of the kids, and the teacher was raising kinds of questions about who created God, and the like, which Paul saw as "risky" in the public schools. Several of the teachers apologized to him for what they were doing. In arithmetic they are going back to addition, subtraction, multiplication, and division in that they did not understand what had been occurring and they thought they would begin all over again. He commented that he sat in on one group while the teacher happened to be out of the room and the kids were wild and into all kinds of trouble. He commented also on the list of rules that apparently have staggered everybody in his eyes. As we stood outside and talked, the kids were going to and from lunch; some of them were in their slippers and some of them were in their stocking feet, and none of them had coats on (12/10).

THE EXTENSION OF FORMALIZATION: SCHOOL RULES

Introductory Comments

The English language contains a number of words that reflect a common core of meaning: customs, mores, social norms, rules, and laws. The essence of these terms refers to the expectations of members of a group, organization, or society that other members of the group will behave in certain ways. These expectations will vary in degree of formality; that is, social norms are commonly understood and rarely verbalized, but laws often are written and codified in considerable detail. Variations occur in the genesis of the understandings. In some instances they accumulate gradually both in acceptance and formality, as has common law. In some instances, the expectations as rules are established by fiat by a powerful individual or subgroup. The breadth of activities covered by the mores and laws varies considerably from group to group. Finally, the amount and kinds of surveillance, and the amount and kinds of rewards and punishments for conformity and deviation varies also.

In a formal organization, expectations in the form of rules function to facilitate goal attainment. In many instances, the rules are functional equivalents to orders or directives that have their genesis in goal attainment. This can introduce a variety of complexities when there are multiple and potentially conflicting goals, or when priorities among goals are not established. If goals are vague, ambiguous, or abstract, similar problems may arise. Furthermore, if the organization is to be democratically governed and administered, questions of who makes what decisions about which rules become critical also. Finally, the broader norms, meta norms, or "rules about rules" become a complicating context for any particular rule. For instance, Kensington's mandate and formal doctrine in accenting freedom and innovation minimized rules and traditions.

Changes at Kensington

Most school personnel, in their franker moments, will speak of rules and control of pupils as a necessity. In its simplest form, control means that pupils comply with school rules and the directives of teachers.[7] The notes on December 9 indicate that problems of compliance to often unstated standards of conduct were occurring and, also, that the individual faculty members held varying standards.

> Both of the men commented, on the way out, about the noise level that existed in the perception core. At that time, by a later count I made, there were about 60 kids working down there.
>
> The kids were rather wild and much more like the first two weeks of school over at the junior high building. Part of this is because the several teachers are out today. Irma and Liz are ill, and Jack is at some kind of a meeting.
>
> David's kids are roaming quite freely, and he lets them come and go as they please. One teacher told me that on Monday David's kids were wandering all over the building (12/9).

[7] For an extended analysis of this phenomenon in a slum classroom see Smith and Geoffrey (1968).

These problems, which were present all fall, were to culminate in a major policy change, the principal's issuance of two sets of rules and regulations. The first occurred on December 8 and the second on December 14. They are included here as Figures 5.1 and 5.2. A careful examination of the "general policies and operating procedures" and the "administrative regula-

---

KENSINGTON ELEMENTARY SCHOOL

December 8

General Policies and Operating Procedures

A. Food Service Program

1. Lunch will be served to the BSD team 2 at 11:00 by the door to room 101. BSD team 4 will be served at 11:10 between the doors to rooms 105 and 106. The serving table will be placed in the Perception Center by room 108 from 11:30 to 1:00 for use by pupils in the TD and ISD.

2. Pupils in the ISD should use the outside walkway and corridor room 108 in going to and from the serving area, except in severe weather, in which case they may pass through the Perception Center.

3. Waste cans and tote boxes for the return of lunch trays will be placed on the outside walkway just outside doors 102, 106, 110, 114, and 117, except in severe weather, in which case they will be placed just inside these doors. Lunch waste, sacks, or milk cartons should not be placed in classroom wastebaskets.

4. Pupils who desire to go home for lunch may do so with the written permission of the parent. Such permission may be granted on a continuing basis if so stated in writing by the parent. Pupils who go home for lunch should not be gone for more than 50 minutes. Pupils may not eat lunch at public eating places other than school. Pupils may eat at the home of a friend only if permission is granted in writing by the parents of both pupils involved. Pupils who leave the school for lunch must not loiter or play on the way to or from lunch, and must abide by high standards of safety.

5. Rest and relaxation periods, but not physical activity, may be scheduled for pupils after lunch.

B. Perception Center

1. The Perception Center should be used in a quiet, dignified, and purposeful manner.

2. Doors from the Perception Center into learning suites should ordinarily be kept closed.

3. Staff members should use discretion in the numbers of pupils sent to the Perception Center. No more than ten pupils should ordinarily be sent to the Perception Center without first consulting with the materials coordinator or library clerk.

4. Permission slips signed by the teacher should be used by pupils who come to the Perception Core. These forms, available from the materials coordinator, may be filled out by pupils for the teacher's signature. Forms should be retained by pupils while using the Perception Center, and turned in at the charging desk upon leaving.

Figure 5.1 Policy statement issued by the principal.

C. Outside Areas

1. Since there is no grass on the playground, pupils should not use or walk on the school grounds until authorization has been given.

2. Arrangements for the use of the covered play shelter will be developed by the physical education resource person.

3. Teachers may take pupils on walks around the covered walkway for outside physical activity.

4. As soon as the condition of the grounds is suitable, the use of outside areas for instructional purposes will be encouraged.

5. Pupils must not climb over the railings onto the covered play shelter.

6. Pupils must not climb on the solar screens or smoke stack. Infractions of this rule will be considered extremely serious whether during or after school hours.

D. Arrival at School

1. Pupils should ordinarily arrive at school no more than fifteen minutes prior to the official beginning of the school day.

2. Pupils will be allowed to arrive early upon written request of the parent when there are legitimate reasons for doing so.

3. Pupils shall be expected to engage in serious and purposeful activities immediately upon arrival at school.

E. Miscellaneous

1. Pupils should ordinarily enter and leave the building by way of the outside doors of their assigned areas.

2. No more than two pupils at a time should ordinarily be in the rest room adjacent to the Perception Center.

3. Pupils are not allowed to go to the Curriculum Center.

4. Pupils should not go to the nerve center or projection room unless permission is specifically granted because of extenuating circumstances.

5. Pupils should not ordinarily go to the office without permission from the teacher.

6. Pupils are allowed in the basement arts and crafts area only during times scheduled by the creative arts resource person or when accompanied by a teacher.

7. Pupils are not allowed in the mechanical equipment room.

F. General Pupil Behavior

1. Pupils should never talk loudly nor yell anywhere in the building.

2. Reasonable quietness should be maintained in the covered play shelter.

3. There should be no running, fighting, scuffling, or "horseplay" anywhere in the building.

4. Pupils are responsible to all adult personnel and are expected to be courteous and cooperative with them.

5. Pupils are expected to use all time profitably.

Implementation of Policies and Procedures

1. Recognizing the need for institutional procedures and normative standards for behavior in any productive society, willing compliance with the policies and regulations of Kensington School is expected from all members of the school.

2. The staff of Kensington School attempts always to operate openly, rationally,

Figure 5.1 (*Continued*)

and democratically. Should policies or regulations ever be considered inappropriate, efforts should be made through proper means to bring about changes. Compliance should be made, however, until such changes are brought about.

3. Staff members of Kensington School should strive continuously to help pupils understand and abide by institutional standards.

4. The infraction of rules should always be dealt with in positive and dignified ways. Rational conferences with pupils who break rules generally serve as an effective means for working out problems.

5. Staff members are encouraged to seek the assistance of the principal in handling serious or chronic behavior problems. In general, this should be done not by sending pupils to the office, but by reporting the problem to the principal. Detailed oral or written reports should be given in cases of serious misbehavior. In cases of chronic misbehavior, the principal should be given a written record of the misbehavior, reporting merely what infractions occurred and when. Such reports will be evaluated by the principal, and generally followed by pupil conferences, conferences with the parent, or exclusion from school. Corporal punishment may be administered in rare circumstances.

Figure 5.1   (*Continued*)

tions" reveals a number of problems in the relationships among administrators, teachers, pupils, and parents in the varying activities in which Kensington was engaged. The significance of the statements is severalfold. First, they were perceived as a major "retreat" from Kensington's mandate and early expressions of the formal doctrine. A brief note from a Transition team meeting illustrates the point:

> This was a team meeting in which Eugene was present and at which time he tried to, or did give, the rules, that he had previously given to the Independent Study Division and to the Basic Skills Division. Dan sees many of these as incongruent to the attitudes that were expressed earlier (12/9).

Second, the origin of the statement of rules was perceived to be from the principal's office. In the context of a more general concern about the school and its program the notes record:

> I do notice a change and a lack of spirit in the overall staff. Whereas earlier there appeared to be hope that we were beginning to move toward a program of education, it now seems that most of the teachers are quite dejected and do not feel that any progress is presently being made. David, at times, seems optimistic about individual phases of his "program" but seems to lose his interest quickly when he discusses the program more generally. It also appears that staff members have lost any faith they had previously in a democratically functioning staff. Several examples of this occurred. One teacher explained to me the new set of rules that had been produced by Eugene. When I asked whether the staff had contibuted toward this she said, "Yes, we were consulted

and we told him what we did not want. After we told him this, he left it in anyway." She did not at all hide her feelings that this had been a fake democratic approach and that he had, in reality, foisted this on them. A second illustration deals with another teacher's explanation of the rules to her pupils. She explained that there would be no going through the perception core when going to lunch and that they must go outside and around the outside building unless it was extremely inclement weather. When a couple of children asked why, she commented, "Mr. Shelby says it is too noisy" (12/10).

KENSINGTON ELEMENTARY SCHOOL

December 14

Administrative Regulations

1. In general, pupils are expected not to take off their shoes at school. Possible exceptions to this are when pupils are using the tumbling mats in physical education or when sitting on the floor for certain kinds of learning activities in their assigned areas.
2. Pupils should not be kept after school for any purpose without the consent of their parents.
3. In general, teachers are discouraged from permitting pupils in the school building outside of school hours. Under no circumstances should a pupil be allowed in the building outside of school hours unless the teacher permitting it is willing to assume full and prudent responsibility for the behavior of the pupil.
4. Equipment or material should never be taken from the perception core, curriculum center or any other area without following proper check-out procedures.
5. Except during severe weather, pupils should ordinarily use the outside covered walkway for passing from one area of the building to another.
6. Whenever it is necessary for pupils to use the inside of the building in moving from one area to another (such as going to the basement art room), this should be done in a very orderly manner without any talking.
7. The perception core is designed for the use of approximately 100 to 120 pupils at a time. For such usage to be possible, it is virtually imperative that pupils work responsibly and quietly in this area. In order to establish proper normative standards for behavior, the use of the perception core will be limited initially to individual activities.
8. Except in cases of emergency, requests for custodial services should be made to the office rather than to custodial personnel. Unless the matron is readily accessible, emergency cleaning needs also should be referred to the office for notifying the matron.
9. Addition to item B4 of library regulations (Dec. 8 bulletin): Pupils who are recognized as being consistently and conscientiously responsible in caring for materials and abiding by regulations may be issued permanent passes to the perception core. Should any such pupil fail to assume his responsibilities, the permanent pass may be withdrawn by the materials coordinator. Permanent passes have been ordered for each child from the Brodart Company.
10. The use of production equipment is restricted to the A-V technician, the instructional clerk, the materials coordinator, and the office secretary.

Figure 5.2 Further clarification of school policy.

Finally, the rules focused on the use of the perception core, which was flooded with pupils leaving the laboratory suites for independent work. The lack of internal corridors precipitated rules regarding pupil movement to lunch, to the basement art room, and to the small rest rooms located on the periphery of the perception core. The problems of noise and sound transfer are referred to in phrases such as "quiet, dignified and purposeful manner" or "in a very orderly manner without any talking." The varied rules on early arrival and playing on the grounds and the frequent use of the noun "permission" carry overtones of most elementary schools.

A Final Note

In the educational psychology literature, the problem of rules has received minimal treatment. Much of this neglect probably relates to a movement away from the harsh punitive autocracy prevalent in some schools in the pre-Deweyian era. The rise of democratic educational philosophy, the concern for the social-emotional climate of the classroom, and the development of pupil mental health are part of this picture as well. In contrast, the organizational sociologists treat rules as an important element of bureaucracy. Gouldner (1954a) cites functions such as: (1) explication, wherein rules become functional equivalents of personally given orders. When the rules are clear and accepted they do away with the necessity of close supervision which often is perceived as punitive. Reactions of hostility and apathy frequently follow close supervision. (2) The screening function of rules hides the latent power and authority in that supervisors can blame the next level up and carry out their responsibilities in terms of being bound by the same requirements. (3) The remote control function enables authority to be used at a distance, from several layers up in the organization. (4) The legitimation of punishment is a fourth function of bureaucratic rules, in that they forewarn individuals about expectations and deviations from expectations. In a sense the rules coincide with a more general cultural norm, that is, prior warning or advance notice regarding behavior. (5) A bargaining or leeway function of rules exists, according to Gouldner, in providing a supervisor room to extend occasional favors and to build informal cooperation from subordinates.

We shall have considerably more to say about rules: in the context of a public school that has a "democratic administration"; in an organization in which multiple groups (pupils, teachers, and parents) are involved; in which objectives relate to socializing younger "not of age" members into a broader society; and in which issues of civil rights are ambiguous. These factors complicated Kensington's and Shelby's attempts to bring order into the social relationships among teachers and pupils.

CHAPTER 6

Unique Physical Facilities: The New Building

INTRODUCTION

Our experience with the nature and conceptualization of material props, physical facilities, and school architecture has been quite limited. However, as we heard people talk about the possibilities inherent in building designs like Kensington's, and as we read glowing accounts of anticipated outcomes in similar new structures, a bit of skepticism began to mount. Children, teachers, and schooling, as we had known them directly (Smith and Geoffrey, 1968), and indirectly as other intensive observers (Jackson, 1968; Barker and Gump, 1964; and Barker, 1968) had reported their experience, seemed less than glowing. In a way, Sommer (1969) expressed it best:

"Frank Lloyd Wright put forth the doctrine that form follows function, which became a useful antidote to needless ornamentation. Yet it is curious that most of the concern with functionalism has been focused upon form rather than function. It is as if the structure itself—harmony with the site, the integrity of the materials, the cohesiveness of the separate units, has become the function. Relatively little emphasis is placed on the activities taking place inside the structure. This is predictable in the case of the architect who, in his training and practice, learns to look at buildings without people in them. . . . It is also common to find lavish descriptions of buildings before they are opened for use. I had occasion to visit the prototype 'flexible school,' a building shell whose internal dimensions can be altered quickly and inexpensively through the use of demountable wall partitions. Thousands of educators had visited the model and read the well-illustrated pamphlets describing the building. Unfortunately, the group of architects and educators who developed the prototype was disbanded even before the first school patterned along the lines of the model opened its doors. The model itself was to be used for other purposes. I am not criticizing this project specifically, for what is involved is standard practice in architecture" (pp. 3–4).

171

Consequently, this chapter consists of two main parts. The first is a lengthy description of the physical plant. Where possible we treat both the physical facilities and their expected behavioral concomitants as specified in the Architectural Design Institute (ADI) document, an account purporting to present "the educational life" within the innovatively designed structure.[1] In addition, we supplement the description of each element with appropriate data from the field notes. The second part of the chapter attempts to conceptualize some of the latent variables involved and to state possible relationships among them. This intellectual process maintains our interest in developing miniature theories of major aspects of school functioning.

THE BUILDING AND ITS UTILIZATION: FACADE AND REALITY

The physical structure of the school, as any other "item," to use Merton's concept, is an element of the total system. As any element of a system, it has its antecedents and consequences. Earlier we clarified the "mandate," the people's wish and the superintendent's action in designing and erecting the building. This physical structure, as with the social structure, has its visible or facade components, which are presented to the varying publics, and its "real" or working components, with which the members of the system, staff and pupils, must deal. In May during the closing days of school our notes relevant to these issues developed in the following manner, and we insert them with only minimal stylistic editing.[2]

The Overview

As part of the summary of the year, I have been looking at the ADI *Sketch* of Kensington, the innovative school. By reading materials from this and then adding reactions as I see the school at this point in time, we will have some interpretive comment taken at the close of the year, which should provide a significant summary of much of what has happened.

For instance, the first page comments in this fashion, "All of the fantastic change in technology and knowledge of the past several decades would be meaningless had it remained a static local affair in each instance. In order to pass from theory to general fact, use, and progress, an idea must be on the working end of communication." The booklet goes on, "This sketch shows

[1] This *Sketch* was a beautifully produced and widely circulated booklet. ADI is an architectual consulting organization specializing in educational buildings.

[2] It seems appropriate to comment that these notes were dictated over Memorial Day a long lazy early summer weekend. Sitting outdoors in the sunshine, the observer as interpreter reflected on the year's experience.

what is happening to new ideas in school planning, program, and construction. It constitutes an index to the working end of communication, and by reaching the local administrators and disseminating the finest new ideas which appear in new school buildings, serves an indispensable part in the development of better schools."

As I think about this, it seems that Kensington has more than achieved goals in this area. The number and kinds of visitors who have been to the school are so numerous that it is difficult to organize and order them. People from the local metropolitan area and from all over the country, people from all kinds of educational enterprises, the public schools, the universities, the commercial companies, and the like, have been in and out of the building at a phenomenal rate. Eugene has a folder of many letters from these people commenting on the program and what it has meant to them when they plan their own buildings and their own ideas and institutions scattered throughout the area. The publicity in the *Daily Star,* the write-up that will come out in *National Weekly,* and the selection of the school as school of the month attest to this prestige, dissemination of ideas, and points of view.

Another significant aspect of this dissemination notion relates to comments that Eugene has made recently and which I think are involved in the recommendations that he submitted to the central administration, that playing this role of high visibility and dissemination has been an expensive one. A good bit of his time and a considerable amount of Tom's time has been spent indoctrinating and guiding such visitors about. He is asking for resources if this is to be done in subsequent years. He has also raised the idea of moving toward a much less visible position, in order to solve internal problems within the school. What has been profit to the district and to the superintendent has been costly and expensive to the day-to-day functioning of the school.

On page 4 of the ADI document "a Spirit of the old Northwest Territory" and "another expedition into unchartered educational territory, new and dramatic approaches" are noted. Ten aspects of the new building are described: "Nothing here is absolutely new and untried, but the startling array of new structural approaches to old educational problems is enough to make even the casual observer ask for reasons—and the answers on why the school is significant." They comment also, "These items do not just arrive from a potpourri of possible new approaches. They arise naturally and organically out of a new sort of program conceived and planned by the community, a program which requires new building concepts, new furnishing and staffing concepts, new problems and new questions."

Without doubt, these ideas were in the air during the early part of the year— August, September, etc. The notes will carry, I think, without contradictions, phrases by Jerl and Eugene among others that the school had much to contribute to education in present-day America. They viewed themselves as breaking ground with new concepts and ideas and approaches to teaching and learning. This vision of pioneering and innovating, a belief system in our terminology, was important and all pervasive. The later disillusionment of people such as David, who perhaps carried the idea the farthest, appeared very dramatically during the course of the winter. One of the significant questions, which it seems to me that we must answer, concerns how and why this vision was lost and what kinds of reasons and rationalizations grew to replace it. One phase of this could be in the rising frequency of statements of "Wait till next year" type comment which is so characteristic of ball clubs having a bad season.

The Classical Shape

The first of the ten items concerns the classical Greek design. The pamphlet characterizes this shape as modern on the one hand, and then compares it to "A Parthenon whose qualities contribute to an effect of organically articulated form rather than mere massiveness, of subtle refinement rather than gross power whose shape is, in fact, a prototype of evolutionary progress in educational growth." They continue to accent the classical yet modern idea with the following comment, "It is a facility offering facility and speed, mobility and flexibility to a non-graded, organic, fluid approach to inquiry."

Once again, without question, it seems to me that the paragraph captures the major thrust of the school. The accent on what came to be called "process" as opposed to "content" has been a major part of the belief system or formal doctrine throughout the year. It also, as our notes will attest, has been a major point of conflict and discussion throughout the year. This probably, as much as anything, represents the major problem of translating ideals into specific, concrete programs of action. The only "real process" that seems to have come to fruition is in the area of reading in the Basic Skills Division. At that point, reading process is so equivalent to content of curriculum that it is very difficult to separate the two and it is perhaps not an appropriate example. More specifically, the processes involved in inquiry in science are, perhaps, the classic case for the school. For some children, and a small number in ISD, there has been a considerable amount of emphasis and actual work in a variety of what might be labeled "interest catchers" or what might be more appropriately called beginning experimentalism in physical and biological science. In the spring our notes will attest to the ISD teachers' disillusionment with Jack who provided again what might be called an excellent illustration of this program in science for, in their estimate, 15 percent of the ISD kids. They were never able to make workable the program for the large majority of the children. In social studies, the process notions are perhaps best illustrated in Kay's unit on the stock market and Liz's unit on communism. The most telling critique probably lies in the issues discussed in the last few days of the notes concerning the inability to make use of the local tax campaign as a significant issue in the instructional program to correlate with the degree of significance it possesses in the lives of the pupils, as they deal with their families and the community.

It seems noteworthy to comment that such glowing words as "facility and speed, mobility and flexibility," while rallying cries for emotional appeals, the actuality is more akin to lack of facility and speed, immobility and inflexibility. Confusion and disarray characterize many events as they occurred.

Teacher Work Center

The next section is entitled "The Teacher Work Center." In effect, this name has not been used; more typically it is called the Curriculum Center. As the *Sketch* comments, "The area was designed to give the staff room to work individually in small groups in preparation for classes . . . from this 'gut' section will come a continual flow of learning materials, varied and unique and limited only by the demands of students' needs and by the capacity of machines and technical specialists employed by the program." In actuality, the work center is much more a gathering place for people to have lunch, drink coffee, and talk informally. The area also has been widely used in the community for a multitude of meetings. The staff, committee, and team meetings, almost always utilize this area. Occasionally, one will see teachers grading papers or preparing materials. The images that come to mind are Alec with his stack of arithmetic papers and Jean or other people from Basic Skills team-4 who often will be checking materials as they sit chatting and drinking coffee. Very little intensive class preparation is done here.

The area contains several other features that deserve comment. First, there are the trapezoidal tables, which have perplexed the staff all year in terms of readily shaping them into a design that will be useful to sit around. On a number of occasions they have served very well to illustrate Eugene's desire to have everything "just right." Second, the area contains the school's professional library, which consists mostly of Tom's books. Very seldom have they been used in any functional way. Only on a rare occasion have I seen anyone with one of the books checking a position or trying to amplify a point of view. Third, the problem of built-in facilities and storage space is also well exemplified. There is no built-in blackboard because this would cut down on the "flexibility" of the area. There are no cupboards except brief space in some of the movable lowboy cabinets. The filing cabinets jut out at an awkward angle and yet are very necessary. Fourth, this area, and the Nerve Center below, has been the one part of the building that has been kept inviolate from the students' access. I do not believe that I have ever seen a pupil up here.

Fifth, this has been the area for congregating in the informal activity of the school. Seldom in the course of the day can one not find a conversation there. John and Tom and more recently Alec are there frequently. They are the ones with the flexible schedules and the ones who can come and go at greater will. Eugene also is a frequent habitue of the place. To tie this point down, one can note that Mary and Carla are practically never there. I do not think that I have seen them there informally during the course of any day. The BSD team-4 are there quite frequently, usually in singles or doubles. They, as we have indicated, perhaps more than any other group, have themselves well enough organized so that somebody has free time someplace almost all of the time. That's a bit too strong. The kindergarten teacher very infrequently is there. Among the Transition teachers there is less use than with Basic Skills team-4. However, Claire and Meg particularly are frequently there. Dan is about mostly at lunch time. In ISD the most infrequent use comes from David, although there was almost no occasion for him to be there in the last couple months. During this interval he has literally withdrawn almost totally from the school staff. Linda, Liz, and Kay, particularly the latter, frequently come up for breaks during the course of the day. Invariably they just "leave" their children. Irma does not use the area to a very great degree, and Jack also does not frequent the place. His absence from school in the last month or six weeks makes that interpretation a little harder to make. The real habitue is John. He is there almost as much as I am.

Another interesting point apropos of this concerns the teaching aides who are almost never up here unless they are working. Until now I had not really thought about that, but Arthur, Joan, Helen, Marjorie, and Inez drink their coffee down below or in the conference part of the office. As I sit here and think about that, I am struck quite dramatically at how clear that break has been. Tom mediates between the groups probably more than anyone, because Arthur and Marjorie both work in his area, and the former works for him, and Helen also works for him. Administratively, most of their work comes through the direct requests of the teachers. Tom also tends to keep Arthur quite busy. The pupils go directly to Helen regarding books and materials. The aides remain at the beck and call of the teachers. The matron seems to associate more with them also. There is another subgroup, the lunch help, which involves three or four women who also do not utilize the curriculum center. They also seem to run fairly independently of the teaching aide staff. There has been such a turnover of janitors that I have very little feel for their place in the organization. The other group that has made a large use of the curriculum center is the central office personnel. The most frequent visitor is Jerl who spends a good bit of his time while he is in the school in the center. Steven, when he comes, usually will have lunch or coffee there. Finally, it is a gathering place for a cup of coffee for many of the visiting educators who have people to talk to or who are being indoctrinated by Eugene. I think here particularly of Janine, the Latin American woman from Ohio, and of Williams from the *National Weekly*. They would interview and write their notes here.

The flow of creative materials described in the sketch has not come about.

This part of the ADI *Sketch* also states "Satisfaction of these planned processes require that the student have 50 percent of his time available for individual study and demand a greater, more uninhibited flow of space and materials between peripheral and internal areas of the building than is available in traditional buildings or in the newer 'loft' concepts of space distribution." Although, I dare say, one-half and even more of the student's time in some parts of ISD have been involved with individual study, the production of materials has not kept pace and might well be called a major flaw in the

implementation of the total program. Later when we talk about needed resources, we shall speak more to this general point. Not only is a technical
staff, such as Arthur and Marjorie needed, but also a professional staff to generate the ideas that then will be implemented by the technicians. The ambiguity in Tom's role perhaps becomes even more dramatic concerning a point
such as this. If he had been defined as the "instructional dean" with specific
responsibilities to facilitate the work of the experienced teachers and to aid
the inexperienced teachers, in a teacher training relationship, then the center
might have worked more as it was hoped for. From early in the year over
in the gym, Tom continuously backed off from assuming a strong directive
role. The notes should contain a number of his comments that he was there
to help them plan and suggest materials for units and program, but that his
job was not to tell them what the units should be or to lay out the dimensions
of the units. As I think about this now, he might have analyzed the situation
and assumed this responsibility, or Eugene, in turn, might have analyzed it
and delegated this responsibility. Administratively, the autonomy of the self-
contained classroom teacher was being violated by the interdependence of
space, and the interdependence of teams and the autonomy of instructional decisions could have been broken into as well. This might have been a more
ideal solution of the problems faced by Liz, David, Linda, Kay, and Dan
in particular. The others who were more experienced and more able, Jack,
Alec, and Irma, could have used this service at a much more equalitarian
level and in its resource aspect than could the previously mentioned
individuals.

Another way of looking at this might well be the lack of university resources.
In a sense, Leslie Roberts was to provide some of this stimulation. Frequently
in the meetings he would talk about sending materials and books and ideas
on the ways to do things. For whatever reason, this never reached the point
of full productivity. If he had been involved full time in actually writing
the materials or had an assistant or two who was available full time to take
ideas and to produce them, then this would have moved much more effectively.
Perhaps he and Tom could have worked out this kind of relationship. As
I think about Leslie's contribution I feel, at this point, that his own interests
gradually moved from being helpful and instrumental in materials and methods to getting much more involved in his conceptualization of teaching reading
and in the measurement of it through content analysis of the tapes, and much
more involved in trying to implement a research program, and much less
in implementing the Kensington program as a program. This, too, accents
the dilution and divergence of an initial and important resource to the curriculum program of the school. Later we shall want to talk about the dilution
into the curriculum committee, and its worry and concern with long-term
objectives instead of with day-to-day materials and units. To have really done
this properly, however, would have required a series of curriculum specialists
probably attached to a university with access to the ideas and to the broader
realms of materials. Perhaps, too, more careful delineation of the resource
person's responsibilities would have helped significantly here. One might con-

sider early discussions of the roles of these two groups, particularly as Jack and David fought about this during the workshop period. If the people could have been marshaled under the leadership of Leslie or Tom, or perhaps even Jerl from the central office, into a smoothly working production team with the major burden of the utilization of materials falling with the individual teachers or academic counselors, then this, too, might have had a chance for more success. The lack of textbooks hurt the teaching program in the same way that the lack of originally produced materials hurt. We might also comment about, later and in the last few months, the problems with budget and with the misuse of materials influencing the lack of paper, stencils, and the like. Continuously tied in with this is the inexperience of the teachers in knowing what to do even though they have the materials. This flow of ideas, and materials to represent the ideas, illustrates a piece of the overall conceptualization and system of variables needed to account for the functioning of an elementary school. Apropos of this type of conception, we need to go back to Charters' (1964) article on workflow, which seems a most important way of viewing the situation.

The Perception Core

The sketch's statement is a vivid picture of unreality. Although fragments of it are part of the vision that once existed, almost none of it is a part of the reality of it now. Specifically, the sketch says this: "Out of this grew the perception core concept which represents an advancement over the instructional materials centers and the resource and research centers just as they were an advancement over the older library concept. Where conventional learning patterns are conceived to begin in the homeroom or the classroom and to proceed to the library and back, the pattern here begins in the perception core area, expands and overflows into what were once called the classrooms but which we must call laboratory suites in order to describe the process adequately. Students entering the building with one-week schedules (as opposed to the contemporary 36-week schedules), go to the outer part of the sanctuary and begin the day individually in special carrels or in small groups as planned. Their special areas of concentration or study may reach through a broad spectrum from a study of live biological specimens in or about the stream (that flows through a portion of the building along the edge of the core) to a study of foreign languages in one of several centers set up throughout the area. The five study centers, each designed to accommodate a specific subject area, consist of bookshelves and study spaces arranged in changeable patterns. The remainder of the perception core is fitted with isolated study booths and shelves for general reading matter and instructional materials, including phonograph records and tape players with headphones; small slide projectors for viewing at a desk by one student; filmstrip projectors; microfilm, microcard and microprint readers; teaching machines; portable television receivers with headphones; small motion picture projectors for small groups; and portable radio receivers with headphones."

Such was the dream of someone. The realities of the perception core are these: first, the area is called the perception core. This term is used by staff and students alike. Second, the central locus of the area is the desk or checkout counter which is very similar to a library checkout counter in any public school or, more specifically, in any good children's library. Helen and her student assistants hang out here. Third, there have never been fish or biological specimens in the aquarium. This was not done in spite of the fact that a local store volunteered to stock the pond. I do not know why this was not accepted. For a time there was water in the pond, and for a time there were problems with children using it as a wishing well and throwing money into it. At this point I do not know why Jack never took the initiative to establish it as a major aquarium and wild life center. Fourth, the east end of the area over near the children's theatre was soon developed into an independent reading area for children from Basic Skills, especially team-4. It also has had wide usage by the Transition groups. In effect, it has become another instructional area for these very crowded division areas. By pulling some 10 to 30 children out of the major instructional area and into this part of the perception core, the load is reduced in the other areas, and here the teachers move about reading with individual children as they, in turn, read from a variety of books at their ability and interest levels. I have very vivid images of Meg, especially, and Claire to some extent there; Jean, Sue, Wanda, Elaine, and Sarah (Elaine's replacement) heavily utilized this area. Although there have been differences between Wanda and Jean, for instance, in the relative accent on having common materials with a text basis, with Wanda arguing for more of this, and with Jean arguing for less, the reading program has been intensive and has involved all of the children in almost a maximal way. Except for the very real difficulty about the unavailability of primer materials, this program has moved hard and has moved in the best individualized or differentiated fashion.

A further dramatic image I have of the perception core concerns the extensive use of encyclopedias. Never in my experience in and out of elementary schools have I seen so many children utilizing encyclopedias on so many different topics on so many different occasions as I have at Kensington. The perception core has had a constant flow of kids looking up Egyptian and Chinese writing, a host of biological things concerning frogs, snakes, and worms, and a variety of other information from literally every aspect of the curriculum.

Also, in the perception core there is an image of a few kids who are perpetually wandering around. I recall one day when Kay and I were watching one of the boys in her class as he moved from table to desk to leaning on the lowboy to punching a kid to bothering somebody else as he hopped from one portion to another portion of the area.

Furthermore, there were times when individual teachers tried to utilize the space. Alec, for instance, tried to teach math there; Jack tried to hold science discussions; and Joe held his Friday morning counseling sessions over in the western corner. This just did not work well. Joe's group was too noisy and uncontrolled, and we have some fine quotes from Helen who tried to shush them once and found she was talking directly to Joe. Alec and Jack tried to set up science and math centers, but this proved to be awkward and unfeasible. Throughout the year the area has contained sign-up sheets for math, science, art, and a variety of other activities. These lists run from long to short with scratch outs of whole sections for total classes by some of the teachers to brief lists of individual pupils on some kind of program or instruction. A final image of the perception core, and one that is older and weaker now, is of the area as a hallway. During the middle of the winter when it was cold outside, the traffic through here was very great and a continuing problem. As far as I know, no plans have been made regarding it for next year.[3] Throughout the middle part of the day from 11:00 to 1:00 there would be kids with trays of food going back and forth. Also it is the only hallway across the way to the theatre, to the art room, to the P.E. shelter, and to the office. Each of these places has maximal usage a good part of the day. More recently with the weather being pleasant, the outside walkway has been used to a very high degree, and this problem is almost nonexistent. This controversy is rich with comments and quotations about whether or not the weather was inclement, and comments and problems regarding the dogs who ate the children's food, and the pneumonia that the parents thought the children were catching.

The statement "students entering the building with one-week schedules (as opposed to the contemporary 36-week schedule)" is reminiscent of the first few days and weeks at the junior high school, and of the perception core itself. The illusion existed that the children could sign up and would sign up and that the organization of the kids could be handled on an individual basis for the whole 200 children. By the time we moved to the building itself, there was no possibility for the students to "begin the day individually in special carrels or in small groups as planned"; they went to their self-contained area in the outside ring of laboratory suites, and through a formal system of signed passes they then could go into the perception core for specific purposes. The traffic flow was a major point of controversy between divisions, each of whom wanted some access to the space and some greater degree of utilization. Particularly this was true of Transition and Basic Skills-4, who felt jammed and cramped into quarters that were inadequate. The commandeering of the east end as a reading area helped to alleviate these problems.

The special areas of concentration or study also has not worked out. Finally, the books were arranged according to the classical Dewey decimal and Library of Congress system, and into appropriate shelves. None were designated as areas of science or social studies or language arts. After a number of patterns were tried, finally a workable arrangement of shelves and tables was achieved. This has remained fairly constant since then. Out here almost no use has

---

[3] Post-year data indicate continued parental complaints regarding the outside walkway.

been made of phonograph records or tape players; occasionally, some small slide projectors or filmstrip projectors have been used. There is no microphone equipment; teaching machines are not available; and portable TV has not been part of this area. Similarly, no portable motion pictures or radio receivers have been utilized.

In effect, much of what was distinctive about the perception core as opposed to a materials center or library has not been achieved generally in the school. However, this is not only a problem of the materials and facilities being available but also there remains a problem of usage. The school has had an ample supply of maps and globes almost since the beginning of school. The use of them has been so close to minimal that only a time or two, and these most recently, have I seen anyone carefully using maps. Part of the problem here is the fact the teachers have taught little geography in a basic group instructional sense or with several pupils. In this regard, they have not needed to make reference to the large maps that exist. Some of them are outstandingly beautiful, and yet when the program is either nonexistent or totally individualized, then one does not need to call on maps as group devices. At this point in time, almost all of the slate globes, which permitted chalking in areas, have been stored and are not in use. I cannot recall now any image of someone utilizing this in ISD. Back in the gym there was a bit of use by Kay, I think. Similarly, almost none of the cycloteachers have been used in recent months. Partly this is because of the teachers' feeling of the inadequacy of some of the programs, partly to the novelty having worn off by their abuse during the first few months in the gym, and partly also to the expense of the paper that is used in the machine. The latter could have been handled, however, by obtaining cheap newsprint and by having Arthur or Marjorie cut them to shape. Occasionally I heard talk about the possibility of these materials being developed into workable units by the teachers and by others. Here, again, time and imagination and energy were lacking. The analogy I see is that of a series of gems scattered about in disuse and ill-repair because there has been no craftsmen to make the setting with its interlocking units into which the gems might fall.

Although I am thinking of the perception core, I might comment about the rest rooms that open off of it. There are no centralized rest rooms for all of the children. Each rest room is a small individual unit that can be used by children individually rather than in total group recess. What has happened here is that these units have become gathering places and playgrounds for the children as they move out of their classroom and in and out of the perception core. There have been continual problems in keeping the kids out of the rooms except when they were necessary for their purposes. On occasion the rooms have been used as dressing rooms for kids who were putting on some kind of performance with costumes in their own areas of ISD. There is a quote or two in the notes about Eugene's contact with the kindergarten teacher who lined her kids up with a whistle in an attempt to march them off to the rest room and then found that there was no rest room for them to march to as a group. In a sense, as intended, this facility also made it very difficult for the teachers to use the more traditional procedures. It forced them, again as intended, to more individualized, differentiated activities. Once again, the difficult link was that the very real intent of how to do these things was never fully elaborated. Only later were they worked out, and here not often well, after intense trial and error. They became part of the content of early spring ISD team meetings.

One final comment concerning the cost of the school. The use of the audio materials, tape recorders, the centralized television, and the like, awaits further financing. This will amount to large blocks of money. Also, the possible development and building of an outside wall around the outside hallway also awaits considerable financial resources. This is a long, long hallway that, I predict, one day will be built to solve the internal problems of passageways. What that would have cost originally as it was added on to the building would be an interesting figure to divide into the price per square foot of floor space.

The Learning Laboratory Suites

The profile sketch reads this way. "The designation of classroom spaces as laboratory suites avoids the association with homeroom and baseroom procedures which are absent in this program." This is patently not so at Kensington. The school has moved continuously toward more and more spaces designated as homeroom and baseroom areas.

The sketch states: "These 20 spaces, equipped with overhead projectors and other electronic and mechanical aides to be described in the section on the 'nerve center,' comprise the outer ring of the area and are divided only by movable, visual dividers; and each class space thus loosely defined is made more mutable by the further possibility of subdivision through complete movability of all furniture and equipment in these spaces." This sentence is generally quite true; there are overhead projectors in most of the areas. However, these projectors are only occasionally used. The teachers have moved much more toward the use of blackboards. As I think about this, the major difference in the blackboard and in the overhead lies in the necessity of pre-prepared transparencies. Here again, we are involved in the same problem that has been indicated in our earlier discussion. The staff has had neither the time, the energy, nor the resources to prepare an accumulating file of transparencies. Perhaps the most widely used ones exist in materials that Eugene uses to talk to groups of people who visit in the program. A gradually developing accumulating file of them implies that there are organized bodies of material that one wants to teach about and that will on later occasions also be taught. Such a file, like notes for lectures or like folders of pictures for particular events, becomes a portion of every teachers' armamentarium. Here the problem is quite acute in that no one will admit to having this kind of a curriculum, which is prebuilt or prepared prior to some particular moment of need. Most of the need or use of these has been of a sort where one writes on them for the moment and then erases them later. This kind of use is more easily adaptable to a blackboard, at least, in terms of the experience of these people. When I think of my own teaching and the possibility of having this kind of material on file, and ready to be pulled out to illustrate or to demonstrate a particular point, then the real value of this equipment comes forth. With the general inexperience of the teachers and the lack of articulation of any kind of program or curriculum, these materials then seem much less essential.

"Instant adhering chalk surfaces of plastic and like features of mobility and display in demonstration facilities satisfy the qualities of fluid space necessary for maximum utility of individual, small group and large group study." As I think of ISD, I am struck by the minimal amounts of this sort of thing. In Basic Skills, and some of the entryway near the administrative suite, considerable display of creative artwork occurs. Very little of this is a part of the learning suites elsewhere. One might comment that Dan typically has piles and piles of "junk" lying around that he uses in his dramatic groups and for some of his instruction, much of this to the dismay and consternation of Claire. Related to this is a comment that I should have made regarding the perception core and the availability of space for displays in it. I have a distinct image of Eugene talking with Tom on two different occasions, one in which Tom was talking about trying to put up bulletin boards on the wall of the perception core. Eugene resisted this because it cut down on the flexibility of the use of the room. An alternative reaction might have been one of distress at the notion of flexibility impeding the solidification of the program in certain desirable ways. It would, as Eugene did indicate, prevent the reorganization of the perception core in other ways. He was arguing dramatically for the use of the bulletin board back of some of the storage cabinets. The second illustration was a situation in which Eugene asked Tom who had given the permission for Liz's group to put up signs regarding *Macbeth,* the play that her group had performed several weeks ago. Tom said that he had given them a general OK in that there seemed to be nothing he could do about it. Eugene was concerned about the loss of aesthetic quality in the development of kind of a junky look to the building. It is hard to emphasize enough how much of this consideration keeps coming into the events of the building. On a number of occasions he has been concerned about the arrangement of tables in the curriculum center and concerned about the looks of the building and what we have called in the notes, "the facade." Also, it should be pointed out that the aesthetic qualities of the building are very, very high in my judgment. The building is and has been a beautiful thing to look at and to work in. However, this aesthetic aspect, especially as interpreted by Eugene, has hindered many usual goals of elementary education.

"Tote trays further enhance the freedom of peripheral activity." These are physical facilities that have not existed in the building and about which there has been almost no discussion. Racks of them might well have provided storage space which was a continuous problem in the gym and which helped precipitate having pupil stations that belonged to individual children. A tote tray or two would have prevented the necessity for assigning kids to individual desks. As

I think about this, I am struck by the larger generalization that very minute items in the materials arrangement that have been neglected have had far-reaching effects on the program and the later structures that have been developed. For instance, if each person had had two of these trays in which he could keep his books and other materials, one for total storage and one to carry with him as he went from activity to activity, then the whole complexion of the program would have been different. They could have been built as low storage units, perhaps, six or eight tote trays high and maybe six or eight tote trays wide, which would have permitted two per person in each of the areas and which could have been back-to-back in the various sections of ISD. With them the kids could have rotated among teachers among instructional areas, bringing just what they needed for whatever purposes they might have. Then they would not have been caught with the problems of needing a desk to store things and the constant quarrels over somebody using my desk or getting into my materials or taking my pencils, and the like. This raises also the more general need for a careful analysis of materials and physical facilities in psychomotor learning and in the analysis of group functioning. It might be well to observe the way in which pupils in high school or junior high school use their lockers or to observe a home economics class as it utilizes tote trays in a more restricted way. There are naturalistic situations in which they do seem to function well and ably. Experiments also could be designed to develop more knowledge about them.

A final comment might be made about the statement "This peripheral movement is even further augmented by a free-flow of traffic (without corridors!) to the central areas through immediate access from the laboratory suites." This flow of traffic, rather than being a free flow in a positive sense, has been chaotic as we have commented, and the demand for corridors is one that has not been well handled.

The description of the learning laboratory suites continues: "The natural flow of the program carries the student from perception core to the laboratory suite where he encounters special teachers and assistants. Where his studies developed along lines of breadth in the core, they now begin to close in on the specifics in reaching for depth." This is so far from reality, it's impossible to make an intelligent comment on it. There is so little formal instruction for the majority of the kids, except for perhaps Irma's section of ISD, that one finds very little evidence of depth in any kind of study. The major exception to this is the large amount of writing on rather brief papers growing out of work with the encyclopedias especially.

"The program for kindergarten and first-year pupils is more directive than that described above, and motion for these children is more nearly confined to specific areas with specific home groups." Without question, Basic Skills is much more organized and much more directive than any of the other areas. This seems true for both the team of two and the team of four. Here again, this is the only place where intensive instruction is given systematically to large groups.

The Children's Theatre

Herein lies the actualized heart of the vista envisioned. Dan, Chris, Elaine, and occasionally Wanda, Carla, and others have made the theatre into a reality. The profile reads as follows: "The perception core is separated from the children's theatre by the life-science stream and a glass wall. The theatre itself is unique. It was designed for the children. A large, open space is surrounded by three simple acting areas, each of which may be used for simultaneous production and two of which are joined by a bridge that crosses the life-science pool, extending into the theatre a short distance. With the 'open stage' concept, drama presentations are to be staged utilizing portable flats designed and built by the students. Creative thought is stimulated in this flexible space, student interest expanded by the acting tower, including an enclosed spiral stairway leading up to a balcony which looks out over the theatre."

In part, the physical description is inadequate. The pool only comes a short way into the theatre. There is no bridge that crosses over it. The phrase "for simultaneous production" is ambiguous. If it means that the areas can be used for different productions at the same time, then, obviously, it does not hold true. The noise and the carrying of voices makes any kind of independent usage impossible. If by this is meant having two areas that can serve as separate scenes for the same play, then this meaning of simultaneous is very true.

The center of the theatre is depressed two steps below the basic floor level of the building, and this area, all of which is carpeted, can be used as a seating area for pupils without bringing chairs from the classrooms. This, too, is a reality. Not only do the kids sit here without chairs, they lounge, they lie, they flounder about on the floor.

The theatre has been, perhaps, the most successful and the most creative part of the school. Just yesterday, for instance, Irma's group of the least able pupils presented a "patriotic program" for Memorial Day. Although the theatre was not used in any novel or original way, it provided a focus for this kind of a meeting. The kids sit comfortably on the carpeted steps, lounge occasionally, and generally relax and partake of the various offerings. The notes contain extended lists of the productions that have occurred there.

The rear view screen facility has been only partially adequate. The movie projector works very well with the attachment that was put on the front of the lens. The slide projector does not work well in that it does not magnify to a great enough degree. The distance is a handicap here. One further unanticipated phenomena concerns the projection from the front as opposed to the rear of the screen, and the fact that one usually needs a monitor in the auditorium with the children. Recently, last week, I observed a film, *The Discriminating Frogs and Toads*, during the noon hour. Arthur was the only adult present. He showed the film from the outside with normal projection procedures. If he had been on the inside of the projection room, then he would not have been able to monitor the children and, in effect, supervise them. The point I am suggesting, I guess, is that the design of many aspects of the building seem more fitting for an older group of children who are better able to care for themselves and who need less supervision.

"The area can also be used for large group instruction or as an auditorium facility." Except for movies and occasional discussions, such as Eugene's recent discussion on the school tax, the auditorium has not been used instructionally. Perhaps the fundamental truth is that there has been no topic that seemed worthy of being instructional for the total group. There have been no instructional assemblies as it were. There have been no lectures for the entire school. On several occasions the room has been used for large parent groups. Most recently, when the slide and audio presentation on the school was presented this spring the children's theatre as an auditorium worked very successfully.

As I continued to listen to the broad generalizations stated by the writers of the *Sketch,* I am struck even more, as I have been on occasion in the past, with the need to ask for specific procedures and practices and examples that fit the overall generalization. Specifically again, the notion of utilization for "large group instruction" sounds nice, seems to fit the jargon of the times, and yet, when you think concretely of what kinds of things are going to be taught to large groups and how are these groups to be managed and how is the content to be integrated, sequenced, and scheduled, then one is up against a whole series of knotty problems. Without the specific, concrete example to think through, then one cannot proceed in any optimal way. It seemed to me that this was characteristic of the thinking and planning all year.

The Physical Education Shelter

The shelter is described in glowing terms: "Combining vast savings over gymnasium construction (which is usually poorly utilized in elementary schools) with the enhancement of proper acoustical form for a community ampitheater and for summer evening band concerts, this shelter is an inexpensive improvement on an old solution. The multi-use concept applied here was deliberately conceived and planned to offset the 'multiuseless' room frequently built into the elementary school. Sides of the open shelter are protected by banks of shrubbery which deflect the winds which are then carried up and over by the shape of the roof."

"The infra-red heating units are ideal for the shelter, because rather than heating the air, which would be intolerably wasteful, these units heat to a comfortable degree the children and the objects which stand or pass beneath them."

It's difficult to know where to begin to describe the illusion and the reality. I, personally, have no data on the degree of utilization of gymnasiums in elementary schools. I would doubt that they are as "poorly utilized" as the ADI sketch describes them. A very simple study could well be set up to determine the adequacy of and the kinds of utilization of gymnasiums. This should be carried out in the context of varying climates. The "California design" of much of this equipment seems inappropriate for a community like Milford, which has intolerably warm summers and damp and sloshy winters. Since I have been in the school, I have heard no remarks regarding the use of the ampitheater for summer band concerts or other kinds of activities. To my knowledge no use of the outdoor facility for any kind of total school gathering has occurred.

The use of labels such as "multi-useless," although frequent in August and in the fall, has almost disappeared recently. On many occasions the staff has had strong reason to wish for inside play and multiple-purpose use of space. John, particularly has been tremendously handicapped in the P.E. program. During the winter the shelter was almost useless for his purposes. The notes are full of many, many conversations with his total concern and defeatism over this.

It's important to note also that it was intended that the shelter would be protected by "banks of shrubbery which deflect the winds which are then carried up and over by the shape of the roof." This may be another of those very simple aspects that for reasons of finance or reasons of forgetting, or for reasons of change in intention, have not been implemented and that may have carried a tremendous burden. There seems to be little question that the shelter area suffered materially during the winter because the wind would blow in the rain and the snow. A bank of densely planted shrubs undoubtedly would have helped this condition. More recently, the shrubs would have shielded the shelter from some of the dust that has blown in from the unpaved and unsodded earth surrounding the area.

The sketch, in describing the heating units, speaks of "intolerably wasteful" in regard to any other kind of heating in this area. While that is a pretty phrase, it is also an inaccurate one. The heating units have been totally inadequate. They are mounted too high, and there are too few of them. What this meant during the winter was that the children played in hats and coats, almost as though they were out on an open playground. Only when one stood directly underneath the unit was it warm enough to be without a coat. And there, typically, it was under the units on the stage rather than in the open play area with its higher ceiling.

In summary, the P.E. shelter has been one of the most widely acknowledged inadequate features of the school building. The wind, as we have commented, has been severe. In the winter it was rain and snow, and in the spring it was dust. The shelter has been a gathering place for dirt and leaves in recent months. My guess is that in the early fall it will become a very serious problem as the leaves fall and blow in. Day after day we have cited in the notes the fact that the area was dusty and dirty and only occasionally were there resources to clean it.

A final observation or comment on the P.E. shelter might well be supplied by the way in which John spoke about his decision to remain at Kensington. The point I would make is that he rationalized, in part, his decision by accenting the relationships he has had with the other teachers and the way in which they have accepted the P.E. program as part of the total curriculum. Although this is very true, it changes the emphasis that he had made earlier when he was considering the Kansas job away from the inadequacies of the shelter, the playground space, and the field. These latter points have been quite crippling, and will take a tremendous amount of money to alter. The school system just does not have that kind of financing. Apropos of these other facilities, it seems to be important to note that the school was not able to organize and to develop a systematic workable program surrounding the use of the parking lot as a playground area or the use of the circle as a playground area; the ideas it seems to me came rather late and, also, the staff was not unified enough to reach a workable agreement here. Without too much difficulty, parking could have been on the street north of the school, on the street west of the school, and potentially in the circle, while the lot remained free as playground space. There may have been other community factors involved here. Similarly, the use of the field was impossible because of the new grass. The erosion also was quite bad. The pond did not become viable as a science center or other activity center. All of these items might best be categorized as difficulties in opening up a new building. They are complicated, however, in that the pond, for instance, could have been cleaned by a couple of the teachers interested in science if these teachers had not been already overly committed to other activities, and did not have the time. The use of kids on Saturdays as working teams to help clean it up and develop it would also have been possible. A very interesting unit on local ecology, bird life, reptile life, microscopic animal life, botanical life in and around the pond and the school ground would have been possible. As I think about that, it could have been a most exciting unit of work.

Visual, Acoustical, and Thermal Treatments

The *Sketch* statement continues: "Though there is little need to defend the use of carpeting and air conditioning on economic grounds, it is significant here that the savings effected by the physical education shelter, the satellite kitchen, the lack of corridors and walls and by the form of the building have more than paid for the initial installation of these items." Economically, we are in no position to make a commentary on these facilities. Unquestionably, space that does not go to corridors might well go for something else. We have commented at some length about the corridor problem. Suffice it to say at this point that when large groups of children move from one location to another location, their path, whatever it be through, becomes a corridor in the best sense of that term.

"Satellite kitchens" is a fancy name for the fact that there is a very small kitchen and dishwashing area in the school. This demands that hot food be brought in daily from other larger and more well-equipped kitchen areas in the district. The notes are replete with statements about the difficulty in orbiting this particular satellite. Ultimately, the kitchen was located in area 105 that the building inspectors had deemed would be a hall and an emergency exit. This space originally was intended as another classroom area. Apparently the legal code also does not recognize the lack of corridors as a functional way of organizing a building. During the course of the midwinter, the people from the kitchen department and the central office were moved and shuffled about as they set up originally in the central portion of the theatre and then later over on one side of the theatre, where kids were prone to hop, skip, and jump up the various levels in the theatre; finally, they ended up in 105, first on the side of an interior wall and then later on the outside wall. Thus, the difficulty in getting a regularly located spot for the serving of meals finally was resolved.

The other half of the situation, that part involving where the pupils would eat, never did reach the same degree of solution. A multipurpose room with tables that fold out from the walls for the lunch hour and where many children can eat at the same time did not exist at Kensington and, in effect, each classroom or laboratory learning suite became a cafeteria. From approximately 11:30 until 1:00 or 1:30 there are children in one area or another who are eating. The original idea of having children drift off individually to have lunch did not work out. In effect, each division then was assigned roughly one-half hour intervals in which most of their eating would be concentrated. This was to prevent jam-ups at 11:30. Perhaps the most basic problem that this created was that it tied the teachers down quite dramatically to the supervision of children. Only in Basic Skills Team-4 and some in Transition was this rotation of teacher supervision handled well. Typically, one teacher and one of the teaching aides would carry on the responsibility of being with the children, and the others, in one shift or another, would be off to the curriculum center for lunch. In ISD it usually meant that the kids roamed around unsupervised through a good part of the period for there was very little trading or watching in any consistent way. This would be contrasted with the more typical public school where one or two teachers would have lunchroom duty supervision one day a week or three days in two weeks, and the like. In effect, the teachers had little total freedom away from the kids without having to keep one eye on the clock for when their turn came or without some guilt that no one was looking after the children at that point.

A further complication was the fact that food was all over the building. Some of this naturally got spilled, dropped, and slopped over. This provoked all kinds of problems, one illustration being an anecdote told by someone, which we have recorded in the notes, about kids carrying hamburgers in their pockets to keep them warm when they made the outside trip. Beyond this, there is one huge streak in the rug in the hallway of the administrative suite. A pupil had dripped a sloppy joe along the way and someone had tried to clean it up by using the wrong technique. This streak has been there for several months, and apparently it will take a major cleaning in the summer to get it out. Litter and garbage cans have accumulated and have been about in many areas. I am reminded here of sitting in Transition just yesterday and noticing under one of the highboy cabinets dust and dirt, scraps of paper, and crayons that seem to have been lying there for weeks, if not months. The major point I would make is that, with the food dispersed all over, the cleaning and maintenance problem is much more acute than it would be if eating were localized.

Perhaps at this point it is appropriate to talk further about the carpeting. Again, I do not know whether ultimately it will be cheaper and more economical than tile. Aesthetically, the carpeting is beautiful and is comfortable to walk on and to view. From the children's point of view, almost uniformly, it seems to me, they have responded very well to the carpeting. They like to run about in their stocking feet or go barefoot on the carpeting, and particularly now, when it is permitted only in the theatre, they enjoy playing their Huck Finn type roles. They enjoy lying and lounging on the carpeting, particularly again in the theatre where it is more permitted. Also, the scuffling, wrestling, horseplay, and roughhousing of the boys benefits maximally from the carpeting in that one can roll, bounce, and tug without skinning elbows or bruising oneself.

On the negative side, the most important consequence of the carpeting, it seems to me, has been in the parental reaction. Uniformly at a meeting where complaints are being voiced about the district or about the school, someone is bound to mention the issue of the carpeting. It has become a rallying cry for those who are against "the monuments" in the district.

The acoustical property of the carpeting, although it may cut the noise, does not really maximize the silence enough that teachers can hold group instruction of several kinds in the same area where there is not a wall between.[4] This was a very serious problem in the junior high gym during the fall and one that people thought would be much better in the school itself. This has not turned out to be true. One of the illusions of the pamphlet is that you can make a room quiet enough in this fashion.

The Nerve Center

"The nerve system, also not so obvious to the casual observer, lies below the teacher work area and the production center at the very heart of the building. In it is housed the instantaneous storage and retrieval system geared to receiving audio or visual information from a number of sources, storing of such information and immediately dispersing it by way of television, recordings or tape, upon command by the dial system, to any part of the building."

As this is stated, it evokes dreamlike images. As one observes, the nerve center reality is very different. Instead of instantaneous storage and retrieval systems, basically we have Arthur, Marjorie, and Tom. Arthur, as we have indicated, is very busy as a general assistant and aide for handling materials, supplies, and equipment. Marjorie is working hard daily on cutting stencils and running the ditto machine. Tom sits at his desk smoking his pipe, paging through

---

[4] Similarly, the acoustically treated ceiling did not contribute to an adequate solution of the sound problems.

catalogs, or writing lengthy statements to commercial companies who might give the school materials of one kind or another.

Metaphorically, the nerve center houses its greatest stimulant in the coffeepot. Here, each day are brewed two urns of very good coffee. Before school the place hums, particularly with the Basic Skills Team-4 teachers in and out with materials and stencils for their program of the day. During the course of the day, the staff is in and out particularly for coffee but for occasional words of comment to the others. Finally, the nerve center is the gathering place of the semiprofessional staff; Arthur and Marjorie are frequently visited by Helen, Joan, and Inez. It is a very busy place and it is very social.

The major problem actually lies in the fact that the school does not have the financial resources to provide the necessary equipment. While the closed-circuit television of Milford County was here, a good bit of experimenting, in the loosest sense of the term (actually, trial-and-error usage of equipment) occurred. There have been no major storage banks of tapes that can be played on call in an individual classroom setting. The major taping cart typically has been in ISD. The individual tape recorders are scattered throughout the building. There has been very little production of materials that have broad universal and cumulative possibilities. Although I do not have an actual count on overhead transparencies, my guess is that there are very few of them, except for the ones used to describe the school, which will have much use in succeeding years. Tom has accumulated and filed an enormous amount of materials for science and social studies by authors, topics, and areas. In the shakedown of the teaching procedures this year, minimal use has been made of this. Arthur and Tom have been extensively involved in retaping materials from the Milford County Audio-Visual Center. Some of this has had considerable use in the school. For instance, just this last week Kay's group was listening to a tape of the story "Wheel on the School." The process of learning about these mountains of potential curricular materials is one of the very real problems for an inexperienced teacher. In effect, the ready supply of resources at one's fingertips is a major hurdle. Presumably these problems are attributable heavily to inexperience and, also, to the general problem of opening the school building.

The Administrative Suite

"The administrative complex is located near the main entrance. It is in immediate viewing range of the Physical Education shelter, satellite kitchen, and ten of the twenty room spaces. The suite is an open space, divided with storage elements to include general and specific areas for principal and secretarial offices, reception area, clinic and guidance or counseling facilities, work space and conference space for parent or other lay conferences."

Little, it seems, needs to be said about the administrative suite. It does not actually open on to 10 of the 20 room spaces as the brochure claims, nor is it divided with storage elements to include general and specific areas. The most fundamental fact of the administrative suite lies in the lack of privacy permitted anyone. As it stands now, the principal's section is partially walled off with cabinets but is basically open, and conversations can be heard while one walks from the front door into the children's theatre or as one stops and picks up his mail in the boxes located in the administrative suite. Similarly, the secretary's desk sits right in the middle of the suite, and the phone rings and conversations can be heard all over the suite. One of the administrative assistants sits directly across from the principal and handles a variety of the routine duties of the school. The nurse and the speech teacher who use the small conference table cabinet walled area also have no privacy. The space has not been adequate for counseling. Because of this, Joe has had his small counseling groups in the perception core instead of in the office area; even in that spot he has had considerable difficulty.

The Atmosphere

"This structure was designed to stimulate creative thinking, to facilitate purposeful motion and to assist thereby the development and flow of critical thinking in the creation of an educational experience such as our best knowledge has long told us was necessary—yet which our children of the past have too seldom had. The structure provides an open-life-place—warm, inviting, and profoundly significant." The rhetoric of the first sentence speaks for itself. It produces no concrete images.

A similar comment, it seems to me, might well be made in terms of the final section of the report entitled "The Citation," in reference to the fact that the yearly school building architectural exhibit at the AASA was awarded a special citation. The citation states: "Imaginative architecture leading to intriguing design. The overall atmosphere is in tune with the interests and imaginations of young children. This building is flexible, free-flowing, and functional."

And Freddy is the outcome.[5] This, then, is the reality sketch of a significant school.

The building was not ready in September, as originally planned and hoped. The temporary quarters were abandoned in early December. We have described some of the problems and issues in the move to the new building. The physical structure of Kensington was imaginative and beautiful in the judgment of everyone. In anticipation before the building was built, the Architectural Design Institute's *Sketch* described Kensington in great detail. In equally great detail we have taken issue with this anticipatory account. We have tried to discriminate the "reality" from the "dream" or, as we called it more formally, "the facade," the view of Kensington that has been presented in many forms to many publics. The weight

[5] In our later discussion of "Humor at Kensington," we observe that the product of Kensington was described by the staff in a warm, good-natured way as "Fully Functioning Freddy."

of this description has been carried by long dictated accounts that appeared in the summary notes near the end of the year. In later interpretive sections we shall quote other aspects of the field notes that provide further illustration and evidence concerning the general interpretation.

PHYSICAL FACILITIES IN SOCIAL THEORY

Introduction

Perhaps, if we had been trained as architects, some of our observations and interpretations on the innovative physical facilities would have been less naive and more fundamental. Perhaps, also, we would have conceptualized the problem differently—or even have been intrigued by a different problem. Be that as it may, we started with the idea from Homans (1950) that the physical environment was important; however, we were not able to obtain from him much in the way of analytical conceptions. Loomis (1960) and Gouldner (1961) helped to some extent. The former comments, "A facility may be defined as a means used to attain ends within the system" (p. 27). Loomis moves the concept little further, since he uses it only as a "residual category." Although his classification includes varied material objects and possessions, his major point is that the focus must be "upon relation of the facility to its utilization, not upon the items as facilities per se" (p. 28). He concludes:

"Regardless of the intrinsic nature of the facility, it is its use, not its intrinsic qualities, which determines its significance to social systems. Whether a given object is used as an altar and considered sacred or as an auctioneer's bench and considered secular, will in large part be determined by its evaluation and the communication of sentiment through utilization" (p. 30).

In our judgment, however, this is only a partial analogy. As means to ends, objects by their "intrinsic" qualities vary in the probabilities by which these means can be attached to certain ends. Thus, the intrinsic quality may affect, limit, or expand the utilization of the facility and obviously may have implications for teacher and pupil behavior. To return to a simple and often overused illustration, school desks that are bolted to the floor are very different from movable desks as soon as instructional procedures and goals shift to ungradedness, small group work, and the like. At Kensington, the modular furniture called "hi boys" and "lo boys" was supposed to serve as mobile cloakracks, bookcases, room dividers, sound barriers, and tackboards. In reality, the shelving and hanging racks were intrinsically too weak to carry the weight of heavy coats or books. The units were too heavy to be moved readily on carpeted surfaces by children or teachers. Finally, as we shall indicate shortly, they absorbed relatively little sound.

Gouldner (1961), in discussing relationships between pure and applied science, points out that sociologists have increasingly neglected aspects of material culture.

". . . pure sociological theory today fails to aid in the analysis of this problem: (1) it has very little to say about, and does not systematically deal with, the role of material props. Even the concept of 'culture,' which at one time involved reference to material traits, is increasingly defined in terms of normative elements alone. The theoretical location of material props, therefore, becomes steadily obscured as it gets thrust into a residual limbo. (2) Present pure sociological theory has given little thought to the relationship between social and cultural systems, and the so-called natural environment" (pp. 86–87).

Fundamentally, we believed that the physical facilities were important to a teacher, and that dimensional concepts of material props and physical facilities, are a needed aspect of educational theory.

Openness, Privacy, Freedom: Major Dimensions

Openness. As was noted earlier, one of the main features of the Kensington building is physical openness; this is clearly illustrated by the learning suites, the perception core, and the administrative offices. In our view the minimization of physical barriers necessitates considering a number of social and behavioral variables that tend to be more stable in traditionally designed buildings.

Lortie (1964) has presented characteristics of a self-contained classroom that, in part, may be attributed to physical design. In the same way, behavioral implications of open-space plans may be cited. Openness creates possibilities for variety and sets up probabilities for a number of interactive sequences that would never occur in a setting with permanent physical barriers. The number and kind of teacher-teacher, student-teacher, and student-student interactions is increased greatly in an open setting. The relationship between openness and opportunities for increased interaction occurs whether the form of instructional organization is a self-contained classroom in an open setting (as the ISD came to be later in the year) or a number of teams operating in the same area. In one respect the openness of the school was parallel to much of the intrateam structure and the interteam relationships. As indicated earlier, no decision-making structure was specified within teams, and there was no formally designated hierarchy. The belief system indicated by both physical design and formal doctrine was the one of pupil freedom, minimal teacher control, teacher-teacher-principal egalitariansim, and minimal rules for the organization. Physical openness was to facilitate these aspects of the school's social structure.

Privacy: A Conflicting Value. In an important sense, privacy is a value, like openness. As such, its behavioral implementation on occasion may conflict with other values—for instance, openness. The issue of privacy as it related to building design was experienced by the faculty and staff in a number of ways.

The low degree of privacy was no more keenly experienced than in the administrative suite that was "open." Initially, students frequented the administrative area. Its being near the main entrance enhanced its chances of becoming a part of the main traffic way. Private conferences were difficult to achieve. Although the movement of students was distracting to other students and teachers, it was also highly visible to visitors. Administratively, it was difficult to specify what visitors would observe. The high visibility in the perception core and ISD made "control" of what visitors would encounter difficult. In one sense, four or five classrooms open to observation simultaneously restricted both the privacy of the individual classroom and of the administration, which might wish to select only certain classes for visitors to observe. Eventually the team operating in the smallest, enclosed area was cited to guests as functioning most like the specifications of the model.

Lack of privacy also characterized the counseling activities. No rooms for private consultation were available, and groups of children were counseled in view of other children.

Finally, adults who have not lived for long periods of time in the company of large numbers of children seldom appreciate the immense gratification that accrues from meeting such simple needs as moments of privacy, conversation—passing the time of day—with another adult, or the leisure of a cigarette. This dimension of a building we referred to as "responsiveness to adult needs." Kensington was to have a small teacher's lounge in the nerve center. Funds were not available to complete this. The Curriculum Center provided a functionally equivalent alternative.

> I would guess also that the curriculum lab on the mezzanine will become a favorite hangout of the teachers because it is somewhat removed and is the only large and convenient lounge-type space. Ultimately, I would guess that the coffeepot will end up there instead of downstairs in the nerve center where it is supposed to be now. Eugene and Tom tried smoking there as I was leaving, and if that works out successfully, then most certainly it will become such a spot (12/7).

The curriculum center did become a place where members of the faculty could eat lunch, work, or plan together. It assured almost complete privacy from student activities.

Freedom. In general, openness and privacy are intermediary values. They are important as antecedents to personal freedom. In schools, the chain of reasoning should lead to learning. Among various kinds of learning, Kensington's emphasis was on intellectual skills and affective goals, such as self-awareness and positive self-evaluation. Our data are intermediary to these final outcomes. We have been struck by the too easy generalization that physical openess, that is, an absence of walls, leads immediately, directly, or simply to freedom in teaching and learning. A case can be made, we believe, that physical privacy provides some major contributions to freedom. These contributions tended to be minimized in the open space design of Kensington.

Sommer (1969) sketches some of the complexities regarding privacy and freedom in legal statutes, social norms, settings such as libraries and pubs, and individual behavior as he speaks out "in defense of privacy." In his analysis the hasty equating of openness with freedom and freedom with an undefined "goodness" is open to serious question. Research on infra-human societies as well as human societies has indicated that, at a minimum, territoriality, dominance, social status (rank), mobility, conflict, and aggression are involved in considerations of space.[6]

Organizational Aspects of Space

Openness, Role-Making, and Formalization. The relationship between physical design variables, organizational variables, and subsequent role behavior illustrates the concepts of role making, formalization, and concern with organizational processes as a series of transactions and negotiations among individuals. An emphasis on interactive processes points to the tendency to create and to change conceptions of self and other-roles. Such a view notes that, since roles vary in the extent to which they are definitive and consistent, individuals, by attempting to define and to make them explicit, create and modify them in the process. To theorists such as Buckley (1967) this then is "role-making" and implies, as a concomitant, role-bargaining or negotiating or contracts among actors. Attending to formal organization regulations, Buckley (1967) states:

"To the extent that the bureaucratic setting blocks the role-making process to that extent is organization maximal, 'variety' of alternatives of

[6] Similar arguments are made by Hall (1966) as he speaks of space as *The Hidden Dimension.*

action minimal, actors cogs in a rigid machine, and the morphogenic process frustrated" (p. 146).

In the case of Kensington, the bureaucratic-organizational constraints were minimal. Opportunities for a variety of alternatives as treated by Buckley seemed optimal. The case may be made, as we did in Chapter 4, that a beginning innovative organization with a number of less formalized new roles may be characterized by a greater degree of role-making than is found in established organizations.

At this point we hypothesize that a setting characterized by physical openness will be accompanied by a greater amount of role-making, negotiating, and bargaining among role occupants than is found in environments that are less open. If shared open spaces have as a concomitant the increased contractual arrangements in the form of teacher-teacher and teacher-student agreements, they, in turn, require additional time for formulation and enforcement. The coordination of activities both within team spaces and in public spaces is required. This, in turn, may alter the timing, the mode of presentation, and the content of instructional material. This would seem to be particularly characteristic of a program that emphasizes the use of new materials and equipment that require sharing by various groups of students and teachers.

In the case of Kensington, the frequent negotiations that involved time and energy expenditures and the lack of uniformity in the acceptance of supposedly agreed-on teacher and pupil behavior culminated in the request for temporary walls and the issuance of rules. As we have indicated, the rules were issued by the principal to regulate the patterns of movement and other behavior specific to the building and were to be enforced by the teachers. For some, the rules violated tenets of the formal doctrine about pupil freedom and teacher-principal equality in the decision-making process. Consequently, the rules received varied degrees of acceptance and adherence. Although the rules attended primarily to the usage of public space, many of the problems, such as sharing, privacy, noise, and coordination of activities, continued.

Proximity to Open Space. Although there was no unassigned enclosed space at Kensington, there were two extra open areas in ISD. Here again, the vagueness of the norms about utilization and sharing were accentuated. In lieu of this, proximity became a significant variable.

Proximity, or nearness in physical distance, looms large as a concept in a social psychological analysis. At the time of the move into the new building several observations and interpretations were made.

> Similarly, in regard to space, the fact that David was able to move over into the other instruction area for his total group work suggests that he will try

to commandeer it strictly through its immediate availability. A disclaimer on that exists, however, since Kay was over there with her group doing an arithmetic lesson about 10:30 this morning. My guess is that she will fight to have some access and use of the space. It should amount to more trouble for Liz, who has to move one section further to use such space (12/7).

Three days later a brief comment recorded in the summary notes follows up on the prior observation.

In terms of the physical aspects of the building and its design, once again the behavior of David illustrates the notion of spreading out over territory. His group is almost constantly in the extra instructional area as well as in its own tuitional area. It will not be long, it seems, until that almost "belongs" to him (12/10).

The issue of the use of unassigned spaces continued and, in one respect, was akin to the questions that arose concerning privacy and private property. As pointed out below, here again, the equalitarian structure of faculty relationships, the absence of walls, which might serve as arbitrators, and the initial dependence on "informal" agreements between teachers on the use of facilities enhanced the need for frequent consultation and negotiations between teachers, even though they were, for the most part, operating as self-contained units.

Patterns of Movement. If a building has locations representing or providing specialized functions or services—play, food, reading, desks for study—then one will have movement within the building. Presumably, doors and hallways were invented or co-opted by architects to facilitate this physical movement. Internally, Kensington did not have hallways. When individuals or groups of individuals went from one part of the building to another part, the issue of "patterns of movement" arose. The observers noticed this shortly after the ISD children came into the building but before the Basic Skills and Transition pupils arrived.

Another aspect of the space situation concerns the fact that the Perception Core is going to turn into one big combined hallway and multiple-purpose room. There was a lot of traffic through it; the lunch materials are at one end and the rest rooms are just off this room also. My guess is, and particularly when there are more kids around, that it will never attain the degree of quiet that one needs to study effectively in such a group setting. I do not know how they will resolve that one. Similarly, the kitchen seems inappropriately located, since all the traffic to and from it will have to go by the principal's area, and this should create some general confusion that is regular and persistent. When the number of children and the number of teachers is more than doubled, this should increase the problems also (12/7).

The absence of traffic patterns specified by the building design and the lack of norms about entering and leaving encouraged idiosyncratic patterns of movement both with regard to timing and location on the part of teachers and students. In the instance of the outdoor walkway, the physical environment became an important variable in the winter months and subsequently altered the patterns of movement within the building.

Thus, initially, in lieu of rules about density, patterns of movement, and entering and leaving spaces, behavior both within and between team areas was largely idiosyncratic and, in some instances, remained so until the close of school. Concomitants were increased distractions, interruptions, and frustration for fellow students and teachers. Although individual movement and activity were congruent with the stated aims of the school, the extent and implications of the idiosyncratic behavior of 200 students under 12 years of age was not fully anticipated. In this respect, our findings concerning the absence of internal traffic-ways fails to correspond to the positive emotional tones in the descriptions of others:

"And there are no halls to funnel children from compartment to compartment at the arbitrary dictate of a bell. Each child finds his own place, creates his own path" (Educational Facilities Laboratory: *Schools Without Walls,* p. 3).

Flexibility in Physical Facilities. Although there is a lack of precision in the use of the term flexibility, we were continuously faced with the need for such a concept in considering the dimensions of physical facilities and materials. As the ISD team altered its social structure, materials that were appropriate for one kind of organization became exceedingly inappropriate for another. The laboratory suite, without walls, for large numbers of students working mostly independently seems appropriate. However, when the organizational structure moves toward self-contained classroom units with some of the staff engaging in formal instruction, the large laboratory suite becomes considerably less adequate. Our findings concerning the relationship between open-school plans and a self-contained form of organization contrast with those of the Educational Facilities bulletin.

"Open space not only works well when the program is self-contained, it even may be especially desirable because it is flexible enough to accommodate traditional schooling while pushing toward change in the future" (p. 49).

Movable soundproof partitions seemed a reasonable compromise, as we speculated in January.

> In thinking about the physical facilities in the discussion this morning it seemed to me that the only real resolution to the problem of space and the organization of the school is to have the foldable soundproof walls separating each of the so-called learning suite areas into separate rooms. This should exist from the

kindergarten through the sixth grade. As teams of people find that they can work together or as ideas for teams of two to teams of six occur, then these walls can be put up or taken down at a moment's notice (1/9).

Further information reveals that walls or partitions of this kind are exceedingly expensive. In Milford, where taxes were high and bonded indebtedness was near the legal limit, the economic aspects of physical facilities were critical.

However, without any arrangement for temporary walls, flexibility, if it may be interpreted to imply adaptability, is not necessarily a characteristic of openness with respect to noise and visibility variables. In fact, frequently, activities were altered in response to the physical design rather than its proving to be highly "flexible" and "adaptable."

Variety of Spaces. Our earlier descriptive account of Kensington's physical facilities indicates not only interesting labels—"laboratory suites," "perception core," and the like—but also suggests that Kensington had varied kinds of space. In the formal documents and in the discussions of the school personnel very little mention occurred regarding the significance of "variety" of space as an alternative to "flexibility" of space. The fact that spaces were as different as the sheltered play area, the perception core, the children's theatre, and the curriculum center poses an important dimension of the building. Buildings can be described in terms of how many kinds of spatial settings are available. Presumably, buildings with high degrees of variety can meet individual differences in educational purposes and educational activities.[7]

Instructional Aspects of Space

Openness to Extraneous Stimuli. Although it is difficult to define "openness to extraneous stimuli," the necessity of such a concept has stayed with us. Kensington presented two situations of extreme openness to extraneous auditory and visual stimuli. Prior to the completion of the new building, the Independent Study Division, with 200 children, was temporarily located (for three months) in a junior high school gymnasium, without walls. In the new school, the lack of walls between classes still represented an extreme position on the openness continuum. In a regular elementary school classroom, about 25 to 35 children work together. When the entire group is engaged in a lesson or recitation, then the extraneous stimuli are primarily in the noise from the playground, traffic, or the tem-

---

[7] Sommer's (1969) discussion of the relation between flexibility and variety is the clearest we have seen. He does not present empirical data that relate variety to utilization variables, apparently because such data do not exist.

perature variations from some modal figure.[8] When children pursue individual topics, the environment is quite open to extraneous stimuli—as every teacher knows when a dozen or so of the class are moving about.

Kensington provided a contrast in both physical design and patterns of teacher-student, student-student, and teacher-teacher interaction. The "laboratory suite" areas of the building were internally open spaces; for ISD it was equivalent to seven classrooms. Shortly after the move to the new building, the following was recorded in the field notes.

> As one of the teachers talked with the principal, she commented that the noise problem was much less severe than it had been in the gymnasium, even though it could still be better. I could hear another teacher across his area when he had discussion early this morning. This kind of thing could not be heard before. However, I also could hear one group all the way down, two teaching stations away from the area where I was sitting.

Anderson (1966), in his discussion of the changing American schoolhouse, makes reference to the problem of noise as a stimulus in the environment of the pupil.

"The question most frequently asked about classrooms without walls is, 'But what about the noise?' Oddly enough, noise problems have not proved severe, partly because floor carpeting and other acoustical devices have been provided, and partly because the teachers have learned to coordinate their schedules and isolate such noise-producing activities as singing. Furthermore, acoustical engineers have concluded that the amount of sound interception necessary between groups may be much less than has been assumed" (p. 145).

In contrast, at Kensington the sound problem occurred early in the temporary quarters and continued in the new facilities, during which time it and its consequences remained a frequent and significant topic at team meetings.

The visual problems remained also. The physical facilities, the open area equivalent to seven classrooms for use by the ISD team, were broken only by modular furniture—cabinets, bookcases, and desks. Smaller areas, equivalent to two or three classrooms, contained Basic Skills (Grades 1 and 2) and Transition (Grade 3). The activities of any one subpart of the team, both children and teachers, were visually and auditorially open to every other part. Changes in these visual and auditory variables, which are correlates of openness, may alter content, kind, and timing of activities, thus varying teacher and student behavior.

---

[8] See the implications of this point in a slum school, as described by Smith and Geoffrey (1968, p. 161).

Density. Part of our concern with a conception like "openness to extraneous stimuli" lies in its relationship to a concept such as "density" which Anderson raises in the sentence that concludes the earlier quotation. He says:

"It also suggests that the overall space must be large enough in relation to the pupil population to permit adequate separation between work groups" (1960, p. 145).

The importance of density as a variable also has been alluded to in the previously cited Educational Facilities Laboratory report on open-plan schools.

"There must be enough space between groups so that the space itself can act as a sound barrier. It is worth noting that at both Dilworth and Fairmont acoustic difficulties showed up only when the spaces were over-populated" (EFL: *Schools Without Walls,* p. 31).

Neither of these analyses presents a criterion indicating when density becomes "over-population."

Density, the ratio of people to space, has been suggested by some social analysts as an important aspect of social systems. Hall (1966), in his monograph, *The Hidden Dimension,* refers to significant psychological and ecological research on overcrowding in the natural habitats of animals and the consequent physiological and social pathology that results. Stable dominance orders are broken, territoriality patterns are disrupted, and the usual nurturant familial patterns are dissolved. Our data suggest that Kensington, with its structure into Divisions (Basic Skills, Transition, and Independent Study) and into instructional teams and the particular allocation of space produced settings of higher density. When one combines the conceptions of "density" and "openness to extraneous stimuli" a further analysis is possible.

From our data we have developed a model (Figure 6.1) that contains an interrelated series of hypotheses regarding the implications of density and openness. If the number of pupils is increased and room size remains constant (or increases more slowly), density increases. As physical barriers, for example, walls, are absent, the openness to extraneous stimuli increases. As density increases and as the environment becomes more open to extraneous stimuli, the frequency of pupil-pupil interaction increases. As each of these increase, then noise and visual levels increase. These higher noise and visual levels promote greater behavioral contagion of pupils and pupil distraction from academic tasks.

We have suggested two broad classes of "contextual variables" (physical

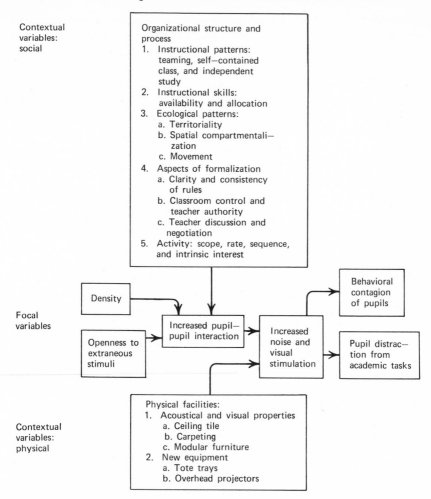

Figure 6.1   The implications of "density" and "openness to extraneous stimuli" in the dynamics of the Kensington School.

and social) that interact with the dimensions in the focal chain. For instance, the high absorption quality of the rugs on the floor and the ceiling tile were supposed to reduce auditory openness. They were better than the hardwood floor of the gymnasium, but they were not adequate. Similarly, modular furniture was to function partly as do walls in reducing visual and auditory openness. This, too, was only partially successful. The absence of movable walls had its impact also.

Organizational changes were pervasive in Kensington, and they had bearing on our analysis of density and openness. The instructional patterns in teaming and independent study and the limits in instructional skills and experience and their allocation resulted in continuing problems which precipitated organizational modifications throughout the year. They contributed to higher frequencies of pupil-pupil interaction. Innovations in classroom control and school rules (toward "democratic" organization) modified the usual consistency and clarity of these dimensions. In turn, these changes compounded issues related to density and pupil-pupil interaction. Finally, the scope, the rate, the sequence, and the intrinsic interest of academic activities were variables of importance in the social context of implications of density and openness to extraneous stimuli.

As Figure 6.1 indicates, when the idiosyncratic patterns of movement interacted with density, they were the source of faculty-faculty and student-faculty interpersonal difficulties and highlighted differences in the beliefs about freedom for pupils and the varied notions about faculty responsibility for the behavior of students other than those assigned to them.

Retrievable Physical Stimuli. Just as the excellence of a library might be an operational definition of the quantity and quality of the ideational structure of a school, the amount of storage space represents the degree of retrievable physical, and ideational, stimuli. Just as an available stored puppet stage may be a useful prop for a language art lesson, thus might other physical items help one to reach instructional goals. Classrooms and school buildings presumably can be placed on such a continuum. Two observations suggest our intent.

> A further comment that came up in the discussions concerned the amount of closet storage space in the building. Although everyone agreed that schoolteachers never felt that they had enough storage space, Howard did comment that the architect was not able to get as much of that in as was originally desired. Tom raised the notion of how desirable it would have been to have a basement under almost all of the building. I am reminded here of the Washington School and the storage closet off the kindergarten (12/10).

Storage space was at a minimum and tended to be movable and, therefore, small. Children's coatracks were open and portable. It was virtually impossible to store and obscure large objects from view. In an open-plan, team setting, this implies some kind of joint decisions and priorities concerning which material props will be retained. These decisions, in turn, have consequences for the kind and form of activities.

Also individuals vary in the degree to which they emphasize neatness and orderliness, and in their tolerance for variation on these dimensions among their team members. An open-space plan with a team teaching organization accentuates the importance of these variables. The amount of storage space as a physical variable may interact with the amount of privacy and the attitudes toward orderliness and neatness.

In Transition Division, Terrifico (the large cardboard robot built by Dan and his pupils) provides an example of the behavioral implications of a low degree of retrievable physical stimuli, an open-space plan, and a team form of organization. The decision to move Terrifico, which was essentially the property of one member of the team, to the new building against the wishes of two of the three-member team was a significant factor in the two-one split that eventually occurred. The lack of storage space for such a large object, the conflicting beliefs about the utility of Terrifico for instructional purposes and his being designated as "clutter," and the subsequent changes in functioning of the team indicate how building design influences organizational structure, individual attitudes, and the amount of privacy.

Conclusion: Conceptualizing Spatial Phenomena at Kensington

A comprehensive educational spatial theory would synthesize learning theory, instructional theory, and organizational theory. We shall not even approximate that synthesis and shall settle for a comment on several major issues that occurred at Kensington and that are intimately connected with a too simplified conception of open-space design in schools.

Figure 6.1 Revisited. In Figure 6.1 we described a set of hypotheses that interrelate density and openness to extraneous stimuli with pupil-pupil interaction, increased noise and visual stimulation, and finally to behavioral contagion and distraction from academic tasks. Although these hypotheses are plausible from our data, they need verification in other settings. Part of our reasoning lies in our two broad categories of contextual variables. Physical changes, notably carpets, acoustical tile, and movable modular furniture (bookracks and coatracks), were introduced to modify the auditory and visual stimuli. In Kensington's case they did not work. In other schools with different treatments they might. Furthermore, the contextual variables that we have labeled social indicate the organizational and instructional elements interdependent with the physical facilities. The kinds of instructional patterns used and the experience of the teachers, as this is represented in availability and allocation of instructional skills, seemed important. The nature of the curriculum, that is the scope, rate, and kind of activities, was unique, as other chapters indicate. The kind of territoriality that developed in the building from the temporary facilities used in the early fall and the stages in which the new building was occupied by divisions played its role. The faculty social structure which had been developing since August most certainly was critical.

Contrasts with Meadowland and Riverbend Schools. A later study (Smith, 1970) characterized several important dimensions in teaching method and administrative strategy related to open-space utilization. We quote from the report of Riverbend and Meadowland Schools:

"The central problem of this project was the determination of patterns of utilization of 'open space' by teachers and children in several new schools. The secondary purpose involved gleaning information about other aspects of the physical facilities which contributed to the open space concept and which posed special problems or opportunities for teachers and children. . . .

"One of the most striking generalizations concerning open space utilization is that each group of teachers develops to a high degree its own style. The reasons are less clear and require more data. In effect, there are multiple resolutions of the problem and opportunity of open space.

"As might be expected, some groups of teachers seem to utilize the open space area almost as though there were invisible walls separating the groups of children. In part this seemed to be a function of choice and of trial and error where joint patterns seemed less satisfactory. In short, they seemed to be functioning much more heavily as regular or standard self-contained classes except they were housed in an open area. (1) The station of each teacher was carefully demarcated. (2) The teacher's desk was with her children's desks. The adjoining work rooms were utilized less and sometimes by itinerant special teachers and not as a conference room. (3) Teacher patterns varied for each 'self-contained classroom' for at times there was total group instruction and at other times there was a small group clustered on the carpet around the teacher while others were engaged in seatwork. In this way intimacy and closeness were achieved. Also, sound problems were handled this way by having the kids sit on the floor while nestled in behind a swiveled chalkboard. Such a pattern was dysfunctional when texts were needed and especially when writing was required.

"Several groups might well be called 'the expanded self-contained classroom.' For a portion of the day it was as though they tried to take 60 or 90 children and teach them in a style similar to a total group recitation in a self-contained classroom. (1) All the children's desks were together. (2) In some settings a microphone-loudspeaker system and/or a lectern had been installed to facilitate each child's hearing. It suffered as a one-way system for the child's response often could not be heard by everyone. The central heating fans complicated this problem. (3) Teaching was partly specialized: science taught by one, social studies by another, and so forth. In some instances lessons were rotated by teachers every other day or according to some pattern. (4) Groups of children were drawn off to peripheral spaces, defined by a limited amount of modular furniture, for some instructional purposes. (5) Often teachers seemed pressed for time; the usual procedures, pupils score their own papers with review of difficult or misunderstood issues, tended to break down. (6) Problems of pupil attention and control exist on occasion in such arrangements, for children on the periphery sometimes are 'lost' and larger numbers of more difficult pupils are grouped together.

"The 'enthusiastic team' colloquially described one of the teams. The teachers are young, confident, and active. During my visits I had the very strong impression that they enjoyed working together and found the team pattern desirable and stimulating. A number of particular observations elaborate this general impression: (1) team planning occurred as they talked informally off and on during the day; (2) heavy utilization of the office space off the main room as a place to study and store curriculum materials; (3) a willingness to let the other teacher or teachers handle 'my' group on occasion; (4) a commonality among the teachers in style of teacher-pupil interaction; the teachers were both quite directive and quite sympathetic toward the children.

"It is important to note that the cooperative teaching involved them only part of the day. Much of the instructional program was handled in the form of self-contained classroom activities.

"A further major factor which needs more analysis is the shift from recitational type lessons and curriculum to project or unit types of curriculum for teaming activities. Social studies or science units wherein the children engage in differentiated reading, resource utilization, data collection, writing, construction and culminating activities were found feasible in some instances. The component teaching skills required, the guidance of individual children into meaningful work, and the coordination of teacher efforts would require considerably more data than I had available. . . .

"An earlier study of an open area school, (Kensington) illustrated an approach to the organization of teachers and pupils in which the teams of 2, 3, 4, and 7 were given groups of 60, 90, 120, and 180 pupils. These large groups of children were then differentiated into smaller groups for particular learning experiences. Such a point of view might be called the *differentiated strategy*. It has several advantages and disadvantages as a means of organizing for team teaching and the utilization of open space.

"In contrast, our inference from the current observations of Riverbend and Meadowland Schools is that an *additive* strategy was more generally used. In this instance groups of pupils (usually 25–30) are identified as being Miss Adam's or Miss Brown's. The teachers are encouraged to develop cooperative teaching in whatever ways seem reasonable and sensible to them as they work together. The consequences of this approach seem to include (1) moving from the familiar to the unfamiliar, (2) tentative exploration, (3) slower changes from traditional styles, (4) less risk taking, (5) higher probabilities of success, and, as we have noted, (6) quite different patterns of utilization."

Our conclusion in that paper remains relevant for the present chapter as well: "The intricacies of the relationships among building design, material props, administrative leadership, staff organizational patterns, curriculum, and teaching styles have only begun to be sketched."

CHAPTER 7

Teaming: Staff Cooperative Interaction

In one of the foremost accounts of team teaching, Shaplin and Olds view the central conception of the approach in this manner: ". . . a type of instructional organization, involving teaching personnel and the students assigned to them, in which two or more teachers are given responsibility, working together, for all or a significant part of the instruction of the same group of students" (Shaplin and Olds, 1964, p. 15). If we define team teaching as cooperative teaching, as does Shaplin in a later statement (1965), then we are in a position to bring to bear theories of cooperation on the problem of staff interaction. Although this account might well have been incorporated in other parts of the Kensington story, since its complexity illustrates very well the issues of organizational change through the unanticipated consequences of purposive social action, we analyze it as an organizational innovation.

Formal Doctrine and Teaming at Kensington

In the Institutional Plan, one statement of Kensington's formal doctrine, teaming was an important component. As we have considered aspects of the doctrine, we believe that internal inconsistencies exist in several elements of the doctrine. In our earlier discussion, we labeled this low integration of doctrine. Furthermore, we believe that the field of educational administration and organization has not analyzed well these latent inconsistencies and no theoretical synthesis exists. Nonetheless, Kensington tried to make these ideas into a workable reality.

For instance, Kensington espoused both a concept of role specialization and a concept of faculty egalitarianism. The latter was a part of the larger conception of the "upside-down authority structure" which we consider intensively in another chapter. The egalitarianship and teaming were to lead to democratic teacher-pupil relationships, individualized instruction, and idiosyncratic teaching styles. The potential for conflict among these conceptions was not anticipated and did occur. Idiosyncratic teaching styles are not always and necessarily democratic. Democratic teacher-pupil relationships have no uniform referent; that is, they may vary from a Rousseauian permissiveness to a benevolent authoritarianism. Individualized instruction can be highly structured and teacher directed or minimally structured and pupil directed. Finally, the degree to which pupil autonomy, responsibility, and independent study are intercorrelated, and the degree to which they flow from the prior variables is not clear.

Within the divisional organization at Kensington, the teachers were subdivided further into teams. This pattern continued throughout the year and was a major innovative thrust of Kensington. At the insistence of several faculty members, the Basic Skills Division split early in August. The team of two, with one third of the Basic Skills children, worked almost totally independently of the team of four. The initial break resulted partly from "personality conflict" and partly from an ideological difference on the traditional-progressive continuum. The team of two developed problems that involved the dominant-subordinate dimension of a dyad. The team of four with strong part-time support, which made it a team of five in many ways, developed very harmoniously, as we have detailed elsewhere. The Transition Division tended to form a dyadic coalition within the triad. Here also the traditional-progressive dimension loomed large. In ISD the changes were frequent and pervasive. The initial "total team" gave way under a variety of pressures, conflicts, and divisions in point of view into departmentalization, two teams of three, then into a dyadic coalition within one team, and finally into almost a total self-contained structure. The latter was characterized by quite varied patterns of teacher-pupil relationships. One class approached a *Summerhill* flavor of total pupil self-direction and initiation. Others approached a more traditional textbook curriculum with high warmth and involvement on the part of the teacher. Many of the details of these events appear earlier in our descriptive accounts of the school.

Illustrative of the complexity of doctrine, practice, and theory is a preliminary interpretation we made into the Summary Observation notes in early May. In effect, it poses an introductory framework for our more careful analysis.

> As I have thought more of team teaching in the last few days I am struck by a number of aspects: first, the administrative overhead gets very large in a big hurry; the integration among persons or among subteams needs to exist and needs to have been worked out in detail at a conceptual level, that is, in the ideas being taught, otherwise there is a lukewarm, forced relationship among the ideas. Second, this raises the general question as to what degree the content ideas really are different and the degree to which they are conceptualized in the same fashion by the individual teachers. Third, I am struck

further by the fact that much team deciding is a series of power politics and related plays. Fourth, I am impressed at how backward everything usually is: the main ingredient here is that often decisions regarding the selection of people to be involved and of the materials to be used comes prior to the careful thinking through of the educational objectives and the means by which you are trying to reach the objectives. This then precludes much of the discussion and much of the integration one wanted to bring about. To keep this kind of rush from occurring, one needs a long prior relationship between two people who have thought through most of the ideas before hand. Fifth, there is the old "philoṣophy" notion as to what is supposed to happen in the teaching-learning situation. For example, is one supposed to slosh around and hope that people will develop "broad integrative concepts," or do you try to teach hard for particular skills and particular ideas in particular areas. Similarly, the priority in which teaming is supposed to be a staff educational device as opposed to the degree as to which it is to be a student educational device raises part of this as well. Any disagreements here are fundamental. Sixth, the degree to which the teacher-pupil relationship is considered the fundamental aspect of instruction influences in an important way the phenomenon of teaming. If one activates contingencies between several layers of teachers and supervisors and through teachers of several areas and subject matters, and only then begins a relationship with the pupils, then the degrees of freedom that are left for the relationship with the pupils are very limited. This point strikes me now as so important and so fundamental that much of the analysis of the team literature will stand or fall right around this thesis. This suggests also that a discussion on the "social psychology of tutoring as an instructional ideal" is precisely the place to focus the analysis of the instructional program at Kensington. Seventh, the degree that one can eliminate the frenetic quality, it seems to me, is also very, very important. A final point I would make concerns the degree to which the hierarchy of authority and dominance easily comes into a team situation. This conflicts mightily with the usual notion of each teacher being his own master (5/4).

Aspects of a Theory of Cooperative Interaction

In a simple, matter-of-fact way, Barnard (1938) begins his analysis of formal organizations and executive functioning by raising questions about cooperative behavior, the phenomenon that lies at the basis of organizations. He states a basic postulate applicable under certain circumstances:

". . . cooperation has no reason for being except as it can do what the individual cannot do. Cooperation justifies itself, then, as a means of overcoming the limitations restricting what individuals can do" (p. 23).

Since we have defined team teaching as cooperative teaching, individuals acting or operating jointly, we explore a number of dimensions on which team teaching as cooperative teaching may be contrasted with other forms of teacher organization. Shaplin has addressed his attention to the same general issue in these terms:

"In this generation in American education, there appears to be a widespread increase in the amount of cooperative or collaborative activity among teachers, particularly of activity directly connected with classroom teaching. . . . Though this collaboration and cooperation takes many diverse forms, there appear to be certain persistent themes, all of which reflect a deep discontent with the standard organization of the school on the basis of the self-contained teacher and the self-contained classroom" (1965, p. 14).

He speaks of themes such as: (1) teachers' desires to teach subjects in which they are more interested, specialized, or talented, (2) teachers' desires for greater flexibility in grouping pupils, (3) a belief in greater efficiency in instructional time through combining classes and (4) desires for joint faculty planning and evaluation. These are important issues in American education.

In this section we deal with several dimensions of cooperative activity: interdependence, coordination, authority, time and place, materials, and specialization. We indicate how each of them is a part of a cooperative system, and we hypothesize some relationships between these dimensions and the utilization of organizational resources. Following this, we illustrate the usefulness of the concepts for exploring the further aspects of team teaching.

Interdependence. Cooperative teaching activity implies interdependence as contrasted with the autonomy that has generally been used to describe the typical organization of teachers. Interdependence in turn requires coordination. Thompson's (1967) delineation of various modes of interdependence and coordination provides a base from which we can examine relationships between these dimensions within teams at various points in time. Thompson begins by distinguishing between three types of interdependence in the following way:

"To assume that an organization is composed of interdependent parts is not necessarily to say that each part is dependent on, and supports, every other part in any direct way. The Tuscaloosa branch of an organization may not interact at all with the Oshkosh branch, and neither may have contact with the Kokomo branch. Yet they may be interdependent in the sense that unless each performs adequately, the total organization is jeopardized; failure of any one can threaten the whole and thus the other parts. We can describe this situation as one in which each part renders a discrete contribution to the whole and each is supported by the whole. We will call this *pooled interdependence.*

"Interdependence may also take a serial form, with the Keokuk plant producing parts which become inputs for the Tucumcari assembly operation. Here both make contributions to and are sustained by the whole organization, and so there is a pooled aspect to their interdependence. But, in addition, direct interdependence can be pinpointed between them, and the order of that interdependence can be specified. Keokuk must act properly before Tucumcari can act; and unless Tucumcari acts, Keokuk cannot solve its output problem. We will refer to this as *sequential interdependence,* and note that it is not symmetrical.

"A third form of interdependence can be labeled *reciprocal,* referring to the situation in which the outputs of each become inputs for the others. This is illustrated by the airline which contains both operations and maintenance units. The production of the maintenance unit is an output for operations, in the form of a serviceable aircraft; and the product (or by-product) of operations is an input for maintenance, in the form of an aircraft needing maintenance. Under conditions of reciprocal interdependence, each unit involved is penetrated by the other. There is, of course, a pooled aspect to this, and there is also a serial aspect since the aircraft in question is used by one, then by the other, and again by the first. But the distinguishing aspect is the reciprocity of the interdependence, with each unit posing contingency for the other" (1967, pp. 54–55).

The self-contained classroom incorporates both pooled and sequential interdependence.[1] In a sense, each teacher operates relatively independently on a day-to-day basis. Sequential interdependence occurs mainly at two points. The beginning and ending of the school year when pupils are retained or "passed" to the next year poses critical problems for internal structure and also provides a major point of contact with the environment, that is, the parents. Long-range interdependence of curriculum also is involved in the levels of textbooks, the supplementary reading materials that "belong" in particular grades, and the enrichment activities that "encroach" on other teachers and other levels. However, team teaching is more likely to be characterized by reciprocal interdependence. The moment-to-moment, the day-to-day, and the weekly and monthly activities of one teacher are contingent on the similar activities of one or more other teachers. In short, the outputs of one teacher become inputs for another.

In some schools the forms of interdependence may represent a degree of unidimensionality for an organization as a whole; however, at Kensington

---

[1] Throughout this discussion, both explicit and implicit comparisons will be made to a self-contained classroom we studied intensively several years ago at the Washington School. This analysis was presented as *The Complexities of an Urban Classroom* (1968).

there was vascillation between modes of interdependency through time. In the ISD alone modes varied from pooled to reciprocal interpendence in the various teams at the same point in time. As a contrast, the team of four in the Basic Skills Division maintained reciprocal forms throughout the year. These varying patterns gave participants a number of changing options and posed a number of decisions to be made.

Coordination: Kinds and Costs. As in the case of interdependency, Thompson views coordination as being secured in three predominant modes: standardization, coordination by plan, and coordination by mutual adjustment.

"Under some conditions coordination may be achieved by *standardization*. This involves the establishment of routines or rules which constrain action of each unit or position into paths consistent with those taken by others in the interdependent relationship. An important assumption in coordination by standardization is that the set of rules be internally consistent, and this requires that the situations to which they apply be relatively stable, repetitive, and few enough to permit matching of situations with appropriate rules.

"In the March and Simon formulation, *coordination by plan* involves the establishment of schedules for the interdependent units by which their actions may then be governed. Coordination by plan does not require the same high degree of stability and routinization that are required for coordination by standardization, and therefore is more appropriate for more dynamic situations, especially when a changing task environment impinges on the organization.

"A third form can be called *coordination by mutual adjustment* and involves the transmission of new information during the process of action. (In March and Simon terms, this is 'coordination by feedback,' but the term 'feedback' has gathered a connotation of super/subordination which unduly restricts it for our purposes. Coordination by mutual adjustment may involve communication across hierarchical lines, but it cannot be assumed that it necessarily does.) The more variable and unpredictable the situation, March and Simon observe, the greater the reliance on coordination by mutual adjustment" (1967, p. 56).

In the school with self-contained classrooms, coordination by standardization is the usual mode. The eight areas of the elementary curriculum prescribe the activities. The number of minutes devoted to each area is further prescribed by the larger organization. Planning occurs most frequently in these schools when there is some specialization of staff and the sharing of these resources. The P.E., art, and music teachers typify such specialities. The scheduling, by plan, for the instruction by these teachers become fixed points in the day and week around which other activities fall. As Thompson indicates, stability and routinization are both antecedents and consequences of such planning.

In a system characterized by a great deal of variety of activity (for example, curriculum, materials, schedules) and of personnel in reciprocal interdependence, as Kensington was, the functions of coordination are enhanced. When this variety is considered as an element of a system, coordination is an attempt to give order. In this sense, increased variety is a concomitant of the establishment of a cooperative effort. Team teaching as a form of organization stands in stark contrast to the self-contained form of organization. Barnard's notion of an ordered combination of personal effort describes well the aspects of cooperation involved in teaming that have implications for coordination. He notes the centrality of coordination for the continuation of cooperative systems. Coordination as "the securing of the appropriate combination of the elements of the organization to produce utilities is the basis for the endurance of cooperative systems."

Barnard's analysis, which suggests continuous adjustments, has further implications for time as a resource of a cooperative system:

"The conditions of the environment . . . are constantly changing the limitations of the environment with respect to cooperative action. . . . Adjustments of cooperative systems are adjustments in the balance of the various types of organizational activities" (Barnard, 1938).

The coordination and adjustment of these activities requires time—and also timing—about which we shall speak shortly. In the case of team teaching, time becomes critical because of the organization per se and because of auxillary functions that often become associated with teaming. For instance, the goals of the Kensington School, especially individualized instruction in contrast to textbook instruction, involved the teams in the preparation and writing of new materials. This exhausting task is not indigenous to team teaching but often arises in conjunction with it for reasons similar to ones that produce dissatisfaction with the self-contained-classroom organization.[2]

Furthermore, the concept of time demands is indigenous in another way. Consider the traditional teacher who plans his work a bit the night before, a bit on the way to school in the morning, and mostly by following the program laid out in the text. This part of his task, planning, demands little time and often is done at odd hours, at the last minute, or on the spur of the moment. In the team-teaching situation, the teacher must consciously rationalize his plans to a higher degree, he must submit them

[2] See especially the analysis by Grannis (1964).

to his fellows for examination, he must examine their plans, and they must reach an amicable compromise on the content and the sequence functional for reaching agreed-on objectives. If this is done seriously, it has implications for daily planning, for weekly or larger unit planning, as well as for semester or yearly planning. This is the essence of coordination by mutual adjustment. This is intrinsic to teaming as cooperative teaching.

Such an increase in time demands is important if one assumes that there are limits to the total time that individuals are willing to devote to the professional part of their lives.[3] Within teaching, little research seems available on the pupil learning consequences of planning per se. None exists on the relative amounts of time spent in planning the teaching act, in executing the teaching act, and in independent activity on the part of the pupil. Presumably, as the planning time increases and the execution time decreases, the impact of specialization must increase to make up for the time decrement. This problem strikes us as an exceedingly critical and practical issue for organizational theory and verificational research.

In short, the nature of mutual adjustment as a form of coordination illustrates a concluding point by Thompson on the costs of increasingly involved coordination:

". . . the three types of coordination, in the order introduced above, place increasingly heavy burdens on communication and decision. Standardization requires less frequent decisions and a smaller volume of communication during a specific period of operations than does planning, and planning calls for less decision and communication activity than does mutual adjustment. There are very real costs involved in coordination" (1967, p. 56).
Our data amply support his conclusion on the relationship between the mode of coordination that is chosen for a cooperative system and the drain on available resources of time and effort. Our notes are replete with comments regarding the tremendous expenditures in "time and energy" as the teams tried to implement an instructional program.

Time, Place, and Materials. Two basic elements of social systems, time and place, are often neglected in discussions of interdependence and coordination. The concept of time as it relates to cooperative activity and scheduling has been described by Barnard as "among the most complex of the processes of coordination." The time at which work is done reaches beyond scheduling and includes the personal characteristic of "dependabil-

---

[3] Without question, total time, 24 hours a day, is limited. At Kensington sharp conflict existed over how much of that time should be devoted to school activities and other, especially family, activities. Furthermore, as we discussed in our analysis of total commitment, important relationships existed regarding true belief in an innovative organization.

ity." This factor, in turn, relates to punctuality and continuity of function in the organization. The implications of the dependability of activity of team members for team effectiveness are discussed later.

In contrasting team teaching as a form of organization with that of the self-contained classroom, the latter requires less teacher-teacher, teacher-student, and student-student coordination of timing than does the former. In some respects, the self-contained form deals with teacher-teacher time units on a yearly basis, but in team teaching, with a mutual adjustment mode of coordination, moment-to-moment allocations of time units are made. This obviously makes for an entirely different "ordered combination of personal effort" with an emphasis on dependability as a means of securing continuity within the activities of the team.

Place as a dimension of cooperative activity has been treated to a certain extent in the chapter on physical facilities, in which we discuss some of the implications of open-space designs for team teaching. The places where work is done may vary from that of the self-contained arrangement, in which units of teacher-occupied space are by and large independent, to settings in which places where most of the activities are performed by partially to totally overlapping patterns of use. The latter has been amply illustrated by the organization of place at Kensington. In instances, time may be viewed in the same way, with team teaching representing joint allocations of time. Barnard notes that dimensions of time and place often have been taken for granted and their significance has been overlooked. However, "the utmost skill and the most refined differentiation of processes will instantly wither if there is failure in time or place."

Similarly, materials as dimensions of cooperative activity may be treated in much the same way as time and place. They incorporate both students and the objects with which work is performed, and either may be the primary responsibility of one teacher, as in self-contained usage, or they may vary from partial to total overlap, as in the instance of team teaching in which props may be "shared" by a number of teachers. Further complications occur with consummable materials such as paints, crayons, paper, and workbooks. If they are allocated in a standardized or planned fashion, as is usual in a self-contained classroom, the individual teacher can adjust her behavior accordingly. In the reciprocal situation with mutual adjustive coordination the dimensions of dependability and trust arise.

The Pupil: Material or Decision Maker. Up to this point, most of our discussion of teaming has focused on the problems of interdependence and coordination of teachers. The analysis of time, space, and materials as elements in coordination suggests that pupils might be categorized similarly, that is, as materials that the school processes as a product. Although this was not Kensington's conception, it might be useful to begin here and later move to the conception of the pupil as an independent and interdependent decision maker.

Classically, in the self-contained classroom organization about 25 pupils are allocated to a teacher for a year. As we have indicated, standardization is assumed and pooled interdependence results. Space, materials, and curricular tasks also are allocated in a standardized fashion with each teacher having her room, her desks, her books, her subjects to teach, and so forth. Within this format, the autonomy-equality pattern as Lortie (1964) describes it, the teacher has considerable freedom to organize her day and her mode of instruction as she desires. For instance, she can be a traditional textbook teacher or a Kilpatrick project teacher. She can integrate science and math or English and social studies into a core curriculum or teach each subject independently. She can proceed abstractly at a verbal level or introduce concrete manipulative materials. She can accent objectives such as the learning of factual material, abstract integrative concepts, or critical and divergent thinking. She can establish relationships with the pupils that go by labels such as democratic or autocratic, learner centered or teacher centered, informal or formal. At the core of these relationships are variations in the degree to which the child initiates and decides what he learns, when he learns, and how he learns.

The usual departmental organization alters the pooled interdependence of the self-contained classroom to a sequential format. The child moves from one hour or period to another teacher, another curricular task, and another physical space. Scheduling is done the first of the year to match pupils, teachers, and space. Such a scheme permits the grouping of pupils in terms of ability—high sections and low sections. As the student grows older, choice is introduced and, depending on interest and ability, the individual can opt for more or less mathematics, science, or music. In curricular areas that demand specialized materials and space—P.E. and gymnasiums, home economics and stoves, science and laboratories—larger masses of often expensive equipment can be assembled. Teachers specialize, focus their training, background, and knowledge, and develop a richer understanding of the ideas and material related to their subject. As with the self-contained format, they develop their own style of relating to pupils. The most serious drawback is that they are involved daily, not with 25 or 35 pupils, but with 100 or 150 pupils. "Getting to know" that many pupils is the proverbial lament of the departmentalized teacher. Pupil choice and decision often lies more heavily in the initial selection of course or instructor rather than in daily or "along the way" alterations in the content and procedures.

Team organization intends to blend some of the advantages of each and to add the very important ingredient of reciprocal interdependence and mutual adjustment. Each team has from 50 to 200 pupils, depending on the number of teachers. Depending on the kind of building they have, all the pupils may be in an open space or in multiple kinds of rooms. Teachers vary in degree of training from aides to master teachers. They may vary in subject matter specialization and competence. And they may vary in instructional skills—tutoring, small group work, to large group lecturing. The most important ingredient, however, is that the team organization forces an increase in teacher interdependence and teacher decision making. In Grannis' words:

". . . team teaching is a structure of givens and alternatives, deliberately fashioned to create options that require decisions and also entailing other decisions that might not have been anticipated in the original design" (1964, p. 125).

One of the most difficult problems confronting the team is deciding which pupils should be where for what kind of instruction. As we have indicated, the self-contained and the departmentalized classroom make some of those decisions before school begins in the fall of the year; for teaming, they are left open. Consequently, the array of activities coordinated by mutual adjustment is very large. As some of our descriptive materials have indicated, each team in each division resolved the issues in very different ways. The sign-up sheets in ISD and the initial grouping by BSD-4 (partly because of the physical room facilities in the temporary quarters at the high school) illustrate the variety of formats possible. We have detailed many of the changes that occurred during the year. Similarly, we have recounted numerous comments by the teachers of difficulties in getting to know pupils with their special problems and individual purposes, the difficulties in building harmonious and cohesive groups, and the difficulties in planning and deciding with the children. In effect, as they achieved the benefits and liabilities of being contingent on their fellow teachers, they found that they were less contingent on the needs and interests of their pupils.

Bounded Rationality. A slight extension of Barnard's (1938) point of perceptual components limiting and necessary to coordinated cooperative behavior moves us to March and Simon's concept of bounded rationality. Barnard means that information about the immediate environment must be present and available to all parties in the joint endeavor. Bounded rationality refers to "the limits of information available to humans and their abilities to use information in their computations" (March and Simon, 1958, p. 203). In short, if mutually adjustive coordination is to occur, all parties to the reciprocal interdependence must possess relevant information. In complex cooperative situations this can result in too much information on some occasions and too little on other occasions.

The goals of Kensington stressed in a variety of ways a concern for the total development of each child, the need to teach him individually, and to program his work cooperatively and individually with him. This produced an information load that would be burdensome for a tutor with one child. A variety of formats of individualized instruction integrate a computer into their schemes for just this reason. For a teacher of 25 children in an all-day self-contained classroom, the burdens are well known and remain a continuing unsolved problem. In team teaching, several conditions maximize the information problem. Each teacher sees more children and each teacher sees each child for a shorter period of time. We hypothesize that the stress on the goal of totality of individual development, in contrast to more limited cognitive goals, means that the focusing of information is more difficult and is compounded by the team-teaching mode of organization. In Kensington, the teaming resulted in continuing laments that "We don't know the children well enough." Although this occurred early in the year particularly, it also was prevalent throughout the year. For instance, in ISD, Irma's group was having oral reports. She had a clipboard with the children's names and she made notes on their presentations. The field notes record the observer's perception and interpretation:

> Irma still stumbles occasionally on a name of a child. (OBS—This seems most significant because they've had these kids for several months now.)

The mechanisms developed to handle the information problems were: (1) team meetings, (2) informal communication, and (3) written records. As we have indicated elsewhere, the formal team meetings varied in the degree to which they were conflict ridden and, consequently, immobilized for information sharing much less the initiation of action. The informal communication occurred well in one team that developed mechanisms for several of the team members to have morning coffee or lunch together. The written records suffered from developmental needs (production of record forms), debate over what should be recorded, and then from limited time to record and to read the recordings of others.

Essentially then, in regard to bounded rationality, the key problem centered on the information overload. The coordination by mutual adjustment increases the amount of information that a participant must consider and, as indicated by Thompson (1967), emphasizes continuous feedback and communication far more than the other modes of coordination. In the case of Kensington, the inadequate mechanisms for processing available information only compounded the problem and confused the key issue.

Inventive Patterns of Activity. Effectiveness of cooperation in most instances requires what Barnard (1938) has called "an ordered combination of personal efforts." The "ordered" element receives elaboration from him in the context of a requirement for inventiveness and the discovery of patterns of interrelatedness of personal efforts. He perceives this inventiveness as a rare and infrequent phenomenon in the history of science and of ordinary experience. At Kensington, an outcome of the summer workshop, or if we were to use evaluative terms—a tragedy of that workshop, was that the staff was still reaching for those concrete patterns on Thursday and Friday of the fourth week, moments before the children were to arrive just after Labor Day. For instance, in ISD the use of self-selected natural friendship groups was not an explicitly defined operational definition of "individualized instruction" until Monday afternoon of the last week of the workshop. The training group and the task group conception did not arrive until Wednesday. On Thursday of that week it was decided that pupil attendance in the training group would take priority over attendance at other groups or activities. As we have related, this led to a particular set of sign-up procedures that was not workable with some children. In turn, the organizational structure was modified in several ways, for example, a self-contained classroom, and so on.

Also, very little careful description exists on the natural history of teaching. Here we have reference to two interrelated phenomena, the flow of events during a semester or a year, and the flow of events during an entire teaching career. If data on these issues were available from the teachers of self-contained classrooms and from teachers in a departmentalized organization, innovations such as team teaching could be conceptualized and evaluated much more readily. Speculations concerning this issue arose in the fall as we talked with Jean Emerson from Basic Skills:

> Jean is ill with a cold and general fatigue. She's putting her time in this week and generally coasting. She'd been invited to a Thanksgiving dinner and was supposed to bring a Jello mold. She just doesn't know whether she's going to be able to get time to do this. With not feeling well and the minimal interests that she expressed later, in cooking, one can get a picture of her current level of functioning. This suggests an important theoretical problem in team teaching, the dips and the plateaus in enthusiasm and in energy and how the other team members must be able to and be willing to pick up at these times and carry more of the weight. In a regular classroom the teacher typically would move into some rather routine busy-work-type activities. If there are such rhythms to teaching, then it seems to be important to think about the team concepts in regard to the rhythms. In paraphrase form, the basic question becomes, "What does the team do when the individual isn't up?"

In effect, our speculation concerns a very mundane kind of problem—the behavior of a teacher who is not feeling good. This kind of influence on cooperative teaching seems important and largely unanalyzed. Barnard's (1938) conception of inventiveness in "ordered" activity seems to catch its focus.

Solutions to aspects of team teaching such as the above that arise from an ordered combination of personal effort have implications for goal attainment or effectiveness of cooperation. In contrast, the BSD-2 team developed an alternative "ordered combination of personal efforts." The problems they found in informal authority, coordination, and inability to know well large numbers of children suggest that the satisfactions were not as high as in alternative situations in which the team members had taught. Barnard, in commenting on this kind of issue, anticipates much of the current work in social exchange theory:

"If the distribution were such that benefits just equaled burdens in each case, which would require ideal precision in distribution, each individual would have no margin of inducement as against other alternatives. The cooperative system must create a surplus of satisfaction to be efficient. If each man gets back only what he puts in, there is no incentive, that is, no net satisfaction for him in cooperation. . . . Efficiency, for the individual, is satisfactory exchange. Thus the process of cooperation also includes that of satisfactory exchange" (1938, p. 58).

Such an analysis suggests also that the persistent themes of deep discontent with the self-contained classroom that Shaplin (1965) described, and which is cited earlier, have their rivals in other kinds of dissatisfaction and discontent within particular teaming or cooperating situations. As our introductory epilogue has indicated, Kensington as a particular system and as a system interdependent with other systems, for example, Milford in the larger context and the divisions and teams within, culminated in almost a total turnover of personnel. The staff opted elsewhere.

"The survival of cooperation, therefore, depends upon two interrelated and interdependent classes of processes: (a) those which relate to the system of cooperation as a whole in relation to the environment; and (b) those which relate to the creation or distribution of satisfactions among individuals" (Barnard, 1938, pp. 60–61).

Thus, inventive solutions that are products or outcomes of a cooperative system may accomplish objectives of the system. The solutions are assessed or "determined with a view to the system requirements." However, they may or may not satisfy individual motives. The latter, which Barnard calls efficiency, may be secured "either by changing motives in individuals . . . or by its *productive* results which can be distributed to individuals." Productive results may be either material, social, or both. For cooperative systems to be efficient, they must create a surplus of satisfaction. In the case of Kensington, the teams varied in both the extent to which inventive solutions were developed and in the amount of satisfaction that was created. If turnover rate, as cited earlier, can be used as an indicator, the surplus of satisfaction, a requisite of efficiency, was not attained for many participants.

Dependability of Activity. One of Barnard's (1938) points on implicit barriers in the ordered combination of activities in cooperation is dependability, that is, a reliability in performance of activities. As a dimension of cooperation, dependability of activity may be treated as a further aspect of time. As was noted earlier, dependability makes for the continuity of function that, in turn, incorporates timing and sequencing of activities.

Reliability in performance of activities was a significant problem for the ISD team and a minor problem in the other teams. The causes were quite varied and seemingly outside the immediate control of the individual members. Throughout the year, Kay was physically below par with the aftereffects of infectious mononucleosis. She missed meetings in the summer workshop, and she was absent from time to time during the year. The problem was seriously complicated by the heavy time and work demands in the Kensington program. Jack had somewhat vague but real responsibilities as a districtwide consultant in science; these duties drew him out of the team in August as well as during the year. He also had Saturday morning college teaching responsibilities, which caused him to miss Saturday staff and team meetings. David had periods of excitement when all things were possible and would be undertaken and periods of doubt and depression when little was attainable. For the team this was a kind of variableness, unreliability, or lack of dependability. Tom, although not an official member of the team, was strongly identified with it and, of course, had his major responsibilities as materials and resource coordinator for the entire school. Frequently in the team, decisions would be made, and the results would be forgotten in the press of a later particular situation, and a further kind of lack of dependability was built into the situation. This again indicates the increased emphasis on moment-to-moment communication and decisions that at Kensington were a concomitant of coordinating teams by mutual adjustment. This seems most clearly relevant to the newness of the organization with its lack of social structure, the abstractness of the formal doctrine, and the absence of close supervision. A few of the faculty developed reputations for being personally undependable. Not only did this create problems of the moment, it also contributed to staff conflict and hostility.

Chester Barnard's observation on the importance of associational attractiveness as an incentive to dependable activity seems extremely insightful in regard to the functioning of Kensington School staff and in regard to the methodology that we used to study the school

"But it seems clear that the question of personal compatibility or incompatibility is much more far-reaching in limiting cooperative effort than is recognized, because an intimate knowledge of particular organizations is usually necessary to understand its precise character. When such an intimate knowledge exists, personal compatibility or incompatibility is so thoroughly sensed, and the related problems are so difficult to deal with, that only in special or critical cases is conscious attention given to them. But they can be neglected only at peril of disruption. Men often will not work at all, and will rarely work well, under other incentives if the social situation *from their point of view* is unsatisfactory" (1938, pp. 146–147).

Our investigation and report bear strong witness to the importance of his generalization. Teams have these consequences. Compatibilities facilitate cooperation; incompatibility tends to be destructive of cooperation. The point is extended from dyadic interactions to individual-group interactions. In Barnard's judgment, the group is a system itself and has influence on the individual's percepts and motives.

Group conflict and discord cause a variety of difficulties in handling mundane chores such as pupil accounting. In a complex organizational structure that involves nongradedness and team teaching, the impact is greater. Casual conversation produced the following data:

> Lunch was delightful: Tom, Arthur, Helen, and I ate together. We were joined by Elaine. A variety of odd bits of information occurred. First, in joking about the attendance, Claire commented that they never have more than one or two absent per class and often no more than one or two for the whole 90 children. There's a standing joke among these three about the attendance at ISD. No one knows how many students are there and not there. I made some comment about "all they have to do is count from the list," and they laughed back "what list?" They, literally, have not been able to account for the children.

> Another item that came out was that one student had moved, had been gone for two or three weeks, before Helen realized that he was. She had been counting him absent all the time. The deciding factor occurred when the receiving school in another state wrote for his records. These mechanics just have not been worked out (12/5).

The inability to dependably carry out various tasks of the organization were issues that plagued the team through the early months of the year.

Among the myriad of activities that one might identify in team teaching, we observed a critical one as "picking up the slack." Essentially, we mean that an individual perceives a task that needs to be done if the group is to reach its goals, and the individual moves in easily and carries out the necessary aspects.

> The staff group seems to enjoy teaching and to enjoy what they are doing. An illustration of this concerned Elaine straightening out the pictures of elves the pupils had drawn and her comment, "If it is all right with the rest of you I'll go ahead and choose ten of these as winners, unless some of you would like to help which I would be happy to have." Individuals pick up the slack this way continuously. Wanda, for instance, also has brought in a bunch of books at the primer level from the county and local libraries. It is interesting how they have been caught in this team on the fact that the ABC Company did not give them any primers. They have all the pre-primers and the first and second grade books, but they do not have the primers. They now need those for most of their children and they have no place to turn to. The primers from the other series are difficult in that the pupils do not know the names of the children or the animals who are in the stories. They have moved very heavily from the experience-type reading to the more formal textbook materials for most of the pupils. In the course of casual conversation, Jean mentioned that she was going to have all of her pupils go through the readers. This would be at whatever rate they could do it. If the fast ones could read it in a day, that would be fine, and then they would go on and read supplementary materials; if it took them several weeks, that would be fine too, and they would work their way through at that pace. To me, it seems that she wants to run her reading program and she is able to move toward this without too much difficulty. This is another illustration of where experience really pays off (1/4).

Such an illustration combines the aspect of dependability with the aspects of compatibility, initiative, and experience. Thus, even though Barnard points out that "the capacity, or disposition, to adhere to time-schedule assignments is possibly the most important single basis of selection of persons," in coordination by mutual adjustment the requisites of dependability far exceed the willingness to adhere to time-schedules. The composition of groups also incorporates characteristics that make for interpersonal compatibility, experience, ability to perceive from available information the tasks and activities that will enhance group effectiveness, and reliability in performing these operations. When emphasis is placed on moment-to-moment communication and activities as in mutual adjustment, dependability becomes a central facet of the coordination of cooperative systems.

Specialization of Activity. An additional significant theoretical issue arises as a problem: what are the varying kinds of efforts, skills, and specializations that individual teachers might contribute to the team and how skilled are these performances? Essentially this means a scheme or taxonomy of teaching tasks. In classical organizational theory this is the division and specialization of labor. Although Barnard's (1938) analysis of this concerns the bases and kinds of specialization, we must put specific teaching content into the outline. As we analyzed our data, we found major differences among the three teams. The Basic Skills team of four brought uniqueness through specialized knowledge, for example, books such as Dr. Seuss for oral reading, which some knew and had access to and which others did not, skills such as puppetry, which Elaine had and the others did not, piano-playing skill by Wanda, a flair for imaginative fantasy, which several possessed but through which Sue was able to make a unique contribution, and the guitar-playing skill of Chris.

On occasion, the potential involved in specialized skills and unique physical facilities created consequences of considerable magnitude.

> As I left the building, Wanda and Elaine commented to me very enthusiastically about the children's theatre. The school has been given some professional sets and scenery developed by a commercial company. Elaine mentioned that the work in the theatre was the "first time" that they had really been able to do some of the things that Kensington was set up to do. The *Hansel and Gretel* play is to be given this afternoon at 2:00 P.M. People with special talents, as these two, have to utilize these talents with large groups of children. Presumably, over the course of the year, most of the 120 kids would have, at least, one opportunity to take part in an activity of this kind under the direct tuition of someone like Elaine. The areas that seem most responsive to this kind of special work are art, music, dramatics and, perhaps, physical education. The way it was done at the Washington School appears to me to be a much less adequate and minimal kind of alternative (1/6).

In the other two teams, the problems of inexperience in teaching proved very significant. Even for those with strong subject matter specialities, for example, Jack Davis in science, the experience had been mostly with secondary pupils. In several instances, the specialties were not of sufficient magnitude and depth to contribute to the program as seems to be implied by Barnard. Since the individuals in Basic Skills-4 had these skills, the unanticipated consequences occurred in providing strength to the program and in creating pupil interest and pupil learning. Second, the skills provided a place, position, and role on the team for each of the persons. This uniqueness and identity facilitated the development of individual confidence and group esprit de corps. The happy combination of talents in Chris' roles in music, informal leadership, and instruction to Sue, we have mentioned at several points. In contrast, the inexperience in Transition and ISD provoked serious problems and prevented a number of kinds of arrangements. We have commented in other parts of the book about how the move to a self-contained structure in ISD raised difficulties for the teachers trained as specialists who, then, had to behave as generalists. At each turn, Blau's (1955) point kept recurring—a social structure that is purposive for certain ends creates other consequences for which later purposive action is taken, and in due course the organization changes.

Atypical of most schools, Kensington had several additional specialized staff roles. The most important of them was the coordinator of curriculum materials. This involved supervision of the large library of individual book titles that replaced the usual textbook materials, the wealth of special equipment, for example, tape recorders and overhead projectors, and a staff of several aides. The aides' roles varied during the course of the year. While in temporary quarters, they typically were assigned to and placed with divisions. Later they served the total school. Their assignments included audiovisual aide, library aide, and instructional clerk. As we have indicated, they were generally inexperienced in their jobs, and they labored intensively to put order into a new and not too well-defined role. Budget cuts with consequent salary reductions led them to look for and find other job alternatives after the first year.

As we commented earlier, not only does an elementay school teaching organization in contrast to other organizations present serious information load problems it also raises questions regarding the degree to which the specialization of function is possible and desirable. Classically, specialization of labor is based on the increased productivity that results when a complex task can be divided into subtasks that can be performed quickly, usually repetitively, and usually with less skilled labor at various points in the production process. Team teaching seems to have elements of a mixed model. Traditionally, in the self-contained elementary school, the teacher is responsible for the children all day and for all activities. Traditionally, the secondary school teacher specializes in activities, subject matter to be taught, and works shorter periods of time with larger numbers of pupils. Departmentalization is the result. The university typically continues this trend. Implicit assumptions seem to be the increasing pupil responsibility and the increasing need for specialized knowledge as the age of the pupil increases. In team teaching, one major division of labor occurs between professional teaching staff and teacher aides. The latter work at the direction of the professional staff, and in our case they assisted in the library, in preparing seatwork materials such as cutting and running ditto stencils, and in showing films. Within the professional staff the division of labor occurred only partially. Most of the teachers carried multiple to total functions except in the case of physical education activities. Only with the older children were attempts made for decided specialization. This tended to break down for several reasons: lack of pupil responsibility and ability to work independently, staff disagreement about the importance of functions (for example, small group process sessions with pupils), and the lack of highly specialized staff training, experience, and competence.

In viewing mutual adjustment forms of coordination as occurring more frequently in settings characterized by a high degree of uncertainty and interdependence, specialization may be considered as an aspect of a cooperative system that contributes to the reduction of uncertainty. The possibility of information overload is also decreased, because individuals perform a less diverse set of tasks for which they have specialized skills. Differential relations among participants then are based on differences in skill and tasks to be performed; the content of mutual adjustment is the process of coordinating these competencies. When, as at Kensington, differentials in skills are minimal and the organizational design is based on specialization, uncertainty in role behavior increases and the content of mutual adjustment becomes that of coordinating efforts of individuals with minimal skills attempting to perform specialized roles. Uncertainty and ambiguity are heightened; in effect, the costs of coordination are increased through drains on the resources of time and effort. Among the outcomes are reduced task accomplishment.

The Fundamental Nature of Teaching as an Activity. In the view of one educational analyst, a teaching team is a secondary group.

"From a sociological view, teams are *secondary* or *instrumental* groups, in contrast to *primary* groups. In secondary groups, the emphasis is upon task orientation, and evaluation is based upon principles of universalism and achievement; whereas *primary* groups emphasize localism, friendship, kinship, and other personal factors. . . . Careful attention is given to the definition of goals and the creation of positions and roles appropriate for reaching the goals" (Shaplin, 1965, pp. 16–17).

Kensington is an interesting anomaly in this context. As we discussed at great length, the formal doctrine was codified and rationalized well beyond what one finds in most elementary schools. Goal definitions were made and organizational positions were defined to a high degree. Yet, the content of the doctrine argued for a minimal authority structure and for a kind of group consensus that had strong informal and primary group qualities. The month's summer workshop contributed strongly to this also.

Also, as we have observed teaching, here and elsewhere (Smith and Geoffrey, 1968; Connor and Smith, 1967), we have been impressed with the phenomenon of personal intimacy that is characteristic of the activity known as teaching. One exposes large and significant portions of one's self as he makes contact or "tries to reach" a particular child in an elementary school. A host of his experiences, his personal resources, and his idiosyncratic point of view about life are expressed. If the relationship is to have an authenticity about it, this seems almost mandatory. Similarly, as one meets with one's colleagues, in a team or in some kind of cooperative relationship involved in instruction, a similar experience becomes evident. Often the only reason one can present for one's approach is "It's me. That's the way I am, the skills I have, and what I know and can do." To underestimate this primary quality of both teams and teaching is to court a series of major consequences. The previous quotation continues:

"For a variety of reasons, it is possible for such a working group to change into a primary group with stress upon the affective needs of individuals in the group, particularly if the goals are unclear or the related roles poorly defined" (Shaplin, 1965, p. 17).

At Kensington, the issues were more complicated. As we have stressed elsewhere, the doctrine, the accumulating social structure and process (for example, beginning with the T-groups), the strong personal needs of some members, and the quality of true belief, as well as the nature of teaching elementary school pupils contributed to the thrust toward the Kensington teams becoming primary groups. In short, the question we are asking is this: Is there something indigenous to the teaching of young children that prevents the development of a focus which is other than the one of a primary group? Does this lead then to a team that of necessity has this quality of a primary group, rather than a secondary, a task, or an instrumental group? These hypotheses seem compatible with our data.

Conflict and Authority. Ultimately, "an ordered combination of personal efforts" is accompanied by the important problem of control or authority. When coordination by mutual adjustment breaks down and conflict results, someone or something must tell or prescribe time, place, and activity. As we have already indicated, this problem is handled typically in several complementary ways; that is, through appeal to rules and their informal equivalent, group norms; and through a particular kind of role specialization, an administrator, executive, or leader.

Team teaching theorists, for instance, Lortie (1964), project two basic organizational patterns for team teaching—horizontal and vertical. In the former, relationships reflect an egalitarianism among team members and, in the letter, the structure is hierarchical. The latter has a built-in additional mechanism for handling coordination and for conflict resolution. The former typifies the more usual "democratic" form of mutual adjustment. At Kensington, team leaders were never selected. An ever-present issue, the search for leadership within the organization, was related to this as well as to the locus of decision-making problem which we treat in detail later. Formally, the staff never moved to a vertical organization. The norm of egalitarianism, characteristic of public schools elsewhere and of Kensington's formal doctrine, asserted itself. Informally, the principal had a "kitchen cabinet" that shifted, really vacillated, over time and that provided discrepant cues to the staff.

However, the teams varied dramatically. For example, in Basic Skills-2 Carla assumed the role of dominance with initial effectiveness but with the ultimate significant disaffection of Mary. In Basic Skills-4, the solution seemed to fall into several complementing channels: the team, as they came to know each other, found common beliefs about teaching which generated norms. Furthermore, they all seemed to be more goal-oriented than status-oriented. Chris Hun, who initially came to them as a part-time consultant, proved to have a flair for informal leadership as well as a considerable range of teaching talents. Sue, the only one without experience who might have posed a major obstacle, was able to ask for help; the team had the resources to give it, and she learned rapidly. And, as we have commented, she came to have a significant flair for some of the specialized skills. The Transition team resolved the authority problems around Meg, who was the only one of the three with experience, and who tended to give direction and to put a final stamp on decisions in terms of their probability of success. ISD had no formal team leader; persons were vying for the informal position from the first day of the summer workshop until the close of school or, more precisely, until they gave up any semblance of trying to be a cooperative unit. Members held such divergent opinions on the goals and methods of teaching that informal norms did not crystallize easily initially, and interpersonal negative sentiments later continued to interfere.

In summary, within the teams the modes of reciprocal interdependence and mutual adjustment characterized the initial relationships. The mutual adjustment interaction was reflected in various patterns of the informal resolution of power and influence differentials. Although in the coordination by standardization or by plan these differentials would have been primarily allocated formally, in a cooperative system that was coordinated by mutual adjustment, the informal resolution of these differences composed much of the content of mutual adjustment. As we have indicated in some instances, a dominant-subordinate relationship developed with one member assuming leadership and directing and assigning tasks for the other members. Coalition also became a pattern of mutual adjustment for some of the groups with two or more participants "taking sides" against another member. A type of pluralistic compromise characterized the adjustment of one team in which an eqalitarian relationship between members was maintained with "give and take" and open communication. When no stable pattern of adjustment was arrived at informally, then the form of both interdependence and coordination had a tendency to be in continual change. The coordination of efforts in the team had the further problem of the context of authority and control within the school. This aspect of Kensington was of such significance that we raise it at length in the chapter on issues in administrative theory.

Professional Issues in Team Organization

Initial Socialization. In addition to a consideration of the attainment of instructional objectives through cooperative activity, a wider context exists for the analysis and evaluation of team teaching. The socialization and induction of individuals into the teaching profession is a critical and little understood process (Connor and Smith, 1967). Beyond the preservice training, with its variety of culminating practicum experiences, lie the important first months and years of experience. This same point has been made, more generally, by Shaplin (1965).

"Perhaps the greatest innovation in technical functions promoted by team organization is in the area of supervision—supervision from within the teaching force rather than from the administration or a special supervisory staff. Within some hierarchical teams—particularly those involving beginning teachers, interns, and apprentices—it is possible to vary teaching loads in accordance with the teacher's energy, ability, and experience and to provide immediate, on-the-job evaluation and help" (p. 19).

We were struck at several points on the varying experiences the young teachers had at Kensington. Conceptually, we were trying to focus on mechanisms within "teaming" and within "administrative supervision." In our field notes we comment on these issues:

> Another aspect of the situation is the minimal amount of active work on the part of the administration and the supervisors in helping a teacher to come to grips with the problems that are giving her troubles. For instance, in thinking about Sue and Liz, who posed some of the same kinds of problems, it looks as if Sue has, in effect, made it, in terms of being able to handle the children and to move a program along. My observation of her the other day would suggest that she was on top of it, that she had learned a bit about the ebb and flow of the process and could handle it pretty well. Liz has not learned this. Neither one got substantial help from formal supervisors, at least, as far as I know. Sue got considerable help from Chris (a part-time team member) during the early parts of the semester. The team was not able to give this to Liz (11/2).

This may be attributed, in part, to the inexperience of other staff members; in addition, as is pointed out elsewhere, the schism between the North and South halves of the ISD team was, by and large, along lines of experience-inexperience. Partly also, experienced persons like Irma were not able to, could not, or did not give extensive help. The isolation of faculty members who were having severe difficulties in teaching with no careful assistance seems to be another part of the laissez-faire leadership and a fundamental dimension of the program organizationally.

At another point we raise in some detail the social-psychological meaning of "helping." This seems to us to be a key issue in administrative process, as administrative resources are turned toward supervision of staff development. Teaming provides a number of quite different possibilities than the self-contained or departmentalized classroom.

Inservice Training. Shaplin has argued further the difficulties in changing the teaching behaviors of inservice teachers. The usual techniques of curriculum committees, inservice programs, workshops, study committees, and supervisory personnel have acknowledged limitations (Pohland and Smith, 1970). As we have indicated, our Kensington data tended to focus on the problems of team survival amidst inexperience in teaching and personality conflicts among teachers. However, as was shown earlier, the socialization of the new teacher was successful in several instances, as Sue's relation to Chris and Claire's relation to Meg well testify. Team teaching through its openness to peer observation, teacher decision making, and multiple roles seem to have a potency for staff development which was minimally tapped at Kensington.

Professional Consequences. As an educational sociologist, Lortie (1964) raises several broader kinds of implications in the issue of team organization. Essentially his view is this: (1) Teachers in contrast to other professionals work in bureaucratic structures. (2) As a consequence, teachers as compared to other professional groups, for example, physicians and lawyers, have relatively little economic or political power. (3) The autonomy-equality pattern has arisen to offset the lack of power they possess in the bureaucratic structures. (4) The autonomy-equality pattern contains elements such as spatial privacy—one's own self-contained classroom—and widely shared norms such as all teachers should be treated as equals, teachers should treat each other in a nonintervening but friendly manner, and teachers should be free from other adults while teaching. (5) The consequences of the autonomy-equality pattern are multiple and important to the individual teacher. In Lortie's analysis, the autonomy-equality pattern allows the teacher to work at her own rate, that is, some do little and some work endlessly. It allows a wide latitude in teaching style and curriculum content. It allows the teacher to establish her own kind of teacher-pupil relationships. It permits considerable variation in the definition of good and bad teaching or professional performance. Elsewhere (Smith and Geoffrey, 1968; Smith, 1967) we have argued that the informal faculty peer group exerts considerable pressure on a teacher to perform in ways congruent to the group's normative structure and, hence, lessens the effect of the autonomy-equality pattern. In part, we are suggesting that the enthusiast for team organization must contend with relationship between these two phenomena, the informal staff clique and the autonomy-equality pattern. More fundamentally, however, we are reraising the more general thrust of Lortie's position: that departures from the self-contained or departmentalized classroom will ripple through many distal events in the profession of teaching.

Summary and Conclusions

Case studies produce important details of social events that are relevant to the practitioner as well as to the social theorist. In general, we have resisted second guessing and advice giving. On occasion, however, we have recorded in the "Field Notes: Summary Observations and Interpretations" discussions we have had with our colleagues. Glaser and Strauss (1967) argue that activity of this kind is important in developing grounded theory. We found also that it sometimes summarizes proposals for practice. This was the case in January when we discussed aspects of teaming with a colleague. We include these notes because they state succinctly a number of ideas that we think are important.

> During the weekend I got involved also in a conversation with a neighbor who may be involved in some team teaching. As we talked a number of interesting generalizations seem to flow: (1) the people have to have a light teaching load. (2) In the year before, the personnel should have a chance to try out lessons, units, and work to find out if they can get along with the people with whom they will be teaming. (3) Only use experienced personnel. (4) Have an extended summer workshop, pretty explicitly guided by the prior year's experience, for working through a variety of lessons and lesson plans. (5) Have budget resources for materials and supplies. (6) Spend a good bit of time clarifying who is going to do what and how the differentiation of labor will be carried out. (7) In team and staff meetings put first things first. (8) Start with small teams and gradually enlarge them. (9) Begin in a very moderate way with only a few teams and a portion of the pupils. (10) Have administrators to carry out as much of the organizational overhead as is possible. Do not burden teachers with problems of that sort. (11) Attend to all of the linkages with other parts of the system; such as grades, report cards, authority patterns in the school, feelings of other teachers, and the like. (12) Retain almost total flexibility of the internal structure of the physical environment. (13) If consultants are to be used, have them available more than a day or two a month and have them spend other time observing all phases of the program. Or, if possible, have the consultant linked in with a half-time research assistant who will do much of the observing and recording so that the consultant can use his time more beneficially. (14) Make it one of the "major projects of the year" instead of one of a number of projects

so that there will be ample supervisory and administrative time available. (15) Obtain hard data on the enterprise through pre- and post-testing and, if possible, a matched group of kids in other sections and other programs (1/18).

Those suggestions take cognizance of the broad problems of experience, the composition of teams, the language available to talk about educational problems, the integration into the rest of the school organization, and the necessary resources.

At a higher level of abstraction, and more congruent with our analysis in this chapter, the reference to quite basic and quite simple theory of cooperation puts team teaching into an important context. This theory suggests a number of facets of teaming that might otherwise be unanticipated or unintended. As these consequences were positive, they contributed to the team's effectiveness and efficiency. As they were negative, they precipitated organizational change. Briefly, it is possible to suggest several generalizations, useful as hypotheses, for further research on team teaching:

1. Teaming requires the most sophisticated form of interdependence, what Thompson (1967) calls reciprocal, and the most difficult kind of coordination, mutual adjustment. This coordination is very time consuming and expensive in communication and decision making. Organizations and individuals with limited resources (time and energy) must divert them from other activities, for example, on occasion productive effort such as teaching itself.

2. As various hierarchical levels of decision making are introduced (for example, teaming) decision-making freedom at the lowest level (teacher-pupil) is constrained. For those who speak of "democracy" in the classroom, teaming raises serious incompatibilities.

3. Unless individual skills are unique in kind or highly developed in degree, teaming as reciprocal interdependence will be higher in cost than it is productive of benefits.

4. As teams increase in size, from two to more than two, for example, seven, these effects are magnified.

5. Because of fadism and emotionalism instead of analysis in professional education, the new elementary education that offers team teaching to the practitioner contains mutual incompatible elements leading to latent and unanticipated negative consequences—dysfunctions.

CHAPTER 8

Dilemmas in Democratic Administration

AN APPROACH TO THE PROBLEM

The social science literature presents only a few careful descriptive and analytical accounts of administrators in action. Perhaps the most exciting of them is Argyris' *Executive Leadership* (1953). As in all case studies, the particular situation in which the administrator operates is a very critical part of the story. This particularistic quality demands that numerous such investigations be carried out and collated if case studies are to have value for a more sophisticated theory of administration. The reader will recall Argyris' executive entering a business enterprise where, in the view of the central administration, the survival of the organization was a real and serious issue, since the company was losing money to a severe degree. Although some phases of worker morale were high, the supervisory personnel were so demoralized that many of the workers in the organization preferred not to be promoted to supervisory positions. Argyris suggests that these positions had been "undermined" because workers had direct access to the former administrator and the intermediary supervisors were effectively bypassed. In this earlier era, the organization was administered informally by a benevolent, kindhearted man. He ran the organization "like a corner drugstore" according to one of the employees.

In his account of the new regime, Argyris neatly describes the administrative process from three points of view: (1) The "neutral" outsider or researcher's position; (2) the private and internal world of the leader himself; and (3) the viewpoint of the supervisors, that group of first line and middle management supervisors whom the leader set out to bolster and to support as key elements in his chain of command. In this particular case, the behavioral picture emerges of an executive who constantly interacts, vigorously commands, lives as though he were totally organization-centered, treats his supervisory subordinates in a highly individualized style, emphasizes the present, and who sets realistic goals. The subjective picture indicates that the leader viewed himself as bold, firm, hard working, and ambitious. He wanted a supervisory staff that was close to him and was respected by their own subordinates. The consequences of this kind of administration were multiple and varied. Production was high. Tension was high also. Most of the supervisors were not conscious of the source of the tension and viewed "the boss" as an excellent leader, "one of the best in the business." Many held ambivalent personal feelings toward him. The supervisors were highly dependent on the leader. The flow of information upward was highly selective. Cooperation among supervisors was minimal; however, hostility was not present. Although many of the men hunted and fished together, Argyris did not find intimacy or close personal friendships.[1] Finally, as the plant became profitable and as the supervisors behaved the way the leader wanted, the leader's behavior began to shift.

In our view, this brief synopsis of Argyris' study indicates: (1) the need for a multitude of specific cases that analyze the administrative process; (2) a desire for concrete descriptions of the varied situations in which administrative behavior takes place; (3) the importance of knowing the schemas and the decision-making processes lying behind the overt administrative behavior; (4) the accent on processes over time, for example, today had a yesterday and will have a tomorrow; (5) the multiple consequences of any administrative act or series of acts; and (6) the fact that these consequences have varying "good-bad" evaluations depending on the several criteria against which they might be, and usually are, compared.

Our phrasing of this chapter as "Dilemmas in Democratic Administration" indicates that we are persuaded that the issues in being a principal of an innovative elementary school are much too complex for simple truisms of advice. Instead, we hold that administering an innovative organization involves an exciting series of very difficult choices, demands a broad repertory of skills and abilities, and raises a concern for events changing over time. The administrative innovations that were attempted at Kensington were among the most interesting and important facets of the Kensington School.

ADMINISTRATIVE SCHEMAS AND PERSONALITY

One of our central tenets involves the linkages among administrative schemas, the consequent thought processes and decision making, the further consequences in administrative behavior, and finally the interplay with organizational processes. After a discussion early in the summer, one of the observers commented in the summary notes:

> Shelby has read rather widely in some of the decision-making literature and has been particularly absorbed with this aspect of administration. To illustrate

[1] Our experience in hunting and fishing suggests limits to Argyris' generalization.

this, he commented at some length about a taxonomy of decision making that a friend of his developed as part of a doctoral dissertation. In this study the man was concerned with superordinate decisions, appellate decisions, and creative principal decisions. Eugene applied some of them to the problems in vetoing decisions by his subordinates and to some of the kinds of problems that this might create. Similarly, he commented with some pride, I think, about two dimensions of his own decision making. A consideration of many relevant factors and the delaying of decisions were the fundamental modes of approach. He illustrated the delaying aspects with his nonselection of team leaders to this point and, also, with holding off on buying books and other text materials. He also indicated that he planned for the worst of the possible contingencies around each of these delays. The many-variable notion he illustrated partly with the team leaders who, on the one hand, would share very closely his own sentiments and, second, who would be able to work well with other staff members (8/8).

At other places in the monograph we discuss issues such as decisions in which he vetoed subordinate ideas, the organizational consequences of supporting the staff members who shared his sentiments, and the programmatic implications of delaying decisions regarding team leaders and the purchase of texts and materials.

Further facets of his conception of decision making also were indicated:

He makes a distinction between an intuitive decision and a rational decision. An intuitive decision is one that is already programmed in, as in typing when one makes a decision to strike a letter with a particular finger but doesn't think about it but behaves intuitively. The rational decision in his eyes is a decision in which one makes a careful check of the consequences. He tends to distinguish this from finding an after-the-fact rationale, or what might be called a rationalization, of the decision. He illustrated this with his decision to have part of the NTL program in the first week. He thought that this was intuitively good and that he could build a rationale after the fact about it. He himself saw his decision as lying heavily on the past experience he has had with people and events connected with the program and what seemed to be significant results there. He got the particular consultant that he wanted essentially through a chain of conversations and telephone calls (8/9).

Further conversations and discussions indicated that Shelby was not only aware of a good deal of what Massie (1965) calls classical management theory but that he possessed a skepticism toward it. Two such concepts were span of control and unity of authority:

Eugene raised another set of things in which he was interested and which lie within administrative theory more generally. He suggested the concepts of span of control and of unity of authority. He indicated that in this situation they were violating both of these concepts and that he was interested in the consequences of this, the repercussions. For instance, he talked about the older elementary kids being responsible to some five different authorities, the four subject matter specialists and the one academic advisor.[2] The individuals will be differentiated by function, but they will not be differentiated by time. In this sense the usual first period of social studies, second period of language arts, and the like, in a platoon school will be departed from. He raised in this same context an analogy to the family and the fact that children were responsible to two different authorities in this instance (*Observer*. To me this may be a fallacious analogy. We discussed the analogy a little bit in terms of final authority and issues of that kind, but I didn't make much progress at this point.) (8/9).

Intermixed in the above was a third concept—organizational specialization. Also included was a process of thought that involved the use of analogies.

As the discussion picked up on the concept of flexibility another potentially significant issue in the cognitive processes of an administrator occurred— the use of relevant but limited illustrations.

Another illustration which he presented related to the concept of flexibility. In his school this past year there was considerable concern about the scheduling of recess at any time the pupils and the teacher wanted to go out. He suggested that they try it. They found that there was no difficulty. The need for everyone to go to recess at a set time was not a necessity. Another illustration of the same point concerns the school he came from in Minnesota, in which the campus was large and there was considerable playground space. He raised the suggestion with his teachers that they might have a recess at any time that the class wanted, for there was room on the grounds. This kind of flexibility in scheduling apparently went very well there also. These were two of the illustrations he used to take some of the sting out of the general skepticism of mine regarding the possible chaos in the situations. They also suggest to me a kind of talent and way of behavior that Eugene has which might be very significant (8/9).

The unanalyzed problems in a psychology of administration which we are pointing toward are severalfold. The kinds of concepts in the heads of educational administrators have not been studied thoroughly. If March and Simon (1958) and Zetterberg (1965) are correct that the classical concepts [for example, those raised in Massie (1965)] are not variates but taxonomic definitions pretending to be principles, then the undone work of the organizational theorist in education presents severe problems for the practicing educational administrator.

The role of analogies in thinking processes also has not been clearly conceptualized. The potential negative as well as the positive transfer of

[2] Notice here also the inconsistency with other statements about who is responsible to whom.

real but limited experience to broader realms and situations is clearly seen in the recess example.

Finally, intense personal experiences, some of which involved broad domains of the organization's activities, suggest further hypotheses regarding administrative cognitive processes.

> Another problem about which he talked at great length was the school district accent on the "conceptual approach to curriculum." Essentially this involves an emphasis away from the learning of certain rote materials and the memorization of these to the child's ability to conceptualize. He described an experience from his own behavior in which he saw an outline of concepts in some of the materials he was teaching and he thought that this was very significant, and he made a list of them and had the children memorize them. This is precisely what he did not want to see happen here. In this vein, he said that he tried to utilize the verb "conceptualize" rather than to utilize the noun "concept." We entered into a fairly extensive discussion as to whether his teachers would know enough to possess the structure of the knowledge that existed in their field. He thought that a number could and that some would not be able to. This also came up in the context of the specialists in their areas and the fact that they more probably would have this ability (8/9).

In summary, we are neither trying to laud Shelby's imagination nor to criticize the degree of integration of his ideas. The two points we wish to make are (1) the thought processes are significant for later decisions, and (2) limited data exist on the thought processes of educational adminitrators.[3]

Although our discussion has focused most heavily on the intellectual processes of the administrator, a broader conception of personality is needed. Need dispositions as they have been pursued by Murray (1938) and have been adapted to the analysis of administrative problems by Getzels and his colleagues (1968) are a major necessary thrust into the solution of organizational processes. Our accent on the intellectual is based on the hypothesis that they are more alterable and more "strategic," to use Barnard's (1938) term, than are need dispositions and psychological traits. However, the latter are important also; one brief excerpt illustrates our point.

> Pat reports that Eugene attended the transition team meeting yesterday afternoon and explained the rules and the need for them. He then took his earlier laissez-faire type role and let them conduct their team meeting by themselves. This swinging from laissez-faire to autocratic and back is a real interesting kind of role. It reflects a consistency going back over many months, however (12/10).

[3] A related analysis regarding teacher decision making occurs in Smith and Geoffrey (1968).

Central to the argument of leadership are concerns for units of analysis. Is the behavior of the leader to be analyzed in moment-to-moment terms? Do these moment-to-moment units add up to definable larger units, or styles? Is there a style about variations in style? We puzzled about this all year. The difficult issues of suiting one's style to one's personality is only part of the problem. Serious further concern comes in then devising mechanisims, for example, information getting, to meet certain demands of the administrative process.

THE LOCUS OF DECISION MAKING IN DEMOCRATIC ADMINISTRATION: THE MAJOR DILEMMA

The Upside-Down Authority Structure

American education for at least the last seventy years has been in turmoil over the concept of democracy. One phase of this occurred in Kensington. The summary notes, reporting a conversation between one of the observers and the principal, a day before the summer workshop, capture its flavor:

> . . . we also got into a discussion of, To whom is the pupil responsible? In general, he is not responsible to the teacher, but more the teacher is responsible to him and the pupil is responsible to himself. The teachers are to be resource persons for the suggesting of ideas and of phenomena and of areas of study, but the pupils' obligations will be essentially to themselves. Perhaps the item that struck me most was the elimination of almost every element of coercion and, along with this, to a very great degree, the element of requiredness or minimum essentials of some kind in the curriculum of the children (8/9).

The notes continue with comments of differences in the reading curriculum versus social studies and science curricula. The former would have some minimums, the latter would not. The observer made interpretive comments that:

> . . . it harks back to the early work in the activity curriculum and in the variety of independent study programs (8/9).

Analytically we have referred to this issue as the locus of decision making. The issue was central to the life of Kensington. It merged several theoretical themes—issues in administrative theory, issues in organizational theory, and issues in curriculum theory.

As we have indicated, authority was not delegated to the pupils. It belonged to them. They were the community, the final authority. In a very real sense Kensington becomes a serious attempt to bring democracy to a public school. Our earlier work in a public school that was autocratic in purpose and operation (Smith and Geoffrey, 1968) led us to speak informally of the "upside-down authority structure" at Kensington. The aspects, implications and consequences, of this educational and organizational innovation were multiple. In a sense, the upside-down authority structure illustrates beautifully the interdependencies of the elements in a social system.

Aspects of Authority at Kensington

Classical management theory (Massie, 1965) refers to our locus of decision-making dilemma as the scalar principle, the idea that ". . . authority and responsibility should flow in a clear unbroken line from the highest executive to the lowest operative" (p. 396). At Kensington, the reversal of this flow had a number of important subtleties. Some of them lay external to the school itself but within the immediate environment of the Milford District. Other complications lay within the faculty perceptions and behavior. The behavior of the incumbent develops further our perspective. Our analysis suggests a number of major problems in attempting to introduce an innovation such as democratic school administration.

Kensington in the Context of the Milford District. Typically when people are in conflict, they tend to interact, engage in discussions, persuade one another, trade, bargain, compromise, and come to agreement. When these processes do not result in agreements, they appeal to "higher authority" to mediate or to arbitrate the decision. This higher authority ultimately must act if the organization is to continue to function. In most organizations, several layers or levels of authority exist. The end point or highest level of authority we have called "the final authority." Typically, organizations have a number of levels of authority and a correlated chain of command or flow of commands.

Formally, in the public schools, in a political democracy such as ours, the final authority lies in the local community. In effect, conflicts among pupils are mediated by the teacher; conflicts between teachers and pupils or among teachers are mediated by the principal. This continues "up the line," until one comes finally to the community.

The members of the school board are duly elected to set school policy for the community. Part of the board's charge is to hire a superintendent who has responsibility to staff the schools and to turn policy statements into workable goals toward which the organization might aspire. As we have indicated briefly in other parts of the book, the majority of the board strongly supported Spanman and he, in turn, strongly supported Shelby. However, the community contained serious conflicting positions regarding the public schools, and these differences had a long history in the community. Similarly, the central staff contained an "old guard" that viewed aspects of Spanman's program, including Kensington, with considerable skepticism. From time to time, the reality of this skepticism and its accompanying conflict had repercussions in the day-to-day conduct of the school. Delays in receiving materials and equipment, conflict over budget allotments, disagreements over requisitions and requisition procedures, and problems in personnel were part of the school. However, the major point we would make is that the usual public school structure conflicts in a major way with the Kensington doctrine.[4]

Intermediate Levels: Ambiguous Internal Lines of Authority. Although Kensington's "upside-down" authority structure was a problem of concern and debate within the school faculty, the Milford central office staff retained a more traditional view of Kensington's authority structure, that is, Eugene was in command. A casual introduction during lunch indicated a further perception of Tom's playing the assistant's role.

> Another interesting comment was Howard's statement at lunch in regard to his introduction of Tom to the former school board member. He mentioned that Tom was kind of second in command when Eugene was not here. Tom backed off from this and said that he was not sure about that. All of this fell on the attendant and listening ears of John (12/2).

The nearest Tom's position came to a formal level occurred when the principal attended an out-of-town professional meeting in early March. The *Bulletin* stated it this way:

"If any unusual matters needing attention should arise during this time which cannot be handled through the normal framework, you may refer them to Tom Mack, who has consented to assume this responsibility" (*Bulletin No. 45, 3/1*).

Several further complexities existed concerning Tom. He was the oldest man in the school. His range of experience was broadest. He had had more administrative experience than anyone else, including Eugene. As the coordinator of curriculum materials he was at the hub of most of the communication network in the school. In addition, he held informal responsibilities in Jerl's aspirations for curriculum organization in the Milford District. Finally, and very significantly, he had, in the best sense of the term, an "old shoe" quality. He was informal, gregarious, helpful, and interested. He was father confessor to the young faculty members and trusted confidant of most of the older teachers.

In general we, as observers, refrained from giving advice, moving into a consultant role, and second guessing the staff at Kensington. In May, the notes deviated from our more usual stance.

---

[4] The further entanglements among school district committees, for example, curriculum, textbook selection, and salary, and the legal framework of the schools we leave to another time and another place.

Another significant point was Tom's absence from the school. In my observation he's been around much less recently. Presumably he's working on summer school and related kinds of things.[5] As I write this I have the feeling that he is something of a fifth wheel in the school at this point. Particularly as it slows down and holds the line until the end of the year. It reraises the importance of the analysis of his role in the development of the school and the opportunity that he might have been the instructional leader and inside man in the operation of the school and actually could have done much of the "teaching of teaching" to Liz, Kay, Dan, and other people. At this point it seems to me he had an option that he did not exercise, that is, he would develop and have materials ready but would not move the next step of actually taking on the supervisory role, which no one ultimately took over (5/4).

The limited resources we have commented on at great length. Alternative utilization has been less a part of our format. The "inside-outside" roles in administration at the superintendent level seem to have their counterpart in an innovative elementary school. This kind of organizational structure, although congruent with the highly differentiated staff roles in the Institutional Plan, conflicted with the egalitarian aspects of the doctrine. The staff's view of Tom probably would have been congenial to the formalization of such a role.

Vetoes: A Complexity in the Authority Structure. Although Shelby spoke of pupil self-determination and although the faculty had considerable autonomy and engaged in terrible and trying struggles for power, there were issues in "final" authority that complicated the Kensington situation. For the observers these issues centered in the Institutional Plan and the veto, although other manifestations occurred. During the first week of the workshop, while the T-groups and the related discussion were underway, casual references to the "Institutional Plan" began to arise. As we described earlier in great detail, this was Shelby's conceptualization of the goals and organizational plan of Kensington. The latent conflict between the superintendent's directives to the staff, "the school is you," "go build a school," etc., and Shelby's thoughtful and provocative prior conceptualization never came to full consciousness and open debate within the staff. Considerable frustration existed when staff suggestions that ran counter to the plan were never operationalized and implemented. Similarly, the occasional use of the word "veto" and the occasional practice of it were never the subject of clear and open discussion. The implications of this complexity on the maintaining of an "invisible but potent structure" on the phenomenon of trust, and staff conflict seemed real, important, and far-reaching.

---

[5] He also was involved in discussions which led, for the following year, to his appointment as a principal in another school in the district.

The Invisible but Potent Structure. If one asks the data, Is the upside-down authority a reality to the staff? one finds evidence of skepticism.

> Along these lines I quizzed one of the teachers specifically about the raising more generally of some of these organizational and procedural issues in the team meeting: (1) whether there was any open discussion about them; and (2) whether he was going to raise them. He indicated no on both grounds. . . . It illustrates, perhaps, best of all that he is operating under a notion that there is a formal organization, and this organization has an attribute of power and authority. As he phrased it in another context, "that's Eugene's responsibility." That section of the write-up might well be entitled "The Invisible but Potent Structure." It suggests also that one of the things that is needed is an analysis of recent textbooks in administration that center on the topic of democratic school administration. The parallels, to the democratic classroom, it seems to me, are very striking (9/24).

Significantly, after four weeks of workshop and three weeks of school, a faculty member retains this conception of principal role responsibilities in the context of a formal organization. In spite of policy declarations, "the principal is principal." This discrepancy between the formal doctrine and perceptual reality becomes part of the context of organizational ambiguity and lack of clarity.

Earlier notes raised further speculation regarding the nature and genesis of this invisible but potent structure.

> Part of the problem locally may fall around the inability of Eugene to delegate responsibility. Although he talks the "group process line" and the group's solving of problems and, in effect, they do carry much of the responsibility, he, himself still retains administrative control. It is almost as if he understood phenomena of group process and small group behavior, but that he had no appreciation for the literature on bureaucracy and the formal organizational structure of a large concern. It is a most interesting kind of blind spot. One might argue that this is a general weakness in some of the group dynamics and small group positions and points of view. I will have to check out his background in this regard. It is quite possible that much of my concern about his personalized authority as opposed to bureaucratic authority lies in ignorance or rejection of this tradition within the social sciences. In the sense that he tries to be a rational man with much of what he does and to rationalize most of his activity, it would suggest that ignorance here would leave the kind of holes that the intuitive administrator would not have and would be responding to quite naturally. This is part of a more general problem that seems to me is a very critical one in training anyone in the behavioral sciences. The general assumption is that as one makes conscious what one does, then one can act more rationally and move the organization, or the individual, or the group to greater effectiveness, defined in terms of one's goals. If, however, the knowledge that one is teaching has major omissions along the line, then the

destruction of the intuitive way of behaving and the substituting of a more rational way will produce a discontinuity and will be the source of some troublesome, continuing, and bitchy problems that one cannot handle in one's system. Just on the surface, this may be one of Eugene's major problems (8/18).

The complications of training, of rationality in organization, of unanticipated consequences from institutions' innovative structures, and the limits in an individual's personal repertory are all very apparent.

Earlier, in our discussion of teaming, we made reference to Barnard's observation that concerns the pervasive and intractable problems of personal incompatibility. As he indicates, one must be intimately involved in the organization to perceive it and to appreciate the degree of difficulty it creates. The larger dimensions of this as it relates to administration and to the latent structure of power and authority in the organization appeared vividly in an ISD team meeting during a Saturday morning in January.

9:12 A.M. Group gathers at 9 A.M. or a few minutes after. Chit-chat of a reserved sort. Eugene raises the illustration of conversation between Conant and Goodlad. Goes on to decision or no decision regarding ISD organization. He would like to make a decision at the time of semester change. "Need to clarify model and what we are trying to do. Other aspects: scheduling, resources, personnel assignments, etc." (The tape recorder is running today. Tom set it up. No discussion of this, this morning.) Group sits quietly and listens. It is not a friendly group.

Eugene wants to start on description of the model. "Need a chalk board. Prefer to hear you develop." He wants to summarize rather than participate. Little reaction.

9:20 A.M. He raises recording and permission: the reasons are Jack Davis' absence, ourselves, and an outsider from State University who is to make a film of the school. No objection although these are all silent head shakes.

EUGENE. Spell out things you think are important in ISD. (Also invites ISD resource persons to contribute—that is John and Tom.)

Silence for *1 and ½ minutes.*

EUGENE. Seem to have trouble getting started. (Asks them to write down items.)

LIZ. Start by describing goals or different organization?

EUGENE. Maybe an example—individual, small group, and large activities where desirable, another, form follow function. Continue with pupil freedom to some degree, sequential math program, etc.

9:26 A.M. TOM. One way, each person here is doing some things. Presumably important. Tell why

ALEC. Decide first on general categories. Some of things Eugene mentioned were how decisions are made, behavioral objectives for pupils, etc.

EUGENE. Easiest way is to start—like sorting peas. Get a few categories.

Silence.

JOHN. I missed the point. What we're doing or hope to do?

EUGENE. Hope to do. I'd like to see some pupils doing depth studies. Wide resources of materials center. Just one other thing. Do we want to start with separate lists or as group?

IRMA. Appears to me that it is such a varied thing. All inclusive.

TOM. All right. Taxonomize later.

Long silence.

ALEC. Might be best if we wrote individually.

9:29 A.M. EUGENE. Things we consider important in ISD program.

Silence.

All begin to write.

(*Observer.* The group is full of passive resistance. In a sense they are so conscious of process and of interpersonal feelings that they are immobilized. Another factor may well be waiting for Eugene to "spring his list"; this has happened frequently. No one calls him on it though. Tom seems to write the most. He also seems to be the only one who was briefed directly. Kay's vague ISD reorganization comments of yesterday suggests that she had gotten wind of some of it.)

9:39 A.M. The silence and the writing continues.

9:42 A.M. Eugene shows me his outline. "This is what I meant to ask." "Did I ask it?"

I nod, "Yes."

9:44 A.M. Silence continues.

(*Observer.* This would make a beautiful situation for a novel. The quiet, the tape recorder relentlessly recording, the silence, the strained countenances. David and Eugene smoking. Eyes cast downward. Only Tom is writing now. The individual thoughts of the participants.)

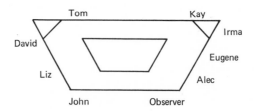

9:46 A.M. EUGENE. "Would you like to have a chairman to get going?

ALEC. I think you ought to be one.

EUGENE. I mean just for this.

ALEC. I mean this.

KAY. I prefer you to enter in as a discussant rather than afterward.

9:48 A.M. David out and in for coffee.

EUGENE. Reflects other's feeling.

LIZ. Yes.

IRMA. You're the only one prepared.

EUGENE. Have feeling I've not been clear—Basic question concerns do we reorganize at semester.

Eugene writes on board:
1. Model.
2. What now doing.
3. If divergence should we handle in present organization or reorganize for greater congruence.
4. If reorganization is in order—how?
5. Assigning staff members not a function of this meeting.

9:50 A.M. EUGENE. Start with no. 1. What are criteria and things we value? Not in order at this time.

Silence.

EUGENE. Who'd like to start?

Silence.

TOM. I have several rather global items. The ability of students to do studies in depth.

Charles writes.

TOM. Acquiring skills which make independent study possible.

EUGENE. Elaborate?

TOM. Not enough to just turn a child loose on Africa, reading maps, almanacs, etc.

EUGENE. Including use of equipment?

TOM. Yes. 3rd, attitudes toward independent study, so we can grant responsibility for these.

EUGENE. Rereads . . . attitudes toward assuming responsibility (1/9).

The meeting continued through the morning until 12:40 that afternoon. Later ISD was extensively reorganized into what was essentially a series of self-contained classrooms with specialized resources in math, science, and physical education. The manner in which an administrator initiates activity remains an important part of the dilemma in the upside-down authority structure of a democratic school.

Conscious Focus on Decision Processes. Self-consciousness is a most interesting phenomenon. On the one hand, some social commentators indicate that the unexamined life is not worth living; other psychologists stress that fact that a highly skilled performance (for example, hitting a golf ball) requires one to "forget" the conscious rules (that is, eye on the ball, overlapping grip, and straight left arm). Kensington was highly self-conscious in all phases of its life, and particularly so in regard to its decision processes. The visability or self-consciousness about the decision-making process arose not only with the staff but also with the parents in the context of the parent council. The morning after the first council meeting the summary notes contained an interpretive comment.

> The council president commented about the school picnic that he said would be a decision that would lie mostly in Mr. Shelby's hands, although Mr. Shelby would want some feedback from the school patrons on this. One of the teachers, who was sitting next to me, commented that "Eugene has them brainwashed." Incidentally, related to this point of who makes the decisions, Eugene has an ungodly flair for maximizing the visibility of that instead of minimizing it. It seems to me that this is very important, since as he makes it evident, it is almost a gauntlet that is being thrown, and an individual, if he is to maintain his own self-respect and sense of autonomy, is going to challenge it and take issue with it. By leaving the final power as a kind of latent variable, you then can jockey back and forth and not draw the lines as sharply as they seem to get drawn. Somehow it seems to keep the working area for cooperation much wider (12/9).

A number of facets contributed to this self-consciousness. Shelby was intensely analytical; he was passionate in the pursuit of rationality. The staff was exceedingly able intellectually and could carry through abstract arguments. Many of the staff were young and were solving the developmental task of building a professional perspective. Kensington was new and complicated, and it posed problems for which no ready guidelines existed. The mandate, "build a school," such experiences as the initial T-group, and such procedures as team teaching focused on analysis and self-consciousness also.

The consequences of this self-consciousness regarding decisions also were multiple. Perhaps the most important was a displacement of attention from the organizational task to be done to focusing on the process itself. Instead of just "pitching in and getting a job done" the staff was continuously preoccupied with: Who has authority? Who has changed status? Is consensus necessary? Why is Mr. X deviating?, and so forth.

Related to this, was the heavy time and energy commitment that this meant the faculty had to assume. In an absorbing and demanding teaching job, this was a considerable additional load.

Beyond highlighting the growing status dimension among the faculty of peers, the self-consciousness also produced an awareness of inconsistency within the principal's relationships with the faculty. They were typified in issues that we have called the Institutional Plan and in the veto power. The staff struggled with this, and yet, in spite of the high self-consciousness, could never get this clarified. The limits in their planning, the conflict with the Institutional Plan, and those decisions which would be vetoed, were not clear.

A further consequence of this self-consciousness was the minimization of some unanticipated latent dysfunctions of a substantive sort. As the faculty talked through issues, they were able to anticipate many problems. Insofar as they then planned around the anticipated difficulties, the organization profited.

Consequences of the Upside-Down Authority Structure

Previously we spoke of the multiple consequences of the upside-down authority structure. An overview of the early consequences of this structure is shown in Figure 8.1.

The model should be read this way. The Institutional Plan, and Shelby's interpretation of it, stated that the decisions should flow from the pupils to teachers to administration. In the August workshop, with no pupils present, the flow of authority was truncated and it went from teachers to the administration. In conjunction with the T-group experience and the undetermined team leadership positions, this led to faculty jockeying for power, a complex faculty committee structure, and numerous problems in priveleged communications and special knowledge (possessed by the principal through his formal contacts in the Milford School System). Further consequences resulted: the Kirkham incident, an unending search for leadership, and the tremendous expenditures of faculty time and energy. We

Figure 8.1   The aspects of authority in Kensington during the August workshop.

present supporting data and a series of more intensive analyses of these events in succeeding pages.

The Quest for Procedure and Leadership. Difficulties in dealing with meeting procedures were not new to the ISD faculty when they encountered divergences throughout the year. An account from an ISD team meeting in mid-August enables one to view a typical leadership and procedural search:

DAVID. I want to see how we should operate as a group.

JACK. Go ahead.

DAVID. I just want to throw it out.

JACK. Let's hear what you have to say.

EUGENE. We could talk about the things the first person throws out.

David pointedly tells Jack he takes the group off the track.

EUGENE. We need a rudder, we can't just discuss the first thing that comes up.

ALEC. I don't feel I have to talk all the time. David, you seem to think all must speak in turn.

DAVID. Do you who haven't spoken feel this way? I don't want to seem so damn dogmatic, but you, (Jack) should see if we're interested.

IRMA. Do we have to take a vote each time we want to talk about something?

DAVID. I agree with you Alec, that all must not talk—but I wasn't in on the decision making.

JACK. David, what should we do then?

DAVID. I don't have to solve it. Let's talk about it. Hell, let's get some things out of the way.

EUGENE. (Mentioned Basic Skills as a smooth operating function.) If it continued like this time, we would have to do something. Do you want a program coordinator?

BILL. I hope not.

JACK. What is our task—identifying procedure?

BILL. No.

EUGENE. That's what you did.

DAVID. (Curtly.) Let him explain himself.

BILL. I wanted to throw out something and see what came.

DAVID. I feel you are experimenting with us.

JACK. Why doesn't anyone speak up.

LIZ. You have to be impolite to get in a word.

JACK. What is our procedure? (Everyone laughs.)

LIZ. I feel this is necessary.

IRMA. Can we iron out procedure.

BILL. We are. (Curtly.)

IRMA. Not to me we aren't.

BILL. That's what we anticipated last week—separate groups. (Bill, David and Liz agree interpersonal relations are important.)

DAVID. Bill, you and I could railroad this group if we wanted to.

IRMA. (Snaps.) I think you're overestimating yourself.

ALEC. How can we get things done if interrelationships take the time?

TOM. Last week we took three days for this and then we got on the ball.

JACK. Sometimes you start with step one or step two or step three.

IRMA. What do you suggest?

LIZ. We felt a need to discuss relationships.

ALEC. As long as one person needs to discuss it, we need to.

LIZ. We are getting closer now.

JACK. Can I pull out of the situation and do something I want to do? (David and Liz tell Jack that this is not a hypothetical situation. Feeling runs a bit high.)

EUGENE. How about starting and stopping times.

DAVID. We need to find procedural patterns.

JACK. We want to find a starting time.

BILL. I feel we've come a long way.

JACK. Not to me.

DAVID. I feel I am much freer than before.

IRMA. I think we should start and stop on time.

JACK. Then anyone can mention when it's time to quit.

General discussion arose and this was never answered, and the principal attempted to summarize.

DAVID. Eugene, I don't feel we should have you summarize all the time. We should learn to do that.

EUGENE. I won't do that again. I was just a member of the group. (Liz concerned with factionalism of whole team and Bill sees danger of becoming prejudiced before he has sufficient information.)

DAVID. I agree, but we want this conflict—it's healthy—we can always subdivide.

EUGENE. (Again summarized.) We made two decisions. (1) Strict time schedule. (2) Meeting at 1:45 P.M.

The August statements regarding agenda, time of meeting, length, content, who makes other procedural decisions, and the importance given to interpersonal relations by some of the staff were identified early as areas in need of decisions. Yet the same queries were echoed throughout September. Here, as is presented later, is a situation in which possible consequences were identified. In late September, as was true in August, the consequences were identified but no action had been taken previously either to preclude further problems and/or to curb the current ones. The continuing problem is indicated by Liz's response to a question as to their team problem at a total-school faculty meeting: "We never agreed until last week as to who calls meetings, obligations to meet, etc. We finally agreed to meet at 2:15 and in a place. How long we must stay, what happens if you leave, and can those remaining make decisions still have to be decided." This lack of definite procedure seems crucial in a collegial team approach.

The lack of procedural guides fostered a great confusion on the individual level. There were no norms, except the lack of rules, at the team level, and there were none regulating the sphere of the individual as an entity within the team. Risks were high, for when one did act, his assumptions and procedures were subject to the scrutiny of the team with no specific team norms, other than that of the doctrine of nondirectiveness, against which to weigh and to evaluate both ideas and behavior. In effect, to act at all came to be identified with a lack of concern with the team procedural structure and risked being charged with directiveness.

Many of the difficulties facing the ISD faculty were those with which, in a great part, a team leader would contend. The sentiments toward having a team leader and their impact and relationship to the development of the division's organizational structure were important.

Evolution of Team Leadership. A central organizational and administrative issue in team teaching revolves around the pattern of organization: vertical-bureaucratic or horizontal-collegial to use Lortie's (1964) phrasing. One of the investigators' early concerns centered on studying the possible incongruency of formal and informal leadership of teaching teams. This problem did not appear for investigation because Shelby elected to have leadership arise more spontaneously from within the faculty during the August workshop. During that period of the school's life he verbalized the point of view that the teachers were the responsible constituency. As we have related, August especially, but early September also, was the occasion for a series of confrontations and struggles for power among the faculty. The initial Curriculum Coordinating Committee, which later was called the Central Committee, had appointed rather than elected membership. A serious struggle arose here as the implications of the potential power of the committee were perceived.

The Independent Study Division was wracked with conflict. Kirkham was an initial central figure in this. Jack Davis' and David Nichols' conflict lay partly here, that is, a struggle for power, as well as in other philosophical and personality differences. Alec Thurman, in turn, tried and was supported in part at various times for team leadership. Transition's leadership, especially after the arrival of the pupils, moved from essentially a discussion and consensus approach, to one of leadership by Meg, the only one of the three with experience. She received considerable coalition-type support from Claire. In Basic Skills, early conflict was more on the bases of power, for example, ideas and ideology versus experience, instead of needs for dominance. Personality differences were critical also. Later, the team of four evolved more gradually, and with considerable compromise, to a large and relatively unperceived degree through the efforts of Chris, a part-time staff member whose personality and behavior blended considerable experience in individualized instruction, an articulate manner of conceptualizing and talking about the program, great skill in working with young children, considerable help to Sue, the neophyte teacher, and a facility for making constructive suggestions in a group without antagonizing team members. In Basic Skills-2, Carla assumed direction and dominance early and eventually to the great consternation of Mary.

As we have indicated, leadership roles, as a product of group experience, grow slowly and frequently with considerable conflict in a new organization. Also, at Kensington, and here there were elements of professional pride and individual autonomy, too, these informal leadership roles never attained the potency of a formal representation in either a governing or in an administrating function. Shelby never had group leaders or representatives of the faculty who would speak for or speak to the divisions or the teams. Throughout the year school-wide matters were handled with the total staff or with individual members.

Upside-down Authority and Deviationism. A striking consequence of the reversal in the usual authority lines is the potency given the other parts of the organization at particular times. Although no prior discussion or precedent existed, the replacement of Bill Kirkham was carried out in the context of a team decision. Although the events leading to the Friday meeting in August had varied complications, the decision was finalized, or at least formalized, in the context of the team meeting. The usual protection from his colleagues that an organizational employee has, in the form of the formal authority of the organization, was not present. In contrast, one might argue that the group could provide protection from the authority usually vested in the formal line relationships. No situations of this kind of defense occurred.

For our analysis, regardless of the justifiable or nonjustifiable quality of the decision, the power of the group to invoke the ultimate sanction of ostracism, replacement in a job (with all the implications of this for a man's work, career, and the like), for deviation seems critical. The classi-

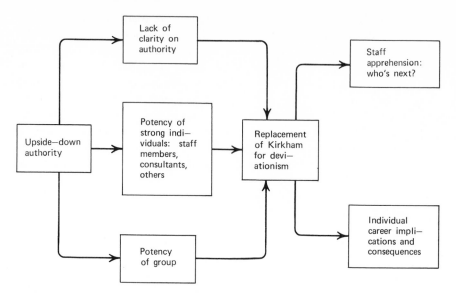

Figure 8.2 The implications of Kensington's authority structure and deviationism.

cal experimental studies of deviation, conformity, and rejection (for example, Schachter et al., 1951) are accurate but pale pictures of this reality.

Rules and the Authority Structure. Although rules are almost an unexamined phenomenon in classical educational psychology, organizational sociologists have been concerned about them (Homans, 1950, Gouldner, 1954).[6] Earlier, we reported on the list of rules established shortly after the move to the new building. One phase of this reappeared along with interpretations by the observer.

> Another interesting phenomenon concerns the rule about no children on the mezzanine. As far as I know, this has not been violated at any time except once when one child was up helping straighten out the books. The most interesting aspect of this to me is that this is the only really clear rule that's ever been drawn dramatically and held to consistently by all of the ISD people and Eugene alike. I have heard no complaints, no problems from the children that this was unfair or uncalled for or somehow impeded their activities. It might become the classic illustration for our argument of the fact that rules, in and of themselves, are not deleterious or fought when they seem reasonable, which means they fit into the prevailing individual, schemas and normative structure, and when there is generalized support among the staff for them.

[6] For a preliminary analysis of rules as belief systems in a slum classroom see the report by Smith and Geoffrey (1968).

A strong orientation on pupil learning and a secondary orientation on things such as teacher privacy, to help her prepare and to get the kids ready to learn, would clarify a good bit of the structure and process that exists in the organization as it now stands (12/14).

The implications of the early negation of rules at Kensington are sketched in Figure 8.3. Thus, a source of the negation of rules was the doctrine concerning flexibility; in reality less flexibility resulted. The occurrence of novel incidents became cases for group decision making, since there were few general or specific rules to which the faculty could appeal. Long and difficult hours were required repeatedly to reach concensus. Increased teacher time expenditure occurred in handling the issues that typically an administrator would perform. This, in turn, meant less time for the preparation of instructional materials, plans, and lessons, which, in lieu of the general absence of textbooks, was vital.

In December, two policy statements regarding rules were issued by the principal shortly after the move to the new building and after long trials and tribulation about "institutional decisions," "teaching decisions," and so forth. The immediate antecedents and consequences appear in Figure 8.4. Responding to criticism from the central office, the anxiety concerning pupil control problems, and in view of partial staff support for concrete guides, Shelby formulated the December rules. The reactions to the rules

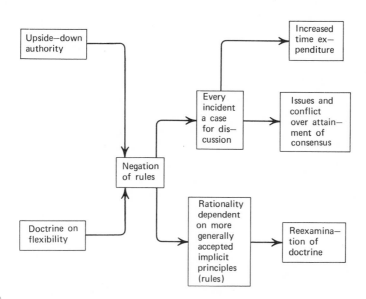

Figure 8.3 The implications of rule negation at Kensington.

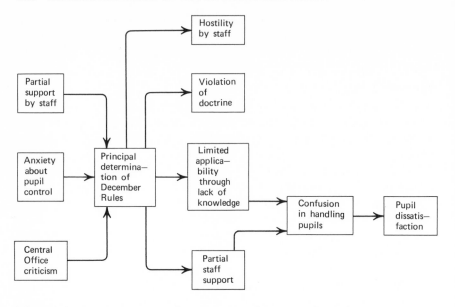

Figure 8.4 The antecedents and consequences of the December Rules.

and the manner in which they were presented were varied. A member from the central office indicated that the rules seemed to reveal that the school was encountering severe problems. There was hostility from staff members who most closely identified with and adhered to early versions of the formal doctrine. The abrupt formation of the rules seemed in violation of written statements that designated the faculty and pupils as the source of decisions like those encompassed in the rules. Hence, the degree of acceptance and application of the rules varied. In turn, this made for differences in pupil behavior. Although the design of the building with a minimum of walls emphasized and increased pupil contact, the differing faculty interpretations and enforcement in their own semi-self-contained groups made for pupil confusion as students observed and interacted with those who were subject to a set of rules at variance with theirs. Although the faculty had more opportunity for contact with and more reason for disciplining others' pupils who wandered into their area, there was great probability that they would request the child to behave in accordance with rules that were not advocated and adhered to by his teacher. This led to both faculty and student dissatisfaction.

Professional Autonomy: the Zone of Indifference. One of the major but, perhaps, underemphasized parts of the Kensington innovative thrust lay in the freedom that was provided the teaching staff. Often at Kensington this point seemed to be lost in the discussions of team teaching, nongraded-ness, or individualized instruction. In some ways, the point seemed to be raised more frequently in the post-experimental-year contacts we had with faculty members who had left the school. As they described current positions and their contacts with their colleagues, the restrictions of principal fiat and central office directives rose as major items of discontent. At Kensington the formal doctrine, the authority structure, and the strong individual needs of teachers for autonomy and self-expression led to a high degree of profes-sional autonomy and freedom on the part of the staff. In turn, for some of the teachers, feelings of satisfaction in teaching arose, numerous coordina-tion and problems of staff conflict occurred, and quite varied styles of teaching—ranging from David's near Rousseauian style to fairly typical textbook instruction—occurred. Interestingly, much of the varied style came in self-contained situations and often came as an unanticipated functional consequence of inability to work as a unit in a team structure (see Figure 8.5).

Summary. In short, democracy and egalitarianism were to be captured in the "upside-down authority structure." Less glowing results, often un-anticipated by the planners of Kensington and the staff of Kensington, occurred. These include a continuous questing for procedures and leader-ship, a kind of formalization, if you like. The evolution of team structure within the Divisions also was influenced in pronounced ways. Rule forma-tion and deviationism occurred and were handled in surprising ways because of the upside-down authority. Finally, the professional autonomy which was not only permitted but encouraged gave rise to a much neglected but im-portant variety of idiosyncratic teaching and classroom styles.

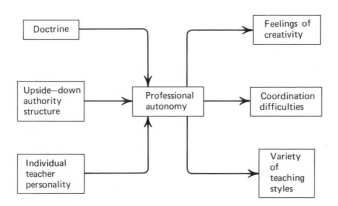

Figure 8.5   The antecedents and consequences of professional autonomy.

Constitutional Arrangements: An Analytic Resolution[7]

All year, Kensington grappled with problems related to democratic administration, authority, and the locus of decision making. Administrative theorists in education also have stated the issue, even though they have not pursued it intensively and analytically.

"Note that the decision to invoke 'group decision' methods is itself a decision. The leader must also decide within what spheres group decisions will be permitted, and to what extent he will be bound by such decisions. Will the group's role be advisory, or will its decisions on every move be a mandate to the administrator" (Halpin, 1966, p. 36).

In a more general critique of T-groups, Whyte (1953) almost discards the issue as inapplicable, at least, in industry:

"Still, let us not kid ourselves about group process in industry. When all is said and done in group discussion, it is up to the boss to make the decision and accept responsibility for it. A skillful leader will seek to avoid decisions that will needlessly antagonize subordinates. He will weigh their ideas and advice most carefully. And, when necessary, after he has made the decision, he will seek for it the sort of support that comes from voluntary cooperation" (p. 42).

However, as we have tried to analyze and make sense conceptually of the issues, we have been struck by the potentiality in Swanson's (1959) concept of constitutional arrangements. It takes us farther than Halpin or Whyte in clarifying Kensington's problems. By constitutional arrangement, he means ". . . the social definitions that state a group's sphere of competence and the proper procedures for making and executing decisions." (p. 48). These procedures or rules of the game have much in common with our concept of group norms. Swanson stresses three kinds or modes of constitutional arrangements.

1. *Parliamentarian:* open discussion and debate, voting on individual issues, *majority* decides. Swanson argues that this is particularly applicable to groups with heterogeneous and often conflicting interests, with equal status of members, and with varying allegiances on specific issues. This arrangement provokes compromise on policy decisions and consensus on procedures.

2. *Participant determining: consensus* obtained for both policy and procedures; assumes equality of members and no fundamental conflicts of

---

[7] Our interpretations here owe an important debt to discussions with Professor Edwin Bridges who has used similar conceptions for the theoretical rationale underlying his experiments in educational administration.

interests. Tends to produce self-examination (individually and collectively), a decline in privacy, and the display of emotional and personal needs.

3. *Democratic centralism:* an elite body, or individual, has final authority to make binding decisions, but he requires judgment and advice of subordinates.

Political sociology (Etzioni, 1966) suggests a fourth constitutional arrangement, a *representational* or multilevel consensus formation structure. In essence, smaller groups of persons settle differences and send a representative to a meeting of representatives who, in turn, reach compromises. Presumably, this group of representatives may behave in any of the ways suggested by Swanson. In his analysis, Etzioni (1966) argues the value of this approach when the conflict is serious, when the interests are heterogeneous, and when the numbers of persons are large. Illustratively, for us, the large numbers of pupils in a school are usually "represented" by their teachers in staff meetings. The principals represent their buildings in meeting with the superintendent. In Kensington two intermediate levels occurred—the divisions and the teams. As we have indicated, Basic Skills contained two teams, Transition had one team, and ISD varied from one team to two teams to self contained classrooms during the course of the year.

As we have commented at several points, Kensington played by each set of rules at one time or another and at one place or another. The observer's notes of the first day in which the divisions met indicates the thrust of "participant determining" (consensus), the implicit parliamentarian (voting), and the democratic centralism (the principal as the final authority).

I will give some random thoughts on the similarities and differences of the three groups that met separately today. Eugene sat in session with each of the divisions. The Basic Skills group met this morning from 11:00 A.M. until 12:00 noon. Eugene opened each of the three sessions by saying that he was not in charge of the group. He explained that his role would be one of resource leader. He made this point in all three sessions. It appeared to me that he served this role best in the first session of the Basic Skills. In this session there was a normal give-and-take discussion. Eugene filled the role of resource leader by answering only direct questions put to him. At times he would comment and then state that these comments represented only the expression of his views, and that they might find it necessary to make changes in this thinking.

The next group that met was the Independent Study group. This was a very fiery session in which David particularly attacked Jack for what he felt was improper procedure in a group discussion. Jack began discussing the individualization of instruction especially as it pertained to the science area. After several comments on this topic, David challenged that this was premature and that they should better spend their time in learning to become a group. The action got rather fast and furious as David and Jack and eventually Bill entered into fiery comments on what should or should not take place in this opening session. Irma felt rather distressed that the time was being taken in this fashion and indicated that she would be much more inclined to discuss problems of a more practical nature. At one time she turned rather sharply on David. He had commented that if they desired, Bill and David could railroad the group. I feel David meant that anyone had the capability of railroading if they so desired but that this was not his intention. Irma, however, turned to him and said, something like "I believe you are overestimating your ability." During this session, Eugene sided rather decisively with David in the turn of events that should be taken in this discussion group. It surprised me because I felt that as principal Eugene would be wishing to get to the matters at hand, namely some very basic questions of just how they would operate, the procedure as a team, the curriculum to be studied and the manner in which they will implement the entire instructional program. Eugene wishes to have these bugs worked out of their relationship now so that they, hopefully, will be able to function as a team in a better fashion. He did not seem in anyway disturbed at the turn of events and in my estimation assisted the agitation by seemingly backing David whenever he could. He did not in anyway dominate this discussion. In fact, he was put back fairly sharply on, at least, two occasions. Once Eugene interrupted Bill with a comment and David immediately snapped, "Let him have his chance to say. You've cut him off before he got to talk." At the conclusion of the session Eugene summarized the steps they had taken in their session thus far, throwing out the various things that had been discussed and naming the decisions they had made. At one time, Eugene referred to a consensus that had been gathered on a particular point when Bill immediately cut him off with this comment, "That was not a consesus. That was one or two people's opinion." Eugene immediately backed off and said, "Yes, that's right."

The third session to meet with Eugene today was the Transition group. This was in many respects a very different session from either of the other two. In this instance, Eugene dominated and took control of the situation. It, from the very start, had a question-and-answer type of atmosphere. The three people in the Transition group would ask and discuss questions of many different topics. They were of practical nature, for instance: What type of organization should we have with the children? How do we have an individualized reading program? What types of free library reading will we have? Just what do you mean by an individualized approach to education?, and the like. The reason for Eugene's handling this group in a completely different manner is not immediately apparent to me (8/17).

Democracy in the public schools goes by many faces. Kensington, both in doctrine and practice, struggled mightily with each of these several views. Because there were several such sides to being democratic, some confusion prevailed. At these points of choice, well-meaning individuals tended to doubt, to inhibit action, to seek clarification, and to struggle to influence the course of Kensington's development. Which kind of democratic constitutional arrangement (if any), in what situations, and when in an organization's life seems to be an exceedingly important issue in a middle range theory of educational administration. If such a theory and its supporting empirical data had been well developed and available in basic and applied social science, Kensington might have been a very different organization.

FURTHER DILEMMAS IN THE ADMINISTRATIVE ROLE

As we observed at Kensington, a number of recurring specific dimensions of the administrative role arose as Shelby defined it. We tried to identify them both conceptually and operationally. From this point, we tried to seek relevant antecedents and consequences. Our theoretical bias suggests that these hypotheses, codified for the most part in pictorial models, are important points of departure for verificational research.

The Statesman Alternative

In his small book entitled *Leadership in Administration,* Selznick (1957) developed the thesis that the higher one is in the administrative hierarchy, the less significant becomes the logic of efficiency, the correlation of means with settled and accepted ends, and the more one needs to shift one's perspective to that of statesman: ". . . a concern for the evolution of the organization as a whole, including its changing aims and capabilities" (p. 5). Although, to our knowledge, Shelby was not aware of the Selznick volume, nor did he phrase his point of view in these terms, his behavior indicates that such a label fits the alternative he pursued. The particular pieces of evidence that seem most persuasive to this interpretation include the selection of the alternative of grandeur or, better, the strong support and the high degree of complementarity of interests on this point among Spanman, Cohen, and Shelby; the creation of the document known as the Institutional Plan; and the persistent pursuit of the Curriculum Committee that struggled throughout the year with the tough issues of the long term goals and broad means of public education. Within professional education, a strong argument for this kind of reconceptualization of the principal's role and a reconstituting of the organizational structure of the school has been made by Schaefer (1967) as he describes the school as a center of inquiry. In his view, the school must change from a dreary factorylike organization into a milieu where students learn to inquire, in part, because inquiry is in the air. That is, they observe and partake of the faculty's inquiry into the exciting and difficult problems of teaching and learning. The administrator's task falls into conceiving, nurturing, and vitalizing this world for staff and students.

As we argued earlier in the case of true belief, the organization as an idea becomes a receptacle of idealism and emotion that antedates the formation of the organization per se. Initially the doctrine, the ideology, and the individual conceptions are built out of individual dreams and partial information instead of out of organizational realities. The day-to-day processes of interaction and adaptation have not occurred and the stuff of firm and continuing institutionalization has not arisen. Consequently, when the organization meets its initial problems, rivalries, disagreements, and failures it has no way to turn but back on the doctrine that provides temporary sustenance, if it be sustenance at all.

In the context, then, of leadership strategies, we would formulate an hypothesis that organizational leadership, the concern for survival, for interpersonal goals, and for efficiency, that is, the technology of adjusting means to given ends, must precede, or be given heavy accent early, in contrast to institutional leadership that must take the surviving and efficient organization and must reformulate its goals toward broader, deeper, or higher objectives. In effect, the kind of administrative incumbent and the time in the organizational history interact significantly. Furthermore, the consequences involved in the election of the statesman alternative must be considered in the light of the initiation and development of an organization, the "true belief" components of vision and statesmanship, the problems of resources, and the mechanisms available for the problems of efficiency.

But even in a school as innovative and as intellectually exciting as Kensington, a reality of administration—the handling of mundane problems—arises. For instance,

> Eugene raised, illustratively, the problems of kids in the theatre tower throwing wads of paper and the jurisdiction over the kitchen help. Later Jerl commented: "You can see the problem he's concerned about." Eugene had no part in hiring the kitchen people, one of whom has a child in Kensington and who pressures the teachers (1/4).

These problems, as specific issues, involved a portion of Shelby's time. The paper throwing was one instance of a group of problems that had led to and then were involved in the development of the December rules for pupil behavior. The tangle of multiple roles and relationships illustrated by the lunchroom personnel was one of a number of these relationships. The superintendent, the principal, one of the aides, and several teachers had children in the school. The varied areas of jurisdiction of who hires and to whom is one responsible complicated the situation further. Finally,

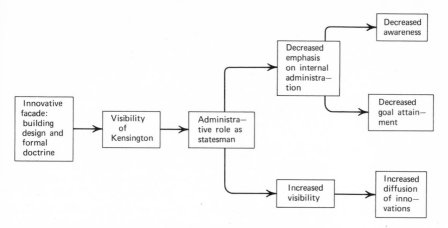

Figure 8.6 The antecedents and consequences of the statesman role.

serving lunch remained a problem; this we discussed at some length in the myths and realities of the satellite kitchens.

Figure 8.6 summarizes a number of hypotheses, as antecedents and consequences, that related to the statesman role at Kensington. A more complete interpretation appears later in our analysis of the "alternative of grandeur," the major innovative strategy and thrust of the Milford District.

Occasions for Intervention

Strategic Times. As we have described, during the last few days of November and the first few days of December, Kensington began to rustle and tremble as the impending move to the new building arrived. To the casual onlooker, moving to new quarters may seem a simple phenomenon. To the investigators, issues of administrative strategies and tactics were apparent; our biases suggested that implications—our notions of anticipated and unanticipated consequences—could accrue from such a change as a move to the new and long-desired quarters.

> Another point of some interest is the way in which Eugene has figured to move. If the building is not totally done, and I still cannot believe that it will be, there is the question of the handling of all the minor inconveniences and the little difficulties, and whether this will impede the program. The question is whether it would be better to wait another week or two weeks and go in full dress or whether it is better to go in and limp awhile in the new quarters. I think my own bias, and I am not sure of the reasons at the moment, would lie with the waiting for it to be totally ready and with the more systematic decision making and planning before you go in. They have limped so

much, for so long, that to engage in more, and in the context of the new building which is supposed to solve many of the problems, seems to me to be a bit on the tragic side, since a move of the more stable units and a solidifying of them then would become an anchor about which you could integrate the more troubled spots.

There are some interesting organizational strategy questions here as to how you play from strength and how you perceive your strength and what particular goals you have (12/3).

Later in the same day, the observers had just finished a brief visit to the building and they commented on the potential consequences of the move.

The building is so far from being ready that it is going to create a good many problems in implementing the program. The issue that keeps coming back to me again and again is that they are getting involved, once again, in situations that are not ready or are not prepared for them. And what should be a beautiful and happy move to a crystallized physical setting that can implement the kind of program they want seems very likely to degenerate into a move to another "almost ready" kind of temporary setting that must be lived with for the moment. This will take some of the edge and some of the excitement and some of the novelty off of the new building. And what could be a real plus in terms of having them get on top of the world again will probably be a minus (12/3).

Further aspects of the strategy of moving arose in the observer's speculations two days later, early on Saturday morning.

This morning I am trying to make sense out of some of the odds and ends left over from the images of the move in the last two days. For some reason the image that gets aroused is that of Sherif's book on the robber's cave experiment, *Intergroup Conflict and Cooperation*. The genesis of the ISD inter-team hostility was on grounds other than the competitiveness introduced by an outsider or by a leader. In a sense, however, the North and the South teams were fighting over the scarce resources. Or better, they soon came to be fighting over that whereas, initially, the problems arose in difficulty in points of view, in ends and means, and in holding to commitments. A very interesting problem would be to try to conceptualize superordinate goals that would, in effect, eliminate this. Perhaps, Eugene missed a very great opportunity. You have a "naturally defined" starting all over again that could have been generalized to a whole series of other things. As far as I know, this has not occurred and the opportunity if it is not taken this morning or this afternoon will be gone forever. This poses an interesting problem for the leader's role in that it puts him in the position of being able to perceive the problem, perceive the alternatives open to the solution of the problem, some of which could be derived from theories such as Sherif's, and then begin to implement them

in some kind of fashion where he has legitimate power and authority. It becomes even more interesting, since Eugene has given away most of that legitimate power and authority. Seemingly, he has lost credits not only because
he gave them away, but because the handling of many of the routine administrative chores has been so troublesome (12/5).

In short, the theoretical point that we seemed to be reaching for concerns
the use of naturally occurring breaks, episodes, which everyone perceives
as such, as an administrative lever, an optimal time for intervention. Presumably, the changing environment presents these opportunities to all organizations, although perhaps more frequently to some than to others. Although the observers did not realize it at the time, this same phenomenon
seemed to be operating in the Transition Division and the Basic Skills
Division. The notes record the issues this way:

> Another item occurred during the coffee break when I was talking with Meg,
> Dan, and Claire. They are concerned about the limited space they will have
> and the fact that they are going to have to work as one large unit. Claire
> and Meg also indicated to Dan that he would not be able to bring along
> his boxes, caves, and whatever. There just would not be space. I was struck
> then, and also later in the general meeting, by what I would call a "shrewish
> wife" mode of addressing and talking to him.

> A couple of incidents occurred that should be mentioned. One of them sur-
> rounds the final agreement among the two representatives of the Basic Skills
> subteams—Carla and Sue—to work together on some kind of a Christmas
> program for the whole Basic Skills Division. Sue even made a comment of
> keeping the spirit of the season, or something very close to that (12/5).

In a sense, the two anecdotes present a negative and a positive illustration
of our more general point.

In a final illustration, we generalize the occasion to any episode characterized by flux.

> All of this is to suggest that once again Eugene has a very clear opportunity
> to move in and shape the policy and the programs of the school. Intuitively,
> the general principle seems to be that whenever there is flux and uncertainty,
> then the chances for influence are increased. Whenever there is an equilibrium
> that is reasonably stable, then the possibilities are correspondingly reduced.
> Latently, I presume that there is an assumption concerning the satisfactions
> that accrue to individuals and the fact that this produces a reasonably stable
> equilibrium. A point of attack on this might well be Kurt Lewin's old notion
> of unfreezing and freezing the quasi-stationary equilibrium. I will have to go
> back and check this and determine the kinds of forces that he argues will
> unfreeze such a group. On the surface it would seem that it must be a very
> significant and potent force. In this particular instance it would be the new
> building, it would be the first time that all the others have been perceived

in operation, and it would be conceptualized as a new start, a beginning (12/14).

This speculation continues our emphasis on the need for a more potent theory of educational administration. When "natural" appearing occasions arise, we hypothesize that members of groups and organizations are more open for "starting again," "beginning on a new foot," "reevaluating old relationships," and so forth. Within the cliches an important principle seems to be lurking. Whether it presumes latent common agreement that all members see problems that they want corrected, and hence the possibility of developing superordinate goals, is not clear. Perhaps also, there is a reawakening or an increased saliency of early idealism that can be drawn on. Perhaps all we are doing is extending Barnard's (1938) concept of strategic factors to include strategic times. Nonetheless, it seems fundamental.[8]

Administrative Awareness: Being on Top of the Situation.[9] In the summary notes, just before the move to the new building, one of the teachers commented seriously about a concern for property destruction (see page 161). This generated in the observer reflections on the communication within the staff. The latter ideas raised an important dimension of administrative behavior, "being on top of the situation."

> Another interesting aspect of her comment is that she obviously was speaking with considerable emotion, considerable concern, and yet she has not raised this with anyone else in the building. In a staff that has a point of view and a philosophy of freedom and of high communication levels, and the like, she is, in effect, giving evidence of the fact that the people do not talk about significant events of this kind. In ISD the divisions are so deep and so great that you, in effect, have an aggregate of people who are interdependent yet isolated. In a sense, this is reflected also in Eugene's relationship to the group. He seems to have no "feel" for the pulse of the Division. One might guess that this is suggested also by his administrative handling of the space allocation and also in what seemed to be implicit in a Basic Skills comment over the moving of the ditto machine. The latter is very vital to them, and they have apparently no control over it. Eugene, apparently without realizing it, is going to create some serious problems for all of them there. In effect, it seems to me that we need a concept of the order of "being on top of the situation," which seems to be having the necessary knowledge about the desires and the

[8] Our account of the end of semester changes illustrates the further practical and theoretical complications within this point.

[9] We make a similar case for teacher awareness in Smith and Geoffrey (1968) and Smith and Kleine (1969). If the generality of these concepts holds true, it strengthens the case for a synthesis of teaching and administrative theory.

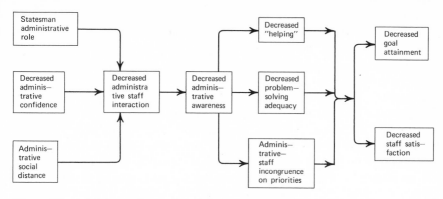

Figure 8.7 A miniature theory of "administrative awareness" at Kensington.

wants of the individuals in the subgroups, having knowledge about how things hook up, and, also, having some kind of resources to control this and to influence it so that you come out in some kind of conglomerate okay fashion (12/4).

Once again, we seem to be in cliché-ridden territory. Figure 8.7 attempts to clarify this. Administrative awareness, the possession of relevant information regarding the organization, seems mandatory for making decisions that move the organization toward its goals and that impinge on organization members in ways that maximize satisfactions and minimize frustration. A further illustration from the field notes suggests the tenor of this argument.

At the close of the school I was to attend a Basic Skills team-4 meeting. This got rearranged because Eugene had someone from the Johnson Publishing Company in to demonstrate a text on program reading. Literally, none of the four was interested in seeing this at this time. They all thought it was more desirable to engage in a team meeting. Wanda, who had gone out of the room and who brought back the word, said that it was not a request, that it was an order. As she put it, there was no choice. Second, the Basic Skills team-4 is operating under pretty much a catch-as-catch-can individual fashion at this point. They have not met during the holidays nor have they met today to any great degree before school started. They were eager to have a team meeting so that they could begin to do some things in correlated fashion. Also, it's the understanding that they will no longer have Chris to help them. I am not sure how firm this is but this is the way they seem to understand it. This means that they have got to redivide the reading groups so that they can pick up the kids she has been working with. This will increase, according to Wanda, the size of their groups to about 30. She believes that this is too large (1/4).

Another old cliché states that one should carry out "first things first." However, the cliché does not specify criteria for determining what is first and what is second. In part, the pressing needs of group members might become such a criterion. An administrator aware of these needs could facilitate the progress of the group.

Resource Utilization: Long and Short Term. A significant event that suggests the broader aspects of the issues in resources occurred in the staff's use of the Christmas holidays. The move to the new building had been completed at all levels. Considerable concern existed about the instructional program. The faculty was tired, frustrated, and in considerable conflict. A number had been ill. The majority of the staff elected to take almost a full vacation.[10]

> Another item that occurred that seems of some importance is the fact that almost all of the teachers are leaving town for all or most of the holidays. As I talked with them today, one of the conversational gambits I used was whether they would be here for the holiday. As I went down the list, I found that almost all of them will be gone. Eugene will be in Alabama, John will be in Ohio, Meg is going to Alabama, Alec, Kay, and Claire are going to Michigan, Wanda is going to Indiana, Dan and Chris are going to Detroit, and David is going to a friend's house. Many will not be coming back until the weekend just before school starts and many will be leaving beginning tomorrow afternoon. This suggests some substantial problems with beginning the new year. At best, the planning that they will be able to do will be mostly individual. At worst, it will amount to almost none (12/22).

Later that same day the notes continue in the same vein.

> In talking with Pat about the possibility of when an organization can be shifted dramatically, I raised the points that were on the first part of today's comments. Almost all of the people will be gone from the city for almost the entire period of the vacation. Some are leaving tomorrow afternoon and some not coming back until Saturday or Sunday the day before school begins. This "fleeing," if it be that, is going to make it almost impossible to plan extensively for the coming months. In the vernacular, this should put them in the soup again all spring (12/22).

Figure 8.8 depicts these hypotheses, and the dilemma underlying them.

The critical importance of time and energy as resources for a social system arose continuously. They possessed limits that set parameters on individual behavior and the contributions to an organization. As such, they

---

[10] We do not have comparative data on general elementary school staff norms regarding vacations. Our guess would be that most elementary teachers use the time for family events and for catching up on nonschool matters.

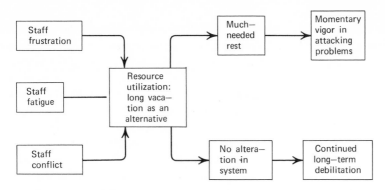

Figure 8.8 The dilemma in the long- and short-term use of resources.

were critical to the analysis of any organization. If our hypotheses are correct, a beginning organization, a changing organization, and an innovative organization put extra heavy demands on these scarce and limited resources. The interplay of this dilemma, our concern for strategic time in administrative intervention and administrative awareness, suggests the very real problems in both the practice and theory of administration.

Monitoring and Sequencing of Decisions. Another phase of the administrative process concerns responsibility for what we have called "sequencing of decisions." An observation arose this way in the notes:

> The early decision to move Irma into a self-contained class looked like an appropriate way to handle some of the problems of the Independent Study Division. Now, however, with the movement of the other children into platoons, it seems to me that this prior move defeats the possibilities for the functioning of the academic counselor concept. With Bill Kirkham gone long ago, with David tied up in the T-groups, and with Irma with her own group, this prohibits any utilization of the academic counselors in the role for which they originally were intended. It seems to me that there is a very real executive responsibility in keeping the sequence of decisions, which seem reasonable at the time of any one of them, from getting you off into spots where it is impossible to reach the organizational goals. If you added the Bill Kirkham situation, the Irma situation, and the Walt Larsen situation, then the Kensington program and philosophy, in every sense of the word, is paralyzed. How to recoup this is a very, very difficult problem (9/15).

The sequencing of decisions refers to the monitoring of the decision-making process so as not to find oneself in an irreversible situation through a series of minor (or major) changes, none of which seem significant at the time but which cumulate quite critically.

Helping: Strategic Factors, Intervention, and Administrative Experience

Strategic Factors. In *The Functions of the Executive,* Barnard presents a "theory of opportunism.[11] By this he means ". . . that no action can take place except in the present, under conditions and with the means presently available." In Barnard's view, this process is essentially a concern about means and finding "strategic factors," the elements of a situation, barriers which prevent the attainment of goals. The shift back and forth between what is or is not a strategic factor depends on where one is in the problem-solving or decision-making process. He uses the illustration of a farmer who wishes to increase his yield of grain. Finding what is needed, for example, potash, is superceded by other limiting conditions.

"Nevertheless, when the need has been determined, a new situation has arisen because of the fact of knowledge or the assumption that potash is the limiting factor; and instead of potash, the limiting factor obtaining potash then becomes the strategic factor; and this will change progressively into obtaining the money to buy potash, then finding John to go after potash, then getting machines and men to spread potash, etc. Thus the determination of the strategic factor is itself the decision which at once reduces purpose to a new level, compelling search for a new strategic factor in the new strategic situation" (p. 204).

We cite this example, not only for its wide generality as a key element in the administrative process but also because of its concrete applicability to the analysis of "helping." If the analogy holds true, Barnard is saying that a problem can be a problem for a long time after the initial diagnosis and decision. If the administrator has responsibility for the total organization and if he perceives difficulties, especially regarding a subordinate's performance, then the sequential focusing and refocusing on the strategic factors must continue until the subordinate, the teacher in this instance, can carry on by himself or until other forces, outside materials or resources, are made available for him to do so.

At several points during the year we groped for a concept of "helping," which seemed to be an important aspect of administrative behavior. Early in December, as the move to the new building was underway, and after a difficult Saturday-morning staff meeting when the faculty argued at length about policies surrounding Christmas parties, tree decorations, and teacher freedom, our speculations developed this way:

> The notion of administrative intervention or breaking into a system and the
> means of conceptualizing this kind of intervention seems best handled by a

[11] His chapter title is "The Theory of Opportunism," but the word opportunism has taken on such strong negative connotations that we prefer to avoid it.

concept such as "helping." Defining "helping" in psychological terms seems a necessary conceptual task. For the moment, the immediate alternative seems to lie in the area of the individual's own definition of his goals and the direction to the goals and what he needs in reaching those goals; better yet in facilitating the goals. The tightrope that the administrator must walk centers on the making of individual goals and group goals congruent. He must fathom the special needs and also the organizational needs and must link them together in a particular action, for example, in terms of whether to install corporal punishment of students, and the like. He might well have implemented this in one room or, at least, have given the teacher this option for helping bring the kids under control. In the other classes, it seems to me, this is not necessary at this point, and it could well come later if need be. The examples drawn from this group would soon filter into all of the other classrooms. Another teacher needs somebody to hold his hand, another needs some textbooks, and so on. Mostly, they need an administrator around to listen, to hear, and to see. Whether Shelby can talk to anybody without moralizing and without a judgmental position is a question (12/7).

Several days later, the same phenomenon was caught.

Eugene spent a good bit of time this morning in laying out physical education schedules with John. This conversation seemed very task oriented and seemed to be a fine example of give and take between two people working on a common problem. There are some real difficulties in what the P.E. objectives will be and how they will be organized among the 20 or so teachers and the 500 children. Apparently, here Eugene is making quite reasonable, adequate, and important contact with one of his teachers (12/10).

At Kensington, the amount of administrative help varied, as our two field note references suggest. With John the problems were minimal, and an extended discussion was sufficient to solve his problems. With other teachers much more complex processes were involved. In instances where the teaching problems were quite severe, several personality processes of the administrator were activated; the most crucial was that of a moralistic-judgmental stance, for example, a teacher *should* be able to handle that problem. On occasion this tendency was evidenced in speaking of a right way and a wrong way for her to handle a situation. These reactions were confounded with the "statesman" outlook instead of an administrative tinkering orientation, with a specific and general loss of confidence as the number of problems multiplied, with the lack of clarity implicit in the "upside-down authority role," and with the mixed emotional reactions he had toward several of the faculty. As these personality processes were aroused, the amount of administrative help decreased. This, in turn, influenced staff esteem and staff role performance. We diagram in Figure 8.9 these aspects as a miniature theory of helping in the administrative process.

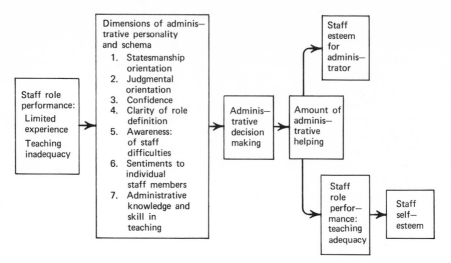

Figure 8.9 A miniature theory of helping in the administrative process.

Conflicting Perceptions and Helping. In literature, one of the most sensitive accomplishments of the past few decades occured in Lawrence Durrell's *Alexandria Quartet.* In four novels Durrell unfolds the lives of a group of people from the individual perceptual frameworks of three members of the group and in a sequel that culminates the experience. In this manner, the totality has a beauty and a subtlety seldom portrayed. As participant observers at Kensington, we were privy to a similar view of a totality. We moved from event to event and conversation to conversation, each time trying to see through the eyes of the particular faculty member. Again and again we were struck by the differences and conflicts in perception that had important implications in the dynamics of the school. For instance, shortly before Christmas, and after the move to the new building, our notes record the following.

> Pat also talked a bit about how the Transition Division members described themselves as the "forgotten division." What these feelings amount to seems to be something like this: back when we needed help over at the Hillside School, none was ever there, and we fumbled and stumbled about. We gradually made sense out of it and began to work out a means of organization and of handling the problems. Now we are gradually getting on top of it, and we do not need or want any help. Also, we do not need and do not want any kind of outside direction that would tell us how we ought to do things.

If this be really true and if Eugene's earlier comments today about his feeling that some of the staff do not appreciate the freedom he's given them also be true, then we have an interesting situation of quite different perceptions of the same events and a good bit of feeling attached to these perceptions. This suggests a very important problem in the basic psychology of conflict, of administrative organization, and possibly of consulting. The differences are not so much in anyone's intrinsic personality problems, but in the relatively simple, but varying, perceptions of the same series or sets of events and the attachment of them with considerable feelings, both positive and negative, and the magnification of them in some kind of spiraling, sequential way that leaves the individuals at a total standoff or with the inability to carry out any kind of common effort. If this is true, it then suggests that there are a whole series of human relations problems that can be solved with minimal effort by providing the experiences that will alter these perceptions either through conversation or through activities of one kind or another (12/22).

Whether more or less of this occurred at Kensington than occurs in any other school or realm of life, we do not know. Nonetheless, we were impressed by its omnipresence and its significance in the functioning of the staff.[12] Presumably, the administrator who has sources of information can contribute to the solution of the perceptual conflict. As these sources are restricted to any great degree, then his processes of decision making and his influence attempts will be correspondingly restricted.

Blau's (1955) general point that the administrator must attend to the "conditions of adjustive development" provides another way of analyzing this part of the concept of helping. In our notes, the incident and interpretation were the following.

11:53 A.M. Kay up for coffee.

(*Observer*. When I contrast her difficulties in relation to Claire and to Sue, both of whom had, in my judgment, lower probabilities of success, I am struck by the impact of the team and of "help" which seems critical for a first-year teacher. They got it and she did not. The power for control that lies in this observation is very high and needs analytical exploitation. It suggests ways to intervene in an ongoing system.) (12/11)

The point we are making is that the fortuitous circumstances of Claire's personal relationship with Meg, an experienced teacher, and Chris' array of skills and willingness to aid Sue were major items in their professional development. Planning and developing teams for such increments in resources would be highly desirable. Whether knowledge is more generally available or whether one has to be "lucky" is an open question. Most

---

[12] This seems particularly significant in a situation where the doctrine accents faculty decision-making perogatives.

assuredly, organizational structures like these can be functional equivalents of administrative action.

Relevant Experience and Skills. The interdependency between a principal's experience and facility in teaching and his instructional leadership role as administrator has been debated widely in education. Late in May we glimpsed aspects of this issue and its relationship to our analysis of helping.

> The most interesting item concerned Eugene's discussion with about 50 of the kids, mostly from ISD, regarding the tax situation. He did what I thought was a beautiful job of raising questions with them, having them state their opinions or having them ask questions, and having other children respond to them. He has a real knack for asking the "Why?" kind of question in which the kids begin to explore the reasons and the varying points of view around what amounts to very difficult positions in government and, in general, morality and ethics. For instance, the kinds of questions that were asked concerned whether it was fair or not that people who send their children to parochial schools must pay taxes for public school kids as well as others. Similarly, should elderly people, who do not have children in school, be required to pay taxes? As these explorations went on, they moved into a whole array of significant social studies ideas. The real tragedy was that, as far as I know, none of the teachers has spent any great amount of time trying to lay a basis for understanding the nature of school levies and how they function and what happens if they do not get passed. Nor has there been any kind of context set that would permit the kids to understand the notions of the "other taxes" which some of them said their parents had to pay, and which caused difficulty with the school taxes as well. The possibilities in political science, government, economics, and the like have not been capitalized on in the school. I keep thinking back to the well-worn illustration which Eugene had early in the year that there would be flexibility in the program so that if some kids in some grade wanted to study the American elections they would not be bound because of the grade they were in. This might well be called the undone social studies project. As he worked with these kids, my guess is that in his own teaching in the upper elementary grades in past years he has been able to carry out much of the kind of program that he has argued for. His attempt to get each kid to state his points of view and then to try to draw some common underpinnings, it seems to me, would fit ideally into the approach that he has had.
>
> All this raises the interesting question as to why he has not been able to teach the others how to do this and how he might have gone about doing it. My own guess is that partly it is inexperience as a principal, and partly inexperience in teacher training, and partly limited experience in teaching per se. This is one of the few times I have seen him actually work with children in an instructional setting, and I came away with strong positive feelings. In the brief discussion I had with Pat afterward she expressed some of the same

sentiments. This might well make a good illustration of the dream that existed. Let me try to recapture more of the specifics as they arose.

First, he handled his daughter, who was one of his pupils, very well in that she was not given any kind of favoritism and at the same time she had a chance to speak her point of view a time or two. One of the points that she made was that she could understand why people who have been in school and who now do not have children in school might be required to pay taxes, but she could not understand yet why people who sent their children to a different school would have to pay taxes. Second, one child raised a very specific point about the education of the parents and the fact that they would not be able to help with the children's homework and that would be too bad. Eugene tried to broaden this to "the larger issue" or "the broader issue," I am not sure of his exact words here, and to move the discussion into more general considerations. Third, he pulled several interesting illustrations out of the hat, one of which was a reference to President Johnson and his education. And another dealt with the fact that people in a democracy needed to know a number of things. Fourth he got on more tenuous ground, from my point of view, when he tried to make the point that they were urging the children to urge their parents to vote either way on this, but that they wanted to present information so that they could discuss it with their parents and could help answer any questions that their parents might have. (*Observer.* My own bias here, and it requires considerable elaboration, concerns the need to have a strong stand taken and argued against other strong stands instead of having much more of what I view essentially as a vacuum. In effect, the pressure group literature and political party literature needs to have some analysis at this point, it seems to me.)

Another point that was part of the start of the discussion centered on who makes what kinds of decisions regarding the school. He asked them who decided whether their building was open or enclosed or whether or not they would have carpets on the floor, and the contrast here was carpets or tile, and several other questions, to which the kids responded, "the school board." And he asked them also who decided on how much money they would spend on the schools, and one of the kids responded "the people." Out of these beginning questions Eugene began to develop his discussion.

Also, in general, he handled almost all comments with interest and concern, tact, and sympathy. His latent agendas did not seem to come out or to get in the way. When occasional factual questions were raised, as when he was asked about the reversion to the one dollar limit, he commented that it was a state law. In effect, he was not adverse to presenting the concrete information as it pertained to the discussion (5/28).

In short, if we can generalize from a brief lesson, Shelby had important skills in teaching for broader intellectual objectives, for the give and take of intensive teacher-pupil discussion, and for the sensitive concern of individual pupils. In its own way this episode becomes a further definition of his conception of Kensington. It was a potential resource that contributed little to the ongoing instruction at Kensington. As such, it raises further questions of helping as an administrative alternative.

Trust

During December, the issue of trust was more generally in the air. A summary comment regarding a staff meeting caught it this way:

> He talked about the "competitive stance" between him and some of the faculty and the need for mutual trust and cooperation. He had mentioned this earlier to me, at least, the competitive part, although he did not say anything about mutual trust (12/15).

Similar statements were made again in January at a team meeting at which the consultant was present. Yet, although the issue was salient, no extended analyses occurred of the sources of the distrust or of the steps to be taken to reduce it. Even though there was little effort to increase trust or to seek for the cause of distrust, a move was made that was to assure specified behavioral outcomes and to lessen the dependence on reciprocal trust. In the summary notes the immediately preceding paragraph began this way:

> Pat called last night and reported the following: Eugene called a last-minute staff meeting some time after I left at 11:00. Many of the teachers were unhappy. He unleashed another whole stack of rules and said that there would be another dittoed sheet of them coming out today. Third, there was some talk of having a committee from each of the divisions to be on a rule-writing group. This apparently was Meg's suggestion, I think, and Eugene did not cotton to it very much. This is surprising in that earlier, yesterday, he had commented about having a broader base for some of the committee and procedure and policy recommendations (12/15).

These observations, however, are only part of a much more complex picture. For instance, in meetings with parents, throughout the year, the teachers were the major elements in describing, explaining, and selling the program. The degree of faith and trust shown here was boundless. Typically, these meetings were opened with a few general remarks by the principal, then the total group broke into smaller units led by the teachers or into totally individualized dyadic conversations between a teacher and a parent. Seldom have the researchers witnessed this degree of faith, confidence, and trust in one's staff.

Other parts of this issue arose around the Institutional Plan. During August, early in the school's history, considerable conflict centered in this domain. The observers' notes reflected the continuing issue of Shelby's reticence about deviating from his extensively thought out conception of Kensington. The dilemma seemed to be an intense conflict between faith and trust in one's carefully considered program and ideas and faith and trust in one's professional staff to create an even more engaging and arresting conception of Kensington. The repercussions of this dilemma and of Shelby's usual choice in favor of the Institutional Plan had further nuances in that some portions of the plan and doctrine emphasized faculty and pupil control of policy and decision making. These incongruities are analyzed in more detail at other points in the monograph.

In its simplest and most direct form, the principal's attitude and concern for the pupils is caught best in a ten-line statement from a staff *Bulletin* in late May when the tax levy was being resubmitted.

"3. *Discussion of Tax Levy With Pupils.* It has been suggested that pupils be informed as much as possible about the forthcoming school tax election. We must be very careful, however, that pupils are not pressured or exploited. It is not uncommon in this area for pupils to be used in questionable ways to get elections passed. We want to avoid such practice, but believe it is quite appropriate for pupils to be well informed about the issues in the district. To make this possible there will be a meeting in the theater at 1:30 Friday afternoon, May 28, for the principal to discuss the tax situation with any interested pupils. Older pupils who are interested and who exhibit some understanding of such matters are invited to attend this meeting" (*Bulletin No. 57, May 25*).

Trust seems to us a most fundamental but little analyzed concept in administrative-staff relationships. Shelby possessed extreme faith and concern in the dignity and responsibility of pupils both as an ultimate goal and as a given for interacting with them. With his faculty the situation was much more complex. He had an ultimate faith that they could explain, interpret, and implement the program. In contrast, he had worked long and hard on the Institutional Plan, which he "trusted" to lead to common goals. No simple resolution was available when these approaches came in conflict. No overarching criteria existed or were developed to indicate which option was to be chosen in which situation.

CONCLUSION

The Theoretical Quest in Educational Administration

Ferment, agitation, and unrest characterize the state of educational administrative theory today. The shift from an evaluative to an analytical orientation began forcefully in 1957 with the first UCEA seminar and the collection of its papers edited by Halpin (1958). More recently, leaders in the field have spoken to a series of issues in the N.S.S.E. Yearbook,

Behavioral Science and Educational Administration.[13] Although we do not pretend to be administrative theorists, we have been interested in leadership, group process, and the psychology of teaching processes for some time, and we found ourselves taking field notes and making interpretive asides about the process of administration. At the start of this study the original research proposal stated our intention this way:

"In the proposed study, the principal's decision-making role will be a focal point in the light of the novel building design, the demand for instructional innovation, and the majority of teachers new to the system. By capitalizing on these events, which should highlight the issues, we should be able to criticize and extend the theory of decision making as it has been applied in education, for example Halpin, *Administrative Theory in Education.*"

In a sense we were listening to the muted voice of Andrew Halpin as he wrote, in his usual deft style,

". . . it is a progress report . . . The fact that these formulations are not all polished to a high gloss does not stop us from sharing our ideas with you. Perhaps you, too, will hear the Lorelei song, and try your own hand at theory development" (1958, p. xiv).

We sailed, heard the song, and know not what rock we have struck and been destroyed upon.

---

[13] Some theorists (for example, Halpin, 1965) feel that the fermentation stopped early and insipidly in this volume.

CHAPTER 9

Individualized Curriculum and Instruction

INTRODUCTION

A discussion of individualized curriculum and instruction at Kensington involves several strands. At one level, we must make an analysis and critique of a very complicated set of issues about which considerable controversy exists in professional education. In its doctrine, Kensington subscribed to what Goodlad (1963) called a "Type C" school in his Project Instruction report for the National Education Association. In a previous chapter we detailed the many facets of that point of view. Taking a stand in the shifting sands of these unsettled issues in professional education became a major consequence for Kensington. In effect, Kensington chose to live with a position that has undergone considerable professional movement, change, and alteration since Goodlad first raised the general stance.

A second major focus we take combines "individualized curriculum and instruction" with an organizational thrust. From its early days in August, Kensington had a curriculum committee that labored through the year on the long-term issues of Kensington's evolving point of view. The story of this committee is a major facet of the Kensington narrative. As it struggled to design, elaborate, and implement Kensington's point of view, it raised the best of Kensington's intentions and hopes. The issues it found knotty and unsolvable are ones that remain frustrating to much of professional education.

Finally, we extend our discussion of the "realities" of Kensington by adding to our cumulative picture presented in earlier chapters. In this manner we further long-term goals such as the descriptive narrative of the interplay between hopes and the operational aspects of the school, theory development in education, and implicit advice to school administrators who wish to anticipate events that are often latent in this particular educational innovation.

279

CURRICULUM: COMMITTEES AND ACTIVITIES

Introduction

Perhaps better than any other part of the organization, the curriculum committees represent the idealism, the enthusiasm, the high hopes, and the limitless aspirations of Kensington. True belief was epitomized individually and collectively in the committee and its members.

Chronology and Membership

The Workshop. The reader will recall that the T-groups of the summer workshop dissolved at the end of the first week and were replaced by a number of committees, the most important of which was the Curriculum Coordinating Committee. *Bulletin No. 3* carried this notice.

"1. *Curriculum Coordinating Committee.* The following staff members have been assigned to the Curriculum Coordinating Committee: Elaine Ross, Mary Radford, Meg Adrian, Bill Kirkham, David Nichols, Irma Hall, and Tom Mack (ex officio). The meeting time for this committee is posted on the workshop calendar" (8/18).

Two days later (in *Bulletin No. 4*) the subcommittees were identified.

"3. *Curriculum Subcommittee Assignments.* An effort will be made at our total staff meeting today to clarify the role of the Curriculum Coordinating Committee and the purpose and functions of the Curriculum Subcommittees. Meetings with several subcommittees have been scheduled with the Coordinating Committee for this morning.

"Assignments to the subcommittees were made as much as possible on the basis of your stated preferences, while at the same time maintaining representation from each of the teams. Assignments are as follows: Language Arts—Liz Etzell, Claire Nelson, Mary Radford (chairman), and Sue Norton; Mathematics—Alec Thurman, Meg Adrian, Carla Young (chairman), and Wanda Ellison; Science—Bill Kirkham, Jack Davis (chairman), Claire Nelson, and Jean Emerson; Social Studies—David Nichols, Kay Abbot (chairman), Dan Hun, Carla Young, and Sue Norton; Creative Arts—Irma Hall, Liz Etzell, Dan Hun, Wanda Ellison, and Elaine Ross (chairman)" (8/20).

As we indicated earlier, the committee assignments were heavy and overlapping. A vast number of meetings were held as staff members explored their varied approaches. Position papers and curriculum guides were not produced by the committees. The problems of curriculum were left on the agenda and were to reappear formally and informally all year.

The Fall Meetings and Activities. For brevity, we again refer to the formal documents, this time the minutes of the October 17 staff meeting, to clarify the continuing work on the curriculum problems and their relationships to other activities. Item No 5 of the minutes read as follows:

"5. *Evaluation.* Eugene Shelby presented a list of descriptive adjectives which could possibly be used to define different types of organizations. This led to a discussion of the need for organization and criteria by which decisions are made. It seemed to be the consensus of the staff that stated procedures are necessary to facilitate the work of the staff in carrying out their various functions.

"Leslie Roberts [the consultant] presented the following categories of decisions:

Curriculum—function of whole school.

Instruction—function of teachers or teams of teachers.

Institutional maintenance—function of principal.

School faculty and how they operate together—function of staff as a whole.

The type of decisions being made with some degree of satisfaction in Kensington at the present seem to fall in the instruction category. Due to the type of curriculum and organization evolving in the schools, the other categories of decisions have not yet reached an adequate operational level. The staff decided to establish two ad hoc committees:

"*Maintenance Committee.* Charged with the responsibility of developing a proposal as to how institutional maintenance decisions will be made. This proposal will be presented at the next Saturday morning staff meeting.

"*Curriculum Committee.* Charged with the responsibility of developing a proposal as to how the curriculum will be developed and how curriculum decisions will be made.

Curriculum Committee	*Maintenance Committee*
Liz Etzell	John Taylor
David Nichols	Jean Emerson
Sue Norton	Claire Nelson
Dan Hun	Tom Mack" (10/17)
Tom Mack	

The opening of school had posed severe problems for the staff and their energies had been devoted mostly to getting the instructional program underway. Formal appointment of new committees implied the moribund status of the original groups. A very brief but significant item in the minutes of the November 7 staff meeting continues the story.

"6. *Curriculum Ad Hoc Committee.* Sue Norton is chairman of this committee. Acknowledged end of curriculum committees as they were set up. This was accepted by the staff. Asked permission to continue task until next total staff meeting. Meeting Monday night of curriculum committee. Others are invited to attend" (11/7).

In effect, the prior structure of committees had been formally dissolved. The staff agreed. Sue Norton became the new chairman.

For the November 23 meeting, Shelby prepared a curriculum bulletin. We have included it in its entirety as Figure 9.1. Briefly, we make several interpretations. First, Shelby's dilemma of forceful ideas and stance versus a more laissez-faire stance reappears. On this occasion, he was presenting ideas to which he had a major commitment. Second, the doctrinal contradictions between "predetermined goals" and spontaneous choices by children or teachers also reappears. Third, Kensington's innovative thrust, goals different from the general educational community, also receives comment. Fourth, and perhaps most notably of anywhere at Kensington, the "locus of decision-making" dilemma appears in full complexity in the paragraph accenting institutional decision making. Subordinates versus superordinates, being "given the authority," and majority vote or consensus illustrate the tangled nature of that dilemma. And, finally, curriculum as a policy-type rationale for making instructional decisions is emphasized.

KENSINGTON ELEMENTARY SCHOOL

November 23

Curriculum Bulletin
1. *On Education.* Learning is experience, the basic unit of education. Since every human being has continuous experience through living within and interacting with his environment, education is natural and automatic. Formal education differs from informal education, however, in that an attempt is made to shape experiences in a particular way to achieve predetermined goals. Although it is impossible to structure any given experience *per se,* the various elements of the environment may be structured in such a way that a desired experience is likely to take place.

The important matters with which the school is concerned, therefore, are what human and material resources should be provided in the learning environment, and how to structure them. Both of these matters are dependent, of course, on the goals of the school. The question is not one of structure or non-structure, but *how* to structure the learning environment. Kensington Elementary School is looking for better ways of structuring learning experiences. It does not necessarily follow that the goals of Kensington are different from the goals of other schools, but as a matter of fact, they probably are.

Figure 9.1 The November 23 Curriculum Bulletin.

2. *On Decision-Making.* One facet of decision-making frequently discussed is the *level* at which decisions should be made. Dr. John Goodlad makes a distinction between the *Institutional* level and the *Instructional* level of decision-making.

I find it more useful to think of decision-making levels in terms of the *Institutional Dimension* and the *Personal Dimensions.* Decision-making at the institutional level takes place within the legal-authority structure of the institution. This does not mean that institutional decisions are necessarily made by superordinates; persons in subordinate positions may make institutional decisions through majority-vote or consensus if given the authority to do so. The distinguishing characteristic of institutional decisions, however, is that they are explicit and openly adopted in some manner provided for by the institution.

In contrast personal decisions are not adopted by the institution. They may be just as open, rational, and explicit as institutional decisions, but may be intuitive and subjective.

Quite obviously, there is a place in the Kensington School for both institutional and personal decisions. Many instructional decisions, for instance, are made at the personal level. Other instructional decisions, such as the adoption of text materials, may be made at the institutional level. (The institution may be viewed as the school district, the local school, or the division or team in Kensington.)

The important thing is to know at what level various decisions should be made. It is probably inappropriate, for instance, to make decisions about goals at the personal level.

3. *On Curriculum.* Curriculum is frequently defined as all the experiences of the learner under the direction of the school. This view is so broad as to be virtually meaningless, since all of the elements of the school—facilities, personnel, time, materials, etc.—help to shape learning experiences.

I find it more useful to think of curriculum as the criteria for making instructional decisions. These criteria include the educational goals, how they are organized (continuity, sequence, integration), establishment of priorities, and guidelines for decision-making.

In general, curriculum decisions should be made at the institutional level.

Figure 9.1 (*Continued*)

The minutes of the staff meeting's consideration of the curriculum committee's report reflect the emphasis from the *Bulletin.* We have reproduced, in toto, this brief statement as Figure 9.2.

The Midwinter Apex

Overview. During January, the curriculum committee was reactivated. The dream of what Kensington might be was rekindled. To the casual

KENSINGTON ELEMENTARY SHOOL

December 1

Minutes from November 23 Staff Meeting.

The staff of Kensington School at the November 23 meeting accepted the following report of the Curriculum Ad Hoc Committee:

The purpose of a curriculum is to provide a rationale for making instructional decisions. This includes a formulation of objectives and the criteria for determining the means of reaching these objectives. The Curriculum Ad Hoc Committee recommends:

A standing Curriculum Committee be formed to:

1. Develop and present to the staff for approval a taxonomy of educational objectives to aid teachers in planning the instructional program.
2. List diagnostic tools and techniques to evaluate the attainment of specific objectives. These would be used as continuing evaluative guides by teachers and pupils.
3. Provide suggestions for materials and activities designed to develop specific skills, cognitive and affective knowledge, and behaviors.
4. Formulate criteria for making instructional decisions in order to bring about congruency between educational objectives and the instructional program.

The following staff members requested that they be allowed to serve on the standing committee and were approved by the staff: Jack Davis, Jean Emerson, Liz Etzell, Tom Mack, Eugene Shelby, and Alec Thurman. Other interested staff members are invited to attend.

Figure 9.2 Minutes of the November 23 staff meeting.

observer, the intertwining threads were not obvious. To the participating members of the staff the enthusiasm was high, the excitement had a sharp edge, and the discussions were savored as good wine. This reality of Kensington had a potency in the lives of the principal and the faculty.

The larger picture was this. After Christmas, now that the school was in the new building, several kinds of outside forces had arisen. The first of these was publicity—both local and national. A local newspaper, the *Daily Star,* sent a photographer to Kensington in early January, and the Sunday supplement, six pages including a full-page cover photograph, appeared in late January. Mr. Williams, an editor from *National Weekly,* spent a week during January at Kensington. He observed, talked with everyone, and attended meetings. His article appeared much later, in early summer, under the title, "A School Where Children Teach Themselves." Later in the spring, a university group, filming innovative schools, spent a few days in the school. Conceptually separate from the publicity, but intermingling in day-to-day reality, were a number of consultants. Dr. Leslie Roberts continued his work and was at Kensington during January when the editor from *National Weekly* was present. Two professors of educational administration consulted for several days during February. The number of observers from universities and public schools was so great that special times for visiting were allocated, and a special orientation talk, usually given by the principal, was developed to acquaint the visitors with Kensington's overall perspective. The largest of the outside influences, however, was the Milford School District's bid for private and federal funds to support a major curriculum reorganization project. This was in the developmental stages from early January until late spring. Consultants from all over the United States were in the district and at the school. Kensington was a major plank in the project. Within the school itself, the principal and the rejuvenated curriculum committee of the staff became the local arm of the program.

In short, these forces—news media, prominent national consultants, and the major thrust of the Milford District—focused on the very exciting and challenging problem of an ideal education for the elementary school child. Kensington was stimulated to a very high degree.

Multiple Stimulation. The field notes indicate the growing excitement during the climactic midwinter weeks.

> The notoriety phenomenon really came out in full blush today. Not only was Mr. Williams of *National Weekly* here, but Leslie Roberts also has been here all morning and finally prepublication copies of the *Daily Star* article were available. This has generated kind of an excitement and a superordinate, or better, a common set of issues, about which the whole group could get involved. Also, this is the last day of school for the semester. In effect, everyone is kind of high. A number of the teachers who got in the pictures, Claire, and Meg, were very pleased about it and excited. There was some concern on the part of several of the people that the old Scott Foresman books were in evidence on the cover picture. Similarly, Meg and Claire were a bit concerned that Dan's "junk pile" was showing in one part, and that the monster was showing in the part of another picture. There is a strong concern on the part of everyone to present the best foot forward in the public image. The girls are all excited about sending copies home, etc. They are wondering how many free copies they get of the newspaper.
>
> As the various people read through the materials they made some semi-cynical comments about some of the presentations. One had a few negative things to say about team teaching, although she was pleased that the article didn't "gush" about it. Another asked where were the individual study carrels that were talked about. Claire was pleased that Transition had made the front page and the cover picture.

The euphoria over this plus the general enthusiasm that Leslie tends to bring, and which he has done again this time, contributed markedly to the "high" quality of the atmosphere. Leslie was effusive in his praise of the "swinging" program in Transition and the fact that Meg and Claire hardly had time to say hello because they were so busy with the children. As he interpreted his word "swinging," he implied the basic learning and quality of the basic learning that was going on. Also, this morning the work of Chris and her guitar in the folk-singing with the ISD South group was marvelous. She is a real pro in that she handles the kids well, she develops their interest, she captures their attention, and they participate with a high degree of enthusiasm. Learning and school activities are fun.

Also, I was impressed with the steady chipping away being done by the Basic Skills team of two. Carla, Mary, and the student teacher all were working all the time, and the kids were reading and writing in fine style.

Contributing also to this general warmth around the lunch table was Sue's comment about going up into the theater to quiet down a bunch of noisy, unsupervised boys so that she could continue her reading group and finding that David was among them pantomiming with machine guns and great energy the activity of the First World War. She did this with good fun and good humor. David, a bit sensitive, made comments about the other play the kids put on, something like the "enchanted fairy or enchanted forest" and also the evaluation sessions that were held in conjunction with the plays. To me the greatest possibilities lie in the continuing accent and in the possible crystallization of a norm around them, that is, there are many different ways to teach children at Kensington. I have not heard this verbalized but it is the kind of growing aspect that seems to be occurring. This may be more me than the situation, however. A second point I would make is that there seems to be some growing equilibrium in style as the bulk of the new teachers learn ways of handling, relating, and getting on with the kids. These teachers are truly gifted individuals both intellectually and in the various special subskills.

This suggests an important principle surrounding the attraction and then the retention of exciting teachers. Kensington had a better shot at this than the run-of-the-mill place (1/21).

As an afterthought, when concluding dictation of the field notes for that day the observer tacked on a comment of a lingering impression.

I still can't get over the effect of the *Daily Star* materials on Meg. The facade is a real reward in the sense of notoriety, and it also tends to reaffirm faith when it lags because of the difficulties of the actual operation. That, I suppose, is one of the major points. In effect, solace when times are tough (1/21).

Mr. Williams of National Weekly. Feature writers, as well as reporters and participant observers, bring a point of view and a stance to their task.

Yesterday morning I met Mr. Williams of *National Weekly*. From my very casual comments with him, and the interview was very short in that I did not open up with any generalizations about the program or how it contrasted with other programs, he seems to be one of the few "visitors" who has scratched well below the surface. He will have spent almost a full week in the school and will have interviewed a good many of the teachers as well as observed a good deal of the day-to-day events. What kind of context he will put it in, I do not know. He is not an educationist, I don't think, in that he had a good bit of misinformation about the Montessori methods which he was offering as a comparison to the Kensington School. He spent a fair amount of time with David and raised the question about "kids teaching each other," which I am sure he got in there. From a very casual remark by Eugene at lunch, and I was with him only a few minutes, he has been on Eugene's back all week, pumping him for information.

In the course of my conversation with Mr. Williams there were people in and out and people who joined us. Sue and John were there as well as Meg, I think, and Claire. Later Elaine and Eugene came up. In the early part, John and Williams and I were sitting at one table while Sue was sitting with several of the girls at another table, and John raised the notion that someone had written him about the shelter area and the overhead heaters and wanted to know what his opinion was. He, I think, is really on the spot, since they have not worked out well and yet he is most reluctant to say so. To this point, he has not raised this kind of thing with Williams. Tom also told me that Williams had not talked with him. That, too, seems to me to be a very significant point in that Williams either is not tuned in or does not care about the social structure of the building. John's statements were of the order that they could save a lot of money with them and that they ought to work or, as I think he said, they "could" work. This is another illustration of the "public image" phenomenon. If John does write a letter of this kind and if it is negative about this one phase of the building, this will become the first major shift in the outside armor, as it were, of the whole approach. As far as I know to this point, there have been no public or outside comments regarding weaknesses in the building or its program.

An additional final word or two about Mr. Williams. He scheduled interviews with many of the teachers and had commented to Jack Davis that he would be seeing him in the afternoon. Williams also got involved in kind of an argument with Jack about the President's poverty program. We had been discussing briefly what the President had said, and I had made a comment or two, and he had sketched out several of his planks. Jack raised some general objection to the notion that there were people out of work who wanted work, and Williams then went into some detail on an article that *National Weekly* is going to do about the employed poor who would not be helped by the program. He then went on to disagree quite pointedly with Jack, and he presented what I perceive to be the liberal point of view. Essentially, it was that there are limited jobs at the skilled-trade levels and that people have differential access to them and that there is kind of a poverty breeding poverty aspect. In this sense, he became a much more significant part of the system than, say, I typically have in arguing with members of the staff. A second aspect, a relevant point, about Mr. Williams, concerns the genesis of the story as it relates to Kensington's facade going out into the hinterlands. He had been roaming around NEA offices in Washington and had seen a picture of the school on the wall of some NEA official and began to chat with him about it. This then led him to make contact with the district, according to Tom, I believe, and now it has become pretty clear that he just is doing an article on Kensington. The symbols by way of pictures and by way of notoriety seem especially significant in making people aware that the phenomenon exists, and perhaps the people who become aware are those who have special roles, such as newspapermen or magazine feature writers who are looking for the unusual, the different that they can capitalize on to pitch stories for their clientele. It seems here also that they are comparable to many of the educators who do a lot of public speaking and who must continually look for novel, interesting, and different "gimmicks" as well as ideas with which they can capture the interest of their audience. This seems particularly appropriate in terms of the genesis of much of the fadish cults in existence today (1/21).

The Climactic Meeting at Kensington.

Capturing the emotional quality of a meeting is always quite difficult. In January, as we have indicated, a confluence of events occurred. The curriculum committee was the locus of much of this activity. The morning-after notes described it this way.

Last night's curriculum meeting ended a little after 10:30, yet people were still standing around talking until we left at eleven o'clock. The number and the interminable quality of the meetings is perhaps unique in elementary school annals. In trying to formulate a point of view about this, the variable[1] that comes to mind is the upwardly mobile quality of most of the staff. In this regard, most of the people have places they want to go and things that they want to do professionally, beyond the Kensington School. This would include about one-half the people in the building. Related to this is the generally youthful quality of the staff and the fact that many of them are thinking through some of these issues for the first time. Third is the relentless quality about Eugene, who just will not give up. At the break, when I went down for a Coke and spoke briefly with Kay, she asked when the meeting would break up, and I commented that there were a few who wanted to go home fairly early and a few who would stay on forever. She laughed and said, "You don't need to name names." Fourth, the staff by and large, I think, is very bright. They are able to handle abstractions and many of them thoroughly enjoy it. Fifth is the fact that the staff is totally new to each other and to the district. Much of what we are witnessing, I think, is the first-time-through phenomenon when everything is kind of up for grabs and due to be settled. In later years few of the people will want to rediscuss some of the same issues.

---

[1] The reader might recast or review this in the context of our discussion of true belief in Chapter 4.

They will have reached an equilibrium in terms of their capacity to make analysis and in terms of the give and take among themselves, and they will not want to redo the same problems. In effect, we may be witnessing here, in its most dramatic form, the problems in the formation and development of a social system. The contrast between this school and most other schools may not be anything more than the contrast between the school that is just beginning to develop and the school that has been in existence for some time. A person wanting to capture or recapture this kind of activity might well have to become involved with new situations periodically. I have visions of the early days of the Graduate Institute of Education at WU (1/22).

Further aspects developed in related conversations.

I had a chance to talk with Jerl. He thinks Eugene is feeling good. He thinks that the program has really been going well this week and feels that there is a whole Hawthorne effect about the new building which is favorable. We talked at some length about this and about the factors involving the newspaper account, Leslie, the *National Weekly* editor, etc., all coming at the same time. He is very pleased with the kind of activity and discussion that has gone on in the curriculum center. As he says, he finds it one of the more enjoyable places in the building (1/22).

And finally:

To return for a moment to the kind of conversations that go on in the school, the contrast between the Kensington School and the Washington School is very marked. As I observed in the other school, the impression I had was that the conversation was very much of a familial type in which people chit-chatted about the latest gossip because they had all the basic problems, points of view, and philosophy settled. The allusion I made was to the Riesman, Watson et al. "Taxonomy on Social Interaction in Conversation." The Kensington conversation is very unlike the Washington School and, in this sense, probably can be traced heavily to the need to work one's way through most of these issues and also to come to some general equilibrium in the social structure, that is, in the ways of handling events.

At the close of the meeting both Williams and Roberts were quite high in their praise of the meeting. William's mode of approach was to raise it in the form of a question: "Is there another school in the country where this kind of thing is going on?" Leslie Roberts' way of phrasing it was the great distances traveled in the very short time they had known each other. Consultants and outside notoriety have some very important functions here. In many ways the school is, as the *Daily Star* account will say, "the most unusual school in Milford County" (1/22).

The group of people[2] in attendance included Mr. Williams of *National Weekly,* the consultant, Leslie Roberts, and one of his graduate assistants

[2] Both of the investigators, Smith and Keith, were present also.

from City University. Late in the evening Jerl Cohen joined them. From the staff were Shelby, Jean and Sue of Basic Skills, Dan from Transition, Jack and Alec from ISD, and Tom, the materials coordinator.

The issues raised in the meeting were broad, involved, and important. Here we merely enumerate them.[3] The initial point of departure was a memorandum of January 19, which we include as Figure 9.3.

The memo illustrates the commitment to rationality and self-consciousness (Item IA) that occurred all year. Item IB suggests the broader issues in spreading the "message" of Kensington to all parts of the educational world. Items IC–IF reemphasize internal aspects of rationality in teaching. Category II restates ultimate goals, "fully functioning," and more proximal goals, "taxonomy of specific educational objectives." In short, the magnitude of the effort is considerable.

The discussion picked up rapidly. The individual internalized conceptions and the need for an institutional or public curriculum were stressed by Shelby. The degree of agreement on the functions of school was challenged briefly as to whether it was "a consensus or ambiguity in definitions." Then, initial statements were made about the "process of knowing," that is, inductive thinking, critical thinking, and creative thinking. Dan and Sue pursued this further with the concept "sensitivity." Various members of the group made comments which we have partially paraphrased:

"difficulty in defining behavioristically"

"in literature it means . . ."

"search for truth"

"common elements in science and humanities. I don't want to make them into a contrast."

"continues on commonality of artists and scientists"

"sees processes as similar . . . what we are trying to develop . . . later children will channel sensitivity in special direction . . . argues for general sensitivity"

One of the observers recorded as an interpretive aside in the field notes:

> (*Observer.* This kind of discussion is really unheard of in a "typical" public elementary school. They are in the middle of Guilford's model and transfer of training problems. Data need to be drawn in here.)

[3] Undercurrents were present even here, however, as the field notes attest:

> 7:55 P.M. Eugene finally arrives, an hour late. The past hour of levity evaporates dramatically. Eugene tries to joke about costing him a five-dollar bet, that is, they would be working on curriculum. Jack comments: "cost us an hour—cheap labor," and then he said that they didn't want to "undo everything after he arrived."

KENSINGTON ELEMENTARY SCHOOL
January 19

Memo: To: Kensington Staff Members   From: Curriculum Committee

At the January 11 meeting of the Curriculum Committee, members considered the nature of its task, various steps in the development of a curriculum, and the possible methods of initiating action. Below in outline form is a resumé of the ideas presented.

I   Reasons for the Development of an Institutional Curriculum:
      A.   To provide a guide for teaching in replacement of internalized curriculum.
      B.   To act as public information resource in explaining institutional program.
      C.   To serve as a guide for determining pupil skills and progress.
      D.   To serve as a guide in the purchasing of materials.
      E.   To provide a guide for pupil evaluation.
      F.   To provide a rationale for making instructional decisions.
II   Organization for the Development of a Curriculum
      A.   Introduction (clarification of criteria)
          1.   Function of Kensington
              a.   Process of knowing
              b.   Conceptual approach to content
              c.   Development of the individual as a fully functioning human being
          2.   Function of a Curriculum
      B.   Guidelines for making instructional decisions and for using the curriculum.
      C.   Development of specific educational objectives in taxonomical form
          1.   Skill objectives
          2.   Trait objectives
          3.   Content objectives
          4.   Process objectives
      D.   Procurement of various diagnostic instruments
      E.   Development, selection, etc., of materials
III Long-range objectives of Curriculum Committee
      A.   Development of a curriculum
      B.   Development of a handbook for the faculty
      C.   Development of a handbook for the pupils

The next meeting of the Curriculum Committee is scheduled for Wednesday, January 20, at 7:00 P.M. The task of the committee at this time will be to discuss ideas related to the introduction and guidelines, and to further develop the categories and subcategories of the taxonomy.

The following evening, then, the group will meet at 7:00 P.M. with Dr. Leslie Roberts. Interested persons are invited to attend either or both of the meetings.

Figure 9.3   The Curriculum Committee memorandum.

The discussion continued into characterization in literature, the use of symbols in the process of developing concepts and feelings, and the difficulties encountered by individual faculty members trying to conceptualize these issues.

Shortly, the discussion veered off into consequences for teacher-pupil relationships. Programming institutional and instructional decisions was suggested as a way of integrating objectives and criteria. A number of illustrations were raised from the use of encyclopedias and SRA Skillbuilders to the multiple and possibly conflicting aspects in traveling to New York—getting there, cheaply, and rapidly.

Issues in continuity and sequence, item IIC in the memo, were introduced. In turn, the problems of any learning experience being "analyzed in terms of these three objectives" and goals were raised. Leslie moved into broad goals; Eugene illustrated with self-discipline; and Leslie accented the point that they are "objectives achieved by inches," and that they are "worked on from the first day the children come to school." He saw children as partially failing, teachers shoring them up, and coming back to the objectives. Tom commented, "I don't buy that. If you have proper diagnostic tools you can set up objectives the pupil can reach. Then you teach him to reset this goal. You don't always have the goals out of reach. I can't see it." Eugene, in reply to Tom, commented: "I think he's disputing Robert Browning." Jack pursued this with "That's the teacher's job in class, the setting of goals."

Shortly, through Eugene's questioning, they confronted: (1) the possibility of scope, continuity, sequence, and integration of curriculum as part of IIC; (2) whether these issues are all part of teacher decision making. And, if so, can it be done by a teacher? Is it realistic when you have 30 pupils? And, (3) the use of a book that then programs decisions.

Alec countered, "Yes, if you have individual programs" and then broadened the issue significantly by commenting, "The only feasible way is child self-evaluation. It must come in. Setting one's own goals lessens the teacher's burden." The discussion drew strong feelings and important ideas. The notes paraphrase the comments.

"Do you let them make bad decisions?"
"If you have a hobby horse . . ."
"No hobby horse. Six years"
"They've got to be able to make mistakes."
"How about inability to compute and dropping out of school?"
"Don't allow this."
"Which things at which levels?"
"What errors would you let them make?"

"Selecting a book which is too difficult?"

"Yes."

"Fifth versus fourth grade math might be a bad decision, but let them make it. But not allow them a 'no math' alternative."

"Allow pupils to waste time."

The illustrations continued. Such general criteria as impact on others, seriousness of the consequences, and revocability of the action were hinted at. Discussions with pupils, the development of IIIC (the pupil handbooks), and the assumption of staff willingness to take responsibility for this activity and for curricular areas where teachers felt less competent were additional parts of the interchange. The discussion included "concern for actions which don't have immediate consequences" and "facing symbolic consequences of acts," which wound back to "part of reflective thinking."

Individuals raised "appeal of decisions" and "problem for me in a team situation." These items were judged beyond "curriculum" and did not get pursued at the moment.[4]

Concerns over "process and content" as objectives caught the committee for the next hour. Once again the imperatives versus the electives arose. The interplay between "old content and subjects" such as spelling, new "theoretical structures of disciplines" such as linguistics, and the skill of communication created considerable excitement. Interspersed were illustrations and analogies from set theory as content and mode of analysis, science as content and classifying, the memorization of poetry, and the modes of analysis of poetry.

The meeting culminated in Roberts' expression of "astonishing productivity of the meeting . . . and . . . amazed at the level of discussion and progress in the short time you've been together . . ." Williams of *National Weekly* was "mightily impressed." The staff agreed to meet next week so that the ideas would not "grow cold."

The Final Tangible Product. On February 11, the Curriculum Committee stapled together a 16-page booklet. The pages were headed by titles reproduced in Figure 9.4. They were blank and were to be used by the faculty for recording incidents and ideas that later would be collated into a curriculum manual. This booklet represented the major tangible product of Kensington's curriculum committees. Instead of spurring further concrete efforts, the booklet terminated the activities of the committee. Coinciding with the climax of the January meetings both in the school and in the district, additional effort seemed mundane and anticlimactic. Furthermore,

---

[4] As important organizational implications of curriculum, it seems to us that they well illustrate the interdependencies of system elements and the impact of innovation in one area having consequences for other areas.

Guidelines for Instructional Decisions

1. Trait Objectives (behavioral manifestations of value)
2. Process Objectives (cognitive processes for acquiring and assimilating knowledge)
3. Skill Objectives
    3.1 Social Skills
    3.2 Technical Skills
    3.3 Computational Skills
    3.4 Communication Skills
    3.5 Fine Arts Skills
    3.6 Physical Education Skills
4. Content Objectives (underlying principles, broad generalizations, major concepts)
    4.1 Social Studies
    4.2 Science
    4.3 Mathematics
    4.4 Language Arts
    4.5 Fine Arts

Figure 9.4   The headings of Kensington's booklet regarding objectives.

the rhythm of the school year, as we report in a later chapter, caught the attention and energy of the faculty in other issues.

Up to this point our evaluative comments have been largely implicit rather than explicit. Instead of pursuing a different stance, we consider only two aspects. First, the magnitude of each of the categories is incredibly large. A Renaissance man, becomes the prototype of the elementary school curriculum and instruction specialist. Only now, after the major national curriculum development projects continue to come to fruition, are the size of the task, the kind of resources required, the integration of multiple specialists, and the time requirements apparent. The potency of true belief, inexperience, enthusiasm, and optimism seems an appropriate side interpretation.

The second aspect we comment on is a more technical issue. The outline provides a structure of elements. The processes involved in linking these elements over time is not clear. The setting of priorities, we argue, is an unsettled political problem. It has a corollary in the confused organizational structure by which constituencies—school boards, administration, faculty, parents, and children—are represented in such decisions. Furthermore, the processes by which they come to decisions—voting, consenting, and advising—were not clear. Also, the classical problems of "scope and sequence" remain in terms of how the elements would be put together into an integrated plan. Finally, as we shall discuss shortly, the implementation of the plan, the "real" reality of curriculum and instruction as it actually occurred at Kensington, presents both congruencies and incongruencies with the ideas generated by the curriculum committees and its antecedents—the formal doctrine and the Institutional Plan.

The Central Office Meetings

A long and involved story in its own right was the districtwide curriculum thrust headed by Jerl Cohen. Because Kensington was so involved in this, Jerl was frequently at the school for conversation and discussion that contributed both clarification and support to his efforts. The magnitude of the dreams and the efforts, as well as the interdependency with Kensington, appeared in early January.

> The major activity of my afternoon, however, was a long curriculum discussion with Jerl, Eugene, and Tom. Eugene and Tom kept getting dragged out for other events, but Jerl and I continued on from a little before 1:00 P.M. until almost 3:30. The gist of the issue, from my point of view, concerns the array of confusion that lies in what might be called the area of curriculum. I am struck with the difficulties that even bright people such as Jerl and Eugene have when they try to make sense out of the interrelationship among ideas such as curriculum objectives, learning experiences, course content, and the like. They are real and difficult and tough issues. Briefly, part of the problem centered on moving from the very airy, abstract seven cardinal principles to the more difficult and complex statements by people like Taba and Tyler, to the more concrete problems faced by the individuals in the district. As I listened to them talk, it seemed to me that considerable thought could go into each of the specific problems and that out of them one could begin to generalize a point of view of more abstract principles. These, then, could be juxtaposed with the various other points of view, Tyler and Taba, for instance, and the more formal statement could be made for the school district. The time and thought that this requires, it appears to me, might well be beyond the resources of the school personnel themselves and, perhaps, of the district, in terms of buying time from consultants outside. This leads, then, into a discussion also of the nature of the consultants and the consulting relationship. The contrast seems very striking between some of the things that Hilda Taba is doing in Contra Costa and what seems to be happening here with the consultant from City University. He is putting in something like one and one-half days a month during the school year and expects to make major changes or, at least, the school people are hoping that major changes will come out of this. As I look at Taba's work with the Contra Costa School District in California in suburban Frisco, the amount of time and effort that must have gone into some of their work seems to run well into the years instead of a period of days per year. Locally, there seems to be very little appreciation of this kind of thing (1/4).

Intertwined in that discussion were several other general points that merit repeating. They were in the field notes from the same day.

1. The impact of the broader district on the school. Kensington is essentially isolated from more general district policy.

2. Eugene reiterated his no prescribed content in Kensington, only conceptual and process objectives. He is unhappy with the "topics," for example, water and nutrition, which he does not consider as concepts. This arose in a discussion of Tyler's specification table in his curriculum syllabus.

3. Jerl is really stymied regarding his job and his curriculum committee. He has a bill of particulars stating the inadequacies of himself, the superintendent, the consultant from State University, building principals, etc. He said, "I don't have an image of what I want done." The particular problems are as diverse as "dropping the advanced shorthand and advanced physics from the curriculum in the high school" to teaching elementary science. The problem is to make the decisions rational. (*Observer.* The latter notion is an interesting starting point for many educational discussions.)

4. Considerable discussion of whether a school district has the resources to carry out major curriculum reform. Jerl picked up a unit from Contra Costa County, with whom Hilda Taba has been working. In his eyes, it is one of the few local curriculum products available. At the state level, only New York and California are active. He teased Eugene by saying, "He's so naive and in the clouds, he thinks a single school can do this." In fact, Kensington has had such aspirations. The problem Jerl has lies in several domains. It is difficult to get a single uniform principle to cover all aspects (1/4).

In short, it is very clear that many of the analyses we have been making of Kensington's aspirations, agendas, and problems have their counterparts in Milford's districtwide curriculum efforts.

The high point of the district's curricular effort occurred in February when representatives of private foundations and the United States Office of Education met with the Milford staff and the local and national consultants. Although many issues were discussed, the goal was curriculum reform; and although many examples of hopes and realities were provided, Kensington was the crown jewel.

The outcomes of curriculum reform were broad. Jerl Cohen's position paper prepared for the conference phrased them this way:

1. Better educational opportunity for boys and girls of Milford.
2. Professional growth and stimulation of personnel involved in curriculum study.
3. Better understanding of the nature of a comprehensive School District as a totality—its curriculum patterns, the administrative enterprise, community responsibility, and staff utilization.
4. The creation of a demonstration School District; not a lighthouse district in the traditional definition of the word where certain exciting innovations are being carried out with culturally advantaged children with educationally

supportive parents; not a lighthouse in the sense that the "truth" has been found, but a lighthouse in the sense that here is a typical district that is genuinely concerned about looking at curriculum and instruction in a meaningful way. The attitude would be for persons to come and observe, not the successes so much, but the types of problems that are encountered along the way and to observe the progress that is being made.

5. Serve as a "seedbed" for theory building, a place for concept testing and empirical studies.

Eleven "top priority problems were identified." The stated objectives for public education in Milford, the social movements influencing curriculum, Kensington's role as a subculture in changing the entire district, the identification of district problems, the conflict resulting from curriculum reform, and the nature of the teacher role illustrate the tenor of the problems.

The conference chairman "argued for building an integrated picture of district activities which then might be brought together for resources to implement the totality." After a preliminary discussion they settled on using Kensington as a focus and as an illustration of the district's problems. The day replayed much of the content that we have raised elsewhere. In a sense the conference was caught in the three separate agendas of the three major figures of Milford. Cohen sought an overall umbrella or conception useful for rationalizing his activities. Spanman sought a structure for action—a means for reaching out into the district with Kensington as a model. Shelby sought pieces of Kensington that would be exportable.

Overall, approximately $200,000 a year for 5 years were the tangible goals. Neither that day nor later in the spring was the funding forthcoming. In retrospect, the failure in the Milford District's attempt for outside financial support of the curriculum project was most critical for Kensington as well as for the district in general.

INDIVIDUALIZED CURRICULUM AND INSTRUCTION

As we commented in our discussion of the dimensions of school buildings, both flexibility and variety can contribute to what is called "meeting individual differences." As an organization, a school can, and usually does, have teachers with quite varied styles and approaches. Also, it can widen the usual limits of its curriculum, for instance, from a "narrow 3 R's" to a much more varied content. By default and by design Kensington possessed elementary forms of both variety and flexibility as strategies.

Independent Study and Its Latent Consequences

Independent Performance. "Fully Functioning Freddy" was both an end and a means to an end. The ideal pupil, at the end of his Kensington experience, was to be able to engage himself creatively and productively with his own independent, self-generated learning activities. In effect, he was to acquire "basic skills" in one division, be in "transition" in another and, finally was to engage in "independent study" in the third division of the school. While this broad process was occurring, the logic of the approach suggested that the pupil who is to become independent must engage in a high frequency of independent activities.

Although a number of issues warrant consideration, the observers saw, initially, analogies to the industrial setting and to graduate school instruction. Speculation arose in the field notes:

> The whole concept of independent study, it seems, needs very careful analysis also. The assumption that they seem to be making is that the materials and the pupils' own talents will be sufficient to engage in the problems of learning. The analogy that seems implicit and fallacious is between this and an assembly line or an industrial setting where there are a set of tasks that recur over and over again and, once they are learned, the individual can take them on and perform them. By its very nature, the task in school is a progressive development and alteration in what is done. This means that there never comes a time when a person is moved toward a stabilized set of activities and, hence, does not need some kind of guidance or direction.
>
> On a very simple level, the same problem, it seems to me, occurs in the university where one can, in effect, do his own research or one can have a group of graduate students and assistants assisting him. In the latter instance, at least, a portion of one's energy must be devoted to a continuous monitoring and supervision and must aid in all phases of the project. This takes some time, actually a good bit, and if one had 30 or 40 of those people, then it would be an impossible situation. This, it seems to me, is the bind of the independent study concept at Kensington. In a sense, even the industrial analogy is not quite appropriate, since there is always the problem of organizational development, the replacement of personnel, and their gradual indoctrination and socialization. An educational setting is, for the pupils, an extreme case of the continuous socialization problem (1/9).

In short, one has a number of children, approximately 40 (in ISD in the spring) whom one must guide individually in one-half dozen areas of the curriculum. In the fall, in the more departmentalized setting, the numbers varied up to 200. As we have indicated elsewhere, the system was too heavy and broke down at a number of points. In science, one of the most well-developed parts of the independent study program, members of the faculty estimated that about 15 percent of the pupils were receiving an excellent individualized program of independent study. The remainder of the children had considerable difficulty. In the other areas of the curriculum, estimates were more difficult to make.

Individual Scheduling. One of the operational techniques utilized for the promotion of independent study and the individualized curriculum was the individual scheduling in ISD. In Chapter 5 we presented some of the descriptive data associated with the procedure. The consequences were severe. The complexity of the problem was underestimated by the staff. The ability of the pupils to carry out the task was overestimated. The coordination of staff schedules with pupil schedules had not been resolved. These early implications are sketched in Figure 9.5. Parenthetically, we would comment that the organizational issues here are dramatic illustrations of our general theoretical position that unanticipated consequences are the primary means of organizational change. As the staff coped with these events, they developed new structures and, thus, changed the basic organization.

Interwoven with the nongraded and individualized approach to education were the "pupil logs," a daily one-page journal of purposes, activities, outcomes, and evaluation. They helped socialize the children, and they provided information to the staff. Additional implications are contained in

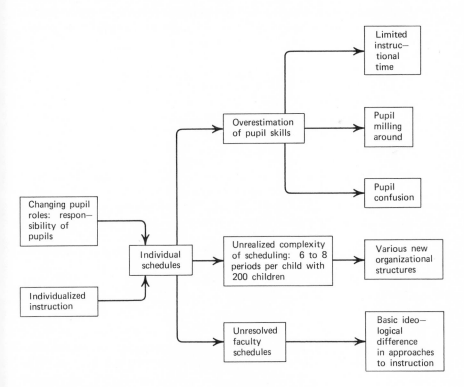

Figure 9.5   Individual schedules in individualized instruction.

Figure 9.6. The unanticipated clerical problems were severe. The communication to the parents was high, and the evidence of parental dissatisfaction with aspects of the program appeared almost immediately.

The continuing and very difficult problem of records in an individualized program recurs in an end of the year staff *Bulletin, No. 58.*

2. *Pupil records.* Pupil records consist of enrollment records, permanent cumulative records, permanent health records, and pupil placement cards. In addition to these records there should be an ongoing work folder for each pupil.

There is a great need for reorganizing the pupil record system at Kensington and throughout the District to make sure that educational needs are adequately and efficiently met. Policies and procedures concerning pupil records need to be developed, clarified, and coordinated.

The following requests are made for the handling of pupil records at the close of this school year:

Enrollment records. Maintained in the office by the general aide.

Permanent cumulative records. Maintained in the file cabinet in the curriculum center. Effort is made to have the general aide record

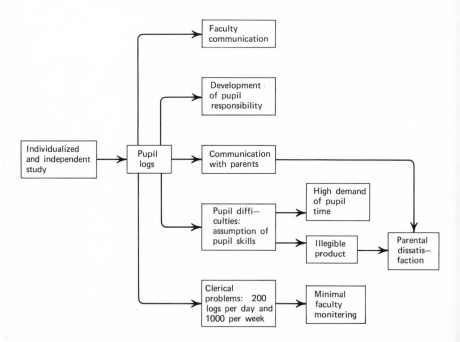

Figure 9.6   Aspects of pupil logs in an individualized program.

as much of the information as possible, such as test scores, etc., but it is necessary for some items to be filled in by teachers. First-semester grades from the report cards have already been recorded by the general aide; it will be impossible for her to record second-semester grades. Teachers are asked to use their professional judgment in recording whatever information is deemed useful and important. Some items of information may be recorded directly on the record form; other information, such as conference reports, anecdotal records, test profiles, etc., should be placed inside the folders.

Permanent health records. Maintained in the curriculum center by the general aide.

Pupil placement cards. Instructions have already been issued for filling out these records. Placement cards should be turned in to the general aide when those sections to be filled in by teachers have been completed.

Pupil work folders. Considerable information is accumulated each year which would have value for the pupil's next teacher but which is not included in the permanent cumulative record. Items such as unfinished SRA pupil record books, records of work completed by pupils, and representative samples of pupils' work in various subjects should be filed in these folders. Folders should be placed in the file cabinet in the curriculum center for the summer. In case you do not already have folders for this purpose, please obtain them from the office. (Swinging-type file folders should be used, but if you are already using manila folders, they will suffice for now.) (5/27)

The comment in the second paragraph suggests the continued frustration in attaining the formalization of one set of procedures. The last sentence indicates the level of detail involved.

The next *Bulletin, No. 59,* phrased the issue more positively and constructively.

5. *Instructions for closing school.* Although the task of providing for the best utilization of school space, equipment, and materials is a continuous one, the closing of school at the end of each year affords an opportunity to set the stage for significant improvements in the handling of these matters. Instructions for closing school will be placed in your boxes today, and your compliance with them will be greatly appreciated.

Pupil Choice and Instructional Styles

In a school commited to the ideals of democracy, the issues of "requiredness" and "pupil choice" are critical. At other points, we have explored the doctrinal positions on these issues, we have analyzed some of the organizational issues in administration and teaming, and now we approach the problems in the context of individualized instruction. We make a basic interpretation that a key dimension of teacher style is the amount of pupil choice that is encouraged and practiced.

Shelby's Definition of Teaching. Burden is an evaluative word and depends on the criteria one brings to the situation. For instance, Shelby's definition of teaching included the following:

> In this high pupil decision-making situation there seems to be another rub or two. One lies in what I call the burden this places on the teachers. From Shelby's point of view, and from his response, the real burden of teaching lies on the teacher who is given a textbook and a study guide and must follow this almost totally. The sharpness of the difference in this approach to education and the approach from downtown headed us into a very interesting and somewhat prolonged discussion. The contrast here is quite dramatic (8/9).

The observer's stance had suggested that a textbook and a teacher's manual was a program of teaching decisions. The topics, the sequencing, and the objectives had been made and collated into a bound volume. The teacher who had such a volume was saved a tremendous amount of preliminary work and thought. Shelby saw this as a constraint and inhibition on the teacher.

Thompson's (1967) theoretical distinctions among coordination by standardization, coordination by plan, and coordination by mutual adjustment seem appropriate. The textbook approach to curriculum and instruction blends the first two, while the freedom from texts accents the latter. As Thompson says:

> ". . . the three types of coordination, in the order introduced above, place increasingly heavy burdens on communication and decision. Standardization requires less frequent decisions and a smaller volume of communication during a specific period of operations than does planning, and planning calls for less decision and communication activity than does mutual adjustment. There are very real costs involved in coordination" (p. 56).

The critical questions become: How much mutual adjustment is needed for which kinds of learning? How much reciprocal interdependence can a teacher tolerate? What blend of what kind of teacher-administrator, teacher-teacher, and teacher-pupil interdependence is necessary and desirable for accomplishing organizational purposes?

Rousseau Writ Large. Throughout this book we have indicated that David Nichols played out a most controversial role in the school. His high energy and creativity were matched early by his commitment and true belief. Later, considerable disillusionment set in. Early in the fall he ran T-groups for pupils. Later in the year, he had a self-contained classroom that possessed a Rousseauian or laissez-faire style. The field notes picture the quality of his orientation.

> Several other aspects of yesterday's observation should be noted: first, David and I engaged in a lengthy tether ball session in which we each won a game and both got tired before we could finish the third and final game. It was great fun. During the course of our play, several of the kids continued to cheer for David and also called him by his first name, for example, "Come on, David." The stretch of informality, a lessening of the social distance, has increased to that point. In my experience this is a very rare phenomenon in public elementary schools. As we went back and forth to the water fountain and to the play area, we crossed his room a time or two, and his pupils seemed to be doing most of the same things that they had been doing through most of the semester, and the year. This includes a few who were painting, a couple who were reading, and a number who were chatting and talking informally on nonschool type affairs. His class continues to be the best example of a laissez-faire situation that I have ever seen in the public schools. A number of the kids have identified very strongly with him, and he seems to be very highly regarded by most of them. It is very hard to get firm data on their reaction (5/4).

A sub-issue in this kind of variety in teaching is the matching of treatments with personality variables. The aptitude-treatment interaction, as it is sometimes called, is mined with conceptual, measurement, and methodological difficulties.[5] Data are meager. We present an item from the notes illustrating an hypothesis that was suggested by our case study data.

> I am reminded also of another parent's statement growing out of a religious discussion. He blames the church and its conservative and moralistic orientation for making him so repressed and for the fact that it is difficult to change this learning which went on for many years. This reminds me of his daughter and the fact that the school has done a wealth of good for her, in my judgment. She has been with David, and the kind of freedom that he permits has opened her up in very fine fashion so that she is "hardly recognizable to her parents," in David's words. She was playing Huck Finn in the play today as I sat in the theatre with their group. She was a far cry from the quiet, timid girl of last fall, and it was marvelous to behold. David's faith in the kids, coupled with a child who seems inhibited and withdrawn, coupled with the total freedom they have, seems very appropriate. The critical educational problem seems to me is matching up the treatment with the child and the teacher. A kid without a strong superego would not benefit as much, I should think (5/24).

[5] See Cronbach and Snow (1969) for the most thorough statement of the verificational difficulties in this kind of research.

The problems in carefully testing such an hypothesis can be seen in opera-tionalizing verbal labels such as timid, withdrawn, and strong superego.

The "Modern Progressive." The formal doctrine tended to negate cur-riculum imperatives, that is, the demands of teaching particular specified content. The staff, however, was split on this approach. In the chance juxtaposition of two conversations the observer caught this as well as the skein of consequences that developed from this problem.

I have just had a long conversation with Jean. We talked some about the curriculum meeting, which Jean heard about just this morning. Apparently the decision was made late yesterday and the word just got out today. She's due over there at 4:15 P.M., which is a very difficult time schedule. They have been having their team meetings in the afternoon and this will cancel that out. Jean is the only one from Basic Skills or Transition who is involved on the curriculum committee. The others are Liz, Jack, Alec, Eugene, and Tom. In talking with Jean, she commented that at least she would not argue with David, since he is no longer on it. This indicates one part of David's withdrawal, which is noted elsewhere. After much other discussion I came around to the point again when she had commented that she was more progres-sive than the teachers at Hillside, the school she taught in last year, and that they were very traditional. In this sense, the sense that she meant it, as she pinned it down, was that they tended to follow the central office directives to the letter rather than do what they wanted to do. She observed that she would tend to close her door and do what she wanted to do. When I con-fronted her with the point that she made about her philosophy and David's being different, I asked her if she could put it on the same continuum or whether it could be put on another continuum. She did not much like being confronted with the issue this way, but she put him on the continuum as an extreme progressive. The difference she saw between herself and him was that he did not think that there were any "imperatives" about things that children should be taught and she did. She found some possible difference between ISD and Basic Skills, but she still thought that there were things that kids should learn. She argued this essentially from her own background and what she would have done as a pupil if she had been totally under self-motivation. In her words, she would know much less about a lot of things that she should know something about.

All of this is interesting, since I had a few minutes of discussion with Dave before I left ISD. He had spent a lonely Thanksgiving and apparently pretty much by himself. He had not, I do not think, gone to any of the parties or the dinners that several of the people were having. He views himself as totally isolated in ISD as well. He commented that it gave him more freedom, that he did not have to go through the team to do what he wanted to do. He also commented that he had spent a lot of time thinking about what he was doing and what the kids were doing. He views the problem as essentially one of using the wrong criteria to evaluate what he was doing and what his

children were doing. For instance, he was concerned that people hold a criterion of how busy the children are in his group. In his eyes, over the long
haul, they will become more involved in different kinds of activities and different kinds of things. He thinks that a use of the traditional criteria would
be a mistake at this point. He talked about how one of the children on last
Wednesday had spent an hour in looking through science material trying to
find out what "diatoms" are. He had set them on some of the prepared slides.
David was very pleased about this. Also, as he and I stood and talked, one
of the children came up and asked him about the word "illegible," which
the child pronounced incorrectly, and David gradually ushered him into a
dictionary to learn how to sound out the word and also to pronounce it cor-
rectly. These materials both came out of the prepared things that exist; in
the latter instance, they were SRA Skill Builders in prefixes. The children
kind of go at this in their own way and at their own rate with a minimal
amount of guidance from him. The possible merits in this approach and the
long-term accumulation of more and more self-direction seem very reasonable.
They sound very much like part of the argument that we were involved in
the other day on the teaching of forms in concept attainment and whether
this inhibits the later invention of categories in concept formation. Just how
these emphases are to be weighted over the long haul, it seems to me, is
a most important and critical educational issue (12/1).

The implications of philosophical and behavioral discrepancies, for instance, those of David and Jean, are important in that they relate to the
division of Basic Skills into two teams. In this instance they permitted
each team to carry out an integrated instructional program. Jean Emerson's
comments continue:

Another comment that she made, to some of my direct questions, concerned
whether the other team members tend to agree with her philosophy. She said
they did. They also say that it is basic that the kids learn the skills, and
they are all actively involved in this. My observations would corroborate this
very well. Almost every time I am sitting in the lounge in Basic Skills somebody is grading an arithmetic, a reading, or a composition paper. The kids
are doing a tremendous amount of this kind of written work around the basic
skills. I asked Jean if the team of two was in agreement. She gave me her
wry little smile and said she did not know. She went on to indicate that they
see so little of the other group and team that she really does not know what
goes on there. She seems to know more about Transition and about ISD than
she does about the other team in Basic Skills. We talked at some length while
her pupils were getting milk and listening to a story. These groups are larger
and give some of the people free time, primarily her and Wanda at this
point. Elaine and Sue were handling the story (12/1).

In short, although Kensington's doctrine seemed to us to be quite anti-
thetical to requiredness, actual practice varied widely among teams and

divisions. The majority of the staff were much less radical than David in their practices and their beliefs. They might be called "modern progressives." They used textual materials to give some scope and sequence to their children's activities, but they interwove experience activities, free reading, and self-selected activities that permitted expression of and attention to pupil interests and abilities.

Requiredness and Choice: A Critical Stance. In an early January coffee discussion among Cohen, Shelby, Mack, and one of the observers, a variety of curricular issues arose and were debated. The notes raise several of them.

> Eugene reiterated his "no prescribed content" in Kensington, only conceptual and process objectives. He is unhappy with the "topics," for example, water and nutrition, which he does not consider as concepts. This arose in a discussion of Tyler's specification table in his curriculum syllabus (1/4).

Here, as on other occasions, the orientation emphasized minimal prescriptions of formal content. Restrictions were made toward dealing with concepts and intellectual processes instead of factual information. An important subproblem lies in the meaning of "concept" and its relationship to a "topic." In short, for an elementary school child what is a concept?

Perhaps, we can clarify theoretically the interrelationships among the doctrine, the realities of the procedures and practices, and pupil learning by reference to a recent systematic position in educational psychology (Ausubel, 1963). Within his introductory chapter, in a section entitled "Responsibility for organizing the curriculum and presenting subject matter," Ausubel seems to be challenging the central tenets of the Kensington position regarding pupil choice. He says:

> "One extreme point of view associated with the child-centered approach to education is the notion that children are innately equipped in some mysterious fashion for knowing precisely what is best for them. . . . According to these theorists, the environment facilitates development best by providing a maximally permissive field that does not interfere with the predetermined process of spontaneous maturation. From these assumptions it is but a short step to the claim that the child himself must be in the most strategic position to *know* and *select* those components of the environment that are most congruent with his current developmental needs, and hence most conducive to optimal growth" (pp. 10–11).

He then proceeds to attack the oft-cited empirical basis—the self-selection of diet by infants; this he says is applicable only in early infancy and only in relationship to physiological needs. ". . . [We] cannot conclude that he is similarly sensitive to cues reflective of psychological and other developmental needs" (p. 11). He continues:

"The battle cry of the progressives that the student must assume responsibility for his own learning has been distorted into a doctrine of pedagogic irresponsibility. It has been interpreted to mean that the student's responsibility is to self-discover everything he has to learn, that is, to locate and organize his own materials from primary sources, to interpret them independently, to design his own experiments, and merely to use the teacher as a consultant and critic. But education is not a process of self-instruction. Its very essence inheres in the knowledgeable selection, organization, interpretation, and sequential arrangement of learning materials by pedagogically sophisticated persons. The school cannot in good conscience abdicate these responsibilities by turning them over to students in the name of democracy and progressivism" (pp. 12–13).

But even psychologists have their psychological critics. Recently, distinctions, for example, Rothkopf's (1968) "calculus of practice" and "management of mathemogenic behavior" have appeared. The former sounds like Ausubel's careful determination, selection, and sequencing of instruction. The latter moves toward producing those intermediate pupil behaviors that lead toward learning and capitalizing on the "adaptive error correcting characteristics" of the pupils. And this, although more abstract, sounds like a sophisticated version of a part of Kensington's aspirations.

Variety of Curricular Materials

No Textbooks. Kensington planned to move toward an individualized program. Since the graded textbooks were perceived as a deterent to such instruction, the school did not order materials of this kind. One book company did loan them a complete set of text materials. In effect, the staff was forced to create new material and to utilize the well-equipped but late arriving library. With the availability of a wealth of materials, a large library, several sets of encyclopedias for every class, SRA individualized reading and skill laboratories, cycloteachers, and the like became the instructional tools. Gaining experience with these materials was a long and arduous task. Similarly, the development of units of work in science and social studies and of transparencies for special instructional purposes consumed large amounts of staff time. The ease of a textbook as a body of sequenced content became very apparent, even if a comparison with the standards of the formal doctrine found it short of the goal of individualized instruction.

In early January, some of the ISD staff moved toward using textbooks to facilitate the math program and also to retain as much individualization as possible.

9:30 A.M. I am currently in ISD-2 where pupils are having a math lesson. Liz, Kay, and Mrs. Gage are working individually with pupils in and around the room, desk-to-desk fashion. Some kids are using ABC texts, some ditto sheets, and some are at the board working "net change" problems by using the stock market reports from the newspapers. The three teachers float through the whole group.

9:34 A.M. Kay is now back at the table with me. She goes over papers, and the pupils walk over individually with questions. For example: "When did we take the base three test?" "Tuesday," she says. "When are we going to get the language arts folders back?" "Today, if I can get finished." She now is reading, remarking in red pencil, and going over papers. The kids continue to raise questions, for example, for a drinking fountain pass and for an arithmetic computation problem (7×10, etc.) involving exponents and equations. The group of children (all 60) are working steadily by themselves or in small groups . . . .

9:57 A.M. Liz is sitting at the table helping one girl with arithmetic. Mrs. Gage is over at the stock sheet on the bulletin board explaining to a boy. Kay is here at the table with a procession of students and questions. The books that are being used are fourth and fifth grade ABC. Some of the kids share a book and work together. At some groupings of desks (4 or 6) the kids may be using different books and everyone is working along. This doesn't seem to bother anyone. The noise level is that of a busy hum. Only occasionally can David's film be heard (this is in the end study area) and only occasionally can Alec's or Irma's class be heard. If I had to rate the class, it would be busy and purposeful activity of a high order.

(*Observer*. As I watch I am reminded again of the similarities among textbooks and programmed materials and textbooks and teachers. If the kids are engaging actively with a text they have many of the advantages of having a teacher.)

10:20 A.M. Two boys are now working at my table. They are fifth graders who are using a fourth grade book. "Miss Etzell put us in this book."

(*Observer*. It is important to notice that they are working on page 9. Most of the kids are working toward the front of the books. This looks like a post-Christmas phenomenon. Second, the potential parental question of why my fifth grader is in a fourth grade book and in the beginning of the book seems very important—especially if their grades are lower than in past years.)

Of the two boys here, one doesn't understand what he is doing at all. Other has to help some . . . .

Later, after a language arts lesson, Kay Abbot joins the observer for a brief comment.

11:20 A.M. Kay is back to my table regarding her arithmetic folders. I comment, "Another stack?" and she replies, "If I don't collect and check them, they (the pupils) don't do anything. They need to be more independent." The latter is expressed with humor and also real feeling. I replied, "That's a problem of our civilization, of which Kensington is but a part." She nods in essential agreement (1/8).

Project-Type Activities. A variety of "project" type activities occurred at Kensington. Some of it was initiated by the teachers, as in the development of the Hansel and Gretel materials, and some of it was instigated by the pupils. Shortly after the move to the new building, a group of ISD pupils began a school newspaper. It was prepared, dittoed, and sold by the pupils with no editing by the staff. The two pages contained a variety of items: cartoons, simple cross word "puzze's," and student opinions. The opinions included such ideas as "People don't like having [sic] to go outside and go to Room 108 to get lunch!" The project was a brief attempt by some of the children to work toward the development of academic skills and ideas in the context of the new building and of the opportunities afforded by curricular variety and freedom.

SRA Labs. Perhaps the most widely and successfully used materials were the ones packaged as "Laboratories" by Science Research Associates. These materials in the language arts were among the first of the commercially available individualized curricula.

10:32 A.M. Now a half-dozen working individually. Three or four with Liz and 25 with Kay. She talks with them about Language Arts folders: missing forms, grades, comments. There is a kind of "test returning stillness" about the group.

Kay talks about daily report forms. "Errors in not being specific enough." Kids raise questions about planning and changing activity. She comments that they have free time in the day for planning. She suggests "overplanning" as better than underplanning.

10:37 A.M. Kay talks about working out a sample plan for a day. Several agree it would be helpful. She allows them the option of returning to stations and doing their own work. About a half-dozen go to the desks. Kay uses the overhead with others.

Source and pages completed:

Purpose:

Evaluation:

Plan for following day:

She pulls a booklet from Reading for Understanding (RFU) number 27 and SRA Gold number 10, and the like, as concrete illustrations.

Several more kids leave as they see what she is beginning to explain. (*Observer.* She does a beautiful concrete job: specific, calls kids by name for information—"What page are you on in *Tall Timber Tales,* Jimmy?" Several further reactions: (1) procedural aspects like this should have been settled months ago. For one-half the group this is so, and they are busy elsewhere. (2) She's neatly picking up on those who still need help—the real essence of individual-ization? (3) She is gearing in for the long, hard Christmas to Easter period when a major block of the year's work must be completed. (4) I am very interested in tomorrow's ISD team meeting: for example, does Eugene know specifically how the group is now moving? Is he going to suggest a host of things appropriate for pre-Christmas but inappropriate now, and so forth?)

10:48 A.M. Kay now has written regarding "Purpose": "to read for understand-ing, to learn new words, to improve handwriting on p's, to read faster, and to learn the form of a fairy tale."

10:55 A.M. A brief check indicates that Liz is in the Perception Core working individually with kids who are working on reports. Mrs. Gage has a group in 120 and does Language Art activities.

10:57 A.M. Kay finishes the evaluation section, and the group is dismissed to begin work. Kay checks about. She then speaks to all those who missed, elected not to partake in, the discussions and asks them to go up and read the outline. (*Observer.* As a device that's a gem. You get the commonality without boredom or force.) (1/8)

The dovetailing of an organizational format (a team of two plus a part-time assistant), a set of learning materials especially prepared for individual work (SRA Labs), and specific teacher skills capture both the beauty and complexities of this kind of individualized instruction.

Special Teacher Prepared Materials. The ditto machines ran constantly at Kensington. In a school with few textbooks, a widely used alternative was the preparation of teacher-made materials. These materials varied con-siderably from copies of standard workbook-type exercises to special instruc-tions that facilitated learning in science, mathematics, social studies, or literature. Teachers and teacher aides regularly spent before school, after school, and between times preparing materials for the children. Well before the school year was over, the usual allotment of "expendable" materials was overdrawn. As we have indicated in other chapters, this created prob-lems between Kensington teachers, who found the cupboards bare and could not carry out lessons which they had planned. Central office problems were created also as charges were raised of waste and inequity vis-à-vis other elementary school buildings. At a mundane level, the expenses of this part of individualized curriculum and instruction are quite high. Educational discussions on the marginal utility of the allocation of budget into varied categories of expenditures have not been entertained.

The creativity that went into some of these materials was quite high. Perhaps the best of this occurred in Basic Skills as they produced, on ditto, "an illustrated booklet" of Hansel and Gretel. The booklets were pre-primers, the content of which was worked out by the children and the teachers as experience lessons. The vocabulary contained verbs such as

"Oh look!
Look Hansel!
Come here and look.
A house. A candy house."

Figure 9.7 A page from the teacher-made Hansel and Gretel booklet.

"come" and "is" and nouns such as "father," "mother," and "candy." The illustrations included the central characters of Hansel, Gretel, and their parents, evergreen trees, a candy house replete with candy canes, lollipops, and a "witch" looking out a window. We include one page from the booklet as Figure 9.7.

The utilization of the materials possessed a flavor of its own. One Monday morning, Elaine greeted a group of Basic Skills children. After a brief five minutes of smooth transition, using one of the pupils and one of her puppets, she cleared up ambiguities regarding her absence on Friday and began a lesson on the Hansel and Gretel materials. The observer recorded a portion of the lesson this way in the notes:

> 9:50 A.M. The kids move into the reading lesson with sight words on a chart on the board:
> "Oh where is Gretel."
> "Come father, mother."

Elaine corrects the second sentence by asking the question: "What do we need?" One boy suggests an "and."

She comments on the new words in the story. She writes "Where is Gretel?" One child reads. She then has them close their eyes, and she pulls over a small desk top forest display. Gretel is found.

She introduces "here," compares to "where," accents "h" sound, similar to the beginning of Hansel, and also compares capital and small letters.

New sentence: "Where is mother?"

She has a child read. Child comes up to the board. The interplay back and forth indicates that the children are actively involved, interested, and learning.

Next: "Where is father?" A child reads and comes up and finds father and puts him on the set.

She has them blindfold their eyes. Some have difficulty doing this.

(*Observer.* The whole lesson is a game. Questions are being asked. Unknowns all around.)

10:00 A.M. "Where is Hansel?"

"Is Hansel here?"

Big game. Billy goes and gets Hansel. "Billy, how did you know? Did Hansel call?" Good humor. The kids are interested and excited (11/16).

The lesson continued with a game in which the teacher chalked the vocabulary on the floor while the children blindfolded themselves by cradling their heads in their arms. Later the children reported where in the room they found the words. The observer concluded "considerable practice given on these words and the discrimination and pronunciation involved." In short, the Basic Skills team created special materials and used them imaginatively in their day-to-day contacts with the children.

Teacher Resources as Material. Sociologists sometimes speak of functional equivalents, two very different elements of a social structure which produce the same consequences or have the same function in an organization. In a classroom an inventive teacher can create and present characters, settings, and plots, just as does a text, a reader, or a storybook. On occasion this occurred at Kensington.

Later when I watched Sue teach I saw her perform as artistically and creatively as an actress. She taught a lesson in numbers by using two imaginary characters from Mars—Numa and Numo, who had come down to the planet and were behaving in very interesting and bizarre ways. This has sources and a genesis many, many weeks ago in the first imaginary bus that was used as a format for the kids when school first began in September. She interwove these imaginary characters into the learning of set theory—if you have a set of two rocks and one turtle and if Numo with his broom pushed all of them into the same square, you would then have a set of three. Throughout the lesson it was "Numo thinks this." or "What would Numo think of that?"

or "Numo did this." or "Can you imagine Numo doing something else?" and the like. I was strongly reminded of a Salinger short story, "The Banana Fish," in which the camp counselor invents and has a continuing theme in the stories that he tells to the children. These kids were captivated in the same fashion. Another part of her lesson was literally teaching in pantomime with no verbal comments at all. It is difficult to describe the quality of this, since she had the kids put a number line on the blackboard and then had various equations of one plus something equals five, and the kids then had to mark the number of loops and hurdles they would have to jump on the number line to get there and then substitute in the number. She would nod to a kid, shake her head at another one who did it wrong; she would frown, she would pucker up, she would smile, and the kids were almost entirely right with her. It was the damnest performance I have seen in ages. If this kind of ability is more general, and Pat seems to think so and Paul saw some of the same things, she has the makings of a first-rate primary teacher (11/13).

The artistic and dramatic elements in teaching are relatively unexplored issues both in traditional and in individualized instruction. The stimulus characteristic in the materials, in the teacher, as in this instance, and in the combination warrant careful analysis. The immediate consequences were high attention and involvement—captivation to cite the observer's description. The long-term consequences are unknown.

Scope of Curricular Content

The Fine Arts. Part of Kensington's concern for "creativity" and "fully functioning" was expressed in an emphasis on the fine arts. ISD's early and intensive use of modeling clay, watercolors, and expensive paper reflected those purposes as well as the more short-range goals of interesting the children and keeping them busy. As we indicated earlier, when supplies ran out and cabinets were empty, team conflict and dissension were increased.

The curricular outcomes varied across divisions and received some of their most important stress in Transition through Dan's efforts. Early in the fall, he and his pupils had created Terrifico, a large robot that he blended into a variety of instructional activities. After the move to the new building, he spent considerable time with the Transition pupils in the basement art room. In February a brief conversation accented his intentions and the structure for actualizing them.

Dan explained his schedule—Monday and Tuesday in art and Wednesday, Thursday, and Friday in drama. All morning: 50-minute periods so that he has all 90 kids. Afternoon language arts. 11:30 to 1:30 lunch, games, and independent study. He comments that they do very little of the latter. We talked of the long-term need to train the kids for this.

As he talked he spoke of "loosening up the kids" and stressing feelings, imagination, and creativity. He tried to get some of the kids to use the watercolor brush less like a pencil or crayon. In drama they have been stressing pantomiming and nonverbal communication. He had them role playing a witch last week. Ultimately he wants to move to role playing other literary characters (2/8).

The "flair" and the "knack" for it was commented on by one of his team members. The products we have described elsewhere.

Drama. The emphasis on creativity in Kensington's goals, the presence of the aesthetically attractive theatre, the special talents of the staff and, perhaps, the amenability of drama to individualized and nongraded instruction in a group setting precipitated an extended program in this aspect of the arts. The notes from the Christmas program with the south one-half of ISD briefly recorded a part of that utilization.

> 1:05 P.M. I am in the theatre with ISD-S. Jack's group is putting on a play for the rest of ISD-S. Essentially, the Mary and Joseph story. About 15 kids are involved (counting a choral group). They use the tower quite effectively as various Inns at which Mary and Joseph knock—window, door, balcony, etc.
>
> 1:08 P.M. The second group, 13 girls and one boy, sing for the group: "Santa Claus is Coming to Town," "Frosty the Snowman," and the like. The theatre holds the 100 kids with no problem, and could easily double the number. Introduce brief dialogue surrounding "what she got for Christmas" as a lead into the "Twelve Days of Christmas." John, Jack, Irma, Alec, Pat and I observe. Eugene and Tom still occupied with observers from local newspaper and another group of 4 or 5 persons. One of the girls introduces entire cast at the end. (*Observer.* She's come a long way during the year—less constricted.)
>
> 1:20 P.M. The third group, seven girls, two boys, go up to sing: "Silent Night," "O Come All Ye Faithful."
>
> 1:25 P.M. Four girls put on a "Week That Was" show from the tower. Santa wants beer and pretzels, Santa on politics, "Ho, Ho, Ho." Headline—"U. S. Mint Happy—Scrooge is Spending." One group of sixth grade boys applaud vigorously, etc.
>
> Eugene stops in for a minute with his visitors.
>
> 1:28 P.M. Kids file out.

The activity varied from traditional to original, from historical to the most recent in commercial television, and from serious to comic. If our casual counting is reasonably accurate, about 50 children out of approximately 100 were involved on this day.

Later in the spring, the Transition Division's accent on drama and the creative arts resulted in a series of productions.

We have just finished watching the Transition group do a dress rehearsal of Ali Baba. Next up is Mary Poppins. Once again, the drama is an exciting part of Kensington. These kids performed very ably. The sets, props, and costumes were very appropriate. The story was done clearly and appropriately. The oil jars made of corrogated paper, the cave, and the other props were all beautifully done. Dan did some of the continuity, and on the screen were flashed several scenes as background in the cave and in the town.

At the end, some of the control problems in Transition became evident. Chris leads the musical interlude of folk songs from the liberal tradition. The dramatic performance is considerably longer, cleverer, and superior to Liz's ISD group the other day. Claire says that they have been working for a month to six weeks. She's a bit sour on the fact that the dress rehearsal takes all morning and one and one-half days of performing.

9:55 A.M. "Mary Poppins Returns." The chimney sweeps, the charwoman, and the boy selling ice cream, "tuppence a cone," are beautifully pantomimed. Chris plays "Chim Chim . . ." and the chimney sweeps sing. All of the audience is very attentive. Hardly a kid stirring.

10:17 A.M. Mary Poppins finishes. In general, the performance is excellent; Mary Poppins' characterization is not as strong as some of the others. Chris plays the intermission music. Dan directs the cast of Mary Poppins to sit down so that the "Terrifico" cast can come up to the stage. The kids are very excited, chatty, and noisy as they get ready.

10:23 A.M. "Adventure in Outer Space." The sound effects are terrific. The props, lights, and transparencies are used beautifully.

11:45 A.M. (approximately). The play ends. Dan continues to explain and to indicate what should be done (5/20).

The observer's involvement and encomium in the notes reflects a strong positive evaluation in his eyes.

Physical Education. From the inception of Kensington, the objectives reflected a concern for a vigorous physical education program in the development of "Fully-functioning Freddie," the "whole child" of Kensington. In John Taylor, the school had a highly trained and experienced teacher. A brief excerpt from the December notes continues the description of his attempts to tailor an individualized program to the special needs, abilities, and interests of the children.

11:10 A.M. We stop by John's instructional class. He is using the overhead projector in the end instructional area of ISD as he describes the records the pupils are to keep on the daily exercise schedule. He speaks clearly, has a point of view, takes questions, etc. The form seems adaptable for the purposes of exercises and physical fitness goals and program.

11:25 A.M. As I talked later with him, he sees this as systematizing the physical fitness part of the program. This commonality would exist for all of the ISD pupils. He pointed out that they can select exercises among a list and that they then do as many or as few as they are able or want to do. He wanted to offer them special sign-up times around repeated lessons on skills, for example, jumping rope (12/11).

A later, and longer, conversation summarizes the important place he found and made in the school. For the purposes of the analysis in this section, it illustrates vividly the further breadth and variety of Kensington's curriculum.

I spent a brief one hour and a half in the school talking mostly with John and Jean. My conversation with John veered off onto many other topics and was quite informative.

He commented also about the satisfactions and dissatisfactions that he found. The physical factors of equipment and space, and the like, loom much less large in his conversation now, as he is planning on staying. The factors that he emphasizes at present are what he calls "freedom" to do what he wanted to do in the P.E. program and also his acceptance—or the acceptance of him and his program—by the other teachers. He contrasted this with his own earlier experience and the experience of the P.E. teachers that he knows in Milford, where too frequently they are saddled with what he calls "a baby-sitting job."

John also went on to talk a little about the fact that he has 20 minutes with the Basic Skills kids, 25 minutes with the Transition kids, and 30 minutes with the ISD children each day. This has provoked no statements of unfairness and no urging for some kind of straight-time equality. Apparently this kind of thing will happen in many schools frequently. As he sees it, with the age change the period should be longer. He also commented that with Basic Skills it gives the teachers a free period, but with Transition and ISD it only raises a redeployment of the personnel in that he draws in ISD from several classes at any one time, and from Transition they break down into smaller groups when he has the kids out. This also suggests a very important point about the Basic Skills people in that the team of four all very much hold to having a break from the kids, and they have worked this, as the notes will record, throughout the semester. They view this as a highlight of their organization. ISD never has reached that level of being able to trade and work cooperatively.

As he talked, the feeling I got was that he is not real close to individual staff members. In this sense, I do not view him as having any really close personal ties within the school, or of a social nature after school. . . . More generally, however, it seems to me he has been held in high esteem ever since the early gymnasium days when he took over the kids for play and P.E. for long periods of time in fairly large groups; when he was willing to run the school safety and patrol boy group; and when he took initiative from time to time to organize and to move the whole enterprise forward a bit. I can still recall vividly Irma commenting then, "He's a real peach."

He mentioned also that the ISD people now regularly have their kids out for one-half hour in the afternoon and occasionally they come out with the kids, and occasionally not. But the kids are well enough behaved that he does not have to worry about them or, as he put it, "otherwise I'd send them on in." Apparently they are very happy to play tether ball and four-square. As we talked about the four-square game we reraised notions about the social psychology of games, and John commented that four-square had been invented at a YMCA summer workshop a few years ago. The kids are very responsive to it and enjoy it. He also talked about another game that he has them play in which they use varying sized rubber balls. One kid bats the ball with his hands and knocks it as far as he can. He has to run around all of the bases, first, second, third, and home, while the defending team has to throw the ball, even though it's caught, to first base, and first base must throw it to second, to third, to home, and in order, to get the kid out. In one game this morning they had 15 runs and couldn't get the other side out, so that he let the other team come to bat, and they had 15 players and made 15 runs without getting the side out. Since then, they have begun to put their better players on the bases and to utilize them defensively (5/5).

All of which is to say that P.E. was a major item in Kensington's attempt to provide individualized instruction toward differentiated goals.

Scope of Goals

Social-Emotional Goals. In recent years labels such as the "Affective Domain" have appeared as educators continue to wrestle with the variety of pupil outcomes other than the three R's and with the cognitive demands which have received considerable emphasis. A long conversation with a Basic Skills teacher posed the issues of social-emotional development.

I also had a fairly extended talk with Carla. In the course of it, I commented that I had heard that she was not going to be back this next year, and I asked her where she would be going. It took us a bit to get over the strain as she commented that she probably will be at another school in the district and would probably be teaching in the primary area. As we stood there, I kind of gave her the lead to talk about it if she wanted to, and I presume that the silence put pressure on her, since she opened up and began to talk about some of the difficulties.[6] The central problems that she describes concern the 67 kids and the great difficulty in getting to know all of them and in somehow trying to teach them. This had ramifications in terms of the need for a folding door between the areas so that the kids could work independently in more self-contained fashion, although she did not use that word, and then be grouped together for films and "things like that." She then made a very eloquent argument for the problems in teaching the kids self-control and in

[6] From other sources we obtained information of conflict with Mary, conflict with Eugene, and isolation from the total faculty.

teaching them how to carry on their own individual work. As she spoke, she commented also that she has always been proud of her ability to work with children and particularly those with emotional problems. She says that she has found that she has been more autocratic this year than she has been in more than 20 or 25 years, and she has been teaching for 28. Her argument was that children do not learn out of the thin air what's right and wrong and what they should do and what they should not do. When I made the comment that you have to teach them that too, she readily agreed. She does not know how to do this with 67 children. She commented also that in the past she liked to keep fairly extended anecdotal records on all of her kids, both academically and in the personal-social areas. With 67 this has been an almost impossible job. Carla's self-image is that of being a very successful teacher. Over the years she's learned how to roll with the punches, to get along with the kids, to meet their needs, and to teach them a good bit. This year she feels like she has been a total failure (5/10).

The size of the group and the constraints of teaming are interdependent, in her view, with knowing the children, keeping careful records of their behavior and activity, and with behaving autocratically. In turn, she felt that she could not help individual children with emotional problems, that she could not aid others in gaining self-control, and that she could not facilitate others in independently carrying out individual work. She was terribly concerned about her perceived lack of success. Finally, she decided not to return to Kensington. These comments were not isolated ones. The other more experienced teachers, for instance, Wanda and Irma, had responded to this part of Kensington's doctrine—a concern for these broader objectives. They, too, had been frustrated in reaching such goals.

Meaningfulness. Interrelated with the conceptions of individualized curriculum and instruction and the scope of the objectives is the conception of meaningfulness. Two basic referents of meaningfulness seem to be widely used and often confused. Structural meaningfulness refers to the conceptual integrity of a body of knowledge. Item X is related to Y and to Z which, in turn, have their own connections. Presumably, when one speaks of the "structure of mathematics" this is the referent for meaningfulness. A second type of meaningfulness is relevance to issues in the life and understanding of the individual child. That which is to be taught has major relationships with questions, problems, and ideas in the mind of the child. Late in May, the principal began a lesson in the theatre with a number of the older pupils. We recorded it this way:

1:17 P.M. Eugene engages in a discussion of taxes—who makes what decisions, boards versus people, and the amount of tax increase. (*Observer*. As far as I know there have been no units in social studies and/or math regarding the problems of local government, the assessment of levies, and the like.)

Eugene encourages discussion, and one pupil raises the fairness to parochial and elderly people. He opens this for general discussion, and the kids mention grandchildren, others paid for us and them, future of the country, etc. The arguments are quite clear and intelligently expressed. A girl reraises the parochial part. The discussion centers in on this.

1:30 P.M. Eugene leaves. Tom Mack picks up the discussion and uses illustration of highways, and the like. A child raises the issue of two cars and more taxes. The questions seem to have all the basic political science questions surrounding the ability to pay, private education as choice and privilege, the responsibility to total community, etc. (*Observer.* These issues might well have been major items. Kay tells me that they dealt with it briefly and tangentially, but not directly.) (5/28)

The issues of school taxes were major items in the community during the year and especially in the spring as proposals were submitted, not passed, and resubmitted. The principal tried briefly to capture the instructional possibilities in a brief lesson. Kay, the social studies specialist, indicates in a brief comment that no systematic or intensive instruction occurred during the year.

Intellectual Processes. Although "process objectives" were part of every phrasing of the formal doctrine and were in every discussion of the curriculum committee, they were less frequent in the day-to-day instructional program. In general, neither materials nor necessary teaching skills were generally available. In regard to teaching skills, the possibilities inherent in analogues to Bruner's (1961) now classic anecdote of a social studies lesson of maps, rivers, and the location of cities were not actualized. For instance, Kensington had available slate globes which invite innumerable discovery-type activities with respect to continents, oceans, climates, civilizations, history, and current events. At no time were they utilized significantly. Beautifully illustrated wall maps lost their utility when geographical imperatives and group instruction were minimized.

Perhaps the strongest emphasis on intellectual processes occurred in science in ISD. Jack Davis had a variety of "packages" of the new elementary science materials, for example, meal worms, molds, electrical circuits, and so forth, which he utilized with the children. On the one hand, these materials were damned by some as "Jack's interest catchers" and lamented by others in that the program was reaching only 15 to 20 percent of the children in ISD.

The potentiality, and some of the limitations, are indicated most vividly in the introduction of some new science materials and equipment. The field notes report briefly:

10:00 A.M. Science lesson. "Why so slow?" "Who can route most complete record?" "Which side lowest?" are some of the initial questions Jack asks as he begins the experiment with the sand table, a stream of water pumped into the source of a river. The illustration of erosion, deltas, the variations in rainfall, etc., are hinted at in minimal fashion.

10:25 A.M. The number of kids has varied from 25 to 3 as attention lags and rekindles. (*Observer.* It's a beautiful graphic illustration. However, for this size group it has serious limitations. . . . Some of the possibilities of careful measuring, the array of concepts, the diffusion of water in soil are lost, through minimal development. I don't know how much was done before and will be done to enhance the learnings.)

Meanwhile the teacher has been helping other children with their individual experiments, projects, and notebooks. The original group moves out and another group enters the science area. The notes pick up once again.

10:35 A.M. The group gradually drifts out and another one comes in. They inspect the sand table. They have a difficult time keeping from poking in the sand, lifting the plastic cloth, etc. About 10:40 Jack groups kids by the blackboard. He passes out science folders. He asks if they have pencil and paper.

Although he clarifies the outline and table of contents for their folders and moves about giving individual help, the observer speculates further on the science materials.

(*Observer.* I am very impressed with the latent and unrealized possibilities of the concrete science project for all sorts of goals: concept development, creative thinking (How many questions can be asked?), and prediction of what will happen when water is turned on. They might have drawn the stream bed and then have guessed at all the consequences. He might have included clay and rock in the soil, trees along the bed, and so forth. Similarly, if references were available and organized, considerable reading could have been integrated.

Interpretatively, the totality seems to be: (1) specific materials (table, pump, sand, etc.), (2) a clear conception of the physical processes, (3) a clear statement of goals on the part of the instructor, and (4) the kids must be controlled through assignment or through participation. If the end product includes How does a scientist behave?, then repetition over several of these experiences seems necssary (11/19).)

As we have indicated, activities of this sort were carried on during most of the year. Although different children were involved significantly at different times, the ISD faculty, in general, expressed concern for the large number of the children who did not get involved.

In February, the notes spoke directly to that issue and raised the organizational confounding.

Another thing that may not have gotten into the notes concerns the behavior of Jack and Alec. They are back on a sign-up arrangement, and Alec has been doing extended testing of the math abilities of the children. This was going on until the middle of last week, and he was picking up stragglers and others. He also has begun to use a good bit of student help to score the papers. The length of time it is taking to get this underway suggests to me once again the problems in trying to have one teacher deal with 200 children. I do not know at this point how the actual instruction is working out nor who is doing it. Jack's intention is to carry almost all of the science instruction. He has sign-up sheets for films, which Liz is unhappy about. "I can order my own films" was her comment. Out of the films come short discussions afterward, and I observed a very interesting one of these on Wednesday. Afternoons and evenings, and other times, are devoted to working on individual projects or on small group projects. Some of the more interested children, it seems to me, will obviously take part extensively in this. The big question comes regarding a variety of those who have minimal science interest and whether they get lost in the shuffle. The beginning date on this will depend, I guess, on talking directly with Jack (2/8).

For the skeptic, one finds Ausubel's position lurking in the background. A related part of Ausubel's analysis argues that meaningful verbal learning, that is, the acquisition of broad structures of knowledge, is *the* most important goal of education in the public schools. The argument covered one further relevant point:

"Another way in which educators have evaded responsibility for programing the content of instruction has been by hiding behind the slogan that the function of the school is to 'teach children how to think—not what to think.' This slogan also states a false dichotomy since the two functions are by no means mutually exclusive. Actually, as will be argued later, the transmission of subject matter can be considered the more primary function of the school. Most of the thinking that goes on in the school is and should be supplementary to the process of reception learning, that is, concerned with having students assimilate subject-matter content in a more active, integrative, and critical fashion. Development of thinking or problem-solving ability can also be considered an objective of schooling in its own right, although it is a lesser objective than the learning of subject matter and is only partly teachable; but under no circumstances is it a proper substitute for reception learning or a feasible primary means of imparting subject-matter knowledge" (1963, p. 13).

As we have indicated, Kensington's formal doctrine tended to negate curriculum imperatives—the demands of the school to teach particular content. None of Kensington's teachers, in belief or practice, approached Ausubel's degree of skepticism and criticism of this part of the doctrine.

Organizational Structures and Individualization

Nongradedness. The graded elementary school, an invention of the nineteenth century and the standard organizational pattern of the twentieth century elementary school, was abandoned at Kensington. In its place were three divisions: Basic Skills, Transition, and ISD. Their goals, as indicated earlier, were a training in basic skills, the three R's, and a transition from this to independent study. Although formal "gradedness" did not exist at Kensington, several comments are in order. The Basic Skills Division worked with 6- and 7-year-olds. Approximately one-half of these children possessed some minimal reading and numerical abilities, since they had been in first grade last year. Most of them were subgrouped together for instruction. In the team of two this tended to be more with basal readers and textbooks than in the team of four. Similarly, the 6-year-olds tended to be grouped together for initial instruction in basic skill areas. The instruction varied from extended experientially developed materials, through individualized library books, to basal reading series textual materials.

Transition, composed of 8-year-olds, third graders, did not have to face the issue of "grade levels" even though the Division contained the usual wide range of individual differences.

ISD had the children who normally would be in fourth, fifth, and sixth grades. Although the organizational patterns changed dramatically over the year, the children typically were never classified by grade levels. Even in the formation of a self-contained class during the second week, not all the pupils were fourth graders. Similarly, when the team split finally into almost total self-contained units in the new building, each teacher worked with some 9-, 10-, and 11-year olds, representing the several grade levels in the pupils' past placement. The specific approaches of the teachers varied widely, as we have indicated.

Anderson (1966), in his discussion of the theory and practice in the nongraded school, comments that the real problems of the new conception are not the small administrative matters but are more fundamental issues which curriculum experts are only beginning to solve.

"The success of the nongraded arrangement depends ultimately on the improvement of curriculum. What is especially difficult about running a nongraded school or a nongraded classroom is *not* how to organize the program, or how to group the pupils, or how to report pupil progress to parents, or how to set up recordkeeping systems, or how to help teachers solve the numerous other administrative problems that arise. What *is* difficult is how to solve the *curriculum* problems that the organizational scheme raises.

"For example, which skill experiences are best arranged through individualized programs in which pupils can proceed at their own rate of speed, and which experiences are best reserved for groups? What topics, presented under what conditions, are appropriate for classes composed of youngsters whose academic potential and achievements range over a wide spectrum? What kinds of experiences can be shared by youngsters in multiage classes in which a great range of responses and contributions is possible? Just how does a spiral curriculum work? How can we better teach for the process goals? These and other questions bedevil the teachers in nongraded schools. Until our curriculum experts begin to attack these problems and produce specific recommendations that teachers can understand, progress will be at a snail's pace" (pp. 50–51).

As we have reported at several points in this monograph, our data suggest that the "numerous" administrative problems have major consequences. Our data indicate also that the Kensington staff struggled mightily with the curriculum issues. The August workshop and the spring curriculum committee could not wait for the future products of "our curriculum experts," whoever they may be. In between times, the staff was "bedeviled," in the several senses of Webster's definition of that term.

Teaming. Although we have devoted a chapter to teaming, most of our comments involved organizational implications. Here we extend our illustrations in several directions but most importantly in terms of the curricular and instructional aspects.

From the notes in the middle of December, we report one-half hour spent with the Transition Division team. They were in the new building in a three-classroom module not separated by movable walls. The excerpt contains a number of particulars important for our conceptualization of teaming and of individualized curriculum and instruction.

10:50 A.M. I am now observing Meg teaching a math lesson.

$$+ \quad = 11$$

She brings kids up front on the floor so they can hear.
MEG. "Who can make a true statement?"

$$5 \quad + \quad 6 \quad = 11$$

Several other volunteers suggest $11 + 0$ and $10 + 1$.

She then introduces a "t" 5 6, etc.

Kids are attentive and responsive. Each question has from six to ten volunteers with the answer.

The noise from Dan's area is pretty loud. As I go down to visit with his group, Claire has her subgroup working steadily. When one of the kids errs in directions, she notes it (10:55) and has someone else correct it. She swings back to Tommy and makes sure he sees his problem. Goes along.

10:58 A.M. Dan is using a filmstrip on telling time. The discussion centers on small and large hands indicating the minutes and hours. As kids respond, most seem to be able to do the lesson. Kids call out answers and he hushes them a time or two. As they count around, he moves too slowly and they get 65 on a 5, 10, 15, etc., count. This provokes some noisy shouting back and forth. (Several from Claire's group look over.) Of his 25 or so kids, he has only about one-half dozen girls in the group.

11:04 A.M. The student teacher joins the group as an observer. Dan takes a long time to make ¾'s equal to 45 minutes. This long, delayed, and over-worked analysis tends to lose some of the kids. Dan sends two kids "who want to sleep" over to lie down in the corner. The filmstrip goes on. As I look around, I see "junk" lining the south wall . . . "Terrifico" is back in a corner and boxes of other stuff lie about.

As Dan continues the film, the group remains relatively nonattentive. He tends to read the questions for the group. He does not bring any enthusiasm to "jazz" things up. Laborious analysis of "How many minutes between 4 and 10?"

There seems to be some confusion between "1 to 12" as the first minute to the 12th and "1" as the 5-minute interval to the "12" as the hour interval. As he has a boy up front for this, he becomes totally engrossed and loses the group. (*Observer.* This seems very important. In contrast, an earlier, three-weeks-ago, observation of Kay flitting about and solving individual problems but always scanning the total group and being responsive to any kind of incipient problems.)

11:15 A.M. Dan makes a generalization that time problems are addition and subtraction problems and that adding and subtracting are the same process. Interlude of interaction with Susan who has wandered off to the resting girls because "I know how to tell time." Several kids around the projector are more interested in it than the lesson. As he calls on Eric, he runs into difficulty for Eric seems quite dull. Others call out "6:45" impatiently. He seems to be working toward the total group meeting a minimum criterion. This seems to frustrate some. He gets involved in a minute or two interchange with one boy who should but does not have his glasses.

11:20 A.M. Lesson continues.

11:22 A.M. I leave.

In summary, we would accent: (1) the noise and distraction from one group to another, (2) the varied competencies in the management aspects of teaching, (3) the consequence of having to live with your team members' style, (4) the impact of limited teaching experience in a team, and (5) the bringing of the goals of individualized education into juxtaposition with a team organization.

A number of contrasting issues arose in the Basic Skills Team of 4 since, as the semester wore on, the Basic Skills Team-4 came to work well together. On their good days they seemed to capture the essence of what Kensington was intended to be. One of those days occurred on Friday, the thirteenth of November. The field notes recorded it this way.

It's now 5:30 P.M.

There are a number of things I would like to say about the Basic Skills Division. After spending a few minutes in Jean's room, I went to have a cup of coffee with Sue. Jean and Wanda had the kids outside for recess and P.E. type activities. Later, we were joined by the substitute and by Chris, who also had free time because of the arrangements for the supervision of the kids by the others. The substitute was there for Elaine who is ill. The substitute played the role of a very interesting prober in that she was curious about what was going on and how it went on. Thus, I was able to sit and listen to someone doing the same thing that I wanted to do and to view it as a third party instead of as a participant. The substitute made a comment that somebody ought to spend a few days "auditing" just to find out how the arrangements went. Wanda commented to this that she should have been here during the early period when nobody knew what was going on, and that everything was very clear and very simple now. In effect, they have worked out the patterns of organization and the movement of the children. Wanda made a comment or two about the trials of teaching first grade and second grade for the first time. She has been a kindergarten teacher in the past. They each made comments, and here I am mixing up my conversation with Sue, Chris, and the substitute and my later conversation with Jean and with Wanda. Jean and Wanda were commenting about how it's possible to teach and handle 50 or 100 kids now. Now the children apparently are able to understand a little bit better about the need for quiet and for organization, and they have accepted some of the responsibilities this way. In effect, their behavior has been shaped toward a criterion that is acceptable. The actual structure of the instruction varies with some of them teaching first-grade reading and second-grade arithmetic and vice versa. In regard to reading, they made comments that a large number of the second-grade kids, and here it was 12 or so, had considerable difficulty with reading and were involved in primary materials only. In Sue's eyes the unhappy aspect was that these kids were homegrown kids from the Hillside School and Milford District. There is also a sizable group of very able readers, many of whom came from outside the district.

Sue and Chris explained to the substitute some of the things that they had been doing in having had the kids dictate their own stories. These stories were then written up by Chris, and today they are supposed to be put in folders. Chris explained very quickly and easily with no pretentiousness about how they might do that by cutting construction paper in half, folding the page for a front and a back, and then stapling it. Chris apparently is full of suggestions and ideas of this sort from her past experience. Sue has no hesitancy at all about accepting this and then amplifying it, which she did when the substitute asked about the kind of decoration and coloring on it, and both Sue and Chris argued for considerable freedom and creativity on the part of the kids. I am reminded here of Shaplin's point about the values of team teaching in bringing teachers into the profession—new teachers that is. Sue was able to take the suggestions of Chris, to amplify them, and to treat them as worthwhile without any hesitancy or without any inferiority feelings on her own part. From some of the comments that she made the other night at the curriculum meeting, she literally worships the ground that Chris walks on. The inference I made then, and which I think is in the notes, is that Chris has been the major instructor and the gal who really saved Sue from the possible debris pile.

In the conversation between Wanda and Jean there was also a feeling of hand in glove working together. By this I mean, essentially, that they hold common goals and that they contribute to the reaching of these goals in an easy, warm, rational style. For instance, Wanda raised a question about what the central concept in math would be for this next week. She's been working on clocks in telling time, and she says it has about run out of all of the different variations she can work out. Jean kind of said she did not know for sure and would have to think about it a bit. Later Wanda was able to weave into the conversation a request to borrow the manual for the modern math book that they have been using. Jean commented freely and easily that it was on her desk and she would be more than welcome to have it for the weekend.

In listing a number of facets of the immediate differences between Basic Skills and ISD, one of the major ones, it seems to me, is that the ISD people are not there to teach and that the Basic Skills people are. There is no question in the minds of the group that they are supposed to teach reading, writing, and arithmetic. They are all excited about the various ways in which this can be done and about the successes that they are having with some children and the kind of problems that they are having with others. In regard to the latter, they talked briefly about one or two pupils who were having considerable difficulty and with whom they are having parent conferences. Chris asked Sue about what the kids were doing and Sue was able to say, pretty specifically, the level the kids were working in, which one was having more difficulties than the other one, and special kinds of problems that each had. The information was passed quickly and easily again in this very free and well-coordinated sequence of interaction (11/13).

Earlier in the same day, the observer formulated hypotheses regarding team teaching from his observations and conversations with the Basic Skills teachers. Most of the ideas relate to curriculum and instruction.

10:25 A.M. I am now in the teachers' lounge and am trying to ascertain the implications of team teaching.

1. It provides the opportunity for teacher-teacher interaction ré school matters: curriculum and instruction. This contrasts with the Washington School.

2. It provides a continuing social dimension to teaching. These five get along very well. This is very reminiscent of the Country Side Pre-school staff.[7] The women enjoy each other's company.

3. The induction of Sue and the student teacher maximizes the several role models in performance and the acquisition of the silent language of teaching.

4. It utilizes, for all pupils, the special talents of teachers, for example, Elaine and Chris.

5. It permits the division of idiosyncratic abilities—learn to do something extra well, for example, Sue's dramatic qualities.

6. It permits some specialization—primary versus second-grade reading, or more math, then reading, and the like.

7. Now that routines are settled, the group can innovate, for example, Chris into "floating" teacher and the use of the teacher aide as a study hall procter. This should cut the "boredom and monotony" down (11/13).

The contrast in these interpretations and those from all the other teams suggests the potency of teaming regarding curriculum and instruction, if the basic organizational problems are settled, if goals and procedures are agreed on, if teachers are experienced, if specialized talent is available, and if there is interest in creative innovation in curriculum and instruction.

Organizational Balance. Early in December, shortly after the move to the new building, the observer walked through the ISD area and made the following interpretation in the field notes:

> After I talked with Alec, I then journeyed on to David's area, I was struck by another issue—viewing the building as a totality. In this light, watching the kids get inductive science from Jack, textbook math from Linda, oral reports from Irma, and mouse playing, Christmas carol singing on tape, and SRA language arts from David, all coalesces into a school that permits, tolerates, and encourages wide variety and high individual differences among teachers and pupils. Within any one day, week, year, or division period, the total accent can be viewed as quite broad and quite in keeping with some of the original goals and intentions (12/8).

The broader point we wish to make comes back to the unit being observed. If the unit under consideration is any one teacher and the child's experience during that year, there may well be restrictions in teacher style, in content, and in emphasis among instructional objectives. If the total school is the unit, then the child has a varied exposure which most educators and parents

---

[7] This is a reference to a local preschool with which we have had extended contact over a number of years.

would consider desirable in the move toward a broadly defined general education. Here, too, one perceives the possibilities latent in the team setting and in the mode of organization. If each child were to experience the totality of the team described above, one might argue for such an experience. Unfortunately, in this regard, Kensington's organizational problems had been so severe as to preclude this; the ISD team was at that time functioning as self-contained classrooms in one large loft-type room, separated only by modular furniture and cabinets.

Later in January, the same issue arose again as the observer moved rapidly through the building in anticipation of an important curriculum meeting in the evening and in anticipation of viewing the context being provided the editor of *National Weekly* who was at Kensington preparing a feature article for the magazine.

> Short discussion with Leslie Roberts from City U., and Mr. Williams from *National Weekly*. Short discussion with John.
>
> 10:05 A.M. I stop to hear Chris and ISD-S sing folk songs: "Crawdad Hole," "Sly Fox," etc. The kids are very excited, attentive here. Teachers also. There is a variation in children selections and the selections from Chris, for example, "The Invisible Fink." She blends in music, discussion, and levity, for example, "What sound would a fink make?" She's a real artist. Brings a dimension to ISD that they have not had. She has a dramatic quality that is reflected in Elaine's performance also. Moving her into a resource with the other divisions has been a real strengthening operation. Kids know many of the songs from school or home, for example, "This Land is My Land," a New Christy Minstrel's song. She has girls sing once, then boys, then both softly. She has the groups leave one by one—each with a song. Also beautifully done.
>
> 10:35 A.M. I am now in BSD-2. A group watches ETV. Carla has a group; she passes out a ditto. Mary moves about individually. I talk briefly with Mary regarding her paper. She finds their team teaching different from the others: (1) no team leader, (2) no homeroom groups, and (3) no teacher aides to grade papers, give tests, etc. Her basic conclusion for self-contained classes or team teaching is fewer pupils. As she says, "We can spot problems—down to the consonants a child needs, through SRA materials. Just don't have time to get to each of them." Also she has not seen nor does she know who Mr. Williams is. He may have been in and out, but he did not talk with her. He has not talked with Carla either, or Carla and she have not talked. This group has been literally isolated from the rest of the school. It has not altered since coming into the new building. Kids are all now doing individual seat work, and the three teachers (Carla, Mary, and the student teacher) move about and help.
>
> Parenthetically, to return to Leslie's conversation with Mr. Williams: Leslie commented about catching the real significance of Kensington in its program and what it was trying to do. He disparaged the visitors who see only the

carpet. Williams sought also from Leslie the teachers who were articulate, outspoken, and creative, at the elementary, the high school, and the college level. Leslie had a name or two to suggest. Leslie accented to Williams the importance of the "climate" here in that it provided security for creative teacher trials that fail, rewards those that succeed, and goads gently the teachers who are reluctant.

(*Observer.* This kind of climate regarding teaching can be as pervasive as the research climate we have at the Graduate Institute of Education. One of the tricks is to establish the breadth of possibilities. At Kensington it can not only tolerate a David but also can encourage it. The most significant detriment to this point has been the inflexibility of the Institutional Plan.)

10:52 A.M. The three teachers continue to circulate throughout the double group. Some kids read, some write, and some work on construction activities. It is a "beehive of buzzing activity." Only an occasional and subdued teacher comment occurs about noise level.

(*Observer.* As I watch and think of the totality, a concept such as "organizational balance" comes to mind. It harkens back to the University of Minnesota Lab School and the principal's comments about his fifth-grade teacher who spent an entire semester on a creative arts—music, drama, writing-project, and his comment that you need one such person. In the present context, if the six-year experience becomes the unit, then you want some mobile and some permanent-type teachers, you want some with strong 3 R's emphasis and some with creative emphasis, some with musical talents and some with P.E., some science and some language arts, etc. This balance should be an optimizing of prerequisites for the product, for example, Fully Functioning Freddy.) (1/21)

Hypothetically this conception would guide personnel selection, implement idiosyncratic teacher personality variables, facilitate specialization, and would provide multiple sources of satisfaction for the individual teacher. For pupil development, the conception suggests also a number of testable hypotheses consonant with Kensington's mandate and formal doctrine.

SUMMARY: ASPECTS OF A MODEL[8]

Introduction

At the root of all the clamor and noise about "meeting individual differences," "differentiated curriculum," and "individualized instruction" lies an exquisitely simple idea and a number of corollaries. The idea is self-evident; the corollaries are in considerable debate.

---

[8] The interpretations have benefited from recent long discussions with colleagues and seminar students. Most particularly, Paul Pohland, Martin Herbert, and Harold Berlak have provided stimulating interpretations.

This central conception is "children differ in a multitude of dimensions." Most people accept this as self-evident. The corollaries, theorems, or deductions all begin with the central statement "because children are different" and follow with a "therefore." The seven major implications about which there is debate include:

∴ 1. The style of teacher-pupil interaction and instruction must differ.

∴ 2. The materials that are used must differ.

∴ 3. The classroom procedures must differ.

∴ 4. Starting points and rates of progress must vary.

∴ 5. The scope of the curriculum must be expanded.

∴ 6. Curricular and instructional goals must vary for individual children.

∴ 7. Pupil choice is essential.

In short, individualized curriculum and instruction possesses many faces. Presumably, the causes and effects of individualized approaches will vary according to which of those faces one attends. In this concluding section, we attempt to clarify the general dimensions underlying the ideas, and we develop a general model that encompasses multiple and partially different particular instances and implications of individualization. As with most of our theoretical interpretations, we think that this is important because educational discussions flounder as persons hold varying referents but utilize similar labels. Furthermore, these labels are often used injudiciously or inadvertently across situations, age levels, and contexts. Overly simple interpretations and overgeneralizations are a consequence.

An Initial Conception

Initially we developed Figure 9.8 to encompass Kensington's curriculum and instruction rationale. In the sense of a Guttman-type scale one can imagine at one level the stylized, traditional, lock-step curriculum wherein all children are engaged at the same time with the same books and materials and are working toward the same goals. If one is looking for ideal types with stereotypic labels, this might be called "the sterile traditional curriculum."

The next level or degree of individualization involves a variation in rate. The pupils move through the same materials toward common goals, but they move more rapidly or slowly. Essentially one attempts to account for differences in general ability and motivation or perseverance.

At the third level one retains the same goals but alters the means or materials as well as the rate of progress through the materials. Many remedial and branching types of programs illustrate such an approach.

Level

5	Pupil choice in goals, materials, and rates	Pupils determine ends, means, and rates of progress. Kensington's ideal.
4	Different goals, different materials, and varying rates	Pupils work toward different ends (for example, enrichment) which involves different materials and varying rates as well.
3	The same goals but varied materials and rates	Children are directed toward the same outcomes but may branch into special material (often remedial).
2	Individualization: variation in rate	Possible variation in starting point; some children move through the material faster.
1	Traditional lock-step	All children in the same books and materials, moving at the same rate toward the same goals.

Figure 9.8 An initial conception of individualized curriculum and instruction.

Much of "modern elementary" probably qualifies here as teachers use some basic text format with a variety of additional supplementary materials.

The fourth level alters goals as well as materials and rates. Pesumably, this can shade slightly from level three as in the instance of enrichment in regular classes; or quite dramatic changes in both content and emphasis can occur as in foreign language study for some pupils.

Finally, the most individualized program, level 5, involves the element of pupil choice in what is studied. At this level the pupils set goals, choose materials, and determine their rate of learning. As our descriptive material has indicated, Kensington sought to individualize at this level.

As we analyzed our data and took issue with the simple model of individualization that Figure 9.8 represents, a number of additional ideas arose that curriculum theorists must attend to, if a clear language is to be available, and if clear propositions are to be developed.

Complications in the Conception

Educational Goals and the Public School Product. Although legal restrictions regarding mandatory school attendance vary across states, most schools currently anticipate a K to 12 interval as their responsibility. Major controversies exist as to the nature of the "socialized" or "educated" or "mature" individual. Even the legal minimums of "law abiding" are undergoing change. The nature of positive mental health or productive citizenry is in high debate. Priorities on individuality versus a sense of community remain open at very abstract levels as well as at less abstract levels—common studies versus an elective program within the schools. In one sense this is a political problem that each community as a local school district resolves to its own satisfaction within certain constitutional limitations. A number of the complications in this area arose in our chapter "Dilemmas in Democratic Administration" where the parallels are quite evident. In the curriculum and instruction areas the contending political groups include pupils, teachers, administrators, PTA's, and school boards.

When pupil choice of goals becomes an element of individualization of curriculum and instruction, one cannot escape the fact that political as well as professional decisions are being made. When educators argue for no or few content imperatives except as chosen by the pupils, they are taking an important political stand with which other contending groups—especially parents and school boards—might wish to quarrel. And which contending groups might use political power and pressure to change.

When all children approach the same goals, a kind of equity or equality exists. Each child has his chance or opportunity for whatever is considered the brass ring. When different goals are set, by teachers or administrators, the same political issues arise as with pupil choice, and the contending groups enter the scene. Two usual procedures occur at this point in public schools.

First, some minimal or common goals for all pupils are stated explicitly. These sometimes will have a grade and subject matter reference, for instance, the primer and the first grade reader for each 6-year-old. The child who masters that or attains the minimal goals is then routed into other experiences aimed often at other goals. For instance, he can do other reading, engage in art activities, or quietly play with another child a game that stresses cooperation, competition, or some other goal. These "additional" or other experiences and their implied individualized goals, if in a framework of broad social acceptability, pose no problems for the decision maker, be he pupil, teacher, or administrator. In general, the scope of the content is broadened and the idiosyncratic choices of the pupils are increased.

Second, considerable care is placed on the criteria underlying the shift in goals. The most pronounced of these criteria is probably general intelligence. If the child is not able to handle ideas, concepts, or skills, different expectations are set. Although many of the expectations involve rate of attainment, they almost always involve attainment levels and goals as well. For instance, higher mathematics (algebra and trigonometry) and foreign language seldom are part of the program of mentally retarded children. Often, too, special procedures, for example, special class placement, are involved. In a sense the area of special education for blind, deaf, physically handicapped, emotionally disturbed, and so forth is an organizational attempt to handle the shift in educational goals and procedures. The political implications of altered goals is apparent to anyone who has ever had contact with these programs and their patrons.

Kensington's continuous search for "criteria in rational decision making" restates the serious problems in varied goals among normal or typical children. "Why should my child not be taught what my neighbor's child is taught?" is a very difficult question to answer when the referent is toward differentiated goals. The differentiated-means question is more easily handled when evidence can be produced, or assumed, that a differentiated program more likely will get the child to the agreed on common goal.

Expanded Goals and Instructional Means. If meaningful verbal learning is the central goal of the "modern elementary" school, as Ausubel and others would argue, then a textbook with its logical substantive organization, a teacher with clarity of exposition, and a recitational style that enables the teacher to monitor attainment and specific barriers to acquisition seem a plausible set of instructional means. Without question such a picture can degenerate into meaningless rote learning as a goal and purposeless drill as the major procedure. The frequency that such a "sterile traditional" program results, in contrast to a more moderate meaningful or modern elementary program, is open to considerable question among educators, parents, and citizens in general.

However, the expansion of educational goals to include independent or idiosyncratic development, attitudinal or affective changes, psychomotor skills in drama, art, and physical education suggests immediately a need for altered means. At Kensington this appeared in mandate, formal doctrine, and day-to-day instructional experiences. The goals in a laboratory science program illustrate explicitly the ends beyond meaningful verbal learning. Affective aspects of curiosity, intellectual skills such as applying, analyzing, and evaluating, and psychomotor skills in handling simple equipment such as screw drivers, battery connections, and microscope slides indicate the breadth of possibilities. If one expands the array and priority of educational goals, then there is a necessary and major impact on instructional means. This seems a simple but exceedingly important point. Also it seems to be ignored or often overlooked.

Means: Instructional Styles, Materials, and Procedures. At a relatively high level of abstraction, the teacher, the books, the materials, and the classroom organization and procedures all can be assimilated under the same general concept "means of instruction." In sociological jargon they are functional equivalents, even though their concrete manifestations are quite dissimilar. This seems a most important generalization and a basic reason for entitling the chapter "Individualized Curriculum *and* Instruction." Too frequently these elements have been separated inappropriately, and confusion has resulted.

The kinds of problems one encounters are shown in Figure 9.9, the role of the teacher in individualized curriculum and instruction. At one end point, the child might interact with no teacher but only with self-instructional materials. Currently a number of curriculum projects are underway in which teachers have minimal involvement. The programmed text, some computer-assisted instruction, and some individualized programs approach or intend to approach a "teacher proof" status. The more usual approach in American elementary schools is the single teacher with a self-contained classroom. A further step on the scale is multiple teachers. Several variants occur: core curriculum such as social studies and English or math and science combinations, departmentalization, and teaming. Kensington was a mixed case in these regards, as we have indicated. Over time, during the school year, the components changed as well.

The conventional categories of pupil organization can be scaled as individuals, subgroups, classes (20 to 40 pupils), and large groups. The categories on such a scale interact in interesting ways with the teacher role. For example, the individual condition may be a tutorial or may be a pupil with his own programmed text. The large group might involve no teacher but an instructional film. The expectations of simple relationships between pupil learning and organizational variables seem naive.

Materials may vary in a multitude of ways, also. Nominally one thinks of books—texts, supplementary readers, and references. "Learning aids" would include maps, globes, science kits, daily newspapers, television, radio, and films. Even more critical are the dimensions of these aids: difficulty level, concreteness, flexibility, relevance, and the like. In a very fundamental sense we are back to an earlier discussion of material props and facilities. The problems there are the problems here.

A very important latent consideration in curriculum and instruction refers to the unit of time under consideration. Generalizations relevant to a daily lesson may be different from the generalizations relevant to a weekly spelling unit, a semester's course of study, a yearly program, or a K-6 curriculum unit. Some of the technical issues underlying this aspect of the problem

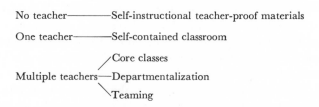

Figure 9.9 Role of teacher in individualized curriculum and instruction.

we have discussed in *"Go, Bug, Go!": Methodological Issues in Classroom Observation* (Smith and Brock, 1970). Also included in that discussion is a concern for the processes of instruction, that is, the flow of curricular and teaching events over time. The contingency of one set of events on another is a major unanswered set of issues in this part of education, the individualization of curriculum and instruction.

The Nature of the Pupil. The discussion of educational goals, instructional means, and individualized curriculum and instruction have an additional complication—the interaction with the nature and personality of the pupil. Although child psychologists have investigated and conceptualized issues here for many decades, adequate representations for educational problem solving and instructional decisions are not available. As a consequence, the Kensington staff's hopes for rationality floundered, in part, because of events beyond their control.

For instance, considerable basic research has been undertaken regarding "levels of aspiration" in children's goal setting. Classical laboratory studies (Sears, 1940) indicate that children who have experienced failure tend to choose unrealistic levels of subsequent achievement, that is, they choose goals that are very difficult and improbable or very simple and easy to attain. The relationship between these events and the day-to-day choices in a program continuing over several months, such as Kensington aspired to, is a phenomenon about which there is almost no data.

Little clarity exists in the interrelationship of specific barriers to learning, the hierarchy of skills in specific learning tasks, and the more general pupil abilities such as mathemagenic behaviors. Each topic is under investigation in the laboratory, but the implications for traditional or individualized curriculum and instruction are not known.

Finally, a comment on a host of age-related variables is appropriate. Stages in ego development and moral values are in considerable controversy. Are there stages? Can stages or levels be skipped? What is the school's contribution to ego development under any circumstances? Does a differentiated approach make a special contribution? Is "fully functioning" a similar concept or does it have important differences? All of these suggest unanswered but latent questions in the Kensington curriculum.

The summary point we make concerns the need for an overall analysis of curricular and instructional strategies as they relate to periods of a child's life such as preschool, primary, upper elementary, junior high, and senior high school. For some individuals, college and graduate or professional schools would be involved as well. To return to our "pupil choice" element, one might argue for progressive movement toward the criterion of full decision making, choice, and adult peer status at eighteen on graduation from high school. If this were accepted, and there is considerable controversy regarding voting, military service, and so forth for young people of this age, then important consequences should occur for the high school program. Schools such as Kensington need both formal doctrine and correlated organizational structures and instructional procedures that integrate with these age-related policies.

Conclusion

More broadly, elementary education does not offer simple or complex solutions for a school like Kensington. Particularly as one pursues "rationality" as a subgoal, which was a large part of Kensington's doctrine and practice, one finds the weak spots in cause-effect chains that lead from immediate practices to long-term goals. Similarly, conceptual and operational weaknesses are exposed. In short, one of Kensington's greatest outcomes is pointing out the limited scholarly underpinnings in much of professional education. When one deviates from the conventional wisdom of self-contained classrooms, common goals, textbooks as central means, then major questions arise for which there are most limited answers.

CHAPTER 10

The Narrative of the Remainder
of the Innovative Year

Most of our descriptive material has focused on the early phases of Kensington's innovative year. And this is as it should be, since the origins of an innovative organization pose critical problems. However, our theoretical interpretations have tended to span the full year. Now it is appropriate to complete the story, since significant events occurred after Christmas and through the spring. One does not have to pose organismic models of organizations to be aware of the rhythmic qualities in the organizational processes of schools. During the spring, teachers receive and sign contracts for the next year. Children and adults look forward to the coming summer vacation and often "hang on," "tread water," "mark time," or occasionally try to "catch up" during the last part of the year. Little is known about the nature and generality of the closing of the year in schools; even less is known about innovative schools. In simple terms we hope to begin to fill these gaps.

MIDWINTER, EARLY SPRING, AND LATE MAY

New Enthusiasm and Old Problems

In early January the notes told of rekindled spirits. The staff came back rested from vacations and from time away from each other, the children, and the school. Discussions were being initiated about Kensington as the locale for the district's summer elementary school. The photographer and reporter from the *Daily Star* were in the building preparing their Sunday supplement feature story on the school. Two sentences catch the flavor of the work.

> Monday, when Jerl was over, and we were engaged in the long discussion on the curriculum, Tom commented that he would have liked to have stayed

but he could not, he had too much to do. This, again, reflects what seems to be the general tenor that everyone is busy and working very hard (1/6).

A later paragraph evokes another image.

> Yesterday was a very exciting day in many respects. By chance I happened to see a Basic Skills play that was given for the rest of the Team-4, not the Division, and for Transition. Some of Elaine's pupils, first and second graders, put on the play "The Golden Goose." The music and the voice on the record and the pantomime of the children and the scenery on the stage and the hominess of the children's theatre made it a superlative event. The theatre held the kids (200) with no strain and enabled them to form a "cozy" group and catch some of the "live" intimacy that occurs in the theatre. For an elementary school, this kind of activity seems like a rare event. The facilities are beautifully adapted for this creativity. The talents of Elaine and Wanda, who helped her, are hard to overstate. This kind of teaching, where one has the facilities, the confidence, and one's own interest and enjoyment, radiates kind of a flair which is a dimension that teaching should have, it seems to me (1/9).

We had the impression that some of this was happening also in ISD, although other difficulties persisted. We commented on the same day:

> Some of the same kind of excitement in teaching seems to be happening with Kay. She develops some of the same excitement that in itself then radiates out to the pupils. Apropos of this was her discussion of beginning a social studies unit on the stock market. This kind of thing is not seen in one of the other ISD teacher's behavior who is much more "going through the paces" and looking for something to do with the children rather than having a number of exciting ideas to do. There seems to be a viscious circle in that as one gets a bit discouraged, then the excitement in one's behavior drops off, and as the excitement in the behavior drops off, the ability to contage the kids drops off, and this makes you more discouraged and the spiral continues downward. Similarly, you can trace it upward (1/9).

However, reorganization was on its way. ISD's Saturday morning team meeting on January 9 went this way:

> It is now 12:45 P.M. and I'm on my way back from the ISD Division meeting.
> The upshot seems to be that Eugene wants to reorganize the division. The new plan essentially involves having a group of four or five academic counselors who, in effect, will become self-contained classroom teachers. There will be two resource persons, Jack and Alec, because of Jack's special talents in science, and Alec, because he teaches mathematics which is a subject matter area allegedly requiring some kind of sequence and special aspects. Also, there will be a creative arts consultant. This will be Chris. And a P.E. resource person who is John. And a materials resource person who is Tom. The drift of the arrangement would be that the academic counselors would have to

work out cooperative relationships with the resource persons, but the relationships among academic counselors, in effect, self-contained teachers, would not be mandatory. They could work out joint arrangements if they desired. Although there was some confusion in the way in which these counselor jobs were described, the essence seems to be that they will be totally responsible for the pupil's program. This kept getting hedged with statements that perhaps the resource person would do all the teaching (1/9).

In *Bulletin No. 33* the reorganization of ISD was described for the total staff:

"*ISD Reorganization.* The Independent Study Division has decided to alter the organization of the Division beginning Monday, February 1. Basically, the new organization consists of 5 Academic Advisors who will be totally responsible for the education program of about 40 pupils each, with two staff members serving as Division resource persons (science and math). Cooperative teaching between Academic Advisors is encouraged and provided for, but will be on an informal rather than official basis.

"There will be a meeting of the ISD Friday at 1:00 to consider: (1) assignment of pupils; (2) roles of Academic Advisors and Resource Persons; and (3) utilization of facilities" (*Bulletin No. 33,* 1/19).

The brief sentence, "Cooperative teaching . . . will be on an informal rather than official basis," indicated the final demise of team efforts in the division. In the same *Bulletin,* a prior item indicated a reorganization of the Physical Education program.

"3. *Physical Education Schedule.* On Monday, January 25, the new Physical Education schedule will go into effect as follows:

9:00–10:15	Transition Division	Daily
10:00–12:30	Independent Study Division	Daily
1:00–3:15	Basic Skills Division	Daily

Please work out any adjustments within the time allotted to each Division with Mr. Taylor" (*Bulletin No. 33,* 1/19).

The full impact of this was to become apparent over the next month or so. The field notes record the issues this way.

Pat reports that John is very upset about the P.E. physical facilities that have not worked out, as we have quoted on a number of occasions and places, and also about the fact that he must work with not only the ISD kids but also with the kids in Basic Skills and Transition. In his eyes the latter keeps him tied up all day and prevents him from implementing any kind of individual program with the ISD children. A thread here, which might be very significant, is to work through the problems of independent study and the time involved as it relates to someone like John, who is probably as skilled a classroom teacher as exists in the building, and who has as well thought out a program as anyone in the building. The gist of the argument might go something like this: he has an individualized program in exercises and physical fitness that he has been working on since before Christmas. He also has some instructional activity around certain games that he has introduced to almost all of the children; and third, he has a number of continuing activities the kids can work on independently and need supervision only from time to time. In a sense he is terribly frustrated that he has not had time to really do the kind of job that he wants done (3/2).

Perhaps, the most significant generalization is that an individualized program is an expensive one and requires a large number of personnel. The teacher-pupil ratio problem probably has not received the attention it deserves in the educational reform literature.[1]

Meanwhile, the Transition Division also was to experience the culmination of the two-one split, which had its origin in the differences in philosophy and approach that team members had expressed as early as the first week of school. The disagreement resulted in one of the team members being out of the classroom area for all of the morning hours. Three groups of 30 students each spent several hours a week working with one teacher in the theatre or in the art room. One of the team indicated that the fine arts program enabled them to get some of the children out of the Transition area so that two of the teachers could carry on the program they wanted. This adjustment not only served the double function of removing the dissident faculty member from the main room for one-half of the school day, but it also reduced the number of children the other two would be teaching at any one time. In addition, it seemed to minimize team conflict.

However, even the two team members who were more content oriented found that parts of the early workshop days were still having an impact. The summary notes indicate the following.

> With all of the students gone from the main area at least one hour a day, although at varying times in groups of 30, I asked whether or not all of the students would study the body systems which one group was doing. One of the team members pointed out that they could not be sure that all students are being exposed to the same thing because some of the pupils are at the same time working on a three-part program in electricity that is being shown on TV. The team member added, "We're really floundering; I'm not so much interested in content now as I am in getting some of the process across."

[1] Notice for instance Robert Anderson's comments in *Teaching in a World of Change* (1966, pp. 36–40).

Even though the ideas of the Transition team members at times seemed to move closer together, at the termination of the school year their differences were still apparently unresolved.

January was a full month. As we have described elsewhere, the Curriculum Committee started meeting again. Considerable publicity for the school was in progress. An open house was held on January 19. The consultant, Leslie Roberts, continued his monthly visits on January 21 and 22. Report cards were distributed and the first semester was over. New staff members—Linda in ISD and Abbie in Kindergarten—joined the faculty.

Gradual Completion of the Physical Facilities

During late winter and early spring, more and more of the building became operational. We have noted that Chris became a general resource person in the creative arts. Facilities for her use as well as for the total faculty received comment in an early February staff *Bulletin.*

"*Use of Art Room.* Although it will be some time before arrangements can be completed for making the basement art room as functional as we would like, considerable use may now be made of this facility. A schedule for reserving this room is posted on the bulletin board in the perception core. The creative arts resource person has priority in the use of the art room, but will not be using it nearly all the time.

"Regulations have been established for using the art room, and you are requested to comply with them conscientiously. It is recognized that the present regulations leave much to be desired in terms of instructional needs, but it is necessary to work within the parameters of the situation as presently exist regarding the building code. We will then want to revise the regulations for using the art room when the building code matter is settled and we are able to obtain additional cabinetry, furniture, and sinks for the room.

"The creative arts resource person will schedule some time each day to instruct designated pupils in the art room; other times will be blocked out during which she will be available to supervise and assist individuals or small groups of pupils who may be sent to the art room for particular purposes. When not being used in either of these ways, the room may be scheduled by other teachers who wish to bring pupils for art activities; pupils must be accompanied by a teacher, however. You are encouraged to use the basement art room rather than classrooms for art activities (particularly messy ones) as much as possible. Pupils must not be permitted to get paints and crayons on the carpeting in classrooms since extreme difficulty is being experienced in removing such stains.

"We are not allowed to place any furniture in the art room at the present time, but carpet scraps are stored in the blue storage room, and may be used for pupils to sit on for art activities. These carpets should be returned to the storage room after use. Neither the art room nor the art supply room should be used by the staff for storing things. As soon as possible, we hope to provide cabinets in the art room for storing uncompleted art projects, etc., but for the time being, please do not leave things, except possibly on the small shelves in the blue storage room. The art room should always be left clean and in good order.

"Pupils going to the art room are encouraged to use the outside entrance from the play shelter as much as possible, particularly when passing in large groups. When using the inside route to the art room, it is essential that quietness and order be maintained when passing through the perception core and down the stairs" (Bulletin No. 39, 2/8).

The references to carpet stains, storage facilities, problems in pupil movement, and budget limitations for furniture and equipment received comment elsewhere in the report.

The new building provoked problems also in regularizing a variety of custodial and maintenance problems. For instance, in the February 9 Bulletin, reference was made to the hiring of a new part-time custodian.

"He will be working in the evenings and Saturday mornings. Although we now have a total of two and one-half custodial personnel, it takes the assistance of everyone in the school to keep the building clean and attractive. Not only for this reason, but also because it is an important educational goal, please encourage pupils to do their part in providing a clean and wholesome school environment. Generally it is wise and helpful to spend the last few minutes of each school day getting the building in order. Since it is difficult to know just when custodians will be vacuuming each room, please have pupils put their chairs on their desks before leaving school each day. If you are certain that your room is not to be vacuumed on a particular day, then this will not be necessary.

"Another way that you can be of considerable assistance is by keeping furniture and accessories distributed properly. Someone moved a table into the theatre last week, for example, and left it there for several days. We would like to ask also that classroom waste baskets be placed directly under the pencil sharpeners in each room. We seem to be having some difficulty in keeping the color-coordinated waste baskets which were purchased especially for the Kensington School in their designated areas. These waste baskets are not to be used in rest rooms, and should not be used for milk cartons or food refuse. At times they have been found with paste, glue, paint, and gum" (Bulletin No. 40, 2/9).

The problems interrelating new kinds of furniture and equipment, the special arrangements for lunch, that is, eating in the classroom areas, and the specialized personnel, custodians in this instance, are readily apparent in the content of the *Bulletins*.

Rules in Educational Organizations

In a school devoted to pupil freedom, the issue of rules provoked a number of dilemmas. We have described some of the problems that occurred in the temporary quarters, especially in the gymnasium with ISD. After the move to the new building in early December, the formalization of rules occurred to a high degree. We have included them as figures in Chapter 5. Staff reactions were varied. However, some saw the rules as being incongruent with attitudes that had been expressed earlier and voiced their feelings accordingly. Others viewed the rules as having been produced by Eugene.

The staff *Bulletins* provide easy access to the issue in the post-Christmas part of the school year. In many instances, the good humor of the staff shines through:

"*School Mascot*. From the looks of things, it appears that the dog is fast becoming our school mascot. We have not checked with Lyndon Johnson yet to see what can be done about the overpopulation of dogs on our campus, but the school board and superintendent are working on the problem. In the meantime, please ask pupils not to feed dogs scraps from their lunches. If pupils own any of our friendly dogs or know their owners, please request that they try to prevent them from coming to school" (*Bulletin No. 34,* 1/21).

The building with its outside walkway, with every classroom opening onto the walkway, and with the need to carry food from the serving area back to the desks seemed to heighten the attendance of the unfettered neighborhood dogs.

The next *Bulletin* took up a different issue.

"*Special Notice*. Please notify our affluent pupils that they are not supposed to throw money in the aquarium. Also, please ask that they not soak their feet in the water" (*Bulletin No. 35,* 1/25).

In early February issues surrounding conferences and pupil movement were recorded in the *Bulletin*.

"*Pupil Conferences with Principal*. From time to time pupils come to the office requesting a conference with the principal. Although provisions should always be made for such conferences, it is important that proper procedures be followed. Pupils should not come to the office without first checking with their teacher or academic advisor. In cases involving such matters as requests for reassignment to another teacher, etc., the teacher should probably have a conference with the principal rather than sending the child to the office. In some cases a pupil-teacher-principal conference might be worthwhile. In summary, pupils should follow appropriate procedures for conferring with the principal, but should not be denied the opportunity to do so" (*Bulletin No. 37*, 2/2).

"*Pupil Movement*. From time to time pupils move from one area of the building to another in fairly sizeable groups. For the most part traffic patterns and movement of pupils is working extremely well. There are a few times however, when pupils need to be especially careful about passing quietly through various areas of the building. One problem area is in using the inside stairway leading to the arts and crafts room. Occasionally pupils are quite noisy also when going to the theatre. Please try to impress upon pupils that common courtesy calls for quiet and orderly movement when passing through quiet areas of the building" (*Bulletin No. 38,* 2/3).

The problems continued to increase, and the organization reacted in an important structural manner. A new unit, the School Policy Committee, was established. Although no formal mention was made of its relationship to earlier committees, the issues with which it was to deal—the development of policies and procedure, the communication of procedures, and the evaluation of regulations, were explicit, and they were reminiscent of earlier efforts. All of *Bulletin No. 41* was devoted to the new committee. We have included the entire *Bulletin* as Figure 10.1. The introductory paragraphs indicate the struggle in developing congruence between the doctrine and the problems of the moment. Such issues we view as major ones, needing conceptualization within organizations. The attempts to obtain clear discriminations among institutional decisions, organizational maintenance decisions, and instructional decisions were not successful. The rules about rules, that is, who makes what decisions, remained unclear. Paragraph four in *Bulletin No. 41* indicates that here the principal is invoking what Swanson (1959) calls "democratic centralism." In this kind of constitutional arrangement a group *advises* the leader who then makes the final decision.[2] The style varied throughout the year.

Humor in Organizations

From the first days in the August workshop through the dinner-party reminiscing in June, a thread of humor ran through the Kensington experience. At times, the humor was full of a youthful and uninhibited joy;

---

[2] Recall that this issue was examined in detail in Chapter 8 as one of the complexities and dilemmas of democratic administration.

1. *Institutional Decision Making.* One of the distinguishing characteristics of the Kensington curriculum under development is an attempt to establish educational criteria and objectives at the institutional level, but avoid the "programming," prescribing, or dictating of instructional decisions. This allows freedom for teachers and pupils to interact in making decisions at the instructional level (which is quite contrary to the way most curriculum programs are designed). We believe that this is the only approach consistent with the design of our program for individualized instruction.

This approach spells out quite clearly that the responsibility for educational decision-making does not lie at the institutional level. At the same time, however, there appears to be some confusion as to the responsibility for making decisions in other areas, notably the area of organizational maintenance. There is ample evidence that broad freedom in this area of decision-making is not only unnecessary but actually detrimental to the success of the school. In order for the five-hundred plus pupils and employees of Kensington to work together effectively and efficiently it is essential to be able to predict the behavior of others (just in the same way that public highways are useful only because driving behavior is predictable). This means, of course, that behavior has to be controlled and that individual freedom must be limited in order to provide greater freedom for everyone.

There is no question as to the need for policies and regulations designed to program decisions and behavior relative to the maintenance and functioning of the institution. Efficiency demands it. There are questions, however, as to how such decisions should be made and implemented. Careful consideration needs to be given to how and by whom policies are developed, how they are communicated, how they are enforced, and how they are evaluated and altered.

Responsibility for dealing with such matters lies with the principal as administrative officer of the school. To assist in carrying out these tasks a *School Policy Committee* has been established. Members of the committee are: Meg Adrian, chairman; Irma Hall; Kay Abbot; John Taylor; Chris Hun; Mary Radford (when available); and Tom Mack ex officio when dealing with matters relative to his field.

The purposes of the School Policy Committee are to:

1. Make recommendations concerning areas where administrative policies and regulations are needed.
2. Assist in the development of administrative policies and regulations through making recommendations and serving as a sounding board.
3. Assist in communicating and interpreting administrative policies and regulations to the total staff.
4. Assist in evaluating administrative policies and regulations.

Figure 10.1   Verbatim reproduction of *Bulletin No. 41,* February 10.

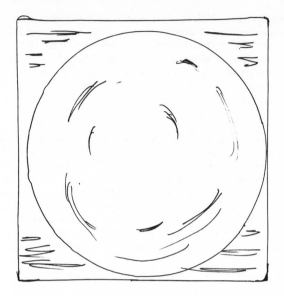

The ☐ is Kensington School
The ○ is the Faculty
Color them incongruently

Figure 10.2   The first page of the coloring book.

at other times it contained the bite of bitterness and disappointment. This part of the story might have been entitled "The Academic Career of 'Fully Functioning Freddy,' " the staff's good-humored early label for the intended product of Kensington's educational milieu. The most vivid illustration of humor occurred at a faculty party in early April. One of the by-products of this was a Kensington Coloring Book, a commentary on the year that was prepared by several of the creative staff. The analysis of the forms and functions of humor within school organizations seems a most necessary task. We have reproduced, as Figures 10.2 and 10.3, two pages, the first and last, from the coloring book. They capture well the flavor of the humor. In between the first and last pages were references such as "This is Basic Skills. Color them primerless," and "These are husbands and wives. Color them neglected." The content of the musical parodies speaks for itself.

Treading Water

A number of items occurred which suggest that at the end of the school year little energy was being directed into vitalizing the concluding experi-

WE'VE GROWN ACCUSTOMED?????

We've grown accustomed to your ways
You make our work-day never end,
We're used to meetings night and noon
And visitors through June,
   Reporters,
   Photographers,
   And silent observers . . .

We've grown accustomed to your shape,
We're going in circles more and more,
By covered walkways we must go
Through wind and rain and snow,
   To work,
   To play,
   To eat each day . . .

We've grown accustomed to no curriculum,
But only skill and trait objectives,
With worksheets we must try
To fill the gap made by
   No texts,
   Or guides,
   But World Books well supplied . . .

They're second nature to us now,
Like breathing out and breathing in,
We were supremely independent and content before we came,
Surely we could always be that way, but just the same,
We've grown accustomed to the teams,
The groups that yell and scream . . .
Accustomed to the scheme.

THIS SCHOOL IS YOUR SCHOOL

This school is your school,
This school is my school,
From the tableless art room,
To the flagless flagpole,
From the fishless fishpond,
To the grassless playground,
This school is made for fools like me.

As I was teaching
In the clockless classroom,
I saw below me
The food stained carpet,
And in the corners

Figure 10.3 The final page of the Coloring Book.

Lay coats and garbage,
This room belongs to you and me.

Now this reminds us
Of that great workshop
Which prepared us for . . . Ho-Ho-Ho-Ho!
The year is ending,
And we are wondering
If this fool was made for Kensington!

Figure 10.3 (*Continued*)

ences of the year. Instead, the focus was toward preparations for the next year. These preparations included staffing, organizational plans, and a concern with the tax campaign. In regard to the former, we have these notes:

> Eugene and I talked some about the drift of the school, particularly ISD, much more toward the direction represented by Irma which Eugene sees as good traditional teaching, but not what he originally had in mind, or really still has in mind for Kensington. He guesses that the new people whom he is interviewing are somewhere between Irma and David but more toward Irma. He does not quite know what he is going to do about this (5/18).

In a relevant but different part of the Kensington system, the notes record an observation, a conversation, and an interpretation.

> Other things that I might comment about during the visit today include the observation of the play shelter area and particularly the stage part, which was literally covered with dust and dirt. I noticed this going in, and Jerl made a comment about it just before we left. As he said, "It would seem to be a very simple thing to have that hosed down every night." I commented back that one man's simple problems are not necessarily another man's simple problems. I commented also that that was a basic principle and that he was free to use it wherever he wanted (5/11).

Finally, on occasion, with some nostalgia and regrets, the thoughts returned to earlier aspects of the year.

> One of the teachers commented that he would like to see a discussion among a number of the people who are leaving as to the "mistakes that each of us made this year." From this he went on into a discussion of some of the things he has learned, and he cited particularly the T-group experience and the fact that the purpose was sound, promoting open communication and building relationships, but that it did not work out that way and, in fact, worked out in just the opposite fashion. He commented also that if he were to go into another school this next year he most certainly would not indicate his feelings and his own personal history to the degree that he did this past

time. He talked at some length about the difficulties of the T-group experience and the fact that it had caused some of the difficulties which it was trying to overcome. He made reference to the very early appearance of people wanting to get at the "real work" and wanting to make decisions about what they were going to do. As he talked about these things, he recounted that it seemed like an eternity ago (5/11).

Decisions were made concerning the flow of pupils in the school. A most important announcement appeared in *Bulletin No. 59*.

"2. *Pupil Placement*. Many pupils are expressing the usual concern for whether or not they will be promoted. It might be wise to explain that all pupils are being promoted, but that they will not be assigned to a given division of the school until the beginning of next year" (5/27).

In effect, no battles were to be fought over retention of pupils.

The problems of dissonance arising from the doctrine and the reality occurred as noted in *Bulletin No. 58,* also issued on May 27.

"Grade placement for next year should be indicated on the back of the report card on the double line just above attendance. Please write the words 'Promoted to grade————.' As discussed in a previous staff meeting, the designation of grade level is not inconsistent with our nongraded program so long as we have flexibility in assigning pupils to instructional groups" (5/27).

So it was. The hope was to pick up and move toward a resolution in subsequent years.

The Deteriorating Social Base

The long reach of the environment, in the form of the tenuous social base possessed by Spanman, Cohen, and Shelby, began to increase in tempo and potency in April and May. The district was in the throes of a tax campaign. The aspects of the situation were multiple: first, the need for increased funding to support the Milford District's new thrust recurred. Second, a new consultant hired by the board argued for a laissez-faire approach, that is, let the community decide what level of expenditure it wanted to make for education. This contrasted with the basic stance of Spanman and several of the businessmen on the board, who were ascendent and forceful and tended to sell hard the products they believed in. Third, as the tax elections failed, scapegoats, among which Kensington was a convenient and plausible possibility, were sought and found. Fourth, this kind of conflict has major consequences in the organizational structure of Milford. Fifth, the impact seeped into the jobs and careers of the major figures in the life of Kensington.

The data supporting these interpretations varied from direct observation of school board meetings, observations of extended meetings of a variety of other school personnel, and long conversations with individuals throughout the system.[3] In one long exchange the notes revealed this information:

> Also he commented about the superintendent's problems, which include several facets. First, he no longer seems to be talking to anybody. Second, the board opposition is more than a troublesome little factor; it could loom very large. He has been advised to do certain kinds of things such as holding the CTA Executive Board meeting before the board meeting tonight and getting a vote of confidence from the Executive Board. It was felt he could not get it from the teachers at large. Interpretively, it seems to me that it is a very significant element that he does not have the backing of his teaching staff either. Also raised at some length were the problems with the central office staff and the fact that in the last three years the superintendent held only a couple of general meetings with them. After the last one he commented that they went so abysmally. Another specific that was cited was the case of a man who has been principal at one of the schools and who next year will be relegated to a teaching contract. Several of the old guard want him to become principal of another of the elementary schools. From his point of view they were stupid. I do not believe that he realizes the full extent of the conflict and the full extent of the revenge that those guys are going to get if they get the power (5/11).

After a long board meeting, the notes record items related to the pressures being generated by the failures of the tax campaign.

> There was some sentiment to resubmit at the 36 cent increase. Some of the teaching staff, who were favoring going for the simple majority at the same rate, were afraid that they would compromise at the 21 cent, which they did not think they would be able to get. They think that one more defeat, and the superintendent will be in serious trouble.

> Another very interesting problem concerning the role of consultants came up, in that the soft sell is essentially the advice of the consultant. This is so contrary to most of the people on the board, for instance, the president is in strong disagreement with the consultant. Also in strong disagreement are most of the activists who earn their living through making programs move in one form or another. It also contrasts with the hard give-and-take of one brand of democracy as opposed to the laissez-faire point of view (5/12).

A week later, after another board meeting, the discussions were as follows.

> I got very different stories from several of the staff about the degree to which Kensington is in the middle of criticism. One tells me that the superintendent

[3] Elsewhere (Smith, 1969) we comment on the comparabilities in this approach and what Campbell and Fiske (1959) call "multimethod-multitrait" approaches to validity.

sees it as central. It sounds to me as if there is a great deal of potential scapegoating here. Another played some of this down and commented favorably about the development of the Parent Council, which he thinks is the only thing that might save Kensington. As he said, the principal keeps turning the criticism of the school over to them and lets them handle the attacks.

It is very difficult for me to piece together the kind of criticisms that are being made about the school. I cannot really get behind the general issue into the specific aspects. The physical plant, especially the carpets, keeps coming up. There seems to be some more oblique reference to the curriculum program and goals of the school. One teacher was telling me, for instance, that the parents do not understand what the school is trying to do, based on last night's meeting, and that there has been very little done by the principal and others to acquaint them with this[4] (5/18).

ARRANGEMENTS FOR NEXT YEAR

Part of the reality of schooling is its rhythmic quality. Although each year is an episode unto itself, the years flow into one another. Mandates and building specifications preceded this first year of Kensington. In the spring, plans began to accelerate for the following year. In part, there were career choices, since individuals had to decide to stay or to move on. In part, the plans involved organizational arrangements for the school for next year.

Career Concerns and Arrangements

Most analyses of teaching and elementary schools as organizations ignore the distant past and the remote future. Our data from Kensington suggested this to be a serious limitation. The need for a concept of career recurred throughout our year. In December, one of the researchers had been observing a physical education class and entered into a brief discussion with the teacher, John Taylor. Later in the notes, the following was recorded.

> John also told me of an assistantship offer for next summer at Midwest U. A woman in elementary P.E. wants him. He is obviously flattered and delighted. The pay is not great but the opportunity—future jobs and movement on his dissertation—would be very high.
>
> (*Observer.* An interesting subtheme running through the whole Kensington experience is the interrelationship between professional training and professional responsibilities. Eugene, John, and Tom have made literally no progress on their dissertations. The local demands are much too heavy. A correlated

---

[4] Notice the content and the time of the year (late May) of this comment for the significance of the item.

problem concerns the conflict between career goals and the manifest functions for which they were hired. Jack and Tom, for instance, have a continual eye on the longer term self-defined "main chances" in the district and in future teacher training institutions. In this sense, they perceive themselves as quite mobile. Sue and Alec also have next step aspirations, and Kensington becomes kind of an interesting vita item. The staff contains few of what I would call "career teachers," for example, Meg and Jean.) (12/11)

An aspect of Kensington that arose in the field notes the first day, which appeared significantly throughout the year, and which remained during the "post-experimental year," was the fact that three members of the faculty had all of their doctoral course work finished and only needed a dissertation to complete their work. All three hoped to develop their papers out of the Kensington experience. None of the three has finished a degree in Kensington. Although such an observation is true, the significance and interpretation is not so easily determined. Our initial thought of "the heavy burden" conveys one position of our reaction. More generally, the observa-

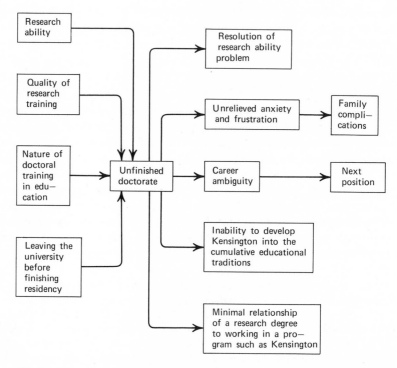

Figure 10.4 The problems associated with "all but the dissertation."

tion strikes us as typifying a major professional education problem that has not received the kind of attention it merits. Figure 10.4 contains hypotheses surrounding this phenomenon. Although preservice teacher education is indicted regularly, less attention is paid to inservice training. The research doctorate, which is given status and lip service, seemed to have little relevance at Kensington. Whether this is the quality of the training, the nature of the people, or an interaction between their graduate program and their abilities, needs, and professional goals is not clear. The consequences of not having completed the degree were apparent in the frustration, anxiety, and varied defense mechanisms used by the individual faculty members. Organizationally, Kensington was not able to influence the broader stream of American education, which had been a fondly held part of the early dream. Perhaps, too, this was a question of talent and organizational resources to implement this dimension of the idea.

A brief notice in the *Bulletin* in the middle of February takes cognizance of the career issue but barely taps the impact of the faculty discussion, gossip, and concern about the plans for the next year.

"Personnel Decisions for Next Year. The personnel office is now in the process of preparing budget information and recruiting personnel for the next school year. In order to work on contracts and recruiting they need as much up-to-date information from present staff members as possible. They have requested that any teacher who definitely does not plan to return to the district next year submit a written letter of resignation at the earliest possible date. Persons who have made no definite decision, but think they may not return to the district, are requested to give this information to the principal informally. The personnel office has also provided an opportunity for teachers who would like to transfer to other schools in the district to make such requests. Forms for this purpose have been sent to each school and are available from the secretary. Any such requests should be submitted as soon as possible. One other request from the personnel office is that the principal verify next year's contract salaries with each teacher. If we have not already conversed with you relative to this matter, would you please check with the principal sometime this week" (*Bulletin No. 42, 2/15*).

We summarized the issue in the early March field notes:

Pat commented at some length on the general discussions of who is going to be back next year, which seem to be rampant in the building. Most everywhere in education, this time of the year is contract time. Since there is such a large group of new teachers at the Kensington School, this becomes very critical indeed. Pat found out that the letters of intent do not apply to the first-year teachers. They must wait out their time, as it were (3/2).

The rumors, the job offers, the graduate fellowships under consideration, and the uncertainty were major factors throughout the spring for the Kensington staff.

Our notes are full of conversations about job opportunities, letters of inquiry to and from faculty members concerning positions in other schools and other communities, and are full of high intensity of affect and concern. Three brief items at the time of the tax crisis and the internal staff crisis, from conversations with Jerl Cohen, are persuasive:

> The critical thing would be the superintendent's replacement. If they replace him with someone like Kaufman or Sullivan, then the whole movement is lost. He said that any one of them would "close down almost all of Kensington." From my understanding of the situation, I have no reason to doubt that that would be so. Jerl's main hope is that they will go outside and that they will get a reasonable person (5/11).

In the same conversation,

> Jerl also made some comments about "his interest" in the affairs. This resides around his own job and the fact that he considers himself as a second person in line to get the axe if Steven goes. He made some comment about whether I knew of anybody who wanted an assistant superintendent interested in curriculum and instruction. He said this jokingly, but I replied with seriousness that I knew that Brookdale was looking for a curriculum director. He countered with the names of two local curriculum men, and I indicated that they were in different districts . . . He asked me who the superintendent was, and I replied that he was new and his name was Joe Ebel from Oregon. He then commented that he would have to give him a call (5/11).

One day later the notes contained this item:

> Jerl also indicated that he had called Joe Ebel yesterday afternoon and that he has an appointment for today. The speed with which that came about suggests that he's very concerned about his own position and about the system generally (5/12).

A week later the notes contained this entry:

> Jerl and I talked at great length about his own career plans. He is looking very hard for a job, essentially because he thinks Steven is leaving, as I have indicated previously in the notes. Basically the alternatives that he proposes for himself are first, a superintendency; second, an assistant superintendency in charge of curriculum; and third, a college or university professorship (5/18).

Paralleling Jerl's decision making were those of every staff member at Kensington. Item No. 8 in *Bulletin No. 58* continues to show the district's efforts to staff its schools.

"8. *Applicants for Principalships.* Any teachers interested in applying for a position as elementary principal have been invited to submit a letter of application to the personnel office" (5/27).

As we have indicated, Tom Mack became principal of Kensington for the summer school, and the following year he assumed the principalship of another school in the Milford District. In passing, we point out that Bill Kirkham, an important figure in the workshop, did not receive a principalship in Milford, nor was he reappointed at Kensington as he wished. He left the district after one year.

The introductory epilogue has sketched the ramifications of teacher turnover, administrative succession, and the decisions to participate.

Bridging the gap between career problems, on the one hand, and the organizational planning for the following year is an item we have called "making teaching livable." In the spring field notes we speculated on this dimension of the educational scene.

> Another aspect that crept in from time to time concerns people like Jean and Meg who are what I would call career teachers, and the ways in which they try to make the job more satisfying to themselves. For instance, although they work hard and put in long after-school hours they would prefer, it seems to me, to have this kind of thing occurring only in peak or stressful points instead of being continuous. They also seem to be on the lookout for various ways in which they can get support that will make the course of their day go more smoothly. For instance, they were talking about having aides who would supervise the kids outside and who would supervise the kids at lunchtime. The intent here is to gain some time free of the kids that can be used for a combination of paper grading and easy socializing among themselves. This appeared (it seems to me) to exist throughout the early Basic Skills days in our temporary quarters at Milford High School. Over there they had things down to a "T," or at least to a coffee break. This fits with my own growing concern for criteria around teaching other than pupil learning but related to satisfactions in the profession. In terms of general learning theory they might well be considered reinforcers that are important in maintaining teacher behavior apart from its acquisition and general development. Most certainly, I would guess that it will be related to staying in the profession.

Those who were staying were trying to shape small parts of the organization in ways that would bring the small but regular satisfactions which make a job livable. Professional education's inability to specify the issues involved remains a major omission to understanding the workings of school organizations.[5]

---

[5] That this aspect can be emphasized and distorted to the point of horror is clearly recognized. In a hospital setting, this dimension in its most extreme and negative form has been described vividly in Kesey's (1962) novel, *One Flew over the Cuckoo's Nest.*

Organizational Events and Arrangements: The May Twenty-Fourth Faculty Meeting

On May 24, Kensington held a faculty meeting for those teachers who anticipated returning the second year and for two new teachers who had already been hired. We reconstruct this meeting in some detail, since the content and structure indicate another view of Kensington. The direct reporting of the items under discussion—the manner in which they were raised, and the reaction to them—has a potency of its own.

At 3:55 P.M., Shelby, the principal, two new staff members for next year, and several of the current staff, Claire and Meg from Transition, Jean and Sarah from Basic Skills, Liz from ISD, and Tom Mack, the materials coordinator, all gathered. They awaited the arrival of Irma. Later, Wanda came in.

The first part of the notes is as follows:

> 3:55 P.M. The meeting awaits Irma and a couple of others. She arrives. Eugene presents the agenda: representatives, strategic objectives of school next year, not the generality of fully functioning nor the specificity of objectives in reading. Introduces two new members: Jan and Barbara.
>
> (*Observer.* The meeting is kind of fun: easy conversation and joking back and forth. Eugene is in good humor. Claire has joked about carpet and the need for vacuuming, etc.)

The seating arrangement was a follows:

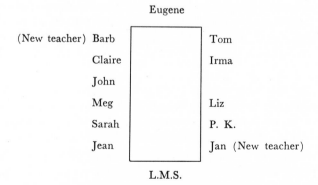

Eugene talks of Parent Council meeting and the need for representatives.
(*Observer.* Hard to get anyone to volunteer.)
(*Observer.* He is playing role of democratic administrator.)

Edith nominates Jean for salary committee. She declines.
John and Claire volunteer for Parent Council.
With humor they nominate back and forth.

4:07 P.M. Wanda comes in.

Discussion continues back and forth. Wanda withdraws her name because of baby-sitting problems. Meg is elected by acclamation.

The Parent Council has four volunteers: John, Claire, Liz, and Tom. Barbara volunteers. Jean does also and says: "Don't know what's involved but I'm game, too." Jan suggests that she and Barbara be alternates, but Eugene pushes for a written ballot.

John and Claire receive the most votes. The others become alternates.

Beyond the interpretations included in the report, we notice several additional aspects: (1) the principal set the agenda; (2) the shift back and forth from good-humored and easy consensus to voting as the procedural methods is still with the staff.

Shelby then speaks of "bringing you up to date on things as I see them." This included items with strong emotional content: "this year has provided a strong foundation . . . move forward next year . . . can say for certain that things will be better next year than this . . . had hardships, struggles, problems and challenges."

A second set of issues dealt with Kensington's relationships with the rest of the Milford District. These ties were financial, political, and organizational. For instance, he commented: "Until the levy is decided we're not sure. . . . Kensington must live within the regular operating budget . . . 40 percent reduction in custodial budget . . . reduction in two teacher aides . . . budget for supplies the same except no longer a new school with contributions from several companies . . . more and better planning in use of materials budget . . . interns turned down by the board . . . one board member said the people were tired of everything going to Kensington." The observer put an interpretive aside into the notes: (*Observer*. Contingent planning is major impact of district-wide problems. Can't really plan.)

The gradual dissolution of the protected subculture, the equity with other district schools, the pressure on resources, and the "more and better planning" seem to be relevant inferences in terms of our broader analytic schemes.

The faculty discussion turned more toward internal issues, the first of which concerned student teachers. It went this way.

Liz asks if there will be student teachers.

Eugene comments, "It depends on whether we want them." Asks for expression of opinion.

Wanda: "I'm for it."

Claire says, "We'll be in better condition to help them. Know better what we'll do."

Liz says one per team in ISD?

Eugene asks, "Any not want one?"
John asks for one also, "I would like one if he's hale and hearty."
Claire comments: "Might not be a he."
Joking and laughter ré male or female, hale and hearty.

Claire's spontaneous comment on helping echoes our interpretations regarding experience, socialization into the profession, and teaming.

Eugene presented a plan for reorganization and indicated that staffing and budgeting could change the plan. Discussion occurred on splitting fourth graders between Transition and ISD and equal numbers of 7-, 8-, and 9-year-olds in two Basic Skills Divisions. Doubts and pros and cons were expressed. The observer wrote the following in an interpretive aside. (*Observer.* The doubts over pupil grouping is a major crack in the nongraded point of view.) The discussion continued on kinds of resource persons—music, creative arts, science, math, and P.E. Jean raised a suggestion for a team of six in Basic Skills instead of two teams of three. She saw this as more flexible. The teacher aides, which they wanted, had been taken out of the budget and could be "bought" only by sacrificing a teaching position and thereby raising the teacher-pupil ratio. The discussion continued through the loss of the administrative intern, the social worker, and the elementary counselor. Wanda expressed concern that the kindergarten room was to be converted to classroom space and she might end up with a basement room, which she does not like.

Plans for a two-week summer workshop were contingent on foundation support. Eugene thought that this was not probable. He hoped they might meet for a few days on their own, especially the new teachers.

In like manner the complications of the materials budget were raised. Eugene commented that he and Tom had been trying to straighten it out. They did not want any of the current money to lapse, and they were "trying to keep new funds unencumbered." The problems lay in this year's $10,000 budget being cut to $2500. The reading committee had already turned in requests of $1800. Approximately $500 of mathematics materials had been requested. As the discussion continued, Eugene indicated that about $1000 of consumable ABC materials had been used this year. (The observer noted: The economy of the text is very critical here. This kind of schooling, individualized curriculum and instruction, is very expensive.) Several "facts" were clarified: no members of the staff were clear about budget limitations; the establishment of priorities had to be made and hard decisions would be required; the bearing of materials or supplies on individualized programs were to be part of Kensington's exploration; and "free" materials were found not to be so free.

At 5 P.M., Claire and John left; the meeting continued. Eugene raised the question of "strategic objectives" for next year. Although he had a list of items that he wanted raised as objectives and issues for next year, he hesitated to present it. He introduced a specific item—Alec Thurman's rationale for decision making. The issue concerned who makes what decisions in a district committed to rational decision making. Jean questioned the meaning of "rationale" in this context and asked if Alec had a specific incident in mind. She commented that she has seen "no clear distinction among decisions by individual staff members, collected staff, and the principal." She referred to the organizational chart handed out earlier in the day and asked, "May I change it this summer?" The conflicts over the use of the theatre and art room were raised. And the voice of the new teachers "not just the old ones deciding" was entertained.

After Eugene wrote "Rationale for decision making" on the chalkboard, the group moved to other problems. Liz raised what became item No. 2, Clarify relationships among professionals, nonprofessionals, and pupils. Meg contributed the third item, More interdivisional work for children, which Irma expanded to include faculty coordination among divisions. As she said, "I never had any idea of what's going on elsewhere." Tom raised No. 4, Program evaluation by staff. Irma countered with, "Is there some need to have program expectations before evaluation, or is that impossible?" which brought smiles to several. Eugene commented, "I was waiting for that one," and wrote No. 5, Curriculum development.

Item No. 6, Inservice training, No. 7, Improve relations with other schools in the district, and No. 8, Community relations, all arose rapidly in the discussion. Eugene had commented that curriculum development "will have to be done locally." In expanding on this, he commented that the school's purposes had included educating the Kensington pupils, helping the Milford District in a number of ways, and making a contribution to American education. He continued, "My own feeling is that next year we should emphasize local need. The other goals require additional financial and human resources. We must be realistic." In the notes, the observer interpreted this as "Critical!!" In this context, visits to other schools were raised by Liz, and Wanda indicated apprentices might be used for this, as the city public schools do. Eugene broadened this to ". . . improving relationships with the other schools in the district." The discussion veered into a brief question as to whether these were curriculum objectives or institutional objectives. Regardless of the label, the group felt they would be useful for evaluation a year from that time.

The final item, No. 10, Formalize record keeping, grew out of a discussion initiated by Irma who was worried that the only official record of the child's work would be on the report card he carried home. Permanent records, cards, and folders entered the discussion, and a considerable lack of clarity was evident in terms of what kinds of records were to be kept, by whom, and which ones had carbons, and who would enter them on the forms. Irma's comment, "I can't trust myself to remember all of them. I feel we've been slipshod this year," was indicative of the problems. Eugene commented that as principal he would not require them to fill in comments along with grades. "If we do, we could make a staff decision. Do you want to make a motion?" The discussion continued regarding diagnostic help and the similarities to brief physician's record cards. The observer noted (*Observer:* This is interesting in contrast with the big diagnostic sheet on all kids that the Curriculum Committee worked on.) Eugene tried once again for a motion. None was forthcoming. He urged them to write comments. Irma expressed concern that she had not kept a summary record of the parent conferences. Eugene reacted, "I didn't know it's been given up." A few additional comments were made and at 5:44 p.m. he asked if there was anything else. There was nothing. He thanked them for attending the first meeting of next year's staff. The meeting was over.

Although we might editorialize on aspects of the meeting, the ten items, the tenor of the meeting, and its format speak for themselves.

THE END OF THE STORY

Field work methodology has few clear rules as to when to end a project. Informally we have argued with our colleagues that the time to quit arrives when one runs out of insights, new ideas, and theoretical hunches. In early March, the field notes record summary observations on an informal coffee klatch conversation.

> After spending part of the morning chatting with several of the teachers, observing very briefly some of the projects and materials that are in the Perception Core, and watching the beginning of the testing in ISD, the major reaction that I have is that I am ready to begin writing about the school. I keep feeling that the same story is coming up again and again as I observe. For instance, as we talked over coffee, we got to discussing the music program and the lack thereof. He commented about how he likes to hear in an elementary school the kids singing from time to time and then, as he put it, "maybe the teachers will learn one day that to take a break and engage the entire group (and he used as an illustration the 90 kids in Transition) in singing would be quite beneficial for the whole program." This immediately raised in my own mind issues about the nature of inexperience and the importance of that phenomenon in the school. This is an old idea and one that I have elaborated on from time to time in the notes, and about which I do not have any more insights. This is interrelated with the team teaching notions of having highly developed skills and specializations among some of the people. This, too, is an old idea and needs to be developed, yet I have no more insights on it than I had a month or two ago. We talked briefly about the

social studies program. His comments centered around his interest and concern about "democracy." He could not detect any kind of experiences that were helping the kids learn respect for individuals, respect for property, and the like. This discussion came out of the issues of the minor disciplinary problems that they were having. He viewed the behavior of the upper grade kids as behavior they long since should have gotten over. Here, too, the critical notions of the conflict between independent study and interdependence is an old part of the story and an issue that they have not resolved and an issue that they do not see clearly conceptually, and is one about which we should be prepared to write. I was struck in the Perception Core by the activity aspects of the program around science projects, with molds, with ants, etc., the art projects that decorate the walls, and the contests that some of the children want to have. This, too, is an old story and one that is ready to be written. We have some clarity also in the kinds of objectives that they set themselves, that is away from a specified content in say science and social studies, and we can talk to the issue of the differences in points of view about goals and within that context put the kinds of means and kinds of experiences that they have been engaging in, for example, Kay's stock market kinds of things, and make sense out of it. In short, what I seem to be saying is that the school's at an equilibrium and that we have a tremendous amount of information about the genesis of that equilibrium. In the vernacular, "It's time to have at it," the analysis and the writing (3/2).

At 3:30 P.M. Friday afternoon, the fourth of June, the observation was finally over. The field notes captured that too.

I can't help but comment as I drive in, off West Milford Boulevard, that everything looks so green and warm and pleasant, and that summer is here. There's almost a pastoral quality to the community. The frantic, innovative year is gone. Life seems to be going on (6/4).

SECTION **IV**

Conclusion

CHAPTER 11

The Kensington Model of Educational Innovation

INTRODUCTION

For many years, public speakers and writers have contended that a speech or an essay should be determined in part by the audience to whom it is directed. More recently, the systems theorists have made a similar point, the elements and relationships built into a system vary dramatically with one's purpose. Hare (1967) illustrates this neatly with a simple road map system that contains two parallel lines and two circles. The elements are the cities and the relationships are the highways. He comments:

". . . the elements and the relationships . . . have been carefully selected to achieve a specific purpose—illustration of the interstate highway system in the area—and the choice of elements and relationships . . . is relevant to that end . . . In defining a system, the matter of relevance is all important. What happens within the boundary of our map could be described in many different ways—by a drawing, by equations, by a physical model, or by a verbal description. *However, unless the elements and relationships to be considered within the map's borders are selected for a specific purpose, an infinite number of connections and combinations would be possible* [Our italics].

"Let us elaborate for emphasis. The observer of this landscape could paint it, draw a topological map, write equations of the traffic flow passing through it, classify the flora and fauna there, develop a history of the area, examine and relate the chemical content of its soil and streams, or make a study of how religious belief affects local law, to mention a few of the projects that could illustrate *some* kind of relationship in the scene. But the investigator would hardly care to undertake all of these projects at one time (p. 14).

The potency of theoretical relevance follows from our affirmation that we want our monograph to be useful to the educational administrator

365

who is contemplating the possibility of innovation in his school. The theory we have been developing is one that will enable him to analyze his situation clearly, to anticipate hazards, and to create mechanisms and solutions to the problems that arise. In essence, we hope to make him more of a professional in the administration of educational organizations than he would be without having read our narrative and having considered our theoretical stance. Consequently, the theory should have some, but less, relevance to parents involved in community action, to teachers who are involved in day-to-day instruction in innovative programs, or to college professors who have ideological commitments to particular innovations. Such has been our choice throughout the book. The last chapter continues that effort. The move toward a summary and conclusion will include aspects of the Milford-Kensington strategy of innovation. We will blend both the manifest, which was verbalized by the district leadership, and the latent, which we found implicit in the activities and interaction of the participants. To these data we bring additional and alternative conceptions that clarify and extend the analysis and complete the picture. To some extent, we review earlier aspects of the analysis.

For purposes of clarity we organize our interpretations into three major discussions. The alternative of grandeur was an overriding strategy of innovation; multiple changes were made in the system. The decision to innovate in this manner had repercussions throughout the system during the entire year—and later as well. Second, widespread use was made of a number of temporary systems. The summer workshop, the protected subculture, and the consultants are exemplars of this strategy. Our data suggest that the broader label and conception that is, temporary systems, were not part of the verbal behavior of the leadership. The third major element we have called "minimal prior commitments." The accent was on youth, inexperience, and the absence of prior structures. Once again, the overall category is ours; the data indicate that the elements were treated as specifics, except insofar as they were part of the alternative of grandeur.

In short, we hope to come full circle in our description and analysis of Kensington and in our interpretation of an anatomy of educational innovation.

THE ALTERNATIVE OF GRANDEUR: A STRATEGY OF INNOVATION

The Rationale and the Realities. When one begins to change a society, an institution, or a school, the system interlinkages present an ever-increasing multiplicity of items open for change. This poses the decision of the degree of change to be attempted. Our observations of Kensington suggest that they chose what we have called "the alternative of grandeur": the change was to be pervasive. This decision had a number of important consequences. As we have stated several times, the strategies of educational innovation were not high in our initial research priorities, although we were intrigued from the start with some of the specific innovative procedures, for example, T-grouping, nongradedness, and team teaching. Nonetheless, our speculations on innovative strategy and tactics began to crystalize in September. Two early interpretations in the notes specify our questioning on Friday of the first week of school.

> It is now 11:15; I have just had a short conversation with Dan who is supervising on the playground at Hillside[1] and a short conversation with Paul who has just come in from Basic Skills. Dan tells me that they have decided for the next few days to group heterogeneously into three smaller sections and to each run what amounts to a self-contained program. Paul says that Chris told him that this was essentially because of the girls' desires and that Dan wanted to keep the large group going for a little while longer. Meg and Claire are upset around the discipline issue. With the large group they find that they have to be too autocratic and too directive and have to tell the kids to stop doing so many things. Neither one of them liked this. Dan commented also that they had not had time to plan and that they did not have enough for the kids to do in the large group activities. He also said that it was very difficult to get any kind of sequence to the lessons. This seems to me to be the essence of the textbook problem versus the hit and miss "activity" type approach. My own guess is that this group will not go back to any systematic team teaching, except for the minimal kinds of things like music and maybe occasionally P.E., because of the difficulty in implementing the curricular areas. The question will come up then as to what sort of pressure is brought to bear by Eugene with regard to the Kensington ideal.
>
> It suggests also that the sequence for innovation might better be to play one's cards hard and strong, that is, through the self-contained classroom, and then move step by step gradually into the shift.[2] As it stands now, the total shift has been overwhelming and the people have retreated (9/11).

The array of difficulties facing the Transition Division seemed to pose insurmountable problems and to force them back to more conventional kinds of adaptations. At this point, our theoretical analysis suggests that the concepts of unanticipated consequences, unintended outcomes, and the magnitude of resources are vital to anyone contemplating change. A more pervasive change is accompanied by more unanticipated events. The more

[1] This is the public school where Transition was located during the first months of school.
[2] At another point we spoke of this as the additive versus the differentiated strategy in moving toward team teaching.

outcomes that are unanticipated, the greater becomes the need for additional resources both to implement the program and to respond to the increased variety introduced by the unintended events. A step-by-step gradual shift would seem to temper this chain of events.

Implicit also in our *in situ* observation is a phenomenon that has received considerably less emphasis, "playing one's cards hard and strong," which seems to mean in more social psychological terms maximizing one's rewards and credits. As a job is done well, it redounds, not only in minimizing the numerous new problems, but it also enables you to build esteem and positive affect among relevant others, for example, pupils and staff. As this esteem increases, one has a resource to spend on less happy, more difficult occasions. This resource amounts to the willingness of participants to accept influence, to discount occasional less adequate future performances, and a willingness to try and to initiate varied activities. Such a resource, so it seems to us, is not one to disregard lightly.

On Monday morning, September 14, the observer, in contemplating the one self-contained class and the modified departmentalization in ISD, made these remarks:

> There is no question but that the school now is much more like a traditional school. There is an instructional program, of some sort, going on in each of the areas. In one teacher's judgment, this is the way they probably should have started and then, as things worked out branched off into the way they wanted to go. This, as we have talked before, is perhaps the most interesting and strategic aspect of innovation that we have come across. It's what I would describe as building from one's strength and then moving into new programs, as opposed to moving dramatically, whole-hog into new programs (9/14).

As we have tried to analyze the change strategy, we developed the conception of the alternative of grandeur. We speculated that such an alternative is a high risk strategy with potentially large rewards. One makes the big gambit, by capitalizing on the high degree of system interdependence. If the pieces are finely honed and the machinery smoothly interlocked, the system takes off; if not, then the problems are momentous.

In December, long after the ISD retreat to more subteaming and self-contained classrooms, original goals were still being pursued by some. As John was trying to move the physical education program forward, he ran into problems that the alternative of grandeur was designed to solve. We recorded it this way:

> Yesterday he and Eugene talked at great length as they tried to lay out objectives, curriculum activities, and schedules. The roadblock lies in most of the ISD teachers wanting the kids out in a block at a particular time. In effect,

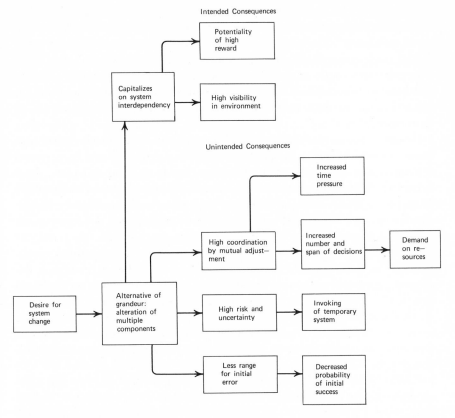

Figure 11.1 The implications of the alternative of grandeur as an innovation strategy.

until they all go on an individualized schedule, he won't be able to. In his eyes, only David is operating in this fashion. (*Observer.* This observation recurs of David as the only one who is in keeping with basic philosophy and mode of approach—as originally conceived—yet he is the one most likely to be replaced.)[3] (12/11)

In short, the simultaneous change in persons, interactions, programs, and structures illustrates the strengths and weaknesses of the high degree of interdependency implicit in the alternative of grandeur.

We developed the model in Figure 11.1 to handle the hypotheses implicit

---

[3] Elsewhere we have described the rising and ebbing of David's enthusiasm, influence, and closeness to Eugene and Kensington.

in the alternative of grandeur. As we have indicated, the major intended consequences seemed to lie in what we have called "capitalizing on system interdependency." The physical education illustration makes the point beautifully. High rewards seem to exist for members of the system when these reorganizations occur and run well. The consequences in terms of visibility and notoriety from being in the mainstream of educational innovation are important, as we have indicated in our discussion of the consequences of Kensington's facade.

However, the harder realities of Kensington appeared as well. By concentrating on the alteration of multiple components, there was a higher level of uncertainty. In settings that are more variable and unpredictable, there is greater reliance on coordination by mutual adjustment as analyzed by Thompson (1967) or on coordination by feedback as presented by March and Simon (1958). Coordination by mutual adjustment is accompanied, in turn, by an increase in unintended outcomes. Changes in a number of components simultaneously, as well as responding to unintended events, increase both the number and span of decisions. Although there is a decreased probability of success in initial activities, there also is an increased demand on both internal and environmental resources. Time pressures increase, and as scholars, for example, March and Simon (1958), argue, spans of attention decrease and time perspectives narrow. Many of the problems we attended to in our discussion of teaming reappear at this broader organizational level.

Gradualism: An Alternative Strategy. After we had phrased the Kensington strategy of innovation as "the alternative of grandeur," we became acquainted with Etzioni's (1966) essay, "A gradualist strategy at work." Our reading of this case-study essay of the European Economic Community, EEC, suggests the broader theoretical significance of the kind of analysis we have been attempting. He contrasts a revolutionary strategy, our alternative of grandeur, with a strategy of gradualism. His broad generalization, "aim high, score low: aim low, score high," supports the gradualist position. In his analysis, a strong negative correlation exists between the level of ambition and the degree of success. The mediating mechanisms underlying these results are several, and they contrast with the dynamics observed at Kensington.

First, he suggests amplifying the close and underplaying the remote. The accent is on the immediate concrete problems instead of on longer range goals and implications. Kensington, it will be recalled, split over the "process-substance" issue, that is, the abstract versus the nitty-gritty, during the first week. Also, many staff members accented a futuristic orientation, a part of the larger issue of crusading and true belief. Second, he argues for "phasing of adjustments," that is, making all the changes, adjustments, and sacrifices into many small and almost insignificant steps. Essentially this reduces resistance to change. Our data suggest it is important because of availability of resources and skills as well. Third, "phasing supranationality" means, in organizational terms, that you allow the development and initial formation of subunits—"institutions, sentiments, and vested interests." In our case the initial accent was on total school policy instead of on initial team or divisional resolutions of issues. Fourth, he introduces the concept of "stretch-outs," giving the participants an opportunity to extend the period of adjustment beyond the initially agreed on interval. Kensington's initial approach argued against this, although when the "retreats" began to occur, the stretch-out conception was invoked, for example, "It'll take a little longer." Fifth, the "multi-path dimension" is an acknowledgement of the cliché, many roads lead to Rome. He argues for allowing for great variety in institutional arrangements. Kensington's complexities in this we have tried to unravel in our analyses of the Institutional Plan and the administrative process. However, as illustrated elsewhere, there was a great variety of approach even within teams. Sixth, provisions for acceleration refers, as it implies, to the fact that if momentum builds up for more rapid change, the system can tolerate it. Kensington had little need for this, since the alternative chosen presupposed immediate total change, that is, maximum acceleration. Seventh, the "locking in system" refers to procedures that prevent regression from gains that have been attained. In Kensington, regression was quite common and few mechanisms existed to prevent retreat. In some instances, the retreat was conceptualized in terms of survival, but in others the lack of surveillance, help, and resources seemed to be dominant factors. Eighth, "provision for institutional spillover" refers to a vagueness about the extent of power possessed by members from their constituents in the original mandates. This enabled the members to seek and acquire more authority and power than initially assigned to them. Once again, Kensington's formal doctrine provided for almost total staff power, but the Institutional Plan circumscribed this sharply, and the principal's style created considerable difficulty in implementing staff spillover. Ninth, the "cushioning" process involves escape clauses which allow individual members who have special problems and grievances a margin of protection. Kensington possessed few of these. We indicated previously the high level of vulnerability among participants. Those who were inexperienced, for instance, received little help.

Such is Etzioni's argument for the gradualist strategy. For the most part, it supports our analysis of Kensington as we presented our initial scheme in Figure 11.1.

In addition, it might be noted that the "one-thing-at-a-time" approach to system change is fundamental to organizational structure and stability.

The implications of attempting to deal with a multiplicity of complex alterations simultaneously seem to be indicated by the following:

"We appeal again to the principle of bounded rationality—to the limits
of human cognitive powers—to assert that in the discovery and elaboration
of new programs, the decision-making process will proceed in stages, and
at no time will it be concerned with the 'whole' problem in all of its
complexity, but always with parts of the problem" (March and Simon,
1958, p. 190).

As we have indicated in the chapter on team teaching, cooperative systems
that are characterized by reciprocal interdependence and are coordinated
by mutual adjustment have as a concomitant a high degree of variety
provided by input from the environment and in terms of the variability
created by the continuous multiplicity of decisions for which there is little
standardization. In contrast, the gradualist alternative, especially when
coupled with strength at a given point in time, maximizes the resources
on smaller changes. The risks are more moderate. The total change of
the system is a long time off and even then might not be easily visible.
One can imagine the skeptic saying: "The organization's not much different

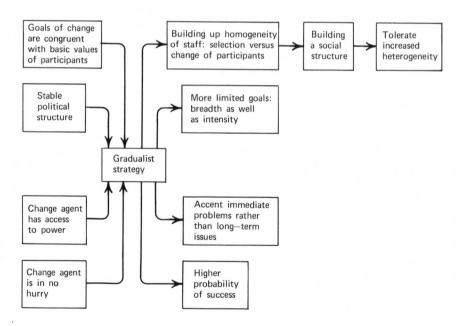

Figure 11.2 The determinants and limits of the gradualist strategy (after Etzioni,
1966, pages 64 to 78).

and always runs itself pretty well." None the less, we hypothesize that a gradualist strategy which implies an alteration of a few components involves (1) lower levels of uncertainty and fewer unintended outcomes, (2) decreased time pressure, (3) an increased interval for major change, (4) limited decisions related to the changes, and (5) decreased demand on resources will have as a concomitant the increased likelihood of success in initial goals. In turn, this increases the opportunity to create a position of strength. For both the organization and the individual incumbents, this reinforces activities, increases esteem, and leads to further change.

In a summary section on the limits of the gradualist strategy, Etzioni places a context around the point of view. Figure 11.2 sketches his latent argument. Some of the characteristics of Milford suggest reasons for the election of the alternative of grandeur as opposed to the gradualist strategy. The Milford District had a history of political conflict over a prior superintendent who was fired, rehired, and later was given a position as a districtwide consultant. Many of the changes sought by the Spanman, Cohen, and Shelby group were not congruent with the lower middle class values of the community. The leaders were cosmopolitans rather than locals; their basic commitments were to the field of education instead of to Milford per se; consequently, time was short. Etzioni's (1966) antecedents of gradualism versus grandeur seem well taken with respect to our data.[4]

TEMPORARY SYSTEMS: INNOVATIONS FACILITATING INNOVATION

Introduction

The flesh and blood of the alternative of grandeur strategy lay in the specific innovations within the school. In a sense, much of what we have related about Kensington might well belong in this section; however, as some items loomed larger and as we unraveled their complexities, we developed more extended analyses and enclosed them in self-contained chapters or larger sections. Here we accent those specific innovations that were "temporary systems," subunits of limited time and scope. Tactics such as the protected subculture, the summer workshop, and the T-group experience were part of the overall alternative of grandeur strategy. They were designed to facilitate the new program, the new organization for instruction, and the new physical plant. Furthermore, they were intended to extend the Milford-Kensington point of view about planned change in American education. Our analysis will treat them essentially as aspects of the school

---

[4] At this point we wish we were political scientists; these items seem to be exceedingly important issues needing analysis from that perspective.

which had implications for the organization as an innovative educational system.

The Protected Subculture as a Temporary System

The Point of View. Throughout the early weeks of our stay at Kensington, we heard references to the school as a "protected subculture." By this, it was meant that the school was to be isolated from the usual pressures, restraints, and directives that most elementary schools face. By categorizing it as unique or different and by treating it this way, the school could develop without the blows and the arrows of a hostile or critical environment. An analogy might be drawn to the rare plant, nurtured in the climate of a greenhouse, away from the onslaught of wind, hail, and lesser elements. More explicitly, the environment of a school is multidimensional, and the protection in a positive and negative sense became that also.

First, the superintendent's office was totally supportive. "Build a school" was his only directive to the faculty in the summer. Second, a school is a part of a bureaucracy composed of policies, rules, and procedures. Kensington had a free hand, unhampered by the usual curricular, program, and personnel requirements. As a protected subculture, Kensington was apart from them; they did not apply. Third, the majority of the school board had been convinced of the worthiness of the school's doctrine and the necessity of giving it a fair trial. A minority member or two attempted to stir up the community but the school was protected from their direct influence. Fourth, although the Milford School District was beset with numerous problems and conflicts, and although Kensington often was cited at board meetings and in the newspapers as an exemplar of the community conflict, the direct pressures went no farther than this during most of the year. The principal and faculty were protected.

Kensington's relationship with its own patrons could not be specified quite so clearly, since the protective mantle was not intended to be applied pervasively. The school worked long and intensively with the parents in open meetings and in the Parent Council. These meetings frequently involved emotional confrontations, since a number of parents felt continuing dissatisfaction with what they perceived to be the instructional program received by their children. A form of protection existed nonetheless from the superintendent and the board president. Both had children in the school and both attended meetings "outside" their organizational roles. They came as supportive parents. Furthermore, the patrons of the school knew explicitly, as did the patrons in the district more generally, that the central administration supported the school.

Comparabilities with TVA. During January, the investigators noted the relevance and parallels of Kensington and Selznick's (1949) account of

TVA as an organization. In a long dictated set of field notes those parallels were explicitly drawn. We include excerpts from those notes as they bear on the protected subculture strategy.

In the official doctrine, Lilienthal appeals to a distinction between centralized government and centralized administration. He argues a need for centralized government but a need for decentralized administration. In this sense, one has the resources to deal with national problems and yet, at the same time, one has the autonomy to deal with the specific regional variations. The latter, hypothetically, develops and enhances initiative, autonomy, and creativity.

This point is reflected in a number of conversations that go back in the Kensington program to the beginning of August. In the superintendent's first remarks he commented to the faculty that they were a "protected community," or something very similar to that. Just yesterday (1/12) in Eugene's comments to Jerl and Steven S. he remarked that the district curriculum policy was applicable to everyone but the Kensington school and staff.

The consequences of having one part of the organization as a special and protected community seem very much in need of analysis. In this sense, the parallels with TVA would be the reaction of other governmental departments and agencies toward a part of the structure that is subject only to the direct control of the President and the Congress and not through a long channel of administrative hierarchy. The reaction of the principals to this in Milford would be most significant.

In Selznick's terms, the minimum essentials for actual decentralization are three: (1) managerial autonomy—the responsible agency in the area of operations is permitted the freedom to make significant decisions on its own account; (2) partnership of TVA in local government—there must be active participation by the people themselves in the programs of the public enterprise; (3) regional unity—the decentralized administrative agency is given a key role in coordinating the work of state, local, and federal programs in its area of operation, and a regional development agency should be given primary responsibility to deal with the resources of the area as a unified whole (pages 28 to 29).

By "managerial autonomy" the TVA people meant essentially freedom from control by the Civil Service Commission in personnel policies, freedom from control by the central accounting office in determining and judging budgets and financial expenses and, third, freedom to apply revenues to current operational expenses. The first two aspects of this seem to apply very heavily to the Kensington program. In the TVA freedom from control by civil service, the intent apparently was to keep hostile people out of the authority and to prevent spying and special profiteering by people from business and power interests. As Selznick reports, there was considerable conflict over this part of the TVA bill. Selznick comments: "The advantages of autonomous control over personnel policy, safeguarded by the merit and efficiency section of the Act, lies in the ability of the agency to choose the kind of men it wants, on the basis of an implicit theory of a close relation between personnel and policy, and thus to shape the character of the organization in the unified direction. The organization may then rely on the weight of personality and group attitudes within its structure for the implementation of policy rather than solely on administrative rules" (1949, p. 32).

Our data would suggest that Kensington has attempted to do the same kind of thing, and that this has provoked considerable friction between Eugene and Howard, one of the people in the central office who does most of the hiring. Insofar as Eugene has not had some control over this, he has been sabotaged, or at least thinks he has, by ineffective people being unloaded on him in secretarial, custodial, and cafeteria personnel. The resolution of conflict that an enclave of this sort seems to establish, as a favorite son, does not seem to be well discussed in the literature.

In the TVA the General Accounting office of the government has the power to assess the legality of expenditures by several departments: "This power is embodied in a procedure which makes it possible for the Comptroller General to disallow expenditures by refusing payment when a particular transaction is deemed illegal" (p. 33). Freedom from this kind of control was deemed necessary by the TVA people. The parallels in the Kensington situation are striking and can be documented throughout the notes of the attempts on Eugene's part to maintain fiscal independence, of Howard's office especially. They have been given gifts of materials and equipment and they have bought materials and equipment far beyond the usual budget restrictions. Eugene's point of view, which he has told me directly, is to buy what he thinks is necessary and to worry about the budget later. He has not attempted to keep supply figures within the grounds usually accepted by the other elementary school principals. Once again, this seems to me to be a major source of his conflict with the lower echelon of the central office and with his peers, the other principals.

Since Kensington has no revenue sources, this general point about TVA seems not to apply.

The one other point that seems most significant in the Kensington situation is the relationship between Jerl Cohen and Shelby. In the curriculum work, insofar as Eugene seems to be a threat, Jerl has attempted to coopt Eugene. From the early comments that Eugene has made about the minor degree of help that Jerl has been to him, my guess is that this would break out into open conflict if Steven Spanman and the rewards he has at his command were not present. Kensington, its Institutional Plan including its curriculum, is Eugene's baby and he has long felt this and does not want anyone interfering or taking credit.

The partnership of TVA and the people's institutions in the official doctrine has both an administrative motivational dimension, that is, participation makes for commitment and, second, a moral dimension reflected in the position that leadership in a democracy must offer people alternatives for free choice instead of ready-made prescriptions elaborated in planning agencies.

On these points, it seems to me that there is a fundamental difference between the TVA program and the Kensington program. In a word, Eugene is no David Lilienthal. However, at the doctrine level there is very little difference in the TVA statements and the Kensington statements. In fact, Kensington might even express it more strongly in that the pupils, then the teacher, and then the principal, must establish the direction and the policy of the work. Perhaps, it is the difference in the working organization rather than in the express policy that is critical here.

Another aspect of this is reflected in the statement, "in developing these relationships [with local governmental institutions] TVA has applied the rule that 'wherever possible, the Authority shall work toward achieving its objectives by utilizing or stimulating the developing of state and local organizations, agencies, and institutions, rather than conducting direct action programs'" (p. 39). In the Kensington situation the parent groups, whether they be PTA's, parent councils, mothers' clubs, or other organizations, have had only a limited invitation to the working of the school. To determine exactly what the doctrine is on this, I would have to check back into the records and the formal statements. In actuality, Eugene has dominated and controlled the formation and nature of the parent council to a very high degree. We have notes and direct quotations concerning the "control" of the agenda, the records, and the policy.

The idea of general participation involves stimulating local responsibility, developing relevent programs, avoiding duplication of efforts, minimizing hostility and resentment, and conserving resources.

The regional unity idea has, in Selznick's words, "a characteristic spiritual lesson." This refers to "a fundamental human responsibility for the prudent utilization of natural resources" (p. 43). The label the TVA puts on this is a concept of "Common Mooring" which comes from a point of view of a man named Morgan who was one of the original members of the TVA board. As Selznick continues to present the doctrine, he comments, "the unified approach made possible by a single agency is a needed antidote for the division of the universe made necessary by specialization" (p. 43).

There are strong overtones of this kind of outlook in the Kensington situation. In a sense, the school with its own local population is attempting to recreate and rethink all of the classical issues of education as they pertain to this group of 500 students. The administrative reorganization, a curriculum reorganization, the teaching reorganization, the materials reorganization, and so forth, suggest the breadth and catholicity of outlook. Interestingly in this regard, I have not heard any special discussion of the particular geographical area and community that Kensington serves. There have been no special comments about the occupational level of the parents, the educational aspirations, or the special conditions that prevail. Last night's meeting with David's parent group would suggest that the parents have a strong concern for the articulation with the junior high program and for the meeting of some kind of minimal standards. Another minority was strong in support of the individual child's opportunity to progress into unusual and more complex activities, as the child is able. To this point there has been no attempt to work with a committee or a group in the junior high school to articulate this program with their program. There has been no attempt to come to grips with parental demands for minimum essentials and meeting with parents regarding these. The tact of independence, own levels, responsibility, etc. is at the heart of the Kensington doctrine and has been spread as such (Field notes, 1/13).

The nature and scope of protected subcultures and the interplay between organizational issues and political issues suggest to us important vistas for educational theorists as well as for the practicing administrator. Seldom does the innovater cast his problems and analysis in these broader terms. The data and the analogy suggest this as highly necessary and desirable.

Implications of Kensington as a Protected Subculture. As we viewed the situation, the protected subculture phenomenon was a major idea in the strategy of innovation of Kensington. Internal unintended negative consequences occurred in the aggrandizement effect, the false overestimation of capabilities and accomplishments. The external consequences lay in the disruption of the usual organizational chains of command, the authority relationships in the central office, and the unfavorable comparisons with other buildings and their staffs, especially the principals. This kind of status incongruency produced considerable negative sentiment, and from these sentiments came some alleged minor sabotage and blocking of Kensington's program. Figure 11.3 contains this analysis.

Interpretations of Temporary Systems: Lewin and Miles. A number of years ago Kurt Lewin (1951) developed a provocative analysis of social change. The major thrust occurred through an analogy: social change involved the unfreezing, moving, and refreezing of group standards. Social devices, and their theoretical counterparts, worked in one or more of the phases. The "unfreezing" or dissolution of prior group standards, he suggests, is facilitated by: (1) "an emotional stir up" such as catharsis, (2) isolation or the creation of "cultural islands," and (3) group decision. Moving or changing the level of group standards has been invoked by lecture methods and group decision. Lewin's (1951) data accent group decision, but these early studies did not separate the group processes from the devices involved. The impact of group decision, according to Lewin, also has a major impact on refreezing group standards.

"The decision links motivation to action and, at the same time, seems to have a 'freezing' effect which is partly due to the individual's tendency to 'stick to his decision' and partly to the 'commitment to a group' " (Lewin, 1951, p. 233).

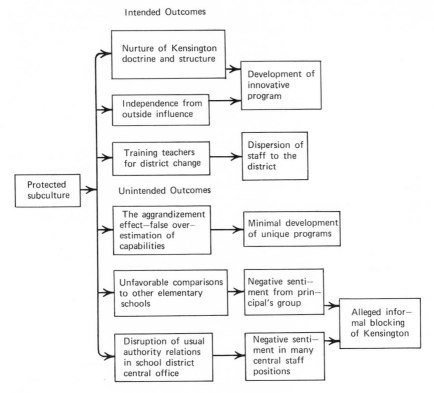

Figure 11.3 The consequences of the protected subculture as a temporary system.

Beyond the group decision, Lewin argues that "refreezing" occurs also because of the institution of new social structures that facilitates and supports the new level. In his example, the housewife who has decided to increase milk consumption puts in a standing order with the milkman. Less attention has been given to the "cultural island" aspect. He comments:

"The effectiveness of camps or workshops in changing ideology or conduct depends in part on the possibility of creating such 'cultural islands' during change. The stronger the accepted subculture of the workshop and the more isolated it is the more will it minimize that type of resistance to change which is based on the relation between the individual and the standards of the larger group" (pp. 232–233).

Throughout our analysis we have indicated how the interplay of activities, interactions, and sentiments constantly generated variety, strain, and stress that contributed to a continuous process of structural elaboration and re-

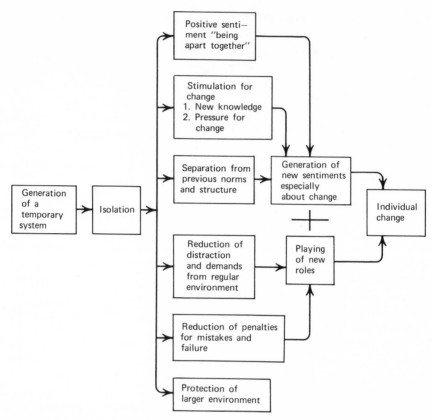

Figure 11.4 An interpretation of the theory underlying the "protected subculture" after Miles (1964) and Lewin (1951).

organization. Purposive concepts such as "freezing," "moving," "refreezing," appear somewhat static and oversimplified in the view that we have generated of the beginnings of Kensington as a complex adaptive system.

Miles' (1964) analysis of isolation in temporary systems builds heavily on Lewin's conception of cultural islands but also adds several important dimensions to the analysis. From his discussion (pp. 454–456) we have abstracted the significant elements regarding the "cultural island" or "protected subculture" dimension of the Milford School District's change strategy. Figure 11.4 hypothesizes some of the relationships that may occur when isolation is selected as a strategy of change. It indicates that sentiments toward participants, that attitudes toward general change, and that levels of knowledge are altered. It shows how separation from the constraints of norms and structures, from the distraction and demands of the day-to-day environment, and from the reduced penalties for error may generate new sentiments about change and may encourage the playing of new roles. At the same time, the larger environment is protected from any major error that may occur within the temporary system. The separation of the school and making it, in part, a temporary system was an element of the alternative of grandeur. Moreover, the notion of protected subculture as a strategy of social change has been utilized long before Kensington; isolation usually has been an integral part of utopian attempts. It is not surprising then that theorists and practitioners concerned with change and innovation would attempt to integrate the concept into their work.

Total Staff Summer Workshop

To our knowledge, a month's workshop for a total staff of an elementary school is an unusual if not unheard of phenomenon. At Kensington, as we described in Chapters 3 and 4, it was a reality. The intended consequences were to build the staff into a smooth-working unit and to develop concrete teaching plans for the year. As it turned out, neither of these objectives was accomplished to a high degree.

In an important sense we have a temporary system, another cultural island, developed within a larger system for the purposes of facilitating the larger system. The timing of the workshop (in August prior to the school year), the content of the workshop (T-groups, team meetings, curriculum meetings, and individual work), and the dynamics of the workshop have been explored in great detail in earlier chapters. An additional issue, in our opinion, must be mentioned—the problems in the language available for examining teaching, children, and school organization. At this point in time, professional education, both as a science and as an art, remains so much a personal kind of experience that it is difficult to talk productively about it without having common concrete experiences. The language is very inexplicit and carries so many multiple referents for each term that it is not until one is in the concrete situation that the intended meanings become clear. Not until this point does one translate ideas into behavioral terms, that is who says what to whom, who does that at what time, and who moves where in what specific situation. The language problems seem so fundamental that any temporary system that comes early, that involves people unknown to one another, and that hopes to produce specific and concrete plans is open to serious question. In an important and real sense, we hope that we have contributed to a resolution of this state of affairs through our descriptive narrative and theoretical interpretations.

The kinds of workshops—their objective, content, organization, participants—need further analysis and empirical investigation. Most educators, we believe, consider workshops as highly desirable, without regard to form and only restricted by limited funds. Our experience suggests that "the total staff summer workshop" does have a time and a place.[5] Kensington's was not as productive as one might hope.

The Consultant Role as a Temporary System

Innovative organizations in public education appear to be creating a new role, that of the well-paid, highly visible consultant. Miles (1964) argues that consultantships can be viewed as temporary systems. Their duration is "state-linked" or "condition-linked" to use his phraseology. That is, the relationship has system change as its goal, and the relationship is terminated when the goals are achieved, not necessarily in a specified time interval as, for instance, a month's workshop. The Kensington case suggests several subtleties that the observers as researchers perceived only gradually. In the spring, prior to the formal observing, the field notes give an account of a meeting.

> Today I met with the superintendent, the Kensington principal, a second principal, the curriculum director, and with a man from the United States Office of Education. Apparently the district is trying to obtain more additional funds related to this project than they have been able to do thus far. As I explained the project to the man from the United States office, I had the distinct feeling that I was running up against a bureaucratic type, a do-you-know-all-of-the-hot-items? sort of guy.
>
> The discussion covered a variety of people and their work: Bruce Biddle's early work at the University of Missouri which actually would be quite relevant and which I had not put into this context. He mentioned also people like Don Campbell's quasi-experimental approaches, Marie Hughes' classroom analysis, and Flanders' interaction process analysis. This very quickly became sort of a one-upmanship game. Although very interesting, I just do not like people who come in very quickly and very readily and very easily and try to tell you how to do what you are trying to do. They do not know the dimensions of the situation as you see them, and they do not know the possibilities within it. The whole implication is that they can do in 5 minutes what you have been trying to do for several weeks in working out a proposal. Presumably, this fellow is trying to be helpful and to indicate things that would improve a project. It is as if a day's talk with some "expert" would solve all of your problems and eliminate all the mistakes that you might make.

---

[5] An attempt to move these ideas further appears in Pohland, P. A., and Smith, L. M., *Pedagogical models underlying teacher workshops.* St. Ann, Mo.: CEMREL, 1970.

This is so in contrast to my own approach as to how people do research and how they improve the quality of it that it tends to make me livid. I keep wanting to ask these characters, as one of my colleagues does, "Just what research and what kind of scholarly activity have you done?"

I had not quite perceived just how much of their lives were built around this assumption that a brief talk will settle all of one's problems. When you attack that, you attack the cornerstone of their existence. (5/7, Pre-experimental year)

The observer's limited perspective toward technical rationality, that is, goal achievement in the internal functioning of the organization, set the standard for his negative evaluation. However, a distinction between the internal and external issues in which consultants engage seems most important. Thompson's (1967) conception of organizational rationality focuses on the relationship of the organization to its environment. The achievement of additional resources and inputs into the organization (in this instance both the Milford School District *and* the Kensington School) was continually on the superintendent's agenda. Consultants were a major ingredient in Spanman's strategy. Galbraith (1967) might argue that this is a special instance of subtleties in the growing technostructure as organizations try to take uncertainty out of the environment. That is, the organization attempts to insure a steady flow of funds into the organization. The twin aspects of direct influence and of a context of doing the most up-to-date prestigious activities help keep one within this part of the *Zeitgeist*.

Although norms are not available for explicit comparisons, Kensington seemed to receive amounts of consultant service that were far greater than that for the usual elementary school. The two T-group trainers were present for a week, Leslie Roberts spent the equivalent of several weeks at the school, and varied persons were available from the many commercial companies who loaned or gave materials to the school. Also, several nationally known educators and social scientists spent a few days in the school or the district. Without question, these people had impact on the school. In the view of most of the staff who also tended to focus on technical rationality, the results were a mixed blessing. At a more general level, the consultants' impact on goal achievement becomes an instance of the problems in relating a temporary system to the permanent system. Miles (1964) makes a few very brief comments under the heading of "linkage failure." When consultants "overstep" the boundaries, as Roberts allegedly did in the eyes of some of the staff in the Kirkham affair, serious negative consequences arise. Similarly, when consultants arrive and take time when one has more pressing survival demands, the effects are minimized. Finally, when one's problems are pervasive interpersonal social skills, as teaching is in part, short-term encounters seem as helpful as dew in a drought.

In summary, at Kensington, technical rationality, the ordering of organizational structures and processes for goal achievement, involved the use of consultants in early staff socialization experiences and in later program and staff modification. Milford's and Kensington's attempts to innovate through the use of consultants was a bold if not highly successful foray.

The internal-external distinction and its corollary, technical rationality versus organizational reality, seems mandatory as we discuss an illustration that falls midway between. Spanman and the Milford Board of Education hired a consultant to help plan the tax campaign. The summary notes relate the event, in part.

> Perhaps the most significant issue in the whole story of the school and the district concerns Walter Cook's old story about the leader of the parade who got more than two blocks ahead of the parade and found that he was no longer leading the parade. In this sense the superintendent and the Kensington idea is a long way ahead of what most of the community wants or wanted at the time. This is illustrated by the fact that there has been some subterfuge and also some manipulation of information and of events. This situation of the hard sell and the movement behind the scenes with the hard sell was terribly complicated when they took the advice of the consultant and decided that what the schools were to be would depend on what the people wanted, and that they should move toward a total soft sell. One of the significant assumptions of the soft sell, as I see it, is that you line up the administration of the schools with the popular desires of the community. In this instance, it then becomes almost a foregone conclusion that you have got to retract from the two-block ahead leadership. My guess also is that this is totally inconceivable in the long run in the eyes of Steven, Jerl, and Eugene. Most certainly, it is not a role that is tenable for the board president who is a very talkative, aggressive guy. The internal contradictions here seem very great (5/11).

As in all case studies, one longs for information that can be obtained only from controlled experiments. However, the need for congruence of consultant "advice" and the "basic" dispositions of the people who must implement the advice seems a fruitful hypothesis.

Finally, the broader point we make is really an extension of Thompson's (1967) internal-external issues. Rephrasing this as the utilization of a consultant because of his name and reputation to influence decision makers requires the minimal integration of values or of means and ends. The limits here are only the ones of conscience and the ability to develop a plausible facade. The relationship is significantly different, if the specialized knowledges, skills, or orientations are going to be implemented or used. At this point a careful synthesis and integration with the organizational structure, process, and incumbents appear to be mandatory.

The Deployment Center: Dispersion of Staff into the District

In addition to being a protected island or enclave, Kensington was to serve a further role in innovation within the Milford School District.[6] We heard about it in conjunction with comments on the uniqueness of the staff:

> One of the teachers, in the course of these comments, raised the notion that in his early discussions with Eugene there was talk of Kensington being the kind of a center in which people were brought through and then deployed out into other parts of the Milford District. This makes it a very different kind of situation in that regard also (8/26).

The consequences of this included a contribution to the high enthusiasm and to the belief that they, the staff, were the chosen ones. In this manner the conception of another temporary system contributes to our earlier analysis of "true belief in an innovative organization."

The farthest extent of this occurred, as we have related, in the spring district-wide curriculum meeting. Discussion took place on the deployment of people and ideas from Kensington to other schools. The reality, however, as our introductory epilogue indicated, involved a high degree of staff turnover and of administrative succession; most of the movement was out of the district.

Furthermore, few teachers from other schools within the Milford District were ever present at Kensington. Even on this matter, diffusion and dissemination, Kensington's orientation was beyond Milford. As previously pointed out, the well-developed façade, the publicity, the high visibility, and the frequent visitors from afar gave substance to this interpretation. Yet, that an elementary school would be conceived as a temporary center for training in innovative skills is, in itself, an atypical approach to change within a school district. However, the school as a protected subculture was not successful enough, nor did the district leadership remain long enough, to give this sequential step a trial. The idea remains as an intriguing one.

Public School Research as an Innovation

An important part of Kensington's ideology and program centered on research. As we have indicated, the teachers were encouraged to innovate and to depart from the traditional in their teaching. In this Deweyian

---

[6] Here as elsewhere the boundaries of the temporary systems shift. At some points the Milford School District is the permanent system and Kensington is the temporary system. At other points, for example, the summer workshop, Kensington is the permanent system.

sense, Kensington was an experimental school. Moreover, the staff had three members who sought doctoral dissertations in the school. In August, the school established a research committee of six interested members. One of the consultants used the school as a clinical setting for trying out his ideas as well as for engaging in formal data collection on individualized reading instruction.[7] In addition, the district contracted with the present investigators (Smith and Keith) who, in turn, contracted with the United States Office of Education for research support. Our central contention is that this amount and kind of research is an educational innovation of major importance.

This part of the story of Kensington involved the central office staff's concern for impartial investigation, description, and, eventually, dissemination of the Kensington doctrine and program. The basic strategy, once again, was the development of a temporary system to carry out the task. In Miles' (1964) terminology this would be "event-linked." In the spring of the year before the school opened, discussions occurred among the principal investigator and the superintendent, curriculum director, and principal. The initiative for the research came *from* the school district.

> In talking about what I might do in the situation, I shied very strongly away
> from the possibility of actually getting involved in a consulting role or a teach-
> ing role in terms of how the staff might function. I argued strongly that I
> was mostly interested in the research analysis role.[8] This I think we got squared
> away very well. Also, I raised very definitely several of the foci of interests
> that I would have: the development of the faculty in terms of how it became
> a working unit, the development of the children as they came to view and
> to respond to the school situation, and then, quite specifically, the principal

[7] These aspects of the research program moved along much less satisfactorialy. The three staff members who had had hopes of completing doctoral dissertations found that their time was consumed totally by the needs for program implementation. The more informal interests in research expressed by several staff during the workshop week did not reach fruition. The consultant, interested in individualized instruction in reading in all divisions, implemented a broad program of tape recording lessons, questioning the staff, and providing feedback through group meetings and interviews. In our judgment, the conception was fascinating and exciting. However, the pressures on staff time, some interpersonal conflicts, the mixing of research and consulting roles, and other commitments which prevented him from being closely in contact with the school contributed to the gradual demise of the project.

[8] Although we did not realize it then, we were opting for the summative role in evaluation instead of the formative role as Scriven (1967) has used these terms. The organizational realities of evaluator cooptation versus evaluator independence of and goal displacement from research and evaluation to program support are issues that he does not handle. Our intuition here stood us in good stead. Our more extended analysis of these issues appears in Smith, L. M., and Pohland, P. A. *Observation of CSMP pilot trials.* St. Ann, Mo.: CEMREL, (In process). We have found the temporary system conception highly facilitative.

as a decision maker in such a setting. At the latter point, I raised specifically the real hazards and the tremendously painful business it is to have somebody shadow you. I told them about Geoffrey's[9] problems and indicated that they would be as great or worse here (4/17, pre-experimental year).

The notes on that discussion concluded this way:

Briefly, to summarize next steps: I am going to draft a copy of the possible research project to be submitted to the United States Office of Education, and the curriculum director will check the superintendent's belief about getting matching funds. All in all, it looks like it probably will go if each of us wants it to (4/17, pre-experimental year).

Several weeks later, the principle investigator met with the superintendent. The brief notes summarizing this conference contain the basic ingredients of the relationship.

Essentially, I presented the kinds of issues that I saw lying in the way of reaching an agreement. This was after a brief comment of the superintendent's of "When do we start?" I raised the point of freedom of access, and he promised complete freedom and even offered spontaneously the use of files and records. I raised also the problem and degree of involvement I would like to have, which would be very high. This he agreed to also. We spoke of the split between the research and the consulting roles, and the fact that my preference lay with the research role instead of with the consulting role. Once again he agreed with this. He talked a little about how other university personnel might be brought in for the consulting aspects. I commented that it was all right with me if it was all right with them (5/6 pre-experimental year).

The activities of the conference included also a consideration of the content of the study.

We went through the report of the first draft of the application that I had written, and both he and Mr. Cohen responded quite positively to it. I left copies with them so that they could make additional comments as they saw fit. All in all the discussions took about one-half hour, and they seemed to go very well. I left feeling quite good and believing that the project could be a most interesting one (5/6, pre-experimental year).

Later the investigator summarized the final part of the preliminary arrangements.

Since then I have clarified the budget and sent copies to them. And, this morning made final arrangements with the curriculum director. He had read

---

[9] Once again the reference is to William Geoffrey, a teacher in a slum school who was coinvestigator in an earlier study (Smith and Geoffrey, 1965, 1968).

the materials again and sent a copy to the principal. The principal's major reaction was that I had accented the building rather than the program, and he thought that the building was the least important or, at any rate, the lesser of the two. Other than that, I did not feel that they had made any fundamental criticisms of the application (5/6, pre-experimental year).

On the first day of the summer workshop, following an initial welcome to the faculty by the superintendent and principal, the research project, which culminated in this book, was explained briefly to the teachers:

> Our intent is to record the problems in the development of a new staff in a unique situation; this morning's questionnaires are a source of baseline data. There will be a final report to the school administration and to the United States Office of Education. No day-to-day information will be fed back to the administrators. The researchers are not consultants (8/10).

Prior to any workshop activity, the faculty completed the two previously mentioned questionnaires, the *Minnesota Teacher Attitude Inventory* (Cook et al., 1951) and the Wehling-Charters (1969) *Teacher Conceptions of the Educational Process.*

In summary, the critical aspects of this temporary system seem to be the following: (1) the school district wanted the research carried out. (2) In every conceivable way the school staff honored their agreements and gave the research team access and support. (3) The principle investigator made a serious misestimation of the cost and time involved.[10] The project was underfinanced and should have run several times as long. The press of other activities and commitments meant that the report was completed a year and one half after the first year of Kensington's operation. It meant also that the United States Office of Education waited more than a year for the final report on its contract. (4) The need to divide research and other operational roles is most important. Research seems to be crowded out if it is carried with other responsibilities.

Those who are unfamiliar with educational organizations and, hence, may not appreciate the atypicality of Milford and Kensington in regard to these summary generalizations should take note of the state of the field as described by Miles in *Innovation in Education.*

"Thus the question of the fate of innovations is an extremely critical one . . . However, the question of adoption and continuation begs the more fundamental question, the one which an innovation's proponents usually answer automatically and positively: Is it really effective?

"Yet . . . a near axiomatic statement is this: Educational innovations are almost *never* evaluated on a systematic basis . . . .

---

[10] Some functional consequences occurred also as the Introductory Epilogue implies.

"To illustrate: it has been pointed out that less than half of one percent of nationally financed experimental programs in a large state were systematically evaluated . . ." (1964, p. 657).

By taking the research initiative, the leaders in the Milford School District were behaving in a unique and innovative fashion. More generally, part of the formal doctrine centered on Kensington's being an experimental school. In the sense of being innovative, of permitting and fostering quite varied and idiosyncratic teaching styles and formats, of being open to considerable brief observation by educators throughout the country, and by subjecting itself to systematic outside observation, Kensington was very much an experimental school.

Concluding Comments

Kensington had a number of components that were organized into temporary subsystems operating in the permanent system. The time limits for some were clear-cut, that is, they were chronological, time-linked.[11] For others, extraction from the system was less well defined; they were event-linked or condition-linked. And in many instances some of what would be designated as characteristics of temporary systems lingered or filtered into the permanent system. They became important issues in what Miles (1964) has called linkage failure, interlocking ". . . temporary and permenent systems effectively, without vitiating the advantages of temporal spatial isolation from the recurring demands of durable organizational life."

The month's workshop for the total school, the Training Groups for faculty and students, the regular contacts with consultants and the researchers, the temporary physical facilities and the strategy of the protected subculture were temporary subsystems at Kensington. Frequently they provided ideas, tension, and stress within and between the interacting units of Kensington that, in turn, formed the basis for additional restructuring and reorganization. Also the temporary systems were to alleviate some of the elements of risk (freedom to make mistakes, for example) and to act as a buffer (that is, the strategy of isolation) between the permanent system and the environment. As we have indicated none of these relationships was simple or unequivocal in actual operation.

Temporary systems were invoked, in part, to cope with what we referred to earlier as Stinchcombe's (1965) concept of the liability of newness. He points out that new organizations must use skills produced outside the organization or must invest in education. At Kensington, the workshop and Training-Groups were attempts at education, change, and socialization

---

[11] Throughout this concluding section, Miles (1964) provocative statement and his vocabulary constitute a point of departure.

of incoming personnel. It was hoped they were a way to implement and to speed up changes that were an integral part of the alternative of grandeur. Also the workshop was intended to help staff members to become acquainted and to ease what Stinchcombe has referred to as the new organization's reliance on social relations among strangers. We indicated in an earlier chapter how the Training Groups were viewed as a mechanism of develop mutual trust, to begin to "become a group." In contrast, some of the origins of mistrust surrounded the dismissal of Kirkham in the before-school activities. In this instance parts of two temporary systems were involved—the workshop and a consultant. The impact of the interaction between the temporary systems and the permanent system was great on the permanent system. Personnel components of one division were altered and the probabilities for structuring the interactions surrounding the roles of the remaining members were changed. Mutual distrust was heightened, and the potency of the belief system as a mechanism for sifting and omitting from the system the incumbents whose "philosophy is not like ours" was demonstrated. In short, the interchanges among the components of temporary and permanent systems resulted in changes in both the components and in both types of systems. We pointed out earlier how the Training Group Sessions, although viewed as a temporary system in themselves, evoked behavior, revelations, expressions of affect, and generally heightened self-examination and awareness that became an important part of the structuring of subsequent interaction. Many of the items were unintended and negative for organizational goal attainment.

Miles has suggested that, in a temporary system, because of the egalitarianism and the limited size of the system, the net influence of an individual can sometimes be substantial. In our data, both Kirkham and Nichols illustrate how individual members may alter the sentiments, activities, subsequent structure, and direction a system may take. The move toward informality and egalitarianism present in the initial temporary subsystem at Kensington led to a lack of attention to procedural concerns in the permanent system. Later, the rules that were issued by the principal complicated the egalitarianism between the faculty and administration. Again, in Kensington's instance, the temporary systems complicated the problems of the permanent system.

As noted earlier, isolation is usually an attribute of a temporary system. As an encapsulated system, Kensington's evolving from the strategies of temporary systems produced difficulties in delineating the boundaries for exchanges with the environment and, subsequently, in securing resources and support. Isolation was to assure the reduction of penalties for making mistakes. At Kensington, the phrase "freedom to fail" was frequently heard. However, there was no information about how long this protection would be adhered to. There was little notion about whether the base of support for the establishment and the maintenance of the protected subculture and other aspects of temporary subsystems were widespread or highly idiosyncratic. So intense was the "protection" that the lines of communication with a number of incumbents in the environment were nonexistent. The searches for resources gave the most abrupt clues that some of the temporary characteristics of the system were, indeed, "temporary."

Although Miles (1964) notes the difficulties that may occur when the attempt is made to link temporary and permanent systems, additional problems are encountered when what is to be a permanent system is organized around temporary subsystems, and when it takes on many of the characteristics of temporary systems with no time lines for shifting from temporary activities to the ones more applicable to a permanent organization. As indicated earlier in the chapter, the alternative of grandeur with its "multiplicity of things at once" had as a concomitant an input overload that often is characteristic of temporary systems. Unrealistic goal setting, which is often cited as descriptive of temporary systems, in the instance of Kensington, was also an attribute of the alternative of grandeur. The "as if" characteristic of temporary systems invited a feeling of infinite possibility—the sense that "the sky's the limit." This facet in the instance of Kensington interacted with the dimension of true belief, with the extreme expenditures of time and effort, and with the strength of the commitment to ideas embodied in the doctrine. A related problem occurs when a temporary system is installed in a system that is to become permanent. "The possibility of the temporary system's becoming permanent is never in the foreground, often remains indeterminate, and is frequently out of the question completely," according to Miles (1964, p. 432). The training group strategy at the beginning of Kensington was to be a temporary attempt; however, it was later expanded to the student body, and groups for parents were considered. The degree of temporality of some of the other systems, with the exception of the workshop, was less clear. This lack of clarity was a further source of uncertainty for the beginning system.

Questions arose constantly over the nature and locus of the "permanent system." For instance, intense involvement and engagement in system activities is a frequent concomitant of initial innovative attempts. As we hypothesized earlier, persons who possess true belief may undertake numerous searches for grails. In a sense, individuals with this orientation may behave as temporary components or subsystems in that, although the grail is rarely obtained, they move on to other settings. In this way they thrive on beginnings with all the proverbial high hopes and aspirations and do not remain to see what may be the outcomes of the aggrandizement effect. It seemed as though the permanent system were a vaguely defined reference group of innovators, and as though Kensington was a temporary system to which they were attached briefly.

In fact, if not in name, temporary systems were a major part of Kensington's approach to educational innovation. This strategy was linked intimately with the alternative of grandeur, the previously analyzed strategy. Our case study illuminates well additional issues in the theoretical positions generated earlier by Selznick, Lewin, and Miles. Furthermore, our case suggests cautions to the practicing administrator who might adopt ideas too quickly and without regard to the subtleties of his own particular situation.

MINIMAL PRIOR COMMITMENTS AS AN INNOVATIVE STRATEGY

Although the label "minimal prior commitments,"[12] holds no special favor in our eyes, the concept seems important. A series of decisions were made that were to be facilitative in the implementation of Kensington's program. We have clustered them into a single conception because they relate to youth, inexperience, and the absence of prior formal interpersonal relationships. As a cluster, minimal prior commitments constitutes Kensington's third major strategy of innovation.

Youth

In spite of the efforts of developmental psychologists, age remains a phenotypical variable containing a variety of latent genotypical issues. Stages of ego development and developmental tasks of different age periods help only a little as one attacks the relevance of age to organizational analysis. In general, the Kensington staff was young, as was the district leadership. Youth brings energy and a capacity for hard work. It brings enthusiasm, and, as we have indicated, often true belief as well. Furthermore, it brings what we have called minimal commitments to many of the usual structures in our society. The investments in long held points of view, in community relationships, and in circles of friends are minimal. As a consequence, the possibilities for the organization are malleable inputs for shaping very different structures and processes. In addition, the organization is increasing uncertainty, since the minimal commitments that are being accented are the very things that help define what one believes, what one can do, and what one is. All of them give an initial identity and stability to a group or an organization. By design, Kensington opted for the minimal commitment of youth.

[12] At a higher level of abstraction, we are involved again with the conception of isolation. The "cultural island" in the present instance is from the orthodoxy of professional education and from the demands of prior personal relationships.

Throughout the workshop, the team meetings, and the committee sessions, the latent agenda of youth was present. Our descriptive accounts in Chapters 1, 3, 5, and 10, to mention only the most extended discussions, emphasize the continual and unending questing for the resolution of personal points of view, professional orientations, and a quite abstract synthesis of the two. Authority, rules, ideal interpersonal relationships among faculty and among administration, faculty, and pupils, the nature of educational aims and goals, and Fully Functioning Freddy, all are specific illustrations and items from this agenda. As such, it is an agenda of youth, an agenda of the examined life, and an agenda of Kensington.

Inexperience

Kensington gambled heavily on inexperienced personnel to launch its innovative program. The decision seems to have followed from the two-horned dilemma of "initial training in desirable directions" versus "breaking old habits and retraining into new directions." Such a two-alternative decision could be increased, at least, twofold to a four option problem. As a third alternative, experienced teachers with skills and experience relevant to the new elementary education and with personal desires for change could have been sought and recruited. Fourth, a situation in which change is the dominant group norm could have been accented. Both of these latter alternatives were in the Kensington blueprint, but inexperience dominated. A number of the teachers, one third, had had no teaching experience beyond student teaching. Also, and quite significantly, several of the experienced teachers were teaching an age level, new to them. For example, Wanda was a kindergarten, not a first or second grade teacher; Mary had taught a fourth grade, not a first or second grade. Jack's experience had been primarily secondary, and later, Lee Gage, who was a long-term substitute for him, had been a secondary teacher. A student teacher from the first semester, Linda, who was inexperienced otherwise, joined the faculty full time at the semester break. Significantly, two additional groups of adults, four teacher aides and three student teachers, a number equivalent to one third of the regular faculty, were inexperienced.

In mid-September, this issue and some additionel implications appropriate for research received interpretative comment in the field notes.

> Another major question I have concerns the use of inexperienced personnel in the carrying out of innovation. A repertory of skills both substantively and in terms of group management seems absolutely mandatory for a person in a free situation of this kind. This was highlighted, perhaps most dramatically, by Liz this morning in that she did not have the materials that she needed. This, as we have argued, then limits the kinds of things that she can do. It also suggests that if a response sequence cannot be played out, then another

sequence must be implemented. She does not have them in her repertory. Consequently, as was noted this morning, she spent a lot of time on bulletin boards and communication boxes, and the like. With her involved in the key area of reading, for which she's had limited training, there is going to be "hell-to-pay" there. Experience should give one a whole series of these repertories that could be utilized whenever other avenues become blocked. In effect, they give you ways to respond when the intended ways are no longer available. Trying to catalogue some of them, the sorts of situations and the ways that one can respond to them, seems to be a much needed research problem. This could be handled experimentally in something like a creativity test where you list a problem and then ask the person to suggest the array of things that he would do. One could put them into an experimental role-playing or simulated situation where you make demands that they carry out some of these procedures. Seemingly, they could be developed with enough complexity and enough realism that they would be very valuable training devices as well as research devices (9/14).

The continuing magnitude of the experience issue is shown further in a brief excerpt from the notes in early May.

Another episode that struck me as very significant was Liz's comment about one of her children whom she had to take from the room. Initially I had overheard her talking with someone else about it, and then I approached her and raised some discussion about the boy in question. Apparently he had been disturbing the others, and she had told him to go to the principal's office. He had refused. She told him, "You're going if I have to drag you every inch of the way!" This kind of assertiveness and follow through on one's position was not at all in her behavior during the fall in the gymnasium. If she has come this far, then she is going to be over the major management problems that she has, and she will be able to move into instructing. As she talked about this, she commented to the effect that sometimes you have to do this (5/4).

We have analyzed this kind of learning in great detail elsewhere (Smith and Geoffrey, 1968; Connor and Smith, 1967; Smith, 1968). The Kensington teacher's resolution coming *at the end of the year* is a major commentary on the strategy of inexperience in an innovative organization.

Forgetting is a delightful psychological mechanism. Those teachers and administrators who began their careers many years ago will have memories that are leveled, selected, and tempered by later experiences. The trials of inexperience interrelate with preservice training, with the induction of new members into the profession, and with a view of teaching careers.

One other item concerning the conversation with one of the new teachers last night. The one real bright spot in her life these days is the thought of skiing with a boyfriend of hers. Most of her life is consumed with "psychologi-

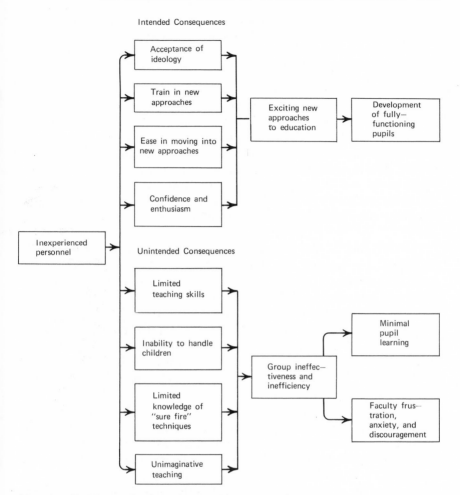

Figure 11.5 The implications of inexperience in teaching.

cal fatigue." She commented about having gone to bed at 7 P.M. two nights this past week. She also has to get up at 6:30 A.M. each morning, which is a tremendous chore for her. At 3:30 in the afternoon she does not want to think about anything. In effect, she makes a very good illustration of the survival criterion in teaching, and the difficult problems one has in making it the first year or so. In the early year or two of one's career, just being able to stay in there and being able to come away reasonably happy might be a most important criterion of teacher effectiveness. Only later are the nuances of teaching open for analysis. It seems to me that this should have major significance for a teacher-training program and for the kinds of things that are done with the undergraduates and in the student teaching. All this is to say that the beginning teacher is probably an understudied phenomenon, and that there are half a dozen or more cases in Kensington that are as illustrative as any that exist. That is another problem that needs a close look.

Such was an early episode in first-year teaching.

As we thought through the inexperience issue, it became apparent that several related but conceptually different aspects had to be isolated. The inexperience in teaching was compounded by: (1) being inexperienced in working together; (2) being part of a new organization without formalization, that is, without social structure; (3) utilizing organizational patterns, teams and divisions, with which no one was familiar; and (4) inhabiting temporary facilities that were awkward—to say the least. These influences culminated in considerable difficulty. Figure 11.5 sketches these ideas.

The variation in the teams is critical on the experience-inexperience dimension. For instance, the ISD problems can be contrasted with the Basic Skills-4 team. As we have indicated, the latter had two highly experienced and creative primary teachers, one experienced kindergarten teacher, and one totally inexperienced teacher. Also, early in the semester they received additional help through the addition of a part-time highly creative and experienced staff member. This brought important resources. Also, Basic Skills, by its early split into two teams, settled its most serious factional quarrel. These aspects belong, however, to another part of the story and were described in previous chapters.

Thus, the dimension of inexperience, which was to have, as a concomitant, an ease in moving into new approaches and a receptiveness to training, thereby, producing further innovative behavior, was often accompanied by an inability to handle children, a limited repertory of skills and, frequently, unimaginative teaching. These outcomes combined with the inexperience in working together, cited earlier, the location in separate, temporary facilities, and a low degree of formalization in terms of procedures (that is, mutual adjustment forms of coordination) were additional sources of difficulty for the participants and uncertainty for the organization.

A Staff Unknown to One Another

Kensington's staff came from throughout the middle western part of the country. Only a few of the people had known one another before. This, too, was an educational innovation of significant magnitude. When one has purposes embodied in a significant break with past traditions, a plausible means is to bring together an aggregate of staff who then would be welded into a new unit. Perhaps, the most significant unintended result of this was the underestimation of the time it takes and the problems

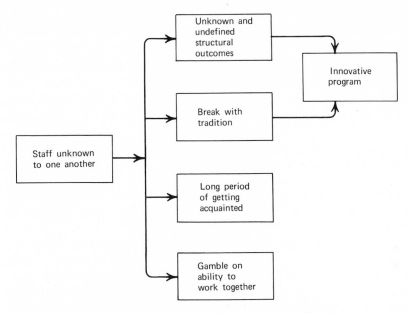

Figure 11.6 The aspects of the "Staff unknown to one another."

involved in building an aggregate of teachers into a workable group, that is, building an institutional core. The complexities involved in the individual personalities attracted to a new enterprise such as Kensington (see our previous discussion of true belief in an innovative organization) and the particular patterns of socialization, workshop and T-groups, are difficult to tease apart. Much of the discussion of issues concerning cooperation, for example, the exploration of who can do what, whom one can trust, and whom one likes, we have put in our discussion of team teaching. In short, the low level of knowledge about one another in terms of competencies, past experiences, friendship patterns, and any number of additional bits of information that members of a system have about each other contributed further to the high degree of uncertainty that characterized the system. Figure 11.6 shows the consequences of the staff new to one another.

Conclusion

An irony, or paradox if you like, existed in the recruitment of individuals characterized by true belief and crusading sentiments. In a sense, they are highly committed rather than minimally committed as we have used the term in this section of our analysis. The commitment, however, was to nonexistent structures, that is, to abstract ideas and ideals at best and, at worst, to vaguer more poorly defined personal needs. Such commitments seemed interwoven with a cosmopolitanism and, consequently, with a reduced localist commitment. In many respects, the consequences of minimal prior commitments are similar to the alternative of grandeur and temporary systems. Uncertainty, isolation, and risk are involved. Freedom, newness, innovativeness not only are desired they also are demanded by these conditions.

SUMMARY: INNOVATION, UNCERTAINTY, AND UNINTENDED CONSEQUENCES

A new organization has a mandate, a charge as it were, and it has the special problems of getting started, that is, coming to terms with the several environments, building a social structure, and facing up to resource limits. An organization with an innovative program complicates this process. In addition, the educational leaders of Milford and Kensington had both a strategy and series of operational tactics, "innovations facilitating innovations," for implementing the innovative program in the new organization. The accent was on planned purposive social action. However, in our descriptions and interpretations, Kensington suggested the phenomenon of social change out of control. The potency of a functionally oriented systems theory kept reappearing.

The alternative of grandeur as a change strategy had, as a corollary, a high level of uncertainty and of unintended outcomes. Uncertainty implies that individuals and their system counterparts do not know the probabilities connecting choices and outcomes. One can hypothesize that uncertainty varies also with the amount of past experience and with the complexity of the decision situation. The alternative of grandeur with its emphasis on changes in a multiplicity of components makes for much greater variety and, hence, increases the complexity of the decision-making process. At Kensington the low level of experience of many of the participants, and other minimal prior commitments, further heightened the level of uncertainty. Uncertainty in terms of getting acquainted, of developing new roles and procedures, and of generating subsequent structures often is characteristic of new organizations. At Kensington there were few mechanisms that effectively reduced these sources of ambiguity. The lack of experience with decision situations in elementary schools, much less an innovative one, the egalitarianism with initial deemphasis on procedures and rules, the high degree of interdependence, the coordination by mutual adjustment, the dimension of true belief and its correlates, the multiplicity of sentiments generated by various procedures, and the façade with its accompanying aspirations and aggrandizement all interacted to increase the level of uncertainty and the number of unintended outcomes. The temporary system strategy, which was highly accented at Kensington, further increased these tendencies. As an illustration, organizational analysts, theorists, and researchers had not at that time generated information regarding the use of T-groups with individuals who were unknown to each other, who were meeting for the first time in the encounter setting, and who subsequently would be working together for a year in a formal organization, albeit a very unusual one.

Not only were probabilities connecting alternatives of behavior choices and environmental outcomes unknown, often the outcomes themselves were unknown, unanticipated, and unintended. Earlier we noted Buckley's (1967) statement that social and psychological structures are generated with "greater or with lesser conscious and delibrate purpose." These "lesser conscious" events in conjunction with the notion of bounded rationality allow that outcomes may be obtained that are unanticipated and unintended.[13] In an early paper, Merton (1957) approached the problem of the "lesser conscious" elements that figure in the generation of structure and later to the stress, strain, and tension that are a part of change. Merton elaborated on the concepts of anticipated-unanticipated consequences and the latent and manifest functions and dysfunctions that they may have for a system. He presented change via the concept of dysfunction, a term that implies the concept of strain, stress, and tension on the structural level, and that provides an analytical approach to the study of dynamics and change. Although we have treated "strain, stress, and tension" at the level of interaction between the components of a system and the exchanges between them and the environment, it seems possible to view unintended outcomes or the ones that result from "lesser conscious and deliberate purpose" as a part of the variety continuously being generated, responded to, sifted, and mapped by the system.

The unintended outcomes are a part of the system; data and information on their implications for the system are fed back to decision-making and control centers as are data resulting from intended, planned outcomes. The difficulties in assessing intended and unintended events and in determining whether consequences are functional or dysfunctional, and for what or whom, are multiple.[14] Although it is assumed that a decision-making

[13] In much of the functionalist literature the labels, unintended, unanticipated, unrecognized, and unwanted, are used interchangeably or overlappingly. Analytical work needs to be undertaken here, since important and discriminable social psychological processes are involved.

[14] In a very important but implicit sense, Barnard (1938) attacked this problem of functional-dysfunctional with his concepts of effectiveness and efficiency. Effectiveness was a goal attainment criterion. Efficiency was a summary "group satisfactions and rewards" internal criterion.

or control center sets certain desired goals and the means by which they may be attained, in some systems, control centers may be difficult to locate. In the case of Kensington the egalitarian relationship formalized in the doctrine was complicated by the Institutional Plan, by changing interpersonal relationships, by the development and demise of committees, by the issuance of rules, and by the multiple meanings and practices of "democratic administration."

In an attempt to conceptualize some of these issues in the nature of consequences, we developed a "2 × 2 × 2" classification system, using the overlapping labels from Buckley (1967) and Merton (1957). As Figure 11.7 indicates, the consequences that are anticipated and functional for the system tend to be congruent with the organizational planning. As an example, team teaching was planned to be a school-wide organizational structure useful as a means for implementing an individualized program. This approach was both anticipated and functional in the development of the Basic Skills team of four members.

If resources are available, mechanisms can be built in to control those anticipated consequences that are foreseen as dysfunctional, that is, negative feedback. It would seem that certain consequences which appear to be

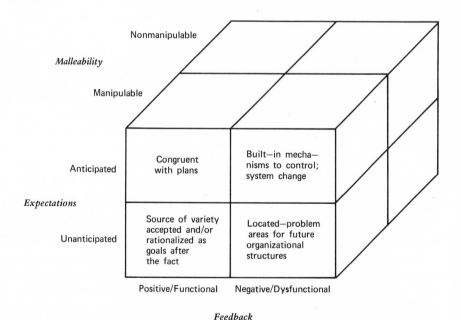

Figure 11.7 The system adaptation related to expectations, feedback, and malleability of outcomes.

dysfunctional may be anticipated but not necessarily intended as Merton has defined the term. As the Kensington data show, the problems surrounding movement to and from the cafeteria illustrate our meaning. The use of the perception core as a corridor was anticipated to be dysfunctional, and other provisions were made which, in turn, had far-reaching ramifications in both the internal and external systems and in the environment. Both flexible facilities and a flexible social structure can be regarded as facilitating the process of built-in control mechanisms. For example, the changes in faculty roles, the regrouping of pupils, and the moveable walls and furniture, anticipated negative feedback or dysfunctions, may be taken into account. Also, it must be recognized that corrective action runs the risk, among others, of overcorrection, that is interference with other goal activities. Shelby's issuance of rules as corrective action for some pupil behaviors undermined some of the belief that an egalitarian relationship existed among members of the staff and the principal and some of the trust of the faculty. In short, corrective output may change the structures to which participants respond and may alter the selections of possible behaviors and the roles for which members may opt. In this way, a system may change or elaborate its structure.

This is essentially the point Blau (1955) has made. We find that his most significant contribution to functional theory lies in the thesis of his study, *The Dynamics of Bureaucracy*: ". . . bureaucratic structures continually create conditions that modify these structures" (p. 9). Essentially he says that rational planning and decision making introduce new structures to reach particular goals. These new structures produce unintended consequences, some of which are dysfunctional. The dysfunctional consequences then precipitate new planning, deciding, and acting (the implementation of new structures). Herein, he says, lies the key to the analysis of organizational change. Illustratively, with respect to Kensington one may ask what the consequences of repeated changes in team statuses and roles appear to be for the system as a whole. What are the intended and unintended consequences of the continued use of the doctrine, the tenets, and the principles surrounding the individualized program, as a mechanism of defense and stability even though the internal structure undergoes rapid change?

Unanticipated outcomes that are viewed as functional for the system or on which some positive feedback has been obtained may be accepted and/or rationalized as goals after the fact. A clear illustration of this was noted earlier in an unanticipated formation of two teams that resulted from informal group influences in the Basic Skills Division. Furthermore, one team, which did not adhere to the doctrine but which was implementing a "successful" program, was later presented as an expanded self-contained classroom and was used to illustrate for visitors the intention of having a variety of teaching styles incorporated in Kensington.

Consequences that are unanticipated for the actors in the system and that are dysfunctional for the system, by definition, lead to further difficulties for the specific organization under consideration and lead to future structures. The unanticipated dysfunctions of the great variation in teaching method as related to intra-classroom structure and to the initial wide range of teacher discretion in decision making serve as examples.

Up to this point, our considerations have suggested that most items of social structure are manipulable, that is, open to control and to change by the system, the decision makers, or the control centers. Most innovators seem to assume such a malleable world.[15] Once again, our data suggest limits to the modification of personality and behavior, at least, to subcomponents such as "teacher personality" or "teacher behaviors." Furthermore, as Barnard (1938) indicated, the sentiments in cooperative systems are often profound and unalterable. Thus it was in our data regarding teams and interpersonal relationships.

The most extended analysis of organizational items leading to nonmalleable unanticipated negative outcomes has been made by Selznick (1949) in what he calls "commitments."[16] He defines it this way:

"A commitment in social action is an enforced line of action; it refers to decision dictated by the force of circumstance with the result that the free or scientific adjustment of means and ends is effectively limited" (p. 255).

He suggests five kinds of enforced lines of action that tend to generate high frequencies of unanticipated consequences. First, organizational imperatives such as order, discipline, unity, defense, and consent may distort the more rational adjustment of means to ends. For instance, in Kensington, faculty consent in procedural issues took such large blocks of time that hasty lesson and unit preparation often resulted and aspects of the individualized program were not met. Second, the social character of the personnel refers to what we have called more generally the role of the incumbents. Once organizational positions are filled, the personality of the incumbents becomes critical. For instance, the building specifications were drawn before Shelby, the principal, was hired. Once hired, his view of Kensington, the Institutional Plan, became very important. Similarly, we have

---

[15] Gouldner (1961) makes the important point that the applied theorist hunts for manipulable variables. Our intent is slightly different in that the innovator may find himself with relatively nonmalleable outcomes.

[16] We have other uses for this label and believe that a more appropriate term might have been chosen by Selznick.

had much to say about true belief in an innovative organization. Our intent in that discussion is to indicate that personnel who join an innovative organization such as Kensington often have orientations similar to Hoffer's conception of true believers, and these orientations create important consequences for the organization.

In his third kind of "enforced line of action," institutionalization, Selznick means that procedural decisions become part of the social structure and constrain future decisions. He illustrates this with reference to precedents, to initial acts committing members to a course of action that is irreversible, and to partially analyzed policy which becomes doctrine. Aspects of this general point were considered in our discussion of Kensington's doctrine and Kensington's early attempts at building an institutional core and the formalization of procedures. Fourth, the social and cultural environment constrains organizational decisions and organizational life. The strife in the Milford community and within the central office staff in the Milford Schools continually played an important part in Kensington. In his fifth kind of commitment, Selznick refers to "centers of interest," the "subordinate and allied groups whose leaderships come to have a stake in the organizational status quo." At Kensington the delegation of power, an antecedent of centers of interest, was not a simple and straightforward phenomenon. Teams never had formal leaders, yet struggles for power and influence went on throughout most of the year. What we have called the upside-down authority structure created a very complex content for the "centers of interest" aspect of Kensington.

Although many of these illustrations are fairly specific items, we hypothesize that the analysis holds true for the larger elements of social structure and process. The major generalization, however, accents the relative frequency of consequences in the eight cells of the model. An innovative system, such as Kensington, by its very nature accented uncertainty and a high frequency of items that were unintended and dysfunctional and nonmalleable. Those who would develop experimental schools, those who would innovate, and those who would seek to implement a vision of a new education for young children might well consider the Kensington narrative and theoretical interpretation.

CONCLUSION

The Kensington model of innovation was rich and highly differentiated. Broad strategies such as the alternative of grandeur intertwined with other ideas, the use of multiple temporary systems, and the gamble on minimal prior commitments. Each of them was composed of quite specific and discriminable units. The step from general models and ideas to the realities of the mundane day-to-day implementation remained a long one. Striking parallels exist in our analysis of Kensington's formal doctrine and Kensington's actual operation, as we presented these earlier in the book. In our phrasing of the Kensington and Milford strategy of innovation, we continued to try to present carefully our records of events as they happened and to integrate them consistently in an ever-broadening framework of ideas developed earlier.

As we commented previously, a concern for recording the events of what Maslow (1965) called ". . . 'natural experiments' that result when some courageous enthusiast with faith in his ideas wants to 'try something out' and is willing to gamble . . ." was also a part of Kensington's design. As our task, we have tried to meet this end by telling the Kensington story and by interpreting it in the context of larger educational issues and of broader social science theory. In short, that is our meaning of an anatomy of educational innovation.

References

Anderson, H. H., and Brewer, H. M. Studies of teachers' classroom personalities, I: Dominative and socially integrative behavior of kindergarten teachers. *Applied Psychology Monographs,* No. 6, 1945.

Anderson, H. H., and Brewer, J. E. Studies of teachers' classroom personalities, II: Effects of teachers' dominative and integrative contacts on children's classroom behavior. *Applied Psychology Monographs,* No. 8, 1946. (a)

Anderson, H. H., Brewer, J. E., and Reed, M. F. Studies of teachers' classroom personalities, III: Follow-up studies of the effects of dominative and integrative contacts on children's behavior. *Applied Psychology Monographs,* No. 11, 1946. (b)

Anderson, R. H. *Teaching in a world of change.* New York: Harcourt, Brace, & World, 1966.

Arensberg, C. M., and MacGregor, D. Determination of morale in an industrial company. *Applied Anthropology,* 1942, **1,** 12–34.

Argyris, C. *Executive leadership.* New York: Harper & Brothers, 1953.

A. S. C. D. *Knowing, perceiving, and becoming.* Washington, D. C.: NEA, 1962.

A. S. C. D. *Individualizing instruction.* Washington, D. C.: NEA, 1964.

Ausubel, D. P. *The psychology of meaningful verbal learning.* New York: Grune & Stratton, 1963.

Barker, R. G. *Ecological psychology.* Stanford: Stanford University Press, 1968.

Barker, R. G., and Gump, P. V. *Big school, small school.* Stanford, Calif.: Stanford University Press, 1964.

Barnard, C. *The functions of the executive.* Cambridge, Mass.: Harvard University Press, 1938.

Becker, H. S. Problems of inference and proof in participant observation. *American Sociological Review,* 1958, **28,** 652–660.

Berelson, B., and Steiner, G. *Human behavior: an inventory of scientific findings.* New York: Harcourt, Brace & World, 1964.

Birnbaum, M. Sense and nonsense about sensitivity training. *Saturday Review,* Nov. 15, 1969, 82–83, 96–97.

Blau, P. M. *The dynamics of bureaucracy.* Chicago: University of Chicago Press, 1955.

Blau, P. M., and Scott, W. R. *Formal organizations: a comparative approach.* San Francisco: Chandler, 1962.

Bloom, B. S. et al. *Taxonomy of educational objectives, Handbook I: Cognitive domain.* New York: Longmans, Green, 1956.

405

Boring, E. G. The use of operational definitions in science. *Psychological Review,* 1945, **52,** 243–245, 278–281.

Bradford, L. et al. *T-Group theory and laboratory method.* New York: Wiley, 1964.

Bridges, E. Personal Communication. 1966.

Bruner, J. S. The act of discovery. *Harvard Educational Review,* 1961, **31,** 22–32.

Buckley, W. *Sociology and modern systems theory.* Englewood Cliffs, N. J.: Prentice-Hall, 1967.

Campbell, D. T., and Fiske, D. W. Convergent and discriminant validation by the multitrait-multimethod matrix. *Psychological Bulletin,* 1959, **56,** 81–105.

Charters, W. W., Jr. An approach to the formal organization of the school. In D. Griffiths (Ed.), *Behavioral science and educational administration.* NSSE 63rd Yearbook. Chicago: University of Chicago Press, 1964.

Connor, W. H., and Smith, L. M. *Analysis of patterns of student teaching.* Washington, D. C.: United States Office of Education, Bureau of Research Final Report 5-8204, 1967.

Cook, W. W. et al. *Manual: Minnesota teacher attitude inventory.* New York: The Psychological Corporation, 1951.

Cronbach, L., and Snow, R. *Individual differences in learning ability as a function of instructional variables.* Washington, D. C.: United States Office of Education Final Report, Bureau of Research No. BR-6-1269, 1969.

Dill, W. R. The impact of environment on organizational development. In S. Mailick, and E. H. Van Ness (Eds.), *Concepts and issues in administrative behavior.* Englewood Cliffs, N. J.: Prentice-Hall, 1962.

DuMaurier, D. *Rebecca.* New York: Doubleday, 1938.

E. F. L. *Schools without walls.* Knoxville, Tenn.: Educational Facilities Laboratory, undated.

Etzioni, A. *A comparative analysis of complex organizations.* New York: Free Press of Glencoe, 1961.

Etzioni, A. *Studies in social change.* New York: Holt, Rinehart, & Winston, 1966.

Festinger, L., Riecken, H., Schachter, S. *When prophecy fails.* New York: Torchbook, 1964. (Originally published by the University of Minnesota Press, 1956.)

Galbraith, J. K. *The new industrial state.* New York: Houghton-Mifflin, 1967.

Getzels, J. W., Lipham, J. M., and Campbell, R. F. *Educational administration as a social process: Theory, research, and practice.* New York: Harper & Row, 1968.

Glaser, B. G., and Strauss, A. L. *The discovery of grounded theory: Strategies for qualitative research.* Chicago: Aldine, 1967.

Glidewell, J. Personal Communication. 1966.

Goodlad, J. *Planning and organizing for teaching.* Washington, D. C.: NEA, 1963.

Gouldner, A. W. *Patterns of industrial bureaucracy.* Glencoe, Ill.: Free Press, 1954. (a)

Gouldner, A. W. *Wildcat strike.* New York: Harper & Row, 1954. (b)

Gouldner, A. W. Theoretical requirements of the applied social sciences. In W. Bennis et al. (Eds.), *The planning of change.* New York: Holt, Rinehart, & Winston, 1961.

Grannis, J. C. Team teaching and the curriculum. In J. T. Shaplin, and H. F. Olds, Jr. (Eds.), *Team teaching.* New York: Harper & Row, 1964.

Hall, E. T. *The silent language.* Garden City, N. Y.: Doubleday, 1959.

Hall, E. T. *The hidden dimension.* Garden City, N. Y.: Doubleday, 1966.

Halpin, A. W. (Ed.), *Administrative theory in education.* Chicago: University of Chicago, 1958.

Halpin, A. W. Essay reviews: *Behavioral science and educational administration* (1964 NSSE Yearbook). *Educational Administration Quarterly,* 1965, **1**, 49–54.

Halpin, A. W. *Theory and research in administration.* New York: Macmillan, 1966.

Hare, V. C., Jr. *Systems analysis: a diagnostic approach.* New York: Harcourt Brace, 1967.

Hemphill, J. *Group dimensions: a manual for their measurement.* Columbus, Ohio: Ohio State University Press, 1956.

Hoffer, E. *The true believer.* New York: Harper & Brothers, 1951.

Homans, G. C. *The human group.* New York: Harcourt Brace, 1950.

Jackson, J. M. Structural characteristics of norms. In NSSE Yearbook, *The dynamics of instructional groups.* Chicago: University of Chicago Press, 1960.

Jackson, P. *Life in classrooms.* New York: Holt, Rinehart & Winston, 1968.

Katz, D., and Kahn, R. *The social psychology of organizations.* New York: Wiley, 1966.

Kesey, K. *One flew over the cuckoo's nest.* New York: Viking Press, 1962.

Kimball, S. The method of natural history and educational research. In G. Spindler (Ed.), *Education and anthropology.* Palo Alto, Calif.: Stanford University Press, 1955.

Klapp, O. E. *Collective search for identity.* New York: Holt, Rinehart & Winston, 1969.

Lewin, K. *Field theory and social science.* New York: Harpers, 1951.

Loomis, C. P. *Social systems: Essays on their persistence and change.* Princeton, N. J.: Van Nostrand, 1960.

Lortie, D. The teacher and team teaching: suggestions for long range research. In J. T. Shaplin, and H. Olds, Jr. (Eds.), *Team teaching.* New York: Harper & Row, 1964.

March, J., and Simon, H. *Organizations.* New York: Wiley, 1958.

Maslow, A. H. Observing and reporting education experiments. *Humanist,* 1965, **25**, 13.

Massie, J. L. Management theory. In J. G. March (Ed.), *Handbook of organizations.* Chicago: Rand McNally, 1965.

Merton, R. K. *Social theory and social structure*. (Rev.) Glencoe, Ill.: Free Press, 1957.

Miles, M. B. *Learning to work in groups*. New York: Bureau of Publications, Columbia University, 1959.

Miles, M. B. On temporary systems. In M. B. Miles (Ed.), *Innovation in education*. New York: Bureau of Publications, Teachers College, 1964.

Murray, H. A. et al. *Explorations in personality*. New York: Oxford University Press, 1938.

Pohland, P. A. An interorganizational analysis of an innovative educational program. Unpublished Ph.D. Dissertation, Washington University, St. Louis, Mo., 1970.

Pohland, P. A., and Smith, L. M. *Pedagogical models underlying teacher workshops*. St. Ann, Mo.: CEMREL, Inc., 1970.

Riesman, D. et al. Sociability, permissiveness and equality: a preliminary formulation. *Psychiatry,* 1960, **23**, 323–340.

Rothkopf, E. Z. Two scientific approaches to the management of instruction. In R. M. Gagné, and W. J. Gephart (Eds.), *Learning research and school subjects*. Itaska, Ill.: Peacock Publishers, Inc., 1968.

Schachter, S. Deviation, rejection and communication. *Journal of Abnormal and Social Psychology,* 1951, **46**, 190–207.

Schaefer, R. J. *The school as a center of inquiry*. New York: Harper & Row, 1967.

Scriven, M. The methodology of evaluation. In R. W. Tyler et al. (Eds.), *Perspectives of curriculum evaluation*. Chicago: Rand McNally & Co., 1967.

Sears, P. Levels of aspiration in academically successful and unsuccessful children. *Journal of Social Psychology,* 1940, **35**, 498–536.

Selznick, P. *TVA and the grass roots*. Berkeley, Calif: University of California Press, 1949.

Selznick, P. *Leadership in administration*. New York: Row, Peterson, & Co., 1957.

Shaplin, J. T. Cooperative teaching: definitions and organizational analysis. *The National Elementary School Principal,* 1965, **44**, 14–20.

Shaplin, J. T., and Olds, H., Jr. (Eds.), *Team teaching*. New York: Harper, 1964.

Sherif, M. et al. *Intergroup conflict and cooperation*. Norman, Okla.: Univ. of Oklahoma Press, 1961.

Simon, H. *Administrative behavior* (2nd ed.). New York: Macmillan, 1957.

Smith, L. M. *Group processes in elementary and secondary schools*. Washington, D. C.: NEA, 1959.

Smith, L. M. The micro-ethnography of the classroom. *Psychology in the Schools,* 1967, **4**, 216–221.

Smith, L. M. *Classroom social systems in teacher education*. Occasional Paper Series No. 4. St. Ann, Mo.: CEMREL, Inc., 1968.

Smith, L. M. *Classroom ethnography and ecology.* Paper presented at the meeting of the ASCD 14th Annual Western Research Institute, San Francisco, April 1969.

Smith, L. M. *Open-space design in elementary schools.* Unpublished mimeo, 1970.

Smith, L. M., and Brock, J. A. M. *"Go, Bug, Go": Methodological issues in classroom observational research.* Occasional Paper Series No. 5. St. Ann, Mo.: CEMREL, Inc., 1970.

Smith, L. M., and Geoffrey, W. *Teacher decision making in an urban classroom.* Washington, D. C.: U. S. Office of Education Cooperative Research Report No. S-048, 1965.

Smith, L. M., and Geoffrey, W. *The complexities of an urban classroom.* New York: Holt, Rinehart, and Winston, 1968.

Smith, L. M., and Hudgins, B. B. *Educational psychology.* New York: Knopf, 1964.

Smith, L. M., and Keith, P. *Social psychological aspects of school building design.* Washington, D. C.: United States Office of Education Cooperative Research Report No. S-223, 1967.

Smith, L. M., and Kleine, P. F. Teacher awareness: social cognition in the classroom. *School Review,* 1969, **77,** 245–256.

Smith, L. M., and Pohland, P. A. CAI Fieldwork methodology: Grounded theory and educational ethnography. In H. H. Russell (Ed.), *Evaluation of a computer assisted instruction program.* St. Ann, Mo.: CEMREL, 1969.

Smith, L. M., and Pohland, P. A. *Observation of CSMP pilot trials.* St. Ann, Mo.: CEMREL, Inc., (In process)

Social Science Research Council. *The behavioral and social sciences: outlook and needs.* Englewood Cliffs, N. J.: Prentice-Hall, 1969.

Sommer, R. *Personal space.* Englewood Cliffs, N. J.: Prentice-Hall, 1969.

Spindler, G. (Ed.), *Education and anthropology.* Palo Alto, Calif.: Stanford University Press, 1955.

Stinchcombe, A. L. Social structure and organizations. In J. March (Ed.), *Handbook of organizations.* Chicago: Rand McNally, 1965.

Stotland, E., and Kobler, A. L. *Life and death of a mental hospital.* Seattle: University of Washington Press, 1965.

Swanson, G. E. The effectiveness of decision making groups. *Adult Leadership,* 1959, **8,** 48–52.

Taba, H. *Teaching strategies and cognitive functioning in elementary school children.* Washington, D. C.: United States Office of Educational Project No. 2404, 1966.

Thompson, J. D. *Organizations in action.* New York: McGraw-Hill, 1967.

Turner, R. H. Role-taking: Process versus conformity. In A. Rose (Ed.), *Human behavior and social processes.* Boston: Houghton Mifflin, 1962.

Tyler, R. W. *Basic principles of curriculum and instruction.* Chicago: University of Chicago, 1950.

Washburne, C. W., and Marland, S. P., Jr. *Winnetka: the history and significance of an educational experiment.* Englewood Cliffs, N. J.: Prentice-Hall, 1963.

Watson, J. A formal analysis of sociable interaction. *Sociometry,* 1958, **21,** 269–280.

Watson, J., and Potter, R. J. An analytic unit for the study of interaction. *Human Relations,* 1962, **15,** 245–263.

Wehling, L. J. An exploration of the organization of teacher conceptions of the educative process. Unpublished Ed.D. Dissertation, Washington University, 1964.

Wehling, L., and Charters, W. W., Jr. Dimensions of teacher beliefs about the teaching process. *American Educational Research Journal,* 1969, **6,** 7–30.

Whyte, W. F. Observational fieldwork methods. In M. Jahoda et al. *Research methods in social relations.* New York: Dryden, 1951.

Whyte, W. F. *Leadership and group participation.* Ithaca: Cornell University, 1953.

Zetterberg, H. L. *On theory and verification in sociology.* (3rd ed.) New York: Bedminster Press, 1965.

Index

411